P9-BZL-873

Clashing Views on

Social Issues

FOURTEENTH EDITION

TAKING SIDES

Clashing Views on

Social Issues

FOURTEENTH EDITION

Selected, Edited, and with Introductions by

Kurt Finsterbusch
University of Maryland

**Contemporary
Learning Series**

A Division of The McGraw-Hill Companies

To my wife, Meredith Ramsay, who richly shares with me a life of the mind and much, much more.

Photo Acknowledgment
Cover image: Buccina Studios/Getty Images

Cover Art Acknowledgment
Maggie Lytle

Manufactured in the United States of America

Fourteenth Edition

23456789QSR/QSR987

Library of Congress Cataloging-in-Publication Data

Main entry under title:
Taking sides: clashing views on social issues/selected, edited, and
with introductions
by Kurt Finsterbusch.—14th ed.

Includes bibliographical references and index.
1. Social behavior. 2. Social problems. I. Finsterbusch, Kurt, *comp.*
302

0-07-351496-9
978-0-07-351496-3
95-83865

Printed on Recycled Paper

Preface

The English word *fanatic* is derived from the Latin *fanum,* meaning temple. It refers to the kind of madmen often seen in the precincts of temples in ancient times, the kind presumed to be possessed by deities or demons. The term first came into English usage during the seventeenth century, when it was used to describe religious zealots. Soon after, its meaning was broadened to include a political and social context. We have come to associate the term *fanatic* with a person who acts as if his or her views were inspired, a person utterly incapable of appreciating opposing points of view. The nineteenth-century English novelist George Eliot put it precisely: "I call a man fanatical when . . . he . . . becomes unjust and unsympathetic to men who are out of his own track." A fanatic may hear but is unable to listen. Confronted with those who disagree, a fanatic immediately vilifies opponents.

Most of us would avoid the company of fanatics, but who among us is not tempted to caricature opponents instead of listening to them? Who does not put certain topics off limits for discussion? Who does not grasp at euphemisms to avoid facing inconvenient facts? Who has not, in George Eliot's language, sometimes been "unjust and unsympathetic" to those on a different track? Who is not, at least in certain very sensitive areas, a *little* fanatical? The counterweight to fanaticism is open discussion. The difficult issues that trouble us as a society have at least two sides, and we lose as a society if we hear only one side. At the individual level, the answer to fanaticism is listening. And that is the underlying purpose of this book: to encourage its readers to listen to opposing points of view.

This book contains 40 selections presented in a pro and con format. A total of 20 different controversial social issues are debated. The sociologists, political scientists, economists, and social critics whose views are debated here make their cases vigorously. In order to effectively read each selection, analyze the points raised, and debate the basic assumptions and values of each position, or, in other words, in order to think critically about what you are reading, you will first have to give each side a sympathetic hearing. John Stuart Mill, the nineteenth-century British philosopher, noted that the majority is not doing the minority a favor by listening to its views; it is doing *itself* a favor. By listening to contrasting points of view, we strengthen our own. In some cases we change our viewpoints completely. But in most cases, we either incorporate some elements of the opposing view—thus making our own richer—or else learn how to answer the objections to our viewpoints. Either way, we gain from the experience.

Organization of the book Each issue has an issue *introduction*, which sets the stage for the debate as it is argued in the YES and NO selections. Each issue concludes with a *postscript* that makes some final observations and points the way to other questions related to the issue. In reading the issue and forming your own opinions you should not feel confined to adopt one or the other of the positions presented. There are positions in between the given views or totally outside them, and the *suggestions for further reading* that appear in each issue postscript should help you find resources to continue your study of the subject. At the back of the book is a listing of all the *contributors to this volume*, which will give you information on the social scientists whose views are debated here. Also, on the *On the Internet* page that accompanies each part opener, you will find Internet site addresses (URLs) that are relevant to the issues in that part.

Changes to this edition This new edition has been significantly updated. There are three completely new issues: *Should Mothers Stay Home with Their Children?* (Issue 5), *Are Boys and Men Disadvantaged Relative to Girls and Women?* (Issue 10), and *Should Biotechnology Be Used to Alter and Enhance Humans?* (Issue 15). In addition, one or both of the selections were replaced to bring a fresh perspective to the debates for the issues on moral decline (Issue 1), crisis of the family (Issue 4), gay marriage (Issue 6), affirmative action (Issue 9), business control of the government (Issue 11), government intervention (Issue 12), welfare reform (Issue 13), public education (Issue 14), the environment (Issue 19), and globalization (Issue 20). Today the world is changing rapidly in many ways so that new issues arise, old ones fade, and some old issues become recast by events.

A word to the instructor An *Instructor's Manual With Test Questions* (multiple-choice and essay) is available through the publisher for the instructor using *Taking Sides* in the classroom. A general guidebook, *Using Taking Sides in the Classroom*, which discusses methods and techniques for integrating the pro-con approach into any classroom setting, is also available. An online version of *Using Taking Sides in the Classroom* and a correspondence service for *Taking Sides* adopters can be found at http://www.mhcls.com/usingts/.

   Taking Sides: Clashing Views on Social Issues is only one title in the Taking Sides series. If you are interested in seeing the table of contents for any of the other titles, please visit the Taking Sides Web site at http://www.mhcls.com/takingsides/.

Acknowledgments I wish to acknowledge the encouragement and support given to this project by Larry Loeppke, former and present list managers for the Taking Sides series, and Nichole Altman, developmental editor.

   I want to thank my wife, Meredith Ramsay, for her example and support. I also want to thank George McKenna for many years as a close colleague and coeditor through many early editions of this book.

Kurt Finsterbusch
University of Maryland

Contents In Brief

Contents

PART 2   SEX ROLES, GENDER, AND THE FAMILY   61

Sociologist David Popenoe contends that families play important roles in society but how the traditional family functions in these roles has declined dramatically in the last several decades, with very adverse effects on children. Sociologist Frank Furstenberg argues that diversity of and change in family forms are common throughout history, and the move away from the unusual family form of the 1950s does not indicate a crisis. It does present some problems for children but the worst problem for children is the lack of resources that often results from divorce or single parenting.

Journalist Claudia Wallis reports that more and more mothers are choosing to quit work and stay home to care for the children. The work demands on professional women have increased to the point that very few can do both work and family. Forced to choose, growing numbers choose family. Communication studies professor Susan Douglas and writer Meredith Michaels attack the media for promoting the mommy myth, that "motherhood is eternally fulfilling and rewarding, that it is always the best and most important thing to do, ... and that if you don't love each and every second of it there's something really wrong with you." They object to the subtle moral pressure that the media puts on mothers to stay home with their children.

America's largest lesbian and gay organization, The Human Rights Campaign, presents many arguments for why same-sex couples should be able to marry. The main argument is fairness. Marriage confers many benefits that same-sex couples are deprived of. Researcher Peter Sprigg presents many arguments for why same-sex couples should not be able to marry. The main argument is that the state has the right and duty to specify who a person, whether straight or gay, can marry so no rights are violated.

Christopher Jencks, professor of social policy at the Kennedy School at Harvard University, presents data on how large the income inequality is in the United States and describes the consequences of this inequality. Christopher C. DeMuth, president of the American Enterprise Institute for Public Policy Research, argues that the "recent increase in income inequality . . . is a very small tick in the massive and unprecedented leveling of material circumstances that has been proceeding now for almost three centuries and in this century has accelerated dramatically."

Author Charles Murray describes destructive behavior among the underclass. Murray asserts that this type of behavior will result in serious trouble for society even though, according to statistics, the number of crimes committed has decreased. Psychology professor Barry Schwartz states that the underclass is not the major threat to American ideals. He counters that "the theory and practice of free-market economics have done more to undermine traditional moral values than any other social force."

Curtis Crawford, editor of the Web site http://www.DebatingRacial Preferences.org, explores all possible options for bettering the situation of disadvantaged minorities in a truly just manner. He argues that the right of everyone, including white males, to nondiscrimination is clearly superior to the right of minorities to affirmative action. Sociologist Lawrence D. Bobo demonstrates that racial prejudice still exists even though it has become a more subtle type of racism, which he calls laissez-faire racism. Though it is harder to identify, it has significant effects that Bobo illustrates. In fact, it plays a big role in current politics.

Journalist Michelle Conlin reviews the many disadvantages of boys and men in school from kindergarten to grad school. Since education is the route to success, men will be less able to compete in the marketplace. Joel Wendland acknowledges the edge that females have over males today in education but argues that females are still disadvantaged in the marketplace.

PART 4   POLITICAL ECONOMY AND INSTITUTIONS   189

Television journalist Bill Moyers describes the harmful consequences of the influence and power of businessess and the rich over government. To him, the stories and evidence that he presents are "something to get mad about." Jeffrey M. Berry, a professor of political science, contends that public interest pressure groups that have entered the political arena since the end of the 1960s have effectively challenged the political power of big business.

Attorneys Eliot Spitzer and Andrew G. Celli Jr. argue that the government plays an essential role in enabling the market to work right. Capitalism runs amuck if it is not regulated to protect against abuse and ensure fairness. John Stossel, a TV news reporter and producer of one-hour news specials, argues that regulations have done immense damage and do not protect us as well as market forces.

Sociologists Scott Winship and Christopher Jencks show that welfare reform and a good economy reduced welfare rolls by more than half and reduced poverty at the same time. They argue that the critics of welfare reform were wrong. Sharon Hayes, professor of sociology at the University of Virginia, got to know many welfare mothers and learned what happened to them since the welfare reform. Her article points out that while quite a few mothers have left welfare since the reform, many cannot hold on to a job and are now worse off than before.

Clint Bolick, vice president of the Institute for Justice, presents the argument for school choice that competition leads to improvements and makes the case that minorities especially need school choice to improve their educational performance. Educator and businessman Ron Wolk argues that school choice and most other educational reforms can only be marginally effective because they do not get at the heart of the educational problem, which is the way students learn. Too much attention is directed to the way teachers teach when the attention should be placed on how to stimulate students to learn more. Wolk advocates giving students more responsibility for their education.

The President's Council on Bioethics was commissioned by George Bush to report to him their findings about the ethical issues involved in the uses of biotechnology. Included in this selection are the expected positive benefits from the biotechnologies that are on the horizon. Political science professor Michael J. Sandel was on the President's Council on Bioethics but presents his private view in this selection, which is very cautionary on the use of biotechnology to alter and enhance humans. Many other uses of biotechnology he praises, but he condemns using biotechnology to alter and enhance humans. In these activities, humans play God and attempt in inappropriate remaking of nature.

PART 5   CRIME AND SOCIAL CONTROL   281

YES: **David A. Anderson,** from "The Aggregate Burden of Crime," *Journal of Law and Economics* XLII (2) (October 1999)   *284*

NO: **Jeffrey Reiman,** from *The Rich Get Richer and the Poor Get Prison: Ideology, Class, and Criminal Justice,* 5th ed. (Allyn & Bacon, 1998)   *292*

David A. Anderson estimates the total annual cost of crime including law enforcement and security services. The costs exceed one trillion, with fraud (mostly white collar crime) causing about one-fifth of the total. His calculations of the full costs of the loss of life and injury comes to about half of the total costs. It is right, therefore, to view personal and violent crime as the big crime problem. Professor of philosophy Jeffrey Reiman argues that the dangers posed by negligent corporations and white-collar criminals are a greater menace to society than are the activities of typical street criminals.

YES: **Ethan A. Nadelmann,** from "Commonsense Drug Policy," *Foreign Affairs* (January/February 1998)   *306*

NO: **Eric A. Voth,** from "America's Longest 'War,'" *The World & I* (February 2000)   *314*

Ethan A. Nadelmann, director of the Lindesmith Center, a drug policy research institute, argues that history shows that drug prohibition is costly and futile. Examining the drug policies in other countries, he finds that decriminalization plus sane and humane drug policies and treatment programs can greatly reduce the harms from drugs. Eric A. Voth, chairman of the International Drug Strategy Institute, contends that drugs are very harmful and that our drug policies have succeeded in substantially reducing drug use.

YES: **Robert H. Bork,** from "Liberty and Terrorism: Avoiding a Police State," *Current* (December 2003)   *322*

NO: **Barbara Dority,** from "Your Every Move," *The Humanist* (January/February 2004)   *329*

Robert H. Bork, senior fellow at the American Enterprise Institute, recognizes that the values of security and civil rights must be balanced while we war against terrorism, but he is concerned that some commentators would hamstring security forces in order to protect nonessential civil rights. For example, to not use ethnic profiling of Muslim or Arab persons would reduce the effectiveness of security forces, while holding suspected terrorists without filing charges or allowing them council would increase their effectiveness. Barbara Dority, president of Humanists of Washington, describes some specific provisions of the Patriot Act to show how dangerous they could be to the rights of all dissidents. She argues that provisions of the act could easily be abused.

Lester R. Brown, founder of the Worldwatch Institute and now president of the Earth Policy Institute, argues the population growth and economic development are placing increasing harmful demands on the environment for resources and to grow food for improving diets. Bjorn Lomborg, a statistician at the University of Aarhus, Denmark, presents evidence that population growth is slowing down, natural resources are not running out, species are disappearing very slowly, the environment is improving in some ways, and assertions about environmental decline are exaggerated.

Author Johan Norberg argues that globalization is overwhelmingly good. Consumers throughout the world get better quality goods at lower prices as the competition forces producers to be more creative, efficient, and responsive to consumers' demands. Even most poor people benefit greatly. Herman E. Daly, professor at the School of Public Affairs at the University of Maryland, does not object to international trade and relations, but he does object to globalization that erases national boundaries and hurts workers and the environment.

Introduction

Debating Social Issues

Kurt Finsterbusch

What Is Sociology?

"I have become a problem to myself," St. Augustine said. Put into a social and secular framework, St. Augustine's concern marks the starting point of sociology. We have become a problem to ourselves, and it is sociology that seeks to understand the problem and, perhaps, to find some solutions. The subject matter of sociology, then, is ourselves—people interacting with one another in groups and organizations.

Although the subject matter of sociology is very familiar, it is often useful to look at it in an unfamiliar light, one that involves a variety of theories and perceptual frameworks. In fact, to properly understand social phenomena, it *should* be looked at from several different points of view. In practice, however, this may lead to more friction than light, especially when each view proponent says, "I am right and you are wrong," rather than, "My view adds considerably to what your view has shown."

Sociology, as a science of society, was developed in the nineteenth century. Auguste Comte (1798–1857), the French mathematician and philosopher who is considered to be the father of sociology, had a vision of a well-run society based on social science knowledge. Sociologists (Comte coined the term) would discover the laws of social life and then determine how society should be structured and run. Society would not become perfect, because some problems are intractable, but he believed that a society guided by scientists and other experts was the best possible society.

Unfortunately, Comte's vision was extremely naive. For most matters of state there is no one best way of structuring or doing things that sociologists can discover and recommend. Instead, sociologists debate more social issues than they resolve.

The purpose of sociology is to throw light on social issues and their relationship to the complex, confusing, and dynamic social world around us. It seeks to describe how society is organized and how individuals fit into it. But neither the organization of society nor the fit of individuals is perfect. Social disorganization is a fact of life—at least in modern, complex societies such as the one we live in. Here, perfect harmony continues to elude us, and "social problems" are endemic. The very institutions, laws, and policies that produce benefits also produce what sociologists call "unintended effects"— unintended and undesirable. The changes that please one sector of the society may displease another, or the changes that seem so indisputably healthy at first turn out to have a dark underside to them. The examples are endless. Modern urban life gives people privacy and freedom from snooping neighbors that the small town never afforded; yet that very privacy seems to breed an uneasy sense of anonymity and loneliness. Take another example: Hierarchy is necessary for organizations to function efficiently, but hierarchy leads to the creation of a ruling elite. Flatten out the hierarchy and you may achieve social equality—but at the price of confusion, incompetence, and low productivity.

This is not to say that all efforts to effect social change are ultimately futile and that the only sound view is the tragic one that concludes "nothing works." We can be realistic without falling into despair. In many respects, the human condition has improved over the centuries and has improved as a result of conscious social policies. But improvements are purchased at a price—not only amonetary price but one involving human discomfort and discontent. The job of policymakers is to balance the anticipated benefits against the probable costs.

It can never hurt policymakers to know more about the society in which they work or the social issues they confront. That, broadly speaking, is the purpose of sociology. It is what this book is about. This volume examines issues that are central to the study of sociology.

Culture and Values

A common value system is the major mechanism for integrating a society, but modern societies contain so many different groups with differing ideas and values that integration must be built as much on tolerance of differences as on common values. Furthermore, technology and social conditions change, so values must adjust to new situations, often weakening old values. Some people (often called conservatives) will defend the old values. Others (often called liberals) will make concessions to allow for change. For example, the protection of human life is a sacred value to most people, but some would compromise that value when the life involved is a 90-year-old comatose man on life-support machines who had signed a document indicating that he did not want to be kept alive under those conditions. The conservative would counter that once we make the value of human life relative, we become dangerously open to greater evils—that perhaps society will come to think it acceptable to terminate all sick, elderly people undergoing expensive treatments. This is only one example of how values are hotly debated today.

Three debates on values are presented in Part 1. In Issue 1, Kay S. Hymowitz challenges the common perception that morals have declined in America, while Robert H. Bork argues for the decliningmorality thesis. Issue 2 examines a major institution that can be seen as responsible for instilling values and culture in people—the media. This issue focuses in particular on whether the news reporters and anchormen report and comment on the news with professional objectivity and relatively bias free. William McGowan argues that the objectivity of most reporters is sacrificed to political correctness, which supports the liberal social agenda. In contrast, Robert W. McChesney and John Bellamy Foster argue that even though newsmen may lean to the left on average, they largely use official sources for their reports, and the net result supports the status quo.

The final culture/values debate, Issue 3, concerns the cultural impact of immigration. Patrick Buchanan argues that current levels of immigration are too high and that immigrant cultures are too different from American culture to be assimilated. Thus, immigration is threatening America's cultural unity. Ben Wattenberg counters that the cultural impacts of immigration will be minor because annual immigration amounts to only a third of a percent of the United States population. Furthermore, he maintains that immigration contributes to America's power and influence.

Sex Roles, Gender, and the Family

An area that has experienced tremendous value change in the last several decades is sex roles and the family. Women in large numbers have rejected major aspects of their traditional gender roles and family roles while remaining strongly committed to much of the mother role and to many feminine characteristics. Men have changed much less but their situation has changed considerably. Issue 4 asks if the traditional family is in crisis. David Popenoe is deeply concerned about the decline of the traditional family while Frank Furstenberg points out that the diversity of current family patterns is not a crisis but such diversity is fairly normal throughout history. Issue 5 considers one of the current strains on mother, the conflict of career and childrearing. Claudia Wallis presents the case for mothers staying home and Susan Douglas and Meredith Michaels argue against those who say that women' place is in the home. Issue 6 debates whether same-sex marriages should be legal. The Human Rights Campaign presents all the arguments in its favor and Peter Sprigg presents all the arguments against it.

Stratification and Inequality

Issue 7 centers around a sociological debate about whether or not increasing economic inequality is a serious problem. Christopher Jencks asserts that it is, while Christopher C. DeMuth argues that consumption patterns indicate that inequality has actually decreased in recent decades.

Many commentators on American life decry the pathologies of the underclass as the shame of America. Charles Murray is a leading proponent of this view and his article is republished in Issue 8. Barry Schwartz critiques Murray's view and argues that the current advanced stage of capitalism is largely responsible for eroding American ideals and producing the underclass.

Today one of the most controversial issues regarding inequalities is affirmative action. Is justice promoted or undermined by such policies? Curtis Crawford and Lawrence D. Bobo take opposing sides on this question in Issue 9.

Issue 10 deals with male-female advantages and disadvantages. Michelle Conlin explains that the way schools operate and the behaviors that they reward or sanction favor females over males. As a result females are graduating from high school, colleges, and most grad schools at higher rates than males. Joel Wendland points out the substantial advantages that males have over females in employment and wages and argues that the gender gap still favors males.

Political Economy and Institutions

Sociologists study not only the poor, the workers, and the victims of discrimination but also those at the top of society—those who occupy what the late sociologist C. Wright Mills used to call "the command posts." The question is whether the "pluralist" model or the "power elite" model is the one that best fits the facts in America. Does a single power elite rule the United States, or do many groups contend for power and influence so that the political process is accessible to all? In Issue 11, Bill Moyers argues that the business elite and the rich have a dominating influence in government decisions and that no other group has nearly as much power. Jeffrey M. Berry counters that liberal citizen groups have successfully opened the policy-making process and made it more participatory. Currently, grassroots groups of all kinds have some power and influence. The question is, how much?

The United States is a capitalist welfare state, and the role of the state in capitalism (more precisely, the market) and in welfare is examined in the next two issues. Issue 12 considers whether or not the government should step in and attempt to correct for the failures of the market through regulations, policies, and programs. Eliot Spitzer and Andrew F. Celli Jr. argues that government intervention is necessary to make markets work well and to prevent various harms to society. John Stossel argue that even well-intended state interventions in the market usually only make matters worse and that governments cannot serve the public good as effectively as competitive markets can. One way in which the government intervenes in the economy is by providing welfare to people who cannot provide for their own needs in the labor market. Issue 13 debates the wisdom of the Work Opportunity Reconciliation Act of 1996, which ended Aid to Families of Dependent Children (which was what most people equated with welfare). Scott Winship and Christopher Jencks show how the welfare reform was a great success because it greatly reduced welfare rolls and dramatically increased the employment of welfare mothers. Sharon Hayes states that the reality is more depressing. The old welfare system helped women who were on welfare to prepare for and obtain good jobs while the new law practically forces women on welfare to take bad jobs at poverty-level wages. The situation of some ex-welfare families has become unmanaged and very stressful.

Education is one of the biggest jobs of government as well as the key to individual prosperity and the success of the economy. For decades the American system of education has been severely criticized. Such an important institution is destined to be closely scrutinized, and for decades the American system of education has been severely criticized and many reforms have been attempted. The main debate on how to improve public schools concerns school choice as presented in Issue 14. Clint Bolick argues that competition improves performance in sports and business so it should do the same in education, and the data support this theory. Also parents should be allowed to send their children to the school of their choice. Ron Wolk prevents a more radical view of school reform. Many reform proposals today, including school choice, will do little to improve schools. He proposes shifting more responsibility for education from teachers to students.

The final issue in this section deals with a set of concerns about the use of present and soon-to-emerge biotechnologies. The value of biotechnologies for therapy, to make well, is accepted by all. Issue 15, however, debates their use to alter and enhance humans. The President's Council on Bioethics presents both pro and con arguments but only the pro arguments are present here. The con arguments are present by Michael Sandel.

Crime and Social Control

Crime is interesting to sociologists because crimes are those activities that society makes illegal and will use force to stop. Why are some acts made illegal and others (even those that may be more harmful) not made illegal? Surveys indicate that concern about crime is extremely high in America. Is the fear of crime, however, rightly placed? Americans fear mainly street crime, but Jeffrey Reiman argues in Issue 16 that corporate crime—also known as "white-collar crime"—causes far more death, harm, and financial loss to Americans than street crime. In contrast, David A. Anderson calculates the full costs of crime, both direct and indirect, and concludes that the costs of murder and theft far exceed the cost of white collar crime. These contradictory findings result from differing definitions of white collar crime. A prominent aspect of the crime picture is the illegal drug trade. It has such bad consequences that some people are seriously talking about legalizing drugs in order to kill the illegal drug business. Ethan A. Nadelmann argues this view in Issue 17, while Eric A. Voth argues that legalization would greatly harm society. Drug use would mushroom and damage many lives, whereas the current war on drugs has considerably reduced drug use. Finally, Issue 18 deals with terrorism, perhaps the major problem in America today. We must defend against and prevent it. To do so effectively requires the expansion of police powers, so we passed the Patriot Act. But did the Patriot Act go too far and trample America's liberties? Barbara Dority examines several provisions of the act and observes how extremely unjust their enforcement has been. On the other hand, Robert H. Bork believes that the complaints of people like Dority have tied the hands of the law in the past and that the grave danger we face today requires the strengthening, not weakening, of the act.

The Future: Population/Environment/Society

Many social commentators speculate on "the fate of the earth." The environmentalists have their own vision of apocalypse. They see the possibility that the human race could degrade the environment to the point that population growth and increasing economic production could overshoot the carrying capacity of the globe. The resulting collapse could lead to the extinction of much of the human race and the end of free societies. Other analysts believe that these fears are groundless. In Issue 19, Lester R. Brown shows how human actions are degrading the environment in ways that adversely affect humans. In contrast, Bjorn Lomborg argues that the environment is improving in many ways and that environmental problems are manageable or will have mild adverse effects.

The last issue in this book assesses the benefits and costs of globalization. Johan Noerberg argues that economic globalization has been a demonstration of the basic economic theory that global markets and relatively free trade economically benefit all nations that participate. Herman E. Daly counters that globalization, which dissolves national boundaries, hurts both workers and the environment.

The Social Construction of Reality

An important idea in sociology is that people construct social reality in the course of interaction by attaching social meanings to the reality they are experiencing and then responding to those meanings. Two people can walk down a city street and derive very different meanings from what they see around them. Both, for example, may see homeless people—but they may see them in different contexts. One fits them into a picture of once-vibrant cities dragged into decay and ruin because of permissive policies that have encouraged pathological types to harass citizens; the other observer fits them into a picture of an America that can no longer hide the wretchedness of its poor. Both feel that they are seeing something deplorable, but their views of what makes it deplorable are radically opposed. Their differing views of what they have seen will lead to very different prescriptions for what should be done about the problem.

The social construction of reality is an important idea for this book because each author is socially constructing reality and working hard to persuade you to see his or her point of view; that is, to see the definition of the situation and the set of meanings he or she has assigned to the situation. In doing this, each author presents a carefully selected set of facts, arguments, and values. The arguments contain assumptions or theories, some of which are spelled out and some of which are unspoken. The critical reader has to judge the evidence for the facts, the logic and soundness of the arguments, the importance of the values, and whether or not omitted facts, theories, and values invalidate the thesis. This book facilitates this critical thinking process by placing authors in opposition. This puts the reader in the position of critically evaluating two constructions of reality for each issue instead of one.

Conclusion

Writing in the 1950s, a period that was in some ways like our own, the sociologist C. Wright Mills said that Americans know a lot about their "troubles" but they cannot make the connections between seemingly personal concerns and the concerns of others in the world. If they could only learn to make those connections, they could turn their concerns into *issues*. An issue transcends the realm of the personal. According to Mills, "An issue is a public matter: some value cherished by publics is felt to be threatened. Often there is a debate about what the value really is and what it is that really threatens it."

It is not primarily personal troubles but social issues that I have tried to present in this book. The variety of topics in it can be taken as an invitation to discover what Mills called "the sociological imagination." This imagination, said Mills, "is the capacity to shift from one perspective to another—from the political to the psychological; from examination of a single family to comparative assessment of the national budgets of the world. . . . It is the capacity to range from the most impersonal and remote transformations to the most intimate features of the human self—and to see the relations between the two." This book, with a range of issues well suited to the sociological imagination, is intended to enlarge that capacity.

On the Internet . . .

Internet Philosophical Resources on Moral Relativism

This Web site for *Ethics Updates* offers discussion questions, a bibliographical guide, and a list of Internet resources concerning moral relativism.

http://ethics.acusd.edu/relativism.html

The National Institute on Media and the Family

The National Institute on Media and the Family Web site is a national resource for teachers, parents, community leaders, and others who are interested in the influence of electronic media on early childhood education, child development, academic performance, culture, and violence.

http://www.mediaandthefamily.com

The International Center for Migration, Ethnicity, and Citizenship

The International Center for Migration, Ethnicity, and Citizenship is engaged in scholarly research and public policy analysis bearing on international migration, refugees, and the incorporation of newcomers in host countries.

http://www.newschool.edu/icmec/

National Immigrant Forum

The National Immigrant Forum is a pro-immigrant organization that examines the effects of immigration on U.S. society. Click on the links for discussion of underground economies, immigrant economies, race and ethnic relations, and other topics.

http://www.immigrationforum.org

The National Network for Immigrant and Refugee Rights (NNIRR)

The National Network for Immigrant and Refugee Rights (NNIRR) serves as a forum to share information and analysis, to educate communities and the general public, and to develop and coordinate plans of action on important immigrant and refugee issues.

http://www.nnirr.org

PART 1

Culture and Values

*S*ociologists recognize that a fairly strong consensus on the basic values of a society contributes greatly to the smooth functioning of that society. The functioning of modern, complex urban societies, however, often depends on the tolerance of cultural differences and equal rights and protections for all cultural groups. In fact, such societies can be enriched by the contributions of different cultures. But at some point the cultural differences may result in a pulling apart that exceeds the pulling together. One cultural problem is the perceived moral decline, which may involve a conflict between old and new values. Another cultural problem in America is whether the media has a bias that is significantly removed from the epicenter of American culture. The final problem is whether current immigrants to the United States bring appropriate values and skills.

- Is American in Moral Decline?

- Does the News Media Have a Liberal Bias?

- Is Third World Immigration a Threat to America's Way of Life?

ISSUE 1

Is America in Moral Decline?

YES: Robert H. Bork, from *Slouching Towards Gomorrah: Modern Liberalism and American Decline* (Regan Books, 1996)

NO: Kay S. Hymowitz, from "Our Changing Culture: Abandoning the Sixties," *Current* (June 2004)

ISSUE SUMMARY

YES: Robert H. Bork, famous for being nominated for the Supreme Court but not confirmed by the Senate, argues that modern liberalism is responsible for the decline in morals.

NO: Journalist Kay S. Hymowitz argues that the permissive culture of the sixties, which led to less respect for authority, crime, sexual promiscuity, and other indicators of moral decline, is waning. The cultural pendulum is swinging back to a more traditional culture of commitment, moderation, and family values.

Morality is the glue that holds society together. It enables people to deal with each other in relative tranquility and generally to their mutual benefit. Morality influences us both from the outside and from the inside. The morality of others affects us from outside as social pressure. Our conscience is morality affecting us from inside, even though others, especially parents, influence the formation of our conscience. Because parents, churches, schools, and peers teach us their beliefs and values (their morals) and the rules of society, most of us grow up wanting to do what is right. We also want to do things that are pleasurable. In a well-functioning society the right and the pleasurable are not too far apart, and most people lead morally respectable lives. On the other hand, no one lives up to moral standards perfectly. In fact, deviance from some moral standards is common, and when it becomes very common the standard changes. Some people interpret this as moral decline, while others interpret it as simply a change in moral standards or even as progress. Take, for example, the new morality that wives should be equal to rather than subservient to their husbands.

The degree of commitment to various moral precepts varies from person to person. Some people even act as moral guardians and take responsibility for encouraging others to live up to the moral standards. One of their major tactics is to cry out against the decline of morals. There are a number of such voices speaking out in public today. In fact, many politicians seem to try to outdo each other in speaking out against crime, teenage pregnancy, divorce, violence in the media, latchkey children, irresponsible parenting, etc.

Cries of moral decline have been ringing out for centuries. In earlier times the cries were against sin, debauchery, and godlessness. Today the cries are often against various aspects of individualism. Parents are condemned for sacrificing their children for their own needs, including their careers. Divorced people are condemned for discarding spouses instead of working hard to save their marriages. Children of elderly parents are condemned for putting their parents into nursing homes to avoid the inconvenience of caring for them. The general public is condemned for investing so little time in others and their communities while pursuing their own interests. These criticisms against individualism may have some validity. On the other hand, individualism has some more positive aspects, including enterprise and inventiveness, which contribute to economic growth; individual responsibility; advocacy of human rights; reduced clannishness and reduced prejudice toward other groups; and an emphasis on self-development, which includes successful relations with others.

The morality debate is important because moral decline not only increases human suffering but also weakens society and hinders the performance of its institutions. The following selections require some deep reflection on the moral underpinnings of American society as well as other societies, and they invite the reader to strengthen those underpinnings.

Many have decried the high levels of crime, violence, divorce, and opportunism, but few argue the thesis of the moral decline of America as thoroughly and as passionately as Robert H. Bork, the author of the following selection. But is he reading the facts correctly? Kay S. Hymowitz presents the counter thesis of moral improvement. The main indicators of morals are reversing, which she explains by the cultural shift from the permissive values of the sixties to more traditional values of today's youth including more respect for parents and traditional values.

Robert H. Bork  **YES**

Modern Liberalism and American Decline

This is an [article] about American decline. Since American culture is a variant of the cultures of all Western industrialized democracies, it may even, inadvertently, be . . . about Western decline. In the United States, at least, that decline and the mounting resistance to it have produced what we now call a culture war. It is impossible to say what the outcome will be, but for the moment our trajectory continues downward. This is not to deny that much in our culture remains healthy, that many families are intact and continue to raise children with strong moral values. American culture is complex and resilient. But it is also not to be denied that there are aspects of almost every branch of our culture that are worse than ever before and that the rot is spreading.

"Culture," as used here, refers to all human behavior and institutions, including popular entertainment, art, religion, education, scholarship, economic activity, science, technology, law, and morality. Of that list, only science, technology, and the economy may be said to be healthy today, and it is problematical how long that will last. Improbable as it may seem, science and technology themselves are increasingly under attack, and it seems highly unlikely that a vigorous economy can be sustained in an enfeebled, hedonistic culture, particularly when that culture distorts incentives by increasingly rejecting personal achievement as the criterion for the distribution of rewards.

With each new evidence of deterioration, we lament for a moment, and then become accustomed to it. We hear one day of the latest rap song calling for killing policemen or the sexual mutilation of women; the next, of coercive left-wing political indoctrination at a prestigious university; then of the latest homicide figures for New York City, Los Angeles, or the District of Columbia; of the collapse of the criminal justice system, which displays an inability to punish adequately and, often enough, an inability even to convict the clearly guilty; of the rising rate of illegitimate births; the uninhibited display of sexuality and the popularization of violence in our entertainment; worsening racial tensions; the angry activists of feminism, homosexuality, environmentalism, animal rights—the list could be extended almost indefinitely.

So unrelenting is the assault on our sensibilities that many of us grow numb, finding resignation to be the rational, adaptive response to an environment that is increasingly polluted and apparently beyond our control. That is what Senator Daniel Patrick Moynihan calls "defining deviancy down." Moynihan cites the "Durkheim constant." Emile Durkheim, a founder of sociology, posited that there is a limit to the amount of deviant behavior any community can "afford to recognize." As behavior worsens, the community adjusts its standards so that conduct once thought reprehensible is no longer deemed so. As behavior improves, the deviancy boundary moves up to encompass conduct previously thought normal. Thus, a community of saints and a community of felons would display very different behavior but about the same amount of recognized deviancy.

But the Durkheim constant is now behaving in a very odd way. While defining deviancy down with respect to crime, illegitimacy, drug use, and the like, our cultural elites are growing intensely moralistic and disapproving about what had always been thought normal behavior, thus accomplishing what columnist Charles Krauthammer terms "defining deviancy up." It is at least an apparent paradox that we are accomplishing both forms of redefining, both down and up, simultaneously. One would suppose that as once normal behavior became viewed as deviant, that would mean that there was less really bad conduct in the society. But that is hardly our case. Instead, we have redefined what we mean by such things as child abuse, rape, and racial or sexual discrimination so that behavior until recently thought quite normal, unremarkable, even benign, is now identified as blameworthy or even criminal. Middle-class life is portrayed as oppressive and shot through with pathologies. "As part of the vast social project of moral leveling," Krauthammer wrote, "it is not enough for the deviant to be normalized. The normal must be found to be deviant." This situation is thoroughly perverse. Underclass values become increasingly acceptable to the middle class, especially their young, and middle-class values become increasingly contemptible to the cultural elites.

That is why there is currently a widespread sense that the distinctive virtues of American life, indeed the distinctive features of Western civilization, are in peril in ways not previously seen. . . . This time we face, and seem to be succumbing to, an attack mounted by a force not only within Western civilization but one that is perhaps its legitimate child.

The enemy within is modern liberalism, a corrosive agent carrying a very different mood and agenda than that of classical or traditional liberalism. . . . Modernity, the child of the Enlightenment, failed when it became apparent that the good society cannot be achieved by unaided reason. The response of liberalism was not to turn to religion, which modernity had seemingly made irrelevant, but to abandon reason. Hence, there have appeared philosophies claiming that words can carry no definite meaning or that there is no reality other than one that is "socially constructed." A reality so constructed, it is thought, can be decisively altered by social or cultural edict, which is a prescription for coercion. . . .

The defining characteristics of modern liberalism are radical egalitarianism (the equality of outcomes rather than of opportunities) and radical individualism (the drastic reduction of limits to personal gratification). . . .

Men were kept from rootless hedonism, which is the end stage of unconfined individualism, by religion, morality, and law. These are commonly cited. To them I would add the necessity for hard work, usually physical work, and the fear of want. These constraints were progressively undermined by rising affluence. . . .

The mistake the Enlightenment founders of liberalism made about human nature has brought us to this—an increasing number of alienated, restless individuals, individuals without strong ties to others, except in the pursuit of ever more degraded distractions and sensations. And liberalism has no corrective within itself; all it can do is endorse more liberty and demand more rights. Persons capable of high achievement in one field or another may find meaning in work, may find community among colleagues, and may not particularly mind social and moral separation otherwise. Such people are unlikely to need the more sordid distractions that popular culture now offers. But very large segments of the population do not fall into that category. For them, the drives of liberalism are catastrophic.

The consequences of liberalism, liberty, and the pursuit of happiness pushed too far are now apparent. Irving Kristol writes of the clear signs of rot and decadence germinating within American society—a rot and decadence that was no longer the consequence of liberalism but was the actual agenda of contemporary liberalism. . . . [S]ector after sector of American life has been ruthlessly corrupted by the liberal ethos. It is an ethos that aims simultaneously at political and social collectivism on the one hand, and moral anarchy on the other." I would add only that current liberalism's rot and decadence is merely what liberalism has been moving towards for better than two centuries.

We can now see the tendency of the Enlightenment, the Declaration of Independence, and *On Liberty*. Each insisted on the expanding liberty of the individual and each assumed that order was not a serious problem and could be left, pretty much, to take care of itself. And, for a time, order did seem to take care of itself. But that was because the institutions—family, church, school, neighborhood, inherited morality—remained strong. The constant underestimation of their value and the continual pressure for more individual autonomy necessarily weakened the restraints on individuals. The ideal slowly became the autonomous individual who stood in an adversarial relationship to any institution or group that attempted to set limits to acceptable thought and behavior.

That process continues today, and hence we have an increasingly disorderly society. The street predator of the underclass may be the natural outcome of the mistake the founders of liberalism made. They would have done better had they remembered original sin. Or had they taken Edmund Burke seriously. Mill wrote: "Liberty consists in doing what one desires." That might have been said by a man who was both a libertine and an anarchist; Mill was neither, but his rhetoric encouraged those who would be either or both. Burke had it right earlier: "The only liberty I mean is a liberty connected with order; that not only exists along with order and virtue, but which cannot exist at all without them." "The effect of liberty to individuals is, that they may do what they please: We ought to see what it will please them to do, before we risque congratulations, which may soon be turned into complaints." Burke, unlike the Mill of *On Liberty*, had a true understanding of the nature of men, and balanced liberty with restraint and order, which are, in truth, essential to the preservation of liberty.

The classical liberalism of the nineteenth century is widely and correctly admired, but we can now see that it was inevitably a transitional phase. The tendencies inherent in individualism were kept within bounds by the health of institutions other than the state, a common moral culture, and the strength of religion. Liberalism drained the power from the institutions. We no longer have a common moral culture and our religion, while pervasive, seems increasingly unable to affect actual behavior.

Modern liberalism is one branch of the rupture that occurred in liberalism in the last century. The other branch is today called conservatism. American conservatism, neo or otherwise, in fact represents the older classical liberal tradition. Conservatism of the American variety is simply liberalism that accepts the constraints that a clear view of reality, including a recognition of the nature of human beings, places upon the main thrusts of liberalism—liberty and equality. The difference, it has been said, is that between a hard-headed and a sentimental liberalism. Sentimental liberalism, with its sweet view of human nature, naturally evolves into the disaster of modern liberalism.

"During the past 30 years," William Bennett writes, "we have witnessed a profound shift in public attitudes." He cites polls showing that "we Americans now place less value on what we owe others as a matter of moral obligation; less value on sacrifice as a moral good, on social conformity, respectability, and observing the rules; less value on correctness and restraint in matters of physical pleasure and sexuality—and correlatively greater value on things like self-expression, individualism, self-realization, and personal choice." Though I think the shift in public attitudes merely accelerated in the past thirty years, having been silently eroding our culture for much longer, it is clear that our current set of values is inhospitable to the self-discipline required for such institutions as marriage and education and hospitable to no-fault divorce and self-esteem training.

Our modern, virtually unqualified, enthusiasm for liberty forgets that liberty can only be "the space between the walls," the walls of morality and law based upon morality. It is sensible to argue about how far apart the walls should be set, but it is cultural suicide to demand all space and no walls. . . .

The Collapse of Popular Culture

The distance and direction popular culture has travelled in less than one lifetime is shown by the contrast between best-selling records. A performer of the 1930s hit "The Way You Look Tonight" sang these words to romantic music:

> *Oh, but you're lovely, /With your smile so warm, /And your cheek so soft, /There is nothing for me but to love you, /Just the way you look tonight.*

In our time, Snoop Doggy Dogg's song "Horny" proclaims to "music" without melody:

> I called you up for some sexual healing. /I'm callin' again so let me come get   it. /Bring the lotion so I can rub you. /Assume the position so I can f. . . you.

Then there is Nine Inch Nails' song, "Big Man with a Gun." Even the expurgated version published by the *Washington Post* gives some idea of how rapidly popular culture is sinking into barbarism:

> I am a big man (yes I am). And I have a big gun. Got me a big old [expletive] and I, I like to have fun. Held against your forehead, I'll make you suck it. Maybe I'll put a hole in your head. . . . I can reduce it if you want. I can devour. I'm hard as [expletive] steel and I've got the power. . . . Shoot, shoot, shoot, shoot, shoot. I'm going to come all over you. . . . me and my [expletive] gun, me and my [expletive] gun.

The obscenity of thought and word is staggering, but also notable is the deliberate rejection of any attempt to achieve artistic distinction or even mediocrity. The music is generally little more than noise with a beat, the singing is an unmelodic chant, the lyrics often range from the perverse to the mercifully unintelligible. It is difficult to convey just how debased rap is. . . .

What America increasingly produces and distributes is now propaganda for every perversion and obscenity imaginable. If many of us accept the assumptions on which that is based, and apparently many do, then we are well on our way to an obscene culture. The upshot is that American popular culture is in a free fall, with the bottom not yet in sight. This is what the liberal view of human nature has brought us to. The idea that men are naturally rational, moral creatures without the need for strong external restraints has been exploded by experience. There is an eager and growing market for depravity, and profitable industries devoted to supplying it. Much of such resistance as there is comes from people living on the moral capital accumulated by prior generations. That capital may be expected to dwindle further—cultures do not unravel everywhere all at once. Unless there is vigorous counterattack, which must, I think, resort to legal as well as moral sanctions, the prospects are for a chaotic and unhappy society, followed, perhaps, by an authoritarian and unhappy society. . . .

The Rise of Crime, Illegitimacy, and Welfare

The United States has surely never before experienced the social chaos and the accompanying personal tragedies that have become routine today: high rates of crime and low rates of punishment, high rates of illegitimate births subsidized by welfare, and high rates of family dissolution through no-fault divorce. These pathologies are recent, and it is now widely accepted that they are related to one another.

The proximate cause of these pathologies is the infatuation of modern liberalism with the individual's right to self-gratification along with the kind of egalitarianism, largely based on guilt, that inhibits judgment and reform. These pathologies were easy to fall into and will be vary difficult to climb out of. There is, in fact, no agreement about how to cure them. It may be, in fact, that a democratic nation will be unable to take the measures necessary, once we know what those measures are.

If radical individualism and egalitarianism are the causes, we should expect to see their various effects produced at about the same time as one another. And that is what we do see. During the same years that popular culture was becoming ever more sordid, the pathologies of divorce, illegitimacy, and crime exploded. The story is well documented and may be quickly summarized. The more difficult question, particularly about illegitimacy and welfare, is how to escape what we have done.

Rates of illegitimate births and the commission of serious crimes began rising together and did so at the same time in both the United States and England. National illegitimacy statistics were first gathered in the United States in 1920. Illegitimate births then constituted 3 percent of all births. The proportion slowly went up to just over 5 percent in 1960, and then shot up to 11 percent in 1970, above 18 percent in 1980, and 30 percent by 1991. These are figures for the entire population. Black illegitimacy started from a higher base than white and skyrocketed sooner, reaching 68 percent in 1991. White illegitimacy had reached a little over 2 percent by 1960 and then shot up to 6 percent in 1970, 11 percent in 1980, and just under 22 percent in 1991. Combined black and white illegitimacy in 1992 was 32 percent. These are national averages; illegitimacy is much higher in lower-income communities and neighborhoods.

Crime displays the same pattern. National records about violent crime in the United States were first kept in 1960. The number of violent crimes in that year was just under 1,900 per 100,000 people; the number doubled within ten years, and more than tripled to almost 6,000 by 1980. After a brief decline, the crime rate began rising again and had reached almost 5,700 by 1992. It is thus apparent that crime and illegitimacy trends began rising at almost the same time and then rose together. . . .

Rising crime, illegitimacy, and student rebellion had a common cause. While the middle-class student radicals turned to dreams of revolution and the destruction of institutions, some of the lower classes turned to crime and sexual license, and probably for the same reasons. That fact bodes ill because it suggests a long-developing weakening of cultural constraints, constraints it will be very hard to put back in place. . . .

Crime rates in a number of areas have stopped rising and in some places have begun to decline. It is possible that the rate of violent crimes has gone down in the nation as a whole. This appears to be partially due to better policing, slightly higher rates of incarceration, and a decline in the number of young males, who are almost entirely responsible for violent crime though more and more women are taking up the practice. But, as the Council on Crime report puts it: "Recent drops in serious crime are but the lull before the coming crime storm." That is because the population of young males in the age groups that commit violent crime is about to increase rapidly, producing more violence than we know at present. It is also likely that the coming young felons will commit more serious crimes than today's juvenile offenders do. According to the report, the literature indicates that "each generation of crime-prone boys is several times more dangerous than the one before it, and that over 80 percent of the most serious and frequent offenders escape detection and arrest." . . .

When physical safety becomes a major problem even for the middle classes, we must of necessity become a heavily policed, authoritarian society, a society in which the middle classes live in gated and walled communities and make their places of work hardened targets. After the Oklahoma City bombing, there were serious proposals in Washington to use the Army to provide security. The mayor of Washington, D.C., proposed using the National Guard to supplement the police in that drug-ridden and murder-racked city. Whites tend to dismiss the violence of the inner cities as a black problem. As the killing and the drugs spread to white neighborhoods and suburbs, as they are doing, the response will be far more repressive. Both the fear of crime and the escalating harshness of the response to it will sharply reduce Americans' freedom of movement and peace of mind. Ours will become a most unpleasant society in which to live. Murray poses our alternatives: "Either we reverse the current trends in illegitimacy—especially white illegitimacy—or America must, willy-nilly, become an unrecognizably authoritarian, socially segregated, centralized state." . . .

NO

Kay S. Hymowitz

Our Changing Culture: Abandoning the Sixties

Sex doesn't sell: Miss Prim is in. No, editors at the *New York Times* "Sunday Styles" section were not off their meds when they came up with that headline recently. Just think about some of the Oscar nominees this year: there was *Seabiscuit,* a classic inspirational story of steadfast outsiders beating huge odds to win the race; *Return of the King: Lord of the Rings,* a mythic battle of good defeating evil, featuring female characters as pure as driven snow; *Master and Commander,* a nineteenth-century naval epic celebrating courage, discipline, and patriarchal authority. And then there was *Lost in Translation,* in which a man in the throes of a midlife crisis spends hours in a hotel room with a luscious young woman, and . . . they talk a lot.

If you listen carefully, you can hear something shifting deep beneath the manic surface of American culture. Rap stars have taken to wearing designer suits. Miranda Hobbs, *Sex and the City*'s redhead, has abandoned hooking up and a Manhattan co-op for a husband and a Brooklyn fixer-upper, where she helps tend her baby and ailing mother-in-law; even nympho Samantha has found a "meaningful relationship." Madonna is writing children's books. Gloria Steinem is an old married lady.

Family Values

Yessiree, family values are hot! Capitalism is cool! Seven-grain bread is so yesterday, and red meat is back!

Wave away the colored smoke of the Jackson family circus, Paris Hilton, and the antics of San Francisco, and you can see how Americans have been self-correcting from a decades-long experiment with "alternative values." Slowly, almost imperceptibly during the 1990s, the culture began a lumbering, Titanic turn away from the iceberg, a movement reinforced by the 1990s economic boom and the shock of the 9/11 terrorist attacks. During the last ten years, most of the miserable trends in crime, divorce, illegitimacy, drug use, and the like that we saw in the decades after 1965 either turned around or stalled. Today Americans are consciously, deliberately embracing ideas about sex, marriage, children, and the American dream that are coalescing into a viable—though admittedly much altered—sort of bourgeois normality. What is emerging is a vital, optimistic, family-centered, entrepreneurial, and yes, morally thoughtful, citizenry.

Not the 1950s

To check a culture's pulse, first look at the kids, as good a crystal ball as we have. Yes, there's reason to worry: guns in the schools, drugs, binge drinking, cheating, Ritalin, gangs, bullies, depression, oral sex, Internet porn, you name it. Kids dress like streetwalkers and thugs, they're too fat, they don't read, they watch too much television, they never play outside, they can't pay attention, they curse like *South Park's* Eric Cartman. The 1950s, this ain't.

Yet marketers who plumb people's attitudes to predict trends are noticing something interesting about "Millennials," the term that generation researchers Neil Howe and William Strauss invented for the cohort of kids born between 1981 and 1999: they're looking more like Jimmy Stewart than James Dean. They adore their parents, they want to succeed, they're optimistic, trusting, cooperative, dutiful, and civic-minded. "They're going to 'rebel' by being, not worse, but better," write Howe and Strauss.

However counterintuitive, there's plenty of hard evidence to support this view. Consider the most basic indicator of social health: crime. The juvenile murder rate plummeted 70 percent between 1993 and 2001. By 2001, the arrest rate for all violent crime among juveniles was down 44 percent from its 1994 peak, reaching its lowest level since 1983. Juvenile arrests for burglary were also down 56 percent in that time period. Vandalism is at its lowest level in two decades. Despite all the headlines to the contrary, schools are a lot safer: school-based crimes dropped by close to half in the late 1990s. According to the Youth Risk Behavior Survey, the percentage of ninth-through 12th-graders who reported being in a fight anywhere in the previous 12 months dropped from 42 percent in 1991 to 33 percent in 2001, while those who had been in a fight on school property fell from 16 percent to 13 percent.

Drinking

Something similar looks like it may be happening with adolescent drinking and drug use, on the rise throughout much of the nineties. But suddenly, around the turn of the millennium, the nation's teens started to climb back on the wagon. Monitoring the Future, an annual University of Michigan survey of the attitudes and behavior of high school students, reports that by 2002 the percentage of kids who reported binge drinking in the last 30 days was close to its lowest level in the 12 years that the survey has been following eighth- and tenth-graders and in the 30 years that it has been following high school seniors. Though during the 1990s marijuana use rose sharply among eighth-graders and less dramatically among tenth- and 12th-graders, by late in the decade the numbers began to fall. More broadly, the Department of

Health and Human Services reports that all illicit teen drug use dropped 11 percent between 2001 and 2003. Ecstasy use, which soared between 1998 and 2001, fell by more than half among high schoolers. A 2003 National Center on Addiction and Substance Abuse study found that 56 percent of teenagers have no friends who drink regularly, up from 52 percent in 2002, and 68 percent say they have no friends using marijuana, up from 62 percent—even though 40 percent of them say they would have no trouble finding the stuff if they wanted it. They're just not interested.

And what about teen sex? Only yesterday, you'd have thought there was no way to wrangle that horse back into the barn. No more. According to the Alan Guttmacher Institute, out-of-wedlock teen pregnancy rates have come down 28 percent from their high in 1990, from a peak of 117 per thousand girls ages 15 to 19 to 83.6 per thousand in 2000. The teen abortion rate also fell—by a third—during the same period. True, American kids still get pregnant at higher rates than those in other major Western nations, but the U.S. is the only country that saw a dramatic drop in teen pregnancy during the last decade.

While American kids are more often saying yes to birth control, even more of them, remarkably, are just saying no to sex, just as they are passing up marijuana and beer. According to the 1991 Youth Risk Behavior Survey, 54 percent of teens reported having had sex; a decade later, the number was 46 percent. The number of high schoolers who reported four or more partners also fell from 18.7 percent to 14.2 percent.

Making the decline in sexual activity more striking is that it began just around the same time that Depo-Provera, a four-shots-a-year birth control technology specifically aimed at teens, came on the market. It's often been said that the birth control pill, which became available to the public in the early 1960s, propelled the sexual revolution. The lesson of Depo-Provera, which was accompanied by a decrease in sexual activity, is that it isn't technology that changes sexual behavior. It's the culture.

If you need more proof, check the surveys not just on kids' sexual behavior but on their attitudes toward sex. Millennial are notably more strait-laced than many of their let's-spend-the-night-together parents. American Freshman, an annual survey of over a quarter of a million first-year kids at 413 four-year colleges, has found that young people have become less accepting of casual sex in the last 15 years. Between 1987 and 2001, those who agree with the statement "If two people really like each other, it's all right for them to have sex if they've known each other for a very short time" fell from 52 percent to 42 percent. Similarly, a recent National Campaign to Prevent Teen Pregnancy survey found that 92 percent of teenagers believe it is important for them "to get strong messages from society that they should not have sex until they are at least out of high school." Twenty-eight percent say they have become more opposed to teens having sex over the past several years, compared to 11 percent who say they are less opposed. It seems that it is adults who are skittish about abstinence, not kids: almost half of the parents interviewed believe it is embarrassing for teens to admit they are virgins, yet only a quarter of teenagers think so.

Keep in mind that these beliefs do not exist in an isolated room of the teen brain marked "sex" or "pregnancy." They are part of a welter of attitudes and values that reinforce each other. . . .

Fed up with the fall-out from the reign of "if it feels good, do it"—not only as it played out in the inner city but in troubled middle-class families across the land—Americans are looking more favorably on old-fashioned virtues like caution, self-restraint, commitment, and personal responsibility. They are in the midst of a fundamental shift in the cultural Zeitgeist that is driving so many seemingly independent trends in crime, sex, drugs, and alcohol in the same positive direction.

Look, for instance, at what's happening to teen alienation. If Millennials have a problem with authority, it's that they wish they had *more* of it. Poll after poll depicts a generation that thinks their parents are just grand. A 2003 *American Demographics* survey shows 67 percent of teens "give Mom an A." They tell interviewers for the National Campaign to Prevent Teen Pregnancy that they want *more* advice about sex from their parents. Summarizing opinion polls, researcher Neil Howe says that this generation is at least as attached to their parents and their values as any generation before. "When it comes to 'Do you get along with your family?' it's never been as high. Same thing for 'Do you believe in the values of your parents?' When they're asked 'Do you trust your parents to help you with important life decisions?' they don't see parents as meddling or interfering," Howe concludes. "They're grateful."

Hallmark Card

In fact, when it comes to families, this generation is as mushy as a Hallmark card. A Harris Interactive survey of college seniors found that 81 percent planned to marry (12 percent already had) at a mean age of 28. Ninety-one percent hope to have children—and get this: on average, they'd like to have three. The 2001 Monitoring the Future survey found 88 percent of male high school seniors and 93 percent of females believing that it is extremely or quite important to have a good marriage and family life. In a survey of college women conducted by the Institute for American Values, 83 percent said, "Being married is a very important goal for me." Over half of the women surveyed said they would like to meet their husbands in college. . . . Americans at or approaching marriageable age—are marriage nuts.

In real life, the number of married-couple families, after declining in the seventies and eighties, rose 5.7 percent in the nineties, according to demographer William H. Frey.

Marrying Later

And in fact, the incredible shrinking married-couple-with-children statistic cited by Kipnis is a statistical mirage, an artifact of two demographic trends, unconnected with American attitudes toward knot tying. First, young people are marrying later; the average age is *25* for women, 27 for men, up from 20 and 23 three decades ago. That means there are a lot more young singles out there than there were in 1970. Further swelling the ranks of these un-Ozzies and Harriets is the vastly increased number of empty nesters, retirees, and widows, beneficiaries of major health-care improvements over the past decades. There are 34 million Americans over 65, and it's a safe bet that only those few living with their adult kids would be counted as part of a married-couple household with children. What it comes down to is that a smaller proportion of married couples with children is no more evidence of the decline of the family than more cars on the road is evidence of a decline in trucks.

Even on the fraught issue of out-of-wedlock births and divorce, there are grounds for hope. In the population at large, the decades-long trend toward family fragmentation has finally halted and, according to some numbers, is even reversing itself. Overall, the proportion of children in married-parent families rose from 68 percent in 1998 to 69 percent in 2002—a tiny boost, to be sure, but the first upward tick in decades. More encouragingly, after plummeting between 1965 and 1992, the number of black children living with married parents rose from 34 percent in 1995 to 39 percent in 2000. Moreover, the longitudinal Fragile Families and Child Wellbeing Study has found that half of the poor, largely black, new mothers it surveys are living with the father at the time of their baby's birth. Two-thirds of them agree "it is better for children if their parents are married," and 77 percent say that chances of marrying their child's father are 50 percent or higher. If history is any guide, most won't; but the fact that so many want to marry and understand that it is better to do so is an unexpected bit of social capital to build on.

Americans are even beginning to look at divorce with a more jaded eye. The divorce rate—statistically hard to pin down—is certainly stabilizing, and possibly even declining from its record high of 50 percent. Not so long ago, orthodox opinion would natter on about marital breakup as an opportunity for adults' "personal growth" or about "resilient children" who were "better off when their parents were happy." For the children of divorce who are now in their childbearing years, such sunny talk grates. They saw their mothers forced to move to one-bedroom apartments while their fathers went off with new girlfriends; they found out what it was like when your father moved from being the love object who read to you every night, to a guy who lives across the country whom you see once a year. When it comes to marriage and children, a lot of these damaged young adults are determined to do better. Nic Carothers, the 18-year-old son of divorced parents interviewed by the *Indianapolis Star*, explained his determination to avoid sex until he marries for life: "My father wasn't a very responsible man. I want to be a better father when the time is right." "I can't tell you how many 30-somethings are still in therapy because of their parents' divorce," Catherine Stellin, of Youth Intelligence, told me. "Now we're hearing that maybe it's a good thing to stay together for the sake of the kids."

Dr. Laura

This change of view is not limited to the heartland. Writing in the mainstream *Atlantic Monthly,* Caitlin Flanagan recently offered mild praise for *The Proper Care & Feeding of Husbands,* by much reviled talk-show host Dr. Laura: "There are many of us who understand that once you have children, certain doors ought to be closed to you forever. That to do right by a child means more than buying the latest bicycle helmet and getting him on the best soccer team. . . . It means investing oneself completely in the marriage that wrought him." Flanagan went on to chastise feminist male-bashing. "Our culture is quick to point out the responsibilities husbands have to wives—they should help out with the housework, be better listeners, understand that a woman wants to be more than somebody's mother and somebody's wife—but very reluctant to suggest that a wife has a responsibility to a husband." Such views didn't sink Flanagan's career; she will now be publishing her marriage-happy essays in *bienpensant New Yorker.*

In fact, applause for the nuclear family is now coming even from the American academy and from left-leaning advocacy groups. For decades, elites jeered at the assumption that changes in family structure would harm children; remember the guffaws that greeted Vice President Dan Quayle's pro-marriage *Murphy Brown* speech in 1992? But by the 1990s, study after study began showing, as Barbara Dafoe Whitehead put it in a landmark 1993 *Atlantic Monthly* article, that "Dan Quayle Was Right"—that, on average, children in married, two-parent families do better than other kids by every measure of success. Once-skeptical experts began acknowledging that the traditionalists had it right all along, and advocates announced, in the words of ChildTrends, that "[m]arriage is one of the most beneficial resources for adults and children." Just a decade ago it seemed impossible to imagine a leftish organization like the Center for Law and Social Policy going on record that "society should try to help more children grow up with their two biological, married parents in a reasonably healthy, stable relationship," but that's what has happened.

Home Alone

Still not convinced that there's anything to cheer about? Think about how much more child-centered Americans have become compared with 15 or 20 years ago—the era of the latchkey kid, when the Nickelodeon children's network touted itself as a "parent-free zone," and *Home Alone* was the signature kids' movie. But by the nineties, soccer moms had the keys to the house and the minivan, which was mounting up thousands of miles on trips to soccer matches, violin lessons, and swim meets. Studies showed a big drop in children's unstructured time. Even older kids came under their parents' hothouse scrutiny: "helicopter parents," in Neil Howe and William Strauss's term, hover over their children even after they leave for college, talking on the phone every day, visiting frequently, and helping them with their papers via e-mail.

The 30-somethings who are today's young parents show every sign of keeping the hearth fires burning bright. According to *American Demographics,* Gen-X parents are "nostalgic for the childhood that boomers supposedly had. It's informed their model of the perfect, traditional marriage." Gen-X women are abandoning Ms. for Mrs.: according to a recent Harvard study, the past decade has seen a "substantial decrease" in the percentage of college-educated brides keeping their maiden names. If they can afford to, these Missuses are also choosing the nursery over the cubicle; by 2000, the number of women in the workforce with infants under one dropped from 59 percent to 55 percent, the first decline in decades. The *New York Times Magazine* has run high-profile stories of six-figure MBAs and lawyers leaving their jobs to be at home with their babies. *Time* published a recent cover story on the trend toward professional-class stay-at-homes, and *Cosmopolitan, of* all places, has found a new group of "housewife wannabes" who would like nothing more than to do a Donna Reed. And these young mothers want big families: *USA Today* reports that "the rate of women having more than two children rose steadily in the late 1990s."

Their traditionalism also embraces old-fashioned discipline. A 1999 Yankelovich survey found that 89 percent of Gen Xers think modern parents let kids get away with too much; 65 percent want to return to a more traditional sense of parental duty. "Character education" is hot in school districts across the country—as are the Girl Scouts, because, as official Courtney Shore told the *Washington Times,* "parents and communities are returning to values-based activities." Today's parenting magazines do a brisk trade in articles with titles like ARE YOU A PARENT OR A PUSHOVER? GET A DISCIPLINE MAKEOVER and TEACHING YOUR CHILD RIGHT FROM WRONG.

Hard Workers

. . .[R]esearchers Howe and Strauss say that Millennials "are the first generation in living memory to be actually less violent, vulgar, and sexually charged than the popular culture adults are producing for them." How can that be?

Generational backlash counts for a lot: what we're seeing now is a rewrite of the boomer years. The truth is, Gen Xers and Millennials have some real gripes about the world their boomer parents constructed. When a 1999 Peter D. Hart Research Associates poll asked Americans between the ages of 18 to 30 what experience had shaped their generation, the most common answer was "divorce and single-parent families." Growing up in the aftermath of America's great marriage meltdown, no wonder that young people put so much stock in marriage and family, their bedrock in the mobile twenty-first century.

The Silent Generation

In fact, in some respects young Gen-X adults resemble their Silent Generation grandparents more than their boomer parents, especially in their longing for suburban nesting as a dreamlike aspiration. . . .

Immigration

Also changing the Zeitgeist is immigration. Marketers often characterize today's young generation by its "diversity"; a better way to put it is to say that it teems with immigrants and the sons and daughters of immigrants. Only 64 percent of Gen Xers and 62 percent of Millennial are non-Hispanic whites, compared with three-quarters of baby boomers. Twenty percent of today's teens have at least one immigrant parent. These kids often have a fervent work ethic—which can raise the bar for slacker American kids, as any high schooler with more than three Asian students in his algebra class will attest. Their parents tend toward traditionalism when it comes to marriage and family, with minuscule divorce and illegitimacy rates among Asians (though not among Hispanics, where families headed by a single mother have expanded rapidly). Immigrant kids are more likely to listen to their parents, and they tend not to be alienated ingrates who take their country's prosperity and opportunities for granted. As a Vietnamese high schooler wrote on PopPolitics.com: "When your parents have traveled thousands of miles to live here, when they spend three hours a day driving you and your siblings to various activities, when they paid hundreds of thousands of dollars for a cramped house they could have bought half-price elsewhere, you feel a debt."

And that drive and seriousness take us to reason number four: the information economy. According to the American Freshman survey, 73.8 percent of college kids say succeeding financially is an important life goal—a huge rise from the 40 percent who thought so in the late 1960s. These kids know they have to be hardworking, forward-looking, and pragmatic. But they know opportunity is out there, having just witnessed one of the most remarkable booms in American history, a time when black family poverty fell from 44 percent in 1992 to 23 percent in 1999, and when an astonishing 23 percent of households began earning over $75,000. Though plenty of Gen Xers lost their shirts when the dot-com bubble burst in 2000, there's little sign that they are souring on the free market. J. Walker Smith, president of the Yankelovich consultancy group, told Adweek that Gen Xers "feel more comfortable than boomers in reinventing themselves—they're more self-reliant and more self-directed. They're at home in an uncertain market and are going to look for a way to reengineer opportunities for themselves right here."

Some argue that we are witnessing the rise of a shallow, money-grubbing generation. After all, the number of kids who say "developing a meaningful philosophy of life" is an important goal has plummeted during the same period in which the number of those valuing financial success has soared. But remember: living in an age of "ecstatic capitalism," middle-class young people, who often have had opportunities to hone their talents in everything from computer science to theater to debate, expect work to be gratifying as well as remunerative. They see work itself as a source of meaning—as well as an engine of self-discipline.

Comfort with the advanced market economy also helps explain how it is that a vulgar popular culture has not had the corrupting influence on behavior that we might have feared. Growing up steeped in entertainment media, the young learn early on to be skeptical toward its blandishments. They don't believe they take their ideas about how to live a decent life from *Dawson's Creek,* or 50 Cent. In a recent survey from the National Campaign to Prevent Teen Pregnancy, for instance, teens were asked who influences their values about sex: only 4 percent answered "the media," while 45 percent answered "my parents." Of course, kids don't necessarily know where they're getting their ideas. And of course popular culture has some influence on their behavior. Presumably, suburban middle-school boys who grab and fondle girls in the halls, while the girls hint at their availability for oral sex, did not learn any of this at the dinner table.

"Bobos"

Even after all these changes, of course, we still live in a post-sexual revolution culture. Nobody pretends we're going back to the 1950s. Americans may have abandoned the credo of "if it feels good, do it," but they still embrace sexual pleasure as a great human good and take pride in advertising their own potential for success in that area. David Brooks coined the term "bobo" to refer to bourgeois bohemians, but the newest generation of bobos might be better described as bourgeois booty-shakers. Young mothers go to "strip aerobics" classes, where they do their workout by pole dancing, before they go off to pick up little Tiffany at kindergarten. Madonna does some provocative tongue wrestling with Britney Spears on national television, but everyone knows that in reality she glories in being a Hollywood soccer mom (and Mrs. Guy Ritchie, as she would have it). An edgy exterior no longer necessarily connotes a radical life-style: not long ago, I watched a heavily pierced couple, as the bride-to-be, with her stringy, dyed red hair, torn jeans, and bright green sneakers, squealed over the pear-shaped diamond engagement ring she was trying on. Go figure.

Gilmore Girls

The popular media has been trying to make sense of these crosscurrents. Some writers seem to grasp that they can bombard their viewers with breast and fart jokes, but in the end people are still interested in how to live meaningful lives. Consider the WB network's popular series *Gilmore Girls.* The main character, Lorelai Gilmore, is a single 30-something who had a baby when she was 16. A motor-mouthed girl-woman, she picks fights with her now-teenage daughter over the size of their "boobs," makes pop-culture allusions as obsessively as any teeny-bopper, and mugs and pouts during her weekly adolescent-style riffs with her own parents. The daughter, Rory, on the other hand, is the proto-Millennial: sober, hardworking, respectful, and chaste. Her hell-raiser mother's jaw drops when she hears that her daughter hasn't really thought about having sex with her boyfriend. Meanwhile, this season Rory is a freshman at Yale, where she writes for the school paper and reads, you know, literature. *(The Sun Also Rises?* On the network that gave us *Dawson 's Creek?)* Yes, this is a piece of pop-culture effluvium, but its point, made weekly, is that Rory has the promising future, while her mother reflects the childish past. . . .

With their genius for problem solving and compromise, pragmatic Americans have seen the damage that their decades-long fling with the sexual revolution and the transvaluation of traditional values wrought. And now, without giving up the real gains, they are earnestly knitting up their unraveled culture. It is a moment of tremendous promise.

POSTSCRIPT

Is America in Moral Decline?

Handwringing over weakening morals has long been a favorite pastime. Yet are Americans less moral today than they were a century ago? Consider that slavery has been abolished, civil rights for minorities have been won and generally accepted, tolerant attitudes have greatly increased, and genocide toward Native Americans ceased a long time ago. How could Americans have made so much progress if they have been getting much worse for hundreds of years? Such reflections cast suspicion over the moral decline thesis. On the other hand, this thesis is supported by many trends, such as the increases in crime and divorce (which have recently declined or leveled off). The issue is important because morality is a distinctive trait of the human species and essential to cooperative interactions. If morality declines, coercive restraint must increase to hold harmful behaviors in check, but self-restraint is much less costly than police restraint.

The issue of the trends in morality requires an examination of the blessings and curses of individualism and capitalism. One tenet of individualism is that the rights of the individual generally have priority over the rights of government or of the community. This may provide the freedom for wonderful human achievements but might also protect hateful and even dangerous speech and weaken society in the long run. Capitalism would be another demoralizing factor because it encourages self-interest and the passion for personal gain. Higher education may be another culprit because it relativizes values. In general, the forces behind the demoralization of society as described by Bork are not likely to be reversed in the medium-term future.

Most of the relevant literature is on aspects of the moral decline. Few works challenge the decline thesis. Examples include Nicholas Lemann's "It's Not as Bad as You Think It Is," *The Washington Monthly* (March 1997), David Whitman, *The Optimism Gap: The I'm OK—They're not Syndrome and the Myth of American Decline* (Walker & Company, 1998), and Gregg Easterbrook's "America the O.K.," *The New Republic* (January 4 & 11, 1999). For an exposition of the moral decline thesis, see Charles Derber's *The Wilding of America: How Greed and Violence Are Eroding Our Nation's Character* (St. Martin's Press, 1996); and Richard Sennett's *The Corrosion of Character* (W. W. Norton, 1998). Richard Stivers attributes the moral decline to a culture of cynicism in *The Culture of Cynicism: American Morality in Decline* (Basil Blackwell, 1994), while Neal Wood attributes it to capitalism in *Tyranny in America: Capitalism and National Decay* (Verso, 2004). Perhaps the solution to whatever decline may exist is moral education, but according to Tianlong Yu in *In the Name of Morality: Character Education and Political Control* (P. Lang, 2004) this may create the potential for some degree of public mind control by the state.

ISSUE 2

Does the News Media
Have a Liberal Bias?

YES: Willam McGowan, from *Coloring the News: How Crusading for Diversity Has Corrupted American Journalism* (Encounter Books, 2001)

NO: Robert W. McChesney and John Bellamy Foster, from "The 'Left-Wing' Media?" *Monthly Review* (June 2003)

ISSUE SUMMARY

YES: Journalist Willam McGowan argues that political correctness pertaining to diversity issues has captured media newsrooms and exerts a constraining pressure on reporters.

NO: Robert W. McChesney and John Bellamy Foster argue that news reporting is bent in the direction of the political and commercial requirements of media owners, and heavy reliance on government officials and powerful individuals as primary sources biases news toward the status quo.

"A small group of men, numbering perhaps no more than a dozen 'anchormen,' commentators and executive producers . . . decide what forty to fifty million Americans will learn of the day's events in the nation and the world." The speaker was Spiro Agnew, vice president of the United States during the Nixon administration. The thesis of Agnew's speech, delivered to an audience of mid-western Republicans in 1969, was that the television news media are controlled by a small group of liberals who foist their liberal opinions on viewers under the guise of "news." The upshot of this control, said Agnew, "is that a narrow and distorted picture of America often emerges from the televised news." Many Americans, even many of those who were later shocked by revelations that Agnew took bribes while serving in public office, agreed with Agnew's critique of the "liberal media."

Politicians' complaints about unfair news coverage go back much further than Agnew and the Nixon administration. The third president of the United States, Thomas Jefferson, was an eloquent champion of the press, but after six years as president, he could hardly contain his bitterness. "The man who never looks into a newspaper," he wrote, "is better informed than he who reads them, inasmuch as he who knows nothing is nearer to truth than he whose mind is filled with falsehoods and errors."

The press today is much different than it was in Jefferson's day. Newspapers then were pressed in hand-operated frames in many little printing shops around the country; everything was local and decentralized, and each paper averaged a few hundred subscribers. Today, newspaper chains have taken over most of the once-independent local newspapers. Other newspapers, like the *New York Times* and the *Washington Post*, enjoy nationwide prestige and help set the nation's news agenda. Geographical centralization is even more obvious in the case of television. About 70 percent of the national news on television comes from three networks whose programming originates in New York City.

A second important difference between the media of the eighteenth century and the media today has to do with the ideal of "objectivity." In past eras, newspapers were frankly partisan sheets, full of nasty barbs at the politicians and parties the editors did not like; they made no distinction between "news" and "editorials." The ideal of objective journalism is a relatively recent development. It traces back to the early years of the twentieth century. Disgusted with the sensationalist "yellow journalism" of the time, intellectual leaders urged that newspapers cultivate a core of professionals who would concentrate on accurate reporting and who would leave their opinions to the editorial page. Journalism schools cropped up around the country, helping to promote the ideal of objectivity. Although some journalists now openly scoff at it, the ideal still commands the respect—in theory, if not always in practice—of working reporters.

These two historical developments, news centralization and news professionalism, play off against one another in the current debate over news "bias." The question of bias was irrelevant when the press was a scatter of little independent newspapers. Bias started to become an important question when newspapers became dominated by chains and airwaves by networks, and when a few national press leaders like the *New York Times* and the *Washington Post* began to emerge. Although these "mainstream" news outlets have been challenged in recent years by opinions expressed in a variety of alternative media—such as cable television, talk radio, newsletters, and computer mail—they still remain powerful conveyers of news.

Is media news reporting biased? The media constitutes a major socializing institution, so this is an important question. Defenders of the media usually hold that although journalists, like all human beings, have biases, their professionalism compels them to report news with considerable objectivity. Media critics insist that journalists constantly interject their biases into their news reports. The critics, however, often disagree about whether such bias is liberal or conservative, as is the case with this issue. In the following selections, Willam McGowan argues that the news media tilt to the left, while Robert W. McChesney and John Bellamy Foster contend that the slant of the news media supports a conservative status quo. Though McGowan focuses on social issues, McChesney and Foster focus on political and economic issues where conservative elite influence can more easily be protrayed.

William McGowan

 **YES**

Coloring the News: How Crusading for Diversity Has Corrupted American Journalism

This book represents an effort on my part to pose unwelcome questions . . . , and to raise intelligent dissent about the disturbing conformity that has spread over the journalistic community. For most of the 1990s I have been intrigued by journalism's attempts to deal with the issue of diversity and have followed efforts at major news organizations all around the country. While it has been interesting to see the effects on the internal workings of the newsroom itself, I have also been most curious about the impact that diversity is having on news coverage itself, particularly coverage of what might be called "diversity issues" of immigration, race, gay rights, feminism, and affirmative action. I think it is fair to say that these are the most important social issues facing the country—the core of what the pundits call "the culture wars." Has diversity helped or hindered American journalism's ability to make sense of them, and by extension, American society's ability to come to terms with them? . . .

With the cultural topography of the country shifting beneath our feet, we need a press capable of framing essential questions and providing honest, candid and dependable answers. But the diversity-driven journalism we are getting has not done this, a failure that has consequences for our policy responses and our politics and our national conversation.

Most of those critical of the news industry's diversity effort have been conservatives offended by what they see as reporting skewed against their values. But liberals should also be dismayed. The identity politics that diversity journalism encourages is hardly the "progressive" force that its champions insist it is; for it runs at odds with the goal of assimilation and integration that progressives have historically championed. Liberals might also lament the way diversity journalism has contributed to liberalism's intellectual stagnation, as well as its debilitating self-righteousness, by depriving it of facts and insights that might encourage a re-thinking of dated positions.

Neither a conservative nor a liberal, I consider myself a pragmatist deeply committed to a frank and fair rendering of facts, to an intellectually honest, balanced debate about controversial diversity-related issues, and to the ideal of objectivity,

Adapted with permission from the publisher, COLORING THE NEWS: HOW POLITICAL CORRECT-NESS HAS CORRUPTED JOURNALISM by Willam McGowan, Encounter Books, San Francisco, California (© 2003).

which has come under fire in journalism and in the postmodern, multicultural university. Even if you are ideologically predisposed to pro-diversity political positions, I'd like to think that the facts I have marshaled will convince you that the journalism I have scrutinized has a slant to it, and that this slant may not be such a good thing for our country. I believe the public deserves unbiased information to help it through the democratic decisions it needs to make—and that journalism has an obligation to put aside its own political biases in the process of providing that information. Our press needs to rediscover a reverence for "armed neutrality in the face of doctrines," as Giovanni Papini, a disciple of the philosopher William James, once phrased it. To the extent that it has not done this, and to the extent that the diversity crusade plays a role in that failure, there is cause for concern—and a purpose for this book.

❧

The coloring of the news is one of those stories that have been happening more or less invisibly for some years. By December 1992, it was not only in the cultural air, but very much on the table at the joint Diversity Summit Meeting of the American Society of Newspaper Editors and the Newspaper Association of America. This get-together had the unmistakable air of a tent revival, full of grim jeremiads, stern calls for repentance and holy roller zeal. Diversity had been fast becoming one of the most contentious issues in American society and in American journalism, responsible for polarizing, if not balkanizing, more than one newsroom around the country. Yet only one side of the issue was present in this crowd. Speaker after speaker got up to declaim in favor of diversity and to warn of editorial sin and financial doom if this cause was not embraced. . . .

On another level, though, the zealotry was entirely understandable. In the preceding few years, the cause of diversity had become a crusade across the length and breadth of the American media, and would be a defining and dominating force in journalism in the decade to come. Almost every day after that 1992 meeting, one could hear echoes from it in newspaper stories and nightly network broadcasts. Diversity was the new religion, and anybody who wanted to be anybody in the news industry had to rally behind it. . . .

❧

During the late 1980s I spent a number of years reporting and writing about South Asia, one of the world's most ethnically riven places. I had no ideological predispositions in the matter of ethnic issues or identity politics when I began working there. After a few years as a frontline witness to the tragedy of ethnic violence, however, I left with the understanding that identity politics could be extraordinarily divisive, capable of polarizing a country's political affairs, undermining its economic productivity, weakening its educational institutions, and straining the bonds that hold people together as one nation. The experience also taught me that journalists can play a role in either accelerating the process of ethnic fragmentation or containing it, depending on how committed they are to resisting identity politics and to eschewing the politicization of information.

Given what my South Asian experience revealed to me, it was unsettling to watch the mounting potential for cultural and political fragmentation here in the United States early in the 1990s. Rapidly changing demographics fed by increasingly nonwhite, Third World immigration were combining with a liberal cult of race, ethnicity and gender to mount a broad attack on the sense of a common American identity and the ideal of race-neutrality in public life.

While Americans once automatically saw themselves as a nation of individuals relating to one another through a common culture forged in "the melting pot," the new multicultural vision demanded that America be viewed as a "nation of nations"—a mosaic composed of separate ethnic, racial and gender blocs, each with its own cultural reference points, and each to be judged with respect to the rest of society by its own distinct values and standards. This was a vision that celebrated differences over consensus, and spurned what historian Arthur Schlesinger, in *The Disuniting of America,* referred to as a "transformative identity" based on "the historic promise of America: assimilation and integration." The multicultural vision also supported ethnic, racial and gender grievances against the oppression borne of "white male hegemony," and demanded compensatory preferences to help the aggrieved groups overcome their injury.

This shift from melting pot to mosaic represented a profound change in the ground rules of society, with far-flung implications for the shape of politics and civic culture. In effect it represented a vast national experiment, calling all the old givens into question. Whereas we used to emphasize the melding of individuals into an American whole and tried as much as possible to shun race and ethnicity as factors in the conduct of public life, now we were stressing group identity as a legitimate consideration in making laws and shaping social policy. Whereas colorblindness was once regarded as an uncontested article of liberal faith and the key to the liberal ideal of equality, it was now being disparaged as a defense of the "unleveled playing field." Liberals were once the champions of racial transcendence; now they were fast becoming the biggest exponents of racial determinism—the belief that race, ethnicity, gender and sexual orientation matter above all else.

As antithetical to the core values of traditional liberalism as the new identity politics was, it also defied the sustaining journalistic ethos that traditional liberalism had shaped. For this reason, the press might have been expected to scrutinize closely the premises and assumptions of identity politics, to challenge its attendant cant, and to point out its undesirable consequences where appropriate. Instead, much of mainstream journalism was giving it a pass or, even worse, becoming a vehicle for it. . . .

Stories that might have explored the downside of diversity, its wobbly, unexamined assumptions, or its internal contradictions were either ignored or reported with euphemism and embarrassment, as through a fog of avoidance. Unpalatable facts got an airbrushing, while critical voices remained unsought or unacknowledged. Instead of questioning whether multiculturalism was something we really wanted, and letting the American public decide, the press treated it as an immutable *fait accompli,* ignoring competing perspectives and contradictory information that might have cast another light on the concept. The sins of omission were as bad as those of commission, and brought to mind Orwell's famous observation that propaganda is as much a matter of what is left out, as of what is actually said.

On immigration, for example, journalists have tended to embrace a highly romantic, sentimental and historically distorted script which assumes immigration to be an unqualified blessing and minimizes its costs. As the urban historian Peter Salins puts it, the core questions associated with immigration are: "What are we going to become? Who are we? How do the newcomers fit in—and how do the natives handle it?" But it's clear that if the press asks itself these questions at all, it does so in only the most superficial fashion, gliding over realities that might otherwise curb its enthusiasm.

This is so even when evidence of the downside is obvious, as it was in 1992 in New York's Washington Heights, when the justified use of deadly force on the part of a white undercover patrolman was labeled police racism by the *New York Times* and the three-day riot by illegal immigrant Dominican drug dealers was portrayed as justified community outrage. The media script also tends to work hard at filtering out uncomfortable realities that might legitimize calls for tighter controls on newcomers, such as alien criminality, high rates of dependency on social services, the adverse impact that high rates of immigration have had on wages and the quality of life in areas where newcomers have concentrated. . . .

The antagonism to assimilation runs across a variety of fronts, but is starkest in the coverage of bilingual education and efforts to reform it. "Reporters just can't see this issue beyond their own ideological bent," said Alice Callahan, a left-wing Episcopal priest who works with Latino sweatshop workers in Los Angeles, most of whom supported Proposition 227, a measure against bilingual education, in 1998. "I have been surprised how unwilling they are to entertain a view of this issue different from their own preconceived view no matter what the facts are." . . .

With respect to gay and feminist issues, diversity's enhanced sensitivity has purged news coverage of many of the pernicious stereotypes that governed reporting and commentary in the past. But it has also given the coverage a decidedly partisan edge. Whether the issue be the integration of gays and women into the military, AIDS, abortion, gay marriage or gay adoption, the press has tended to side with gay and feminist interest groups, trimming its news-gathering zeal to filter out realities that might undercut the cause.

The script on gays and feminists also tends to depict any objections to their causes—however well grounded in constitutional, moral or institutional traditions—as outright bigotry, worthy of cartoonish portrayal. Those journalists who voice conservative perspectives—or defend those who do—know they can expect blowback, as much from gay activists in the community as from those within news organizations themselves. After writing a column criticizing gay activists at Harvard in 1997, for instance, conservative *Boston Globe* columnist Jeff Jacoby was attacked by gay newsroom colleagues—including two of his copy editors—as well as the paper's ombudsman, who called Jacoby's work "offensive" and "homophobic." Describing the "chilling effect" such internal criticism has, Jacoby said: "A lot of gay activists think that any point of view different from theirs is not only wrong, but so illegitimate and beneath contempt that it doesn't even deserve to be considered. I know up front that if I want to write about this topic, I have to be prepared to run a gauntlet and to jump a lot of hurdles—not among the readers who I think mostly agree with me, but right here in the newsroom."

In terms of bias, though, no subject bears the mark of the new diversity orthodoxy more than the emotionally divisive issue of affirmative action and the politics of racial preference. For years, most of the national press treated affirmative action with little journalistic rigor and scant regard for contradictory facts. No matter how weighty (or grim) the evidence . . . , most of the journalistic establishment has not been above performing a little cosmetic surgery of its own in order to preserve the correct image.

In recent years there has been more readiness to examine the operational details of preference programs, mainly because of newsworthy efforts on the state and national level to roll back such programs. But the press continues to demonstrate its ideological attachment to affirmative action in the energy it spends discrediting efforts to eliminate preferences, such as California's Proposition 209 in 1996 and Washington State's Initiative 200 in 1998. "There was a reflex in the coverage that started with the assumption that people in [the pro-209 movement] had bad motivations, racial motivations," observed Ronald Brownstein of the *Los Angeles Times*. The ideological slant comes through as well in the hysterical, exaggerated way the short-term consequences of these rollback efforts get reported, as in the much-hyped 1997 "Resegregation of Higher Education" story. Contrary to what so many journalists predicted, steps to end racial preferences in university admissions did not result in "lily-white" campuses. In fact, Asian students, not whites, gained in percentage representation, and those minorities who were displaced from the elite schools actually ended up in places more appropriate to their academic qualifications, where they would graduate at higher rates than before. And by mid-2000, the percentage of minority students throughout the University of California system, the focus of most of the "resegregation of higher education" coverage, was up overall. . . .

Efforts to expand newsroom representation by ethnicity, gender and race have not been accompanied by any corresponding effort to expand or enhance intellectual or ideological diversity or an appreciation for it. Diversity, it turns out, is only skin deep. Surveys done over the course of the last two decades consistently show that journalists on the whole are today more liberal than the average citizen, and that the influx of women and minorities has only accentuated that imbalance since these groups are measurably more liberal than others. At some news organizations, especially those most committed to diversity, having liberal values has practically become a condition of employment. People with more traditional or conservative views have a hard time getting through the door, and if they do get through, they are wary of revealing their views.

The problem is not an active liberal conspiracy. Rather, it is one of an invisible liberal consensus, which is either hostile to, or simply unaware of, the other side of things, thereby making the newsroom susceptible to an unconscious but deeply rooted bias. The answer is not affirmative action for conservatives, but rather a recognition that this bias exists and serves as an invisible criterion affecting the hiring process.

Journalism is a profession that prides itself on its maverick outspokenness and its allergic reaction to preconceived notions. Yet in today's media climate, some notions are considered beyond scrutiny—including the merits of the diversity agenda. "I deplore the fact that the issue is so sensitive that reporters don't want to talk by name," one Washington bureau chief told me, hastening to add, "I don't want to contribute to that, but I would rather not be noted by name either." Indeed, in many ways news organizations have become the same kind of dysfunctional cultures as those found on the multicultural university campuses, where transgressions against the dominant line of thought can result in hostility and ostracism. . . .

The fear of being labeled racist, sexist or homophobic makes many white reporters reluctant to challenge this newsroom advocacy. As a *New York Times* reporter told a writer for *Esquire,* "All someone has to do is make a charge of racism and everyone runs away." And instead of taking hard-line stances against racial and ethnic cheerleading or the prickly hypersensitivity that mistakes rigorous editing for prejudice, many managers respond with solicitude because they don't want open ethnic conflict on their staff or they are worried about jeopardizing their careers. One of my *Los Angeles Times* sources said that "a large responsibility lies with the fifty-year-old, white males who find it easier, as a company, to give in to these groups than to deal with the real problems."

Not to be ignored in assessing the impact of diversity doctrine is the false perception reigning in the profession that this cause is the moral successor to the Civil Rights Movement of the 1960s. Many top editors who cut their teeth as young reporters covering civil rights in the South seem still to be fighting the last war in their effort to reconfigure the newsroom, ignoring today's more complicated ethnic and racial picture.

Among other things, the conflation of civil rights with diversity has extended the shelf life of the outdated paradigm of white oppression and non-white victimization, which the media invokes to justify a compensatory system of group preferences. It has also allowed diversity supporters to rationalize and excuse their own excesses and failings. When asked about complaints that the diversity campaign encouraged news organizations to go easy on minority groups, the *New York Time's* Arthur Sulzberger Jr. told *Newsweek's* Ellis Cose, "First you have to get them on the agenda."

Most significantly, though, seeing diversity as the next phase of the Civil Rights Movement has also given the whole media debate about it an overly righteous, moralistic air. This has made it difficult to discuss more subtle issues with the dispassion they require, and has also tended to encourage racial McCarthyism toward critics of the effort by dividing the world between "an enlightened us and unenlightened them," as one *Philadelphia Inquirer* reporter put it. As a result, "the whole debate gets lowered to a grade school level of oversimplification" with little effort expended to see the other side, complained former *Los Angeles Times* reporter Jill Stewart. . . .

In the end, though, the press's diversity crusade has performed its greatest disservice to the country's broader civic culture by oversimplifying complicated issues and by undermining the spirit of public cooperation and trust without which no multiethnic and multiracial society can survive. Instead of making public discourse intellectually more sophisticated, the diversity ethos has helped to dumb it down. Instead of nurturing a sense of common citizenship, the emphasis on diversity has celebrated cultural separatism and supported a race-conscious approach to public life. And instead of enhancing public trust—a critical element in the forging of consensus on the thorny social issues we face—the press's diversity effort has manufactured cynicism through reporting and analysis distorted by double standards, intellectual dishonesty and fashionable cant that favors certain groups over others.

The task of building a workable multiethnic and multiracial society is daunting, but by coloring the news, the diversity crusade has made it even more problematical. As one perceptive reporter at the *San Francisco Chronicle* reflected: "The ultimate goal is a society with as much racial and ethnic fairness and harmony as possible, but we can't get there unless we in the press are ready to talk about it in full."

NO

**Robert W. McChesney
and John Bellamy Foster**

The 'Left-Wing' Media?

If we learn nothing else from the war on Iraq and its subsequent occupation, it is that the U.S. ruling class has learned to make ideological warfare as important to its operations as military and economic warfare. A crucial component of this ideological war has been the campaign against "left-wing media bias," with the objective of reducing or eliminating the prospect that mainstream U.S. journalism might be at all critical toward elite interests or the system set up to serve those interests. In 2001 and 2002, no less than three books purporting to demonstrate the media's leftward tilt rested high atop the bestseller list. Such charges have already influenced media content, pushing journalists to be less critical of right-wing politics. The result has been to reinforce the corporate and rightist bias already built into the media system. . . .

The current attack on media content is presented as an attempt to counter the alleged bias of media elites. In reality, however, it is designed to shrink still further—to the point of oblivion—the space for critical analysis in journalism. In order to understand the form and content of the conservative onslaught on the media it is necessary to have some comprehension of the role played by professional journalism beginning in the early twentieth century.

Prior to 1900, the editorial position of a newspaper invariably reflected the political views of the owner, and the politics were explicit throughout the paper. Partisan journalism became problematic when newspapers became increasingly commercial enterprises and when newspaper markets became predominantly monopolistic. During the Progressive Era—as was chronicled in these pages a year ago—U.S. journalism came under withering attack for being a tool of its capitalist owners to propagate anti-labor propaganda.[1] With profit-making in the driver's seat, partisan journalism became bad for business as it turned off parts of the potential readership and that displeased advertisers. Professional journalism was born from the revolutionary idea that the link between owner and editor could be broken. The news would be determined by trained professionals and the politics of owners and advertisers would be apparent only on the editorial page. Journalists would be given considerable autonomy to control the news using their professional judgment. Among other things, they would be trained to establish their political

From *Monthly Review*, vol. 55, no. 2, June 2003, pp. 1–16. Copyright © 2003 by Monthly Review. Reprinted with permission.

neutrality. Monopoly control over the news in particular markets was not especially important—so the argument went—since, whether or not there were multiple newspapers, trained professionals would provide similar reports, to the extent that they were well trained. There emerged a professional code that, following *The Elements of Journalism*, by Bill Kovack and Tom Rosenstiel, might be reduced in its most ideal form to nine principles:

1. Journalism's first obligation is to the truth.
2. Its first loyalty is to citizens.
3. Its essence is a discipline of verification.
4. Its practitioners must maintain an independence from those they cover.
5. It must serve as an independent monitor of power.
6. It must provide a forum for public criticism and compromise.
7. It must strive to make the significant interesting and relevant.
8. It must keep the news comprehensive and proportional.
9. Its practitioners must be allowed to exercise their personal conscience.

Needless to say, such principles are mere ideals in a society where the media are ultimately controlled by those who hold the purse strings. Under these circumstances, the field for the application of journalism's professional code is narrow, and it has been altered to conform to the political and commercial requirements of the media owners, and the owning class in general. In practice, professional journalism has adopted three biases that have tended to institute an establishment bias: (1) government officials and powerful individuals are regarded as the primary legitimate sources for news; (2) to avoid the controversy associated with providing context, there has to be a news hook or news peg to justify a news story, which further tilts the news toward established institutional actors; and (3) journalists internalize how to "dig here, not there," as Ben Bagdikian put it. In other words, stories about corporate malfeasance are far less likely to be considered newsworthy than stories about government malfeasance.

To be sure, professional journalists puts a premium on fairness and social neutrality, but such principles are notoriously difficult to define since there is always a question of where to put the baseline. This has created a situation where the standards maintained are skewed toward the controlling business elites. The present rightward drift is making this even more of a reality.

The conservative critique is based then on four propositions: (1) the decisive power over the news lies with the journalists—owners and advertisers are irrelevant or relatively powerless; (2) journalists are political liberals; (3) journalists abuse their power to advance liberal politics—thus breaking the professional code; and (4) objective journalism would almost certainly present the world exactly as seen by contemporary U.S. conservatives. For their basic argument to hold the first three propositions must be valid. Moreover, for conservatives to continue to maintain a commitment to professional journalism, the media system would have to meet the standard of "objectivity" expressed by the fourth proposition—this is the unstated assumption underlying their entire argument. But this would spell the end of professional journalism as it is now understood. Indeed, it is our thesis that the conservative critics, while relying on the notion of bias (the violation of the professional code of neutrality) as the basis of their criticism of allegedly left-wing media, are not actually concerned with defending professional journalism at all but with eliminating it—as a no longer necessary concession on the part of those who own and ultimately control the media.

The first proposition is intellectually indefensible and is enough to call the entire conservative critique of the liberal news media into question. No credible scholarly analysis of journalism posits that journalists have the decisive power to determine what is and is not news and how it should be covered. In commercial media, the owners hire and fire and they determine the budgets and the overarching aims of the enterprise. Successful journalists, and certainly those who rise to the top of the profession, tend to internalize the values of those who own and control the enterprise. Sophisticated scholarly analysis examines how these commercial pressures shape what become the professional values that guide journalists. Indeed, the genius of professionalism in journalism is that it allows journalists to adopt the commercial/professional values of the owners, yet, because they are following a professional code, they are largely oblivious to the compromises to authority that they are making. They are taught that there is a legitimate spectrum of opinion, conforming to the range of discussions among those who actually own and control the society. Their professional autonomy, such as it is, does not allow them to go outside that spectrum *in the framing* of stories—no matter how far this removes the resulting journalism from the realities experienced by a majority in the United States and the world.

In the formative period of professionalism, especially in the 1930s, journalists like George Seldes and Haywood Broun, through their union, the Newspaper Guild, strove to establish a professional code which would be progressive and emphasize the need to advance the interests of those outside the power structure. They fought to keep the hands of the owners entirely off the content of the news. We will not keep you in suspense. They lost. The eventually dominant professional code for journalism was small-*c* conservative; its call for reliance upon official sources as the basis of legitimate news, and its definition of official sources as those in power meant it could hardly be otherwise. This episode suggests that a more powerful labor movement and, in particular, more powerful media workers' unions are crucial to protecting the integrity of journalism in a capitalist media system.

The most striking example of the deep flaws built into the professional code comes in the area of coverage of U.S. foreign policy and militarism. The range of legitimate debate in U.S. journalism has been and is the range of debate among the elite. Hence the U.S. right to invade any nation it wishes for any reason is never challenged in the press, because to our elites this is a cardinal right of empire. Likewise, the U.S. equation of capitalism with democracy, or, more specifically, U.S. dominated capitalism with democracy, is also a given among our elites and therefore in professional journalism. For journalists to question these matters on their own reveals them to be partisan and unprofessional, so it is not done. This highlights the severe limitations of professional journalism as a democratic force. With the emergence of global news media, this has presented institutions like CNN with a particular dilemma. If they broadcast their rah-rah U.S. news outside the United States it is dismissed as so much blatant propaganda; if they broadcast critical journalism in the United States it is dismissed as unprofessional. With little sense of irony, during the current Iraq war and occupation, CNN has adopted a two-track approach to its journalism, with the United States and the rest of the world getting very different pictures.

Yet, even with this truncated professional code, the rise of professionalism did grant journalists a degree of autonomy from the immediate dictates of owners. The high-water mark for journalist autonomy was from the 1950s to the 1970s. The great unreported story in journalism of the past quarter century, ironically enough, has been the attack upon journalist autonomy by media owners. Increasingly, the massive conglomerates that have come to rule the U.S. news media have found that the professional "deal" struck in the first half of the twentieth century no longer serves their needs. They have slashed resources for journalism and pushed journalists to do inexpensive and trivial reporting. In particular, expensive and not commercially lucrative investigative and international coverage was reduced if not effectively eliminated. To the extent the conservative critique of the liberal media was based upon a concern about journalists having too much power over determining the news, they have won that battle. Journalists have markedly less autonomy today than two or three decades ago.

In fact, conservatives tacitly acknowledge the transparently ideological basis of the claim that journalists have all the power over the news. The real problem isn't that journalists have all the power over the news, or even most of the power, it is that they have *any* power to be autonomous from owners and advertisers. For conservatives, the influence of owners and advertisers is not a problem since they have both the proper political worldview, and unique rights as owners. The conservative critics thus focus on journalists as a kind of fifth column attacking conservative values from within the media. Newt Gingrich, with typical candor and a lack of PR rhetoric, laid bare the logic behind the conservative critique: what needs to be done is to eliminate journalistic autonomy, and return the politics of journalism to the politics of media owners. This also helps to explain why U.S. rightists tend to be obsessed with pushing public broadcasting to operate by commercial principles; they know that the market will very effectively push the content to more politically acceptable outcomes, without any need for direct censorship.

The second proposition of the conservative critique—that journalists are liberals—has the most evidence to support it. Surveys show that journalists tend to vote Democratic in a greater proportion than the general population. In one famous (though highly criticized as methodologically flawed) survey of how Washington correspondents voted in the 1992 presidential election, something like 90 percent voted for Bill Clinton (the favorite of the larger population that year, and hardly a raging progressive). To some conservative critics, that settles the matter. But, the weakness of the first proposition undermines the importance of how journalists vote, or what their particular political beliefs might be. What if owners and managers have most of the power, both directly and through the internalization of their political and commercial values in the professional code? Surveys show that media owners and editorial executives vote overwhelmingly Republican. An *Editor & Publisher* survey found that in 2000 newspaper publishers favored George W. Bush over Al Gore by a 3 to 1 margin, while newspaper editors and publishers together favored Bush by a 2 to 1 margin. In addition, why should a vote for Al Gore or Bill Clinton be perceived as a reflection of leftist politics? On many or most policies these are moderate to conservative Democrats, very comfortable with the status quo of the U.S. political economy.

Already a problem with the argument is apparent . . . : the terms "liberal" and "left-wing" are used interchangeably. In the conservative argument, the great divide in U.S. politics is between conservatives and the "left," a group that spreads unambiguously from Al Gore and Bill Clinton to Ralph Nader, Nelson Mandela, Noam Chomsky, and Subcommandante Marcos. To listen to the shock troops of the current conservative assault on the journalistic profession, support for Gore or Clinton is virtually indistinguishable from being an anarcho-syndicalist or a Marxist. Bernard Goldberg, author of the recent bestseller *Bias* that purports to demonstrate left-wing media bias, associates, albeit flippantly, political strategists for Clinton with Marx in their contempt for the rich, and adds that, "Everybody to the right of Lenin is a 'right-winger' as far as the media elite are concerned."

To the extent there is any basis whatsoever for such claims, it has to do with the fact that conservatives see any concession to social welfare needs as evidence of creeping socialism. Clinton Democrats and radical leftists become the same because of the conservative measure of what it means to be a leftist. It is based almost exclusively upon what are called social issues, such as a commitment to gay rights, women's rights, abortion rights, civil liberties, and affirmative action. And indeed, on these issues a notable percentage of journalists (like most educated professionals) tend to have positions similar to many of those to their left. For Goldberg "the real menace, as the Left sees it, is that America has always been too willing to step on its most vulnerable—gays, women, blacks. Because the Left controls America's newsrooms, we get a view of America that reflects that sensibility."

But this is absurd. Not only do newsrooms *not* project such sensibilities for the most part, the real divide in U.S. politics is not about issues such as affirmative action and thus between the liberal and conservative sides of elite opinion, but between elite opinion and those outside the elite, especially the left (using the term to refer mainly to those who challenge the system itself). Traditionally, journalists have had some autonomy to carry out news investigations and raise questions—as long as they stayed within the legitimate spectrum of debate established by elite opinion. The actual record of the U.S. news media is to pay very little direct attention to the political left as outside that spectrum, and this applies not only to socialists and radicals but also to what would be called mild social democrats by international standards. What attention the left actually gets tends to be unsympathetic, if not explicitly negative. Foreign journalists write about how U.S. left-wing social critics, who are prominent and respected public figures abroad, are virtually non-persons in the U.S. news media.

The Achilles heel for this conservative critique of journalist liberalism, and therefore entirely absent from their pronouncements, however, is a consideration of journalists' views on issues of the economy and regulation. Here, unlike with social issues, surveys show that journalists hold positions that tend to be more pro-business and conservative than the bulk of the population. It is here, too, that the professional code has adapted to the commercial and political concerns of the owners to generate a stridently pro-capitalist journalism. In the past two decades, labor news has all but been eliminated as a legitimate branch of U.S. journalism. In the 1940s and 1950s there were hundreds and hundreds of full time labor editors and reporters on U.S. daily newspapers; today the total of labor journalists in the mainstream media, including radio and TV, runs in single digits. Business news has vaulted to prominence, to the point where it equals and may well exceed traditional political journalism. And the increased attention to the affairs of business has not generated a wellspring of critical investigative coverage of the political economy; to the contrary, much of the coverage approaches the hagiography of a kept press toward its maximum leader. Today most journalists do not consider the affairs of poor people, immigrants, ethnic minorities, and working people the fodder of journalism, whereas the interests (and happiness) of investors are of supreme importance. . . .

Indeed, any serious look at how questions surrounding class and economic matters are treated would quickly free the journalistic profession from any charges of left-wing bias. Over the past two generations, journalism, especially at the larger and more prominent news media, has evolved from being a blue-collar job to becoming a desirable occupation of the well-educated upper-middle class. Urban legend has it that when the news of the stock market crash came over the ticker to the *Boston Globe* newsroom in 1929, the journalists all arose to give Black Monday a standing ovation. The rich were finally getting their comeuppance! When the news of the stock market crash reached the *Globe* newsroom in 1987, however, journalists were all frantically on the phone to their brokers. As recently as 1971 just over one-half of U.S. newspaper journalists had college degrees; by 2002 nearly 90 percent did. The median salary for a journalist at one of the forty largest circulation newspapers in the United States in 2002 was nearly double the median income for all U.S. workers. Journalists at the dominant media are unlikely to have any idea what it means to go without health insurance, to be unable to locate affordable housing, to have their children in underfunded and dilapidated schools, to have relatives in prison or the front lines of the military, to face the threat of severe poverty. They live in a very different world from most Americans. They may be "liberal" on certain issues, but on the core issues of political economy, they are hardly to the left of the U.S. population. Populist views are anathema to them by training and they tend to be quite comfortable with the corporate status quo. To the extent that their background and values determine the news, it is naive to expect journalists with their establishment-centered professional training to be sympathetic with anything more than a kind of elite centrism, far away from progressive left-wing policies and regulations.

As for the third proposition, that journalists use what limited autonomy they have to advance liberal-of-center politics, the evidence is far from convincing. One of the core points of the professional code is to prevent journalists from pushing their own politics on to the news, and many journalists are proud to note that while they are liberal, their coverage tended to bend the stick the other way, to stave off the charge that they have a liberal bias and are unprofessional. As one news producer stated, "the main bias of journalists is the bias not to look like they favor liberals." "One of the biggest career threats for journalists," a veteran Washington reporter wrote in 2002, "is to be accused of 'liberal bias' for digging up stories that put conservatives in a bad light." It is worth noting that in the current U.S. media environment, few journalists have any such concern about not revealing a pro-conservative bias. Such is done roundly and with little concern about accusations of bias, except from marginalized, ignored, and disgruntled leftists. . . .

As for the final proposition, that truly objective journalism would invariably see the world exactly the way Rush Limbaugh sees it, this points to the ideological nature of the exercise. Despite the attention paid to the news, there has never been an instance of conservatives criticizing journalism for being too soft on a right wing politician or unfair to liberals or the left. It is a one-way street. Conservatives sometimes respond to such criticisms that this is what all media criticism is about—whining that your side is getting treated unfairly. In 1992, Rich Bond, then the chair of the Republican Party, acknowledged that the point of bashing the liberal media was to "work the refs" like a basketball coach does, with the goal that "maybe the ref will cut you a little slack on the next one." Honest scholarship attempts to provide a coherent and intellectually consistent explanation of journalism that can withstand critical interrogation. The conservative critique of the liberal news media is an intellectual failure, riddled with contradictions and inaccuracy.

So why is the conservative critique of the liberal news media such a significant force in U.S. political and media culture? To some extent this is because this critique has tremendous emotional power, fitting into a broader story of the conservative masses battling the establishment liberal media elite. In this world, spun by right-wing pundits like Ann Coulter and Sean Hannity, conservatives do righteous battle against the alliance of Clinton, Castro, bin Laden, drug users, gays, rappers, feminists, teachers unions and journalists, who hold power over the world. As one conservative activist put it, the battle over media is a "David and Goliath struggle." At its strongest, and most credible, the conservative critique taps into the elitism inherent to professionalism and to liberalism though this right-wing populism turns to mush the moment the issue of class is introduced. To be sure, some conservative media criticism backs away from fire breathing, and attempts to present a more tempered critique, even criticizing the rampant commercialization of journalism.

The main reason for the prominence of the right-wing critique of the liberal news media, however, has little or nothing to do with the intellectual quality of the arguments. It is the result of hardcore political organizing and it takes a lot of financial backers with deep pockets to produce that result. The conservative movement against liberal journalism was launched in earnest in the 1970s. Conservative critics claimed that the liberal media was to blame for losing the Vietnam War. Pro-business foundations were aghast at what they saw as the anti-business sentiment prevalent among Americans, especially middle-class youth, usually a core constituency for support. Mainstream journalism, which in reporting the activities of official sources was also giving people like Ralph Nader sympathetic exposure, was seen as a prime culprit. At that point the political right, supported by their wealthy donors, began to devote enormous resources to criticizing and changing the news media. Around one-half of all the expenditures of the twelve largest conservative foundations have been devoted to the task of moving the news rightward. This has entailed funding the training of conservative and business journalists at universities, creating conservative media to provide a training ground, establishing conservative think tanks to flood journalism with pro-business official sources, and incessantly jawboning any coverage whatsoever that is critical of conservative interests as being reflective of "liberal" bias. The pro-business right understood that changing media was a crucial part of bringing right-wing ideas into prominence and politicians into power. "You get huge leverage for your dollars," a conservative philanthropist noted when he discussed the turn to ideological work. There is a well-organized, well-financed and active hardcore conservative coterie working to push the news media to the right. As a *Washington Post* White House correspondent put it, "the liberal equivalent of this conservative coterie does not exist." . . .

The crucial change in the news media has not been the increased marginalization of the left—that has always been the case—but, rather, the shrinkage of room for critical work in journalism—what was best about the professional system—and the accompanying shift in favorable coverage toward the conservative branch of elite opinion. Looking at the different manner in which the press has portrayed and pursued the political careers of Bill Clinton and George W. Bush reveals the scope of the conservative victory. A Nexus search, for example, reveals that there were 13,641 stories about Clinton avoiding the military draft, and a mere 49 stories about Bush having his powerful father use influence to get him put at the head of the line to get into the National Guard. Bill Clinton's small time Whitewater affair justified a massive seven-year, $70 million open-ended special investigation of his business and personal life that never established any criminal business activity, but eventually did produce the Lewinsky allegations. Rick Kaplan, former head of CNN, acknowledged that he instructed CNN to provide the Lewinsky story massive attention, despite his belief that it was overblown, because he knew he would face withering criticism from the right for a liberal bias if he did not do so.

George W. Bush, on the other hand, had a remarkably dubious business career in which he made a fortune flouting security laws, tapping public funds, and using his father's connections to protect his backside, but the news media barely sniffed at the story and it received no special prosecutor. His conviction for driving under the influence of alcohol barely attracted notice. One doubts the head of CNN goes to sleep at night in fear of being accused of being too soft on Bush's business dealings or his past record of inebriation.

The conservative propaganda campaign against the liberal media is hardly the dominant factor in understanding news media behavior. It works in combination with the broader limitations of professional journalism as well as the commercial attack upon journalism. Conservative ideology and commercialized, depoliticized "journalism" have meshed very well, and it is this combination that defines the present moment. Subjected to commercial pressures not seen for nearly a century, if ever, and under attack from conservatives, journalism as we know it is in a perilous state. This may not, however, be a total tragedy, given the fact that such professional journalism has done more to support power than to question it, more to quell democracy than invigorate it. In the wake of the destruction of the old media system it is time to construct a new one. And this time around it should be our media—that of democratic forces—not theirs. In other words, we have to begin the struggle all over again, challenging once again big business domination of the media and the corrosive logic it has produced.

Note

1. See Robert W. McChesney and Ben Scott, "Upton Sinclair and the Contradictions of Capitalist Journalism," *Monthly Review* 54, no. 1 (May 2002): 1–14.

POSTSCRIPT

Does the News Media
Have a Liberal Bias?

As the opposing arguments in this issue indicate, we can find critics on both the Left and the Right who agree that the media are biased. What divides such critics is the question of whether the bias is left-wing or right-wing. Defenders of the news media may seize upon this disagreement to bolster their own claim that "bias is in the eye of the beholder." But the case may be that the news media are unfair to both sides. If that were true, however, it would seem to take some of the force out of the argument that the news media have a distinct ideological tilt at all.

Edward Jay Epstein's *News from Nowhere* (Random House, 1973) remains one of the great studies of the factors that influence television news shows. In *Media Events: The Live Broadcasting of History* (Harvard University Press, 1992), Daniel Dayan and Elihu Katz argue that live television coverage of major events helps to create the events and serves an important integrative role for society by deepening most citizens' experience of a common history. A study by S. Robert Lichter et al., *The Media Elite* (Adler & Adler, 1986), tends to support McGowan's contention that the media slant leftward, as does Ann Coulter in *Slander: Liberal Lies about the American Right* (Crown Publishers, 2002), and Bernard Goldberg in *BIAS: A CBS Insider Exposes How the Media Distort the News* (Regency Publishing, 2002), whereas Ben Bagdikian's *The Media Monopoly* 6th edition (Beacon Press, 2000); Mark Hertsgaard's *On Bended Knee: The Press and the Reagan Presidency* (Schocken, 1989); Eric Alterman's *What Liberal Media? The Truth about Bias and the News* (Basic Books, 2003); and Robert Waterman McChesney, *The Problem of the Media: U.S. Communication Politics in the Twenty-First Century* (Monthly Review Press, 2004) lend support to McChesney and Foster's view. A more recent S. Robert Lichter book, coauthored with Linda Lichter and Stanley Rothman, is *Watching America* (Prentice Hall, 1991), which surveys the political and social messages contained in television "entertainment" programs. Several recent memoirs of journalists are very useful for the debate on media bias. See Tom Wicker's *On the Record* (Bedford/ St. Martin's, 2002); Ted Koppel's *Off Camera* (Alfred A. Knopf, 2000);

and Bill O'Reilly's *The No-Spin Zone* (Broadway Books, 2001). David Halberstam's *The Powers That Be* (Alfred A. Knopf, 1979), a historical study of CBS, the *Washington Post, Time* magazine, and the *Los Angeles Times,* describes some of the political and ideological struggles that have taken place within major media organizations.

ISSUE 3

Is Third World Immigration a Threat to America's Way of Life?

YES: Patrick Buchanan, from "Shields Up!" *The American Enterprise* (March 2002)

NO: Ben Wattenberg, from "Immigration Is Good," *The American Enterprise* (March 2002)

ISSUE SUMMARY

YES: Political analyst Patrick Buchanan asserts that the large influx of legal and illegal immigrants, especially from Mexico, threatens to undermine the cultural foundations of American unity.

NO: Ben Wattenberg, senior fellow at the American Enterprise Institute, argues that the United States needs a constant flow of immigrants to avoid population decline and also to avoid the diminishment of power and influence.

Before September 11, 2001, many Americans favored the reduction of immigration. After the terrorist attacks on the World Trade Center and the Pentagon by immigrants, some felt even stronger about limiting immigration. But is immigration bad for America, as this sentiment assumes, or does it strengthen America?

Today the number of legal immigrants to America is close to 1 million per year, and illegal ("undocumented") immigrants probably number well over that figure. In terms of numbers, immigration is now comparable to the level it reached during the early years of the twentieth century, when millions of immigrants arrived from southern and eastern Europe. A majority of the new immigrants, however, do not come from Europe but from what has been called the "Third World"—the underdeveloped nations. The largest percentages come from Mexico, the Philippines, Korea, and the islands of the Caribbean, while European immigration has shrunk to about 10 percent. Much of the reason for this shift has to do with changes made in U.S. immigration laws during the 1960s. Decades earlier, in the 1920s, America had narrowed its gate to people from certain regions of the world by imposing quotas designed to preserve the balance of races in America. But in 1965 a series of amendments to the Immigration Act put all the world's people on an equal footing in terms of immigration. The result, wrote journalist Theodore H. White, was "a stampede, almost an invasion" of Third World immigrants. Indeed, the 1965 amendments made it even easier for Third World immigrants to enter the country because the new law gave preference to those with a family member already living in the United States. Since most of the European immigrants who settled in the early part of the century had died off, and since few Europeans had immigrated in more recent years, a greater percentage of family-reuniting immigration came from the Third World.

Immigrants move to the United States for various reasons: to flee tyranny and terrorism, to escape war, or to join relatives who have already settled. Above all, they immigrate because in their eyes America is an island of affluence in a global sea of poverty; here they will earn many times what they could only hope to earn in their native countries. One hotly debated question is, What will these new immigrants do to the United States—or for it?

Part of the debate has to do with bread-and-butter issues: Will new immigrants take jobs away from American workers? Or will they fill jobs that American workers do not want anyway, which will help stimulate the economy? Behind these economic issues is a more profound cultural question: Will these new immigrants add healthy new strains to America's cultural inheritance, broadening and revitalizing it? Or will they cause the country to break up into separate cultural units, destroying America's unity? Of all the questions relating to immigration, this one seems to be the most sensitive.

In 1992 conservative columnist Patrick Buchanan set off a firestorm of controversy when he raised this question: "If we had to take a million immigrants next year, say Zulus or Englishmen, and put them in Virginia, which group would be easier to assimilate and cause less problems for the people of Virginia?" Although Buchanan later explained that his intention was not to denigrate Zulus or any other racial group but to simply talk about assimilation into Anglo-American culture, his remarks were widely characterized as racist and xenophobic (related to a fear of foreigners). Whether or not that characterization is justified, Buchanan's question goes to the heart of the cultural debate over immigration, which is the tension between unity and diversity.

In the selections that follow, Buchanan contends that immigrants are harming the United States both economically and culturally. He argues that the sheer number of immigrants from other cultures threatens to overwhelm traditional safeguards against cultural disintegration and that this foreign influx is changing America from a nation into a collection of separate nationalities. Ben Wattenberg counters that immigration will benefit the United States, especially by making it a "universal" nation that will be better able to compete in a future that is increasingly global.

 **YES**

Shields Up!

In 1821, a newly independent Mexico invited Americans to settle in its northern province of Texas—on two conditions: Americans must embrace Roman Catholicism, and they must swear allegiance to Mexico. Thousands took up the offer. But, in 1835, after the tyrannical General Santa Anna seized power, the Texans, fed up with loyalty oaths and fake conversions, and outnumbering Mexicans in Texas ten to one, rebelled and kicked the tiny Mexican garrison back across the Rio Grande.

Santa Anna led an army north to recapture his lost province. At a mission called the Alamo, he massacred the first rebels who resisted. Then he executed the 400 Texans who surrendered at Goliad. But at San Jacinto, Santa Anna blundered straight into an ambush. His army was butchered, he was captured. The Texans demanded his execution for the Alamo massacre, but Texas army commander Sam Houston had another idea. He made the dictator an offer: his life for Texas. Santa Anna signed. And on his last day in office, Andrew Jackson recognized the independence of the Lone Star Republic.

Eight years later, the U.S. annexed the Texas republic. An enraged Mexico disputed the American claim to all land north of the Rio Grande, so President James Polk sent troops to the north bank of the river. When Mexican soldiers crossed and fired on a U.S. patrol, Congress declared war. By 1848, soldiers with names like Grant, Lee, and McClellan were in the city of Montezuma. A humiliated Mexico was forced to cede all of Texas, the Southwest, and California. The U.S. gave Mexico $15 million to ease the anguish of amputation.

Mexicans seethed with hatred and resentment, and in 1910 the troubles began anew. After a revolution that was anti-church and anti-American, U.S. sailors were roughed up and arrested in Tampico. In 1914, President Woodrow Wilson ordered the occupation of Vera Cruz by U.S. Marines. As Wilson explained to the British ambassador, "I am going to teach the South Americans to elect good men." When the bandit Pancho Villa led a murderous raid into New Mexico in 1916, Wilson sent General Pershing and 10,000 troops to do the tutoring.

Despite FDR's Good Neighbor Policy, President Cárdenas nationalized U.S. oil companies in 1938—an event honored in Mexico to this day. Pemex was born, a state cartel that would collude with OPEC in 1999 to hike up oil prices to $35 a barrel. American consumers, whose tax dollars had supported a $50 billion bailout of a bankrupt Mexico in 1994, got gouged.

⋅⚙⋅

The point of this history? Mexico has an historic grievance against the United States that is felt deeply by her people. This is one factor producing deep differences in attitudes toward America between today's immigrants from places like Mexico and the old immigrants from Ireland, Italy, and Eastern Europe. With fully one-fifth of all people of Mexican ancestry now residing in the United States, and up to 1 million more crossing the border every year, we need to understand these differences.

2. The number of people pouring in from Mexico is larger than any wave from any country ever before. In the 1990s alone, the number of people of Mexican heritage living in the U.S. grew by 50 percent to at least 21 million. The Founding Fathers wanted immigrants to spread out among the population to ensure assimilation, but Mexican Americans are highly concentrated in the Southwest.

3. Mexicans are not only from another culture, but of another race. History has taught that different races are far more difficult to assimilate than different cultures. The 60 million Americans who claim German ancestry are fully assimilated, while millions from Africa and Asia are still not full participants in American society.

4. Millions of Mexicans broke the law to get into the United States, and they break the law every day they remain here. Each year, 1.6 million illegal aliens are apprehended, almost all of them at our bleeding southern border.

5. Unlike the immigrants of old, who bade farewell to their native lands forever, millions of Mexicans have no desire to learn English or be-come U.S. citizens. America is not their home; they are here to earn money. They remain proud Mexicans. Rather than assimilate, they create their own radio and TV stations, newspapers, films, and magazines. They are becoming a nation within a nation.

6. These waves of Mexican immigrants are also arriving in a different America than did the old immigrants. A belief in racial rights and ethnic entitlements has taken root among America's minorities and liberal elites. Today, ethnic enclaves are encouraged and ethnic chauvinism is rife in the barrios. Anyone quoting Calvin Coolidge's declaration that "America must remain American" today would be charged with a hate crime.

Harvard professor Samuel P. Huntington, author of *The Clash of Civilizations*, calls migration "the central issue of our time." He has warned in the pages of this magazine:

> If 1 million Mexican soldiers crossed the border, Americans would treat it as a major threat to their national security. . . . The invasion of over 1 million Mexican civilians . . . would be a comparable threat to American societal security, and Americans should react against it with vigor.

Mexican immigration is a challenge to our cultural integrity, our national identity, and potentially to our future as a country. Yet, American leaders are far from reacting "with vigor," even though a Zogby poll found that 72 percent of Americans want less immigration, and a Rasmussen poll in July 2000 found that 89 percent support English as America's official language. The people want action. The elites disagree—and do nothing. Despite our braggadocio about being "the world's only remaining superpower," the U.S. lacks the fortitude to defend its borders and to demand, without apology, that immigrants assimilate to its society.

Perhaps our mutual love of the dollar can bridge the cultural chasm, and we shall all live happily in what Ben Wattenberg calls the First Universal Nation. But Uncle Sam is taking a hellish risk in importing a huge diaspora of tens of millions of people from a nation vastly different from our own. It is not a decision we can ever undo. Our children will live with the consequences. "If assimilation fails," Huntington recognizes, "the United States will become a cleft country with all the potentials for internal strife and disunion that entails." Is that a risk worth taking?

A North American Union of Canada, Mexico, and the United States has been proposed by Mexican President Fox, with a complete opening of borders to the goods and peoples of the three countries. *The Wall Street Journal* is enraptured. But Mexico's per capita GDP of $5,000 is only a fraction of America's—the largest income gap on earth between two adjoining countries. Half of all Mexicans live in poverty, and 18 million people exist on less than $2 a day, while the U.S. minimum wage is headed for $50 a day. Throw open the border, and millions could flood into the United States within months. Is America nothing more than an economic system?

⚜

Our old image is of Mexicans as amiable Catholics with traditional values. There are millions of hard-working, family-oriented Americans of Mexican heritage, who have been quick to answer the call to arms in several of America's wars. And, yes, history has shown that any man or woman, from any country on the planet, can be a good American.

But today's demographic sea change, especially in California, where a fourth of the residents are foreign-born and almost a third are Latino, has spawned a new ethnic chauvinism. When the U.S. soccer team played Mexico in Los Angeles a few years ago, the "Star-Spangled Banner" was jeered, an American flag was torn down, and the U.S. team and its few fans were showered with beer bottles and garbage.

In the New Mexico legislature in 2001, a resolution was introduced to rename the state "Nuevo Mexico," the name it carried before it became a part of the American Union. When the bill was defeated, sponsor Representative Miguel Garcia suggested to reporters that "covert racism" may have been the cause.

A spirit of separatism, nationalism, and irredentism has come alive in the barrio. Charles Truxillo, a professor of Chicano Studies at the University of New Mexico, says a new "Aztlan," with Los Angeles as its capital, is inevitable. José Angel Gutierrez, a political science professor at the University of Texas at Arlington and director of the UTA Mexican-American Study Center, told a university crowd: "We have an aging white America. They are not making babies. They are dying. The explosion is in our population. They are shitting in their pants in fear! I love it."

More authoritative voices are sounding the same notes. The Mexican consul general José Pescador Osuna remarked in 1998, "Even though I am saying this part serious, part joking, I think we are practicing La Reconquista in California." California legislator Art Torres called Proposition 187, to cut off welfare to illegal aliens, "the last gasp of white America."

"California is going to be a Mexican State. We are going to control all the institutions. If people don't like it, they should leave," exults Mario Obledo, president of the League of United Latin American Citizens, and recipient of the Medal of Freedom from President Clinton. Former Mexican president Ernesto Zedillo told Mexican-Americans in Dallas: "You are Mexicans, Mexicans who live north of the border."

·❀·

Why should nationalistic and patriotic Mexicans not dream of a *reconquista*? The Latino student organization known by its Spanish acronym MEChA states, "We declare the independence of our *mestizo* nation. We are a bronze people with a bronze culture. Before the world, before all of North America . . . we are a nation." MEChA demands U.S. "restitution" for "past economic slavery, political exploitation, ethnic and cultural psychological destruction and denial of civil and human rights."

MEChA, which claims 400 campus chapters across the country, is unabashedly racist and anti-American. Its slogan—Por la Raza todo. Fuera de La Raza nada.—translates as "For our race, everything. For those outside our race, nothing." Yet it now exerts real power in many places. The former chair of its UCLA chapter, Antonio Villaraigosa, came within a whisker of being elected mayor of Los Angeles in 2001.

That Villaraigosa could go through an entire campaign for control of America's second-largest city without having to explain his association with a Chicano version of the white-supremacist Aryan Nation proves that America's major media are morally intimidated by any minority that boasts past victimhood credentials, real or imagined.

⋅◦⟨◉⟩◦⋅

Meanwhile, the invasion rolls on. America's once-sleepy 2,000-mile border with Mexico is now the scene of daily confrontations. Even the Mexican army shows its contempt for U.S. law. The State Department reported 55 military incursions in the five years before an incident in 2000 when truckloads of Mexican soldiers barreled through a barbed-wire fence, fired shots, and pursued two mounted officers and a U.S. Border Patrol vehicle. U.S. Border Patrol agents believe that some Mexican army units collaborate with their country's drug cartels.

America has become a spillway for an exploding population that Mexico is unable to employ. Mexico's population is growing by 10 million every decade. Mexican senator Adolfo Zinser conceded that Mexico's "economic policy is dependent on unlimited emigration to the United States." The *Yanqui*-baiting academic and "onetime Communist supporter" Jorge Casteñada warned in *The Atlantic Monthly* six years ago that any American effort to cut back immigration "will make social peace in . . . Mexico untenable. . . . Some Americans dislike immigration, but there is very little they can do about it." With Señor Casteñada now President Fox's foreign minister and Senator Zinser his national security adviser, these opinions carry weight.

The Mexican government openly supports illegal entry of its citizens into the United States. An Office for Mexicans Abroad helps Mexicans evade U.S. border guards in the deserts of Arizona and California by providing them with "survival kits" of water, dry meat, granola, Tylenol, anti-diarrhea pills, bandages, and condoms. The kits are distributed in Mexico's poorest towns, along with information on where illegal aliens can get free social services in California. Mexico is aiding and abetting an invasion of the United States, and the U.S. responds with intimidated silence and moral paralysis.

With California the preferred destination for this immigration flood, sociologist William Frey has documented an out-migration of African Americans and Anglo Americans from the Golden State in search of cities and towns like the ones in which they grew up. Other Californians are moving into gated communities. A country that cannot control its borders isn't really a country, Ronald Reagan warned some two decades ago.

Concerns about a radical change in America's ethnic composition have been called un-American. But they are as American as Benjamin Franklin, who once asked, "Why should Pennsylvania, founded by the English, become a Colony of Aliens, who will shortly be so numerous as to Germanize us instead of our Anglifying them?" Franklin would never find out if his fears were justified, because German immigration was halted during the Revolutionary War.

Theodore Roosevelt likewise warned that "The one absolutely certain way of bringing this nation to ruin, of preventing all possibility of its continuing to be a nation at all, would be to permit it to become a tangle of squabbling nationalities."

Immigration is a subject worthy of national debate, yet it has been deemed taboo by the forces of political correctness. Like the Mississippi, with its endless flow of life-giving water, immigration has enriched America throughout history. But when the Mississippi floods its banks, the devastation can be enormous. What will become of our country if the levees do not hold?

❦

Harvard economist George Borjas has found no net economic benefit from mass migration from the Third World. In his study, the added costs of schooling, health care, welfare, prisons, plus the added pressure on land, water, and power resources, exceeded the taxes that immigrants pay. The National Bureau of Economic Research put the cost of immigration at $80 billion in 1995. What are the benefits, then, that justify the risk of the balkanization of America?

Today there are 28.4 million foreign-born persons living in the United States. Half are from Latin America and the Caribbean, one fourth from Asia. The rest are from Africa, the Middle East, and Europe. One in every five New Yorkers and Floridians is foreign-born, as is one of every four Californians. As the United States allots most of its immigrant visas to relatives of new arrivals, it is difficult for Europeans to be admitted to the U.S., while entire villages from El Salvador have settled here easily.

- A third of the legal immigrants who come to the United States have not finished high school. Some 22 percent do not even have a ninth-grade education, compared to less than 5 percent of our native-born.
- Of the immigrants who have arrived since 1980, 60 percent still do not earn $20,000 a year.
- Immigrant use of food stamps, Supplemental Security Income, and school lunch programs runs from 50 percent to 100 percent higher than use by the native born.
- By 1991, foreign nationals accounted for 24 percent of all arrests in Los Angeles and 36 percent of all arrests in Miami.
- In 1980, federal and state prisons housed 9,000 criminal aliens. By 1995, this number had soared to 59,000, a figure that does not include aliens who became citizens, or the criminals sent over from Cuba by Fidel Castro in the Mariel boat lift.

Mass emigration from poor Third World countries is good for business, especially businesses that employ large numbers of workers at low wages. But what is good for corporate America is not necessarily good for Middle America. When it comes to open borders, the corporate interest and the national interest do not coincide; they collide. Mass immigration raises more critical issues than jobs or wages—immigration is ultimately about America herself. Is the U.S. government, by deporting scarcely 1 percent of illegal aliens a year, failing in its Constitutional duty to protect the rights of American citizens?

Most of the people who leave their homelands to come to America, whether from Mexico or Mauritania, are good, decent people. They seek the same freedom and opportunities our ancestors sought.

But today's record number of immigrants arriving from cultures that have little in common with our own raises a question: What is a nation? Some define a nation as one people of common ancestry, language, literature, history, heritage, heroes, traditions, customs, mores, and faith who have lived together over time in the same land under the same rulers. Among those who pressed this definition were Secretary of State John Quincy Adams, who laid down these conditions on immigrants: "They must cast off the European skin, never to resume it. They must look forward to their posterity rather than backward to their ancestors." Woodrow Wilson, speaking to newly naturalized Americans in 1915 in Philadelphia, declared: "A man who thinks of himself as belonging to a particular national group in America has yet to become an American."

But Americans no longer agree on values, history, or heroes. What one half of America sees as a glorious past, the other views as shameful and wicked. Columbus, Washington, Jefferson, Jackson, Lincoln, and Lee—all of them heroes of the old America—are under attack. Equality and freedom, those most American of words, today hold different meanings for different Americans.

Nor is a shared belief in democracy sufficient to hold a people together. Half the nation did not even bother to vote in the Presidential election of 2000. Millions cannot name their congressman, senator, or the justices of the Supreme Court. They do not care. We live in the same country, we are governed by the same leaders. But are we one nation and one people?

It is hard to believe that over one million immigrants every year, from every country on earth, a third of them entering illegally, will reforge the bonds of our disuniting nation. John Stuart Mill cautioned that unified public opinion is "necessary to the working of representative government." We are about to find out if he was right.

Ben Wattenberg

Immigration Is Good

Many leading thinkers tell us we are now in a culture clash that will determine the course of history, that today's war is for Western civilization itself. There is a demographic dimension to this "clash of civilizations." While certain of today's demographic signals bode well for America, some look very bad. If we are to assess America's future prospects, we must start by asking, "Who are we?" "Who will we be?" and "How will we relate to the rest of the world?" The answers all involve immigration.

❧

As data from the 2000 census trickled out, one item hit the headline jackpot. By the year 2050, we were told, America would be "majority non-white." The census count showed more Hispanics in America than had been ex-pected, making them "America's largest minority." When blacks, Asians, and Native Americans are added to the Hispanic total, the "non-white" population emerges as a large minority, on the way to becoming a small majority around the middle of this century.

The first thing worth noting is that these rigid racial definitions are absurd. The whole concept of race as a biological category is becoming ever-more dubious in America. Consider:

Under the Clinton administration's census rules, any American who checks both the black and white boxes on the form inquiring about "race" is counted as black, even if his heritage is, say, one eighth black and seven eighths white. In effect, this enshrines the infamous segregationist view that one drop of black blood makes a person black.

Although most Americans of Hispanic heritage declare themselves "white," they are often inferentially counted as non-white, as in the erroneous *New York Times* headline which recently declared: "Census Confirms Whites Now a Minority" in California.

If those of Hispanic descent, hailing originally from about 40 nations, are counted as a minority, why aren't those of Eastern European descent, coming from about 10 nations, also counted as a minority? (In which case the Eastern European "minority" would be larger than the Hispanic minority.)

But within this jumble of numbers there lies a central truth: America is becoming a *universal nation,* with significant representation of nearly all human hues, creeds, ethnicities, and national ancestries. Continued moderate immigration will make us an even more universal nation as time goes on. And this process may well play a serious role in determining the outcome of the contest of civilizations taking place across the globe.

And current immigration rates are moderate, even though America admitted more legal immigrants from 1991 to 2000 than in any previous decade—between 10 and 11 million. The highest previous decade was 1901–1910, when 8.8 million people arrived. In addition, each decade now, several million illegal immigrants enter the U.S., thanks partly to ease of transportation.

Critics like Pat Buchanan say that absorbing all those immigrants will "swamp" the American culture and bring Third World chaos inside our borders. I disagree. Keep in mind: Those 8.8 million immigrants who arrived in the U.S. between 1901 and 1910 increased the total American population by 1 percent per year. (Our numbers grew from 76 million to 92 million during that decade.) In our most recent decade, on the other hand, the 10 million legal immigrants represented annual growth of only 0.36 percent (as the U.S. went from 249 million to 281 million).

Overall, nearly 15 percent of Americans were foreign-born in 1910. In 1999, our foreign-born were about 10 percent of our total. (In 1970, the foreign-born portion of our population was down to about 5 percent. Most of the rebound resulted from a more liberal immigration law enacted in 1965.) Or look at the "foreign stock" data. These figures combine Americans born in foreign lands and their offspring, even if those children have only one foreign-born parent. Today, America's "foreign stock" amounts to 21 percent of the population and heading up. But in 1910, the comparable figure was 34 percent—one third of the entire country—and the heavens did not collapse.

We can take in more immigrants, if we want to. Should we?

꒰◉꒱

Return to the idea that immigrants could swamp American culture. If that is true, we clearly should not increase our intake. But what if, instead of swamping us, immigration helps us become a stronger nation and a *swamper of others* in the global competition of civilizations?

Immigration is now what keeps America growing. According to the U.N., the typical American woman today bears an average of 1.93 children over the course of her childbearing years. That is mildly below the 2.1 "replacement" rate required to keep a population stable over time, absent immigration. The "medium variant" of the most recent Census Bureau projections posits that the U.S. population will grow from 281 million in 2000 to 397 million in 2050 with expected immigration, but only to 328 million should we choose a path of zero immigration. That is a difference of a population growth of 47 million versus 116 million. (The 47 million rise is due mostly to demographic momentum from previous higher birthrates.) If we have zero immigration with today's low birthrates indefinitely, the American population would eventually begin to *shrink*, albeit slowly.

Is more population good for America? When it comes to potential global power and influence, numbers can matter a great deal. Taxpayers, many of them, pay for a fleet of aircraft carriers. And on the economic side it is better to have a customer boom than a customer bust. (It may well be that Japan's stagnant demography is one cause of its decade-long slump.) The environmental case could be debated all day long, but remember that an immigrant does not add to the global population—he merely moves from one spot on the planet to another.

But will the current crop of immigrants acculturate? Immigrants to America always have. Some critics, like Mr. Buchanan, claim that this time, it's different. Mexicans seem to draw his particular ire, probably because they are currently our largest single source of immigration.

Yet only about a fifth (22 percent) of legal immigrants to America currently come from Mexico. Adding illegal immigrants might boost the figure to 30 percent, but the proportion of Mexican immigrants will almost surely shrink over time. Mexican fertility has diminished from 6.5 children per woman 30 years ago to 2.5 children now, and continues to fall. If high immigration continues under such circumstances, Mexico will run out of Mexicans.

California hosts a wide variety of immigrant groups in addition to Mexicans. And the children and grandchildren of Koreans, Chinese, Khmer, Russian Jews, Iranians, and Thai (to name a few) will speak English, not Spanish. Even among Mexican–Americans, many second- and third-generation offspring speak no Spanish at all, often to the dismay of their elders (a familiar American story).

Michael Barone's book *The New Americans* theorizes that Mexican immigrants are following roughly the same course of earlier Italian and Irish immigrants. Noel Ignatiev's book *How the Irish Became White* notes that it took a hundred years until Irish-Americans (who were routinely characterized as drunken "gorillas") reached full income parity with the rest of America.

California recently repealed its bilingual education programs. Nearly half of Latino voters supported the proposition, even though it was demonized by opponents as being anti-Hispanic. Latina mothers reportedly tell their children, with no intent to disparage the Spanish language, that "Spanish is the language of busboys"—stressing that in America you have to speak English to get ahead.

◦◦❦◦◦

The huge immigration wave at the dawn of the twentieth century undeniably brought tumult to America. Many early social scientists promoted theories of what is now called "scientific racism," which "proved" that persons from Northwest Europe were biologically superior. The new immigrants—Jews, Poles, and Italians—were considered racially apart and far down the totem pole of human character and intelligence. Blacks and Asians were hardly worth measuring. The immigration wave sparked a resurgence of the Ku Klux Klan, peaking in the early 1920s. At that time, the biggest KKK state was not in the South; it was Indiana, where Catholics, Jews, and immigrants, as well as blacks, were targets.

Francis Walker, superintendent of the U.S. Bureau of the Census in the late 1890s, and later president of MIT, wrote in 1896 that "the entrance of such vast masses of peasantry degraded below our utmost conceptions is a matter which no intelligent patriot can look upon without the gravest apprehension and alarm. They are beaten men from beaten races. They have none of the ideas and aptitudes such as belong to those who were descended from the tribes that met under the oak trees of old Germany to make laws and choose chiefs." (Sorry, Francis, but Germany did not have a good twentieth century.)

Fast-forward to the present. By high margins, Americans now tell pollsters it was a very good thing that Poles, Italians, and Jews emigrated to America. Once again, it's the *newcomers* who are viewed with suspicion. This time, it's the Mexicans, Filipinos, and people from the Caribbean who make Americans nervous. But such views change over time. The newer immigrant groups are typically more popular now than they were even a decade ago.

Look at the high rates of intermarriage. Most Americans have long since lost their qualms about marriage between people of different European ethnicities. That is spreading across new boundaries. In 1990, 64 percent of Asian Americans married outside their heritage, as did 37 percent of Hispanics. Black-white intermarriage is much lower, but it climbed from 3 percent in 1980 to 9 percent in 1998. (One reason to do away with the race question on the census is that within a few decades we won't be able to know who's what.)

⋅❦⋅

Can the West, led by America, prevail in a world full of sometimes unfriendly neighbors? Substantial numbers of people are necessary (though not sufficient) for a country, or a civilization, to be globally influential. Will America and its Western allies have enough people to keep their ideas and principles alive?

On the surface, it doesn't look good. In 1986, I wrote a book called *The Birth Dearth.* My thesis was that birth rates in developed parts of the world— Europe, North America, Australia, and Japan, nations where liberal Western values are rooted—had sunk so low that there was danger ahead. At that time, women in those modern countries were bearing a lifetime average of 1.83 children, the lowest rate ever absent war, famine, economic depression, or epidemic illness. It was, in fact, 15 percent below the long-term population replacement level.

Those trendlines have now plummeted even further. Today, the fertility rate in the modern countries averages 1.5 children per woman, 28 percent below the replacement level. The European rate, astonishingly, is 1.34 children per woman—radically below replacement level. The Japanese rate is similar. The United States is the exceptional country in the current demographic scene.

As a whole, the nations of the Western world will soon be less populous, and a substantially smaller fraction of the world population. Demographer Samuel Preston estimates that even if European fertility rates jump back to replacement level immediately (which won't happen) the continent would still lose 100 million people by 2060. Should the rate not level off fairly soon, the ramifications are incalculable, or, as the Italian demographer Antonio Golini likes to mutter at demographic meetings, "unsustainable . . . unsustainable." (Shockingly, the current Italian fertility rate is 1.2 children per woman, and it has been at or below 1.5 for 20 years—a full generation.)

The modern countries of the world, the bearers of Western civilization, made up one third of the global population in 1950, and one fifth in 2000, and are projected to represent one eighth by 2050. If we end up in a world with nine competing civilizations, as Samuel Huntington maintains, this will make it that much harder for Western values to prevail in the cultural and political arenas.

The good news is that fertility rates have also plunged in the less developed countries—from 6 children in 1970 to 2.9 today. By the middle to end of this century, there should be a rough global convergence of fertility rates and population growth.

⚜

Since September 11, immigration has gotten bad press in America. The terrorist villains, indeed, were foreigners. Not only in the U.S. but in many other nations as well, governments are suddenly cracking down on illegal entry. This is understandable for the moment. But an enduring turn away from legal immigration would be foolhardy for America and its allies.

If America doesn't continue to take in immigrants, it won't continue to grow in the long run. If the Europeans and Japanese don't start to accept more immigrants they will evaporate. Who will empty the bedpans in Italy's retirement homes? The only major pool of immigrants available to Western countries hails from the less developed world, i.e., non-white, and non-Western countries.

The West as a whole is in a deep demographic ditch. Accordingly, Western countries should try to make it easier for couples who want to have children. In America, the advent of tax credits for children (which went from zero to $1,000 per child per year over the last decade) is a small step in the direction of fertility reflation. Some European nations are enacting similar pro-natal policies. But their fertility rates are so low, and their economies so constrained, that any such actions can only be of limited help.

That leaves immigration. I suggest America should make immigration safer (by more carefully investigating new entrants), but not cut it back. It may even be wise to make a small increase in our current immigration rate. America needs to keep growing, and we can fruitfully use both high- and low-skill immigrants. Pluralism works here, as it does in Canada and Australia.

Can pluralism work in Europe? I don't know, and neither do the Europeans. They hate the idea, but they will depopulate if they don't embrace pluralism, via immigration. Perhaps our example can help Europeans see that pluralism might work in the admittedly more complex European context. Japan is probably a hopeless case; perhaps the Japanese should just change the name of their country to Dwindle.

Our non-pluralist Western allies will likely diminish in population, relative power, and influence during this century. They will become much grayer. Nevertheless, by 2050 there will still be 750 million of them left, so the U.S. needs to keep the Western alliance strong. For all our bickering, let us not forget that the European story in the second half of the twentieth century was a wonderful one; Western Europeans stopped killing each other. Now they are joining hands politically. The next big prize may be Russia. If the Russians choose our path, we will see what Tocqueville saw: that America and Russia are natural allies.

We must enlist other allies as well. America and India, for instance, are logical partners—pluralist, large, English-speaking, and democratic. We must tell our story. And our immigrants, who come to our land by choice, are our best salesmen. We should extend our radio services to the Islamic world, as we have to the unliberated nations of Asia through Radio Free Asia. The people at the microphones will be U.S. immigrants.

We can lose the contest of civilizations if the developing countries don't evolve toward Western values. One of the best forms of "public diplomacy" is immigration. New immigrants send money home, bypassing corrupt governments—the best kind of foreign aid there is. They go back home to visit and tell their families and friends in the motherland that American modernism, while not perfect, ain't half-bad. Some return home permanently, but they bring with them Western expectations of open government, economic efficiency, and personal liberty. They know that Westernism need not be restricted to the West, and they often have an influence on local politics when they return to their home countries.

Still, because of Europe and Japan, the demographic slide of Western civilization will continue. And so, America must be prepared to go it alone. If we keep admitting immigrants at our current levels there will be almost 400 million Americans by 2050. That can keep us strong enough to defend and perhaps extend our views and values. And the civilization we will be advancing may not just be Western, but even more universal: American.

POSTSCRIPT

Is Third World Immigration a Threat to America's Way of Life?

Former representative Silvio Conte (R-Massachusetts) said at a citizenship ceremony, "You can go to France, but you will never be a Frenchman. You can go to Germany but you will never be a German. Today you are all Americans, and that is why this is the greatest country on the face of the earth." At one time America's open door to immigrants was one of the prides of America. For some people, like Wattenberg, it still is. He thinks that an integrated, multicultural society is a culturally rich society and that immigration is making America stronger. Many people disagree because they fear the consequences of today's immigration. Buchanan worries that, although the new immigrants may want to assimilate, they have reached such a critical mass that the United States has lost the ability to absorb everyone into its own, slowly dissipating culture. The result is that immigrants are encouraged to maintain and promote the cultures that they arrive with, which further dilutes the original culture of America. The issue is based on what one thinks will happen as America becomes more diverse. Buchanan sees America as coming apart and Wattenberg sees America as leading the world.

Stanley Lieberson and Mary C. Waters, in *From Many Strands* (Russell Sage Foundation, 1988), argue that ethnic groups with European origins are assimilating, marrying outside their groups, and losing their ethnic identities. Richard D. Alba's study "Assimilation's Quiet Tide," *The Public Interest* (Spring 1995) confirms these findings.

Several major works debate whether or not immigrants, on average, economically benefit America and can assimilate. Sources that argue that immigrants largely benefit America include Julian L. Simon, *The Economic Consequences of Immigration,* 2d ed. (University of Michigan Press, 1999) and *Immigration: The Demographic and Economic Facts* (Cato Institute, 1995).

Sources that argue that immigrants have more negative than positive impacts include George Borjas, *Heaven's Door: Immigration Policy and the American Economy* (Princeton University Press, 1999); Roy Beck, *The Case Against Immigration* (W. W. Norton, 1996); Patrick Buchanan, *The Death of the West: How Dying Populations and Immigrant Invasions Imperil Our Country and Civilization* (Thomas Dunne Books, 2002); and Otis L. Graham, Jr., *Unguarded Gates: A History of American's Immigration Crisis* (Rowman and Littlefield, 2004). For a more even-handed discussion, see *Not Just Black and White: Historical and Contemporary Perspectives on Immigration, Race, and Ethnicity in the United States* (Russell Sage Foundation, 2004) edited by Nancy Foner and *America's Newcomers and the Dynamics of Diversity* (Russell Sage

Foundation, 2003) by Frank D. Bean and Gilian Stevens. On the issue of Mexican immigration, see Douglas S. Massey, Jorge Durand, and Nolan J. Malone's *Beyond Smoke and Mirrors: Mexican Immigration in an Era of Economic Integration* (Russell Sage Foundation, 2003) and Victor Davis Hanson's *Mexifornia: A State of Becoming* (Encounter Books, 2003).

American Men's Studies Association

The American Men's Studies Association is a not-for-profit professional organization of scholars, therapists, and others interested in the exploration of masculinity in modern society.

http://mensstudies.org

American Studies Web

The American Studies Web site is an eclectic site that provides links to a wealth of resources on the Internet related to gender studies.

http://www.georgetown.edu/crossroads/asw/

Feminist Majority Foundation

The Feminist Majority Foundation Web site provides affirmative action links, resources from women's professional organizations, information for empowering women in business, sexual harassment information, and much more.

http://www.feminist.org/gateway/sdexec2.html

GLAAD: Gay and Lesbian Alliance Against Defamation

The Gay and Lesbian Alliance Against Defamation (GLAAD), formed in New York in 1985, seeks to improve the public's attitudes toward homosexuality and to put an end to discrimination against lesbians and gay men.

http://www.glaad.org/org.index.html

International Lesbian and Gay Association

The resources on the International Lesbian and Gay Association Web site are provided by a worldwide network of lesbian, gay, bisexual, and transgendered groups.

http://www.ilga.org

SocioSite: Feminism and Women's Issues

The Feminism and Women's Issues SocioSite provides insights into a number of issues that affect family relationships. It covers wide-ranging issues regarding women and men, family and children, and much more.

http://www.pscw.uva.nl/sociosite/TOPICS/Women.html

PART 2

Sex Roles, Gender, and the Family

*T*he modern feminist movement has advanced the causes of women to the point where there are now more women in the workforce in the United States than ever before. Professions and trades that were traditionally regarded as the provinces of men have opened up to women, and women now have easier access to the education and training necessary to excel in these new areas. But what is happening to sex roles, and what are the effects of changing sex roles? How have men and women been affected by the stress caused by current sex roles, the demand for the right to same-sex marriages, and the deterioration of the traditional family structure? The issues in this part address these sorts of questions.

- Is the Decline of the Traditional Family a National Crisis?
- Should Mothers Stay Home With Their Children?
- Should Same-Sex Marriages Be Legally Recognized?

ISSUE 4

Is the Decline of the Traditional Family a National Crisis?

YES: David Popenoe, from "The American Family Crisis," *National Forum: The Phi Kappa Phi Journal* (Summer 1995)

NO: Frank Furstenberg, from "Can Marriage Be Saved?" *Dissent* (Summer 2005)

ISSUE SUMMARY

YES: Sociologist David Popenoe contends that families play important roles in society but how the traditional family functions in these roles has declined dramatically in the last several decades, with very adverse effects on children.

NO: Sociologist Frank Furstenberg argues that diversity of and change in family forms are common throughout history, and the move away from the unusual family form of the 1950s does not indicate a crisis. It does present some problems for children but the worst problem for children is the lack of resources that often results from divorce or single parenting.

T he state of the American family deeply concerns many Americans. About 40 percent of marriages end in divorce, and only 27 percent of children born in 1990 are expected to be living with both parents by the time they reach age 17. Most Americans, therefore, are affected personally or are close to people who are affected by structural changes in the family. Few people can avoid being exposed to the issue: violence in the family and celebrity divorces are standard fare for news programs, and magazine articles decrying the breakdown of the family appear frequently. Politicians today try to address the problems of the family. Academics have affirmed that the family crisis has numerous significant negative effects on children, spouses, and the rest of society.

Sociologists pay attention to the role that the family plays in the functioning of society. For a society to survive, its population must reproduce (or take in many immigrants), and its young must be trained to perform adult roles and to have the values and attitudes that will motivate them to contribute to society. Procreation and socialization are two vital roles that families traditionally have performed. In addition, the family provides economic and emotional support for its members, which is vital to their effective functioning in society.

Today the performance of the family is disappointing in all of these areas. Procreation outside of marriage has become common, and it has been found to lead to less than ideal conditions for raising children. The scorecard on American family socialization is hard to assess, but there is concern about such issues as parents' declining time with and influence on their children and latchkey children whose parents work and who must therefore spend part of the day unsupervised. The economic performance of two-parent families is improving because more mothers are entering the labor force, but this gain is often related to a decline in emotional support. Single-parent families tend to perform less well on both counts. Overall, the high divorce rate and the frequency of child and spousal abuse indicate that the modern family fails to provide adequate social and emotional support.

Although most experts agree that the American family is in crisis, there is little agreement about what, if anything, should be done about it. After all, most of these problems result from the choices that people make to try to increase their happiness. People end unhappy marriages. Married women work for fulfillment or financial gain. Unwed mothers decide to keep their children. The number of couples who choose to remain childless is growing rapidly. These trends cannot be changed unless people start choosing differently. As yet there is no sign of this happening in a big way. Does this mean that the weakening of the family is desirable? Few would advocate such an idea, but perhaps some weakening must be accepted as the consequence of embracing other cherished values.

In the selections that follow, David Popenoe argues that the family is the key institution in society. Since it plays many important roles, its functional decline, which is largely due to cultural trends, has many adverse social impacts, including greatly harming children. He concludes by suggesting what needs to be done to strengthen families and family life. Frank Furstenberg provides a much different assessment of the present state of the family as compared with earlier times. The nuclear family was "The gold standard for what constitutes a healthy family" only for a brief time in the 1950s. Diversity is the normal pattern for the family. In light of historical research, it can be said that the current family is not in crisis.

David Popenoe  **YES**

The American Family Crisis

Throughout our nation's history, we have depended heavily on the family to provide both social order and economic success. Families have provided for the survival and development of children, for the emotional and physical health of adults, for the special care of the sick, injured, handicapped, and elderly, and for the reinforcement of society's values. Today, America's families face growing problems in each of these areas, and by many measures are functioning less well than ever before—less well, in fact, than in other advanced, industrialized nations.

The most serious negative effects of the functional decline of families have been on children. Evidence suggests that today's generation of children is the first in our nation's history to be less well-off psychologically and socially than their parents were at the same age. Alarming increases have occurred in such pathologies as juvenile delinquency, violence, suicide, substance abuse, eating disorders, nonmarital births, psychological stress, anxiety, and unipolar depression.

Such increases are especially troubling because many conditions for child well-being have improved. Fewer children are in each family today; therefore, more adults are theoretically available to care for them. Children are in some respects healthier and materially better off; they have completed more years in school, as have their parents. Greater national concern for children's rights, for child abuse, and for psychologically sound childrearing practices is also evident.

Family Origins and History

As the first social institution in human history, the family probably arose because of the need for adults to devote a great amount of time to childrearing. Coming into the world totally dependent, human infants must, for a larger portion of their lives than for any other species, be cared for and taught by adults. To a unique degree, humans nurture, protect, and educate their offspring. It is hard to conceive of a successful society, therefore, that does not have families that are able to raise children to become adults who have the capacity to love and to work, who are committed to such positive social values as honesty, respect, and responsibility, and who pass these values on to the next generation.

Infants and children need, at minimum, one adult to care for them. Yet, given the complexities of the task, childrearing in all societies until recent years has been shared by many adults. The institutional bond of marriage between biological parents, with the essential function of tying the father to the mother and child, is found in virtually every society. Marriage is the most universal social institution known; in no society has nonmarital childbirth, or the single parent, been the cultural norm. In all societies the biological father is identified where possible, and in almost all societies he plays an important role in his children's upbringing, even though his primary task is often that of protector and breadwinner.

In the preindustrial era, however, adult family members did not necessarily consider childrearing to be their primary task. As a unit of rural economic production, the family's main focus typically was economic survival. According to some scholars, rather than the family being for the sake of the children, the children, as needed workers, were for the sake of the family. One of the most important family transitions in history was the rise in industrial societies of what we now refer to as the "traditional nuclear family": husband away at work during the day and wife taking care of the home and children full time. This transition took place in the United States beginning in the early 1800s. The primary focus of this historically new family form was indeed the care and nurturing of children, and parents dedicated themselves to this effort.

Over the past thirty years, the United States (along with other modern societies) has witnessed another major family transformation—the beginning of the end of the traditional nuclear family. Three important changes have occurred:

- The divorce rate increased sharply (to a level currently exceeding 50 percent), and parents increasingly decided to forgo marriage, with the consequence that a sizable number of children are being raised in single-parent households, apart from other relatives.
- Married women in large numbers left the role of full-time mother and housewife to go into the labor market, and the activities of their former role have not been fully replaced.
- The focus of many families shifted away from childrearing to the psychological well-being and self-development of their adult members. One indication of this latter focus is that, even when they have young children to raise, parents increasingly break up if their psychological and self-fulfillment needs are unmet in the marriage relationship.

We can never return to the era of the traditional nuclear family, even if we wanted to, and many women and men emphatically do not. The conditions of life that generated that family form have changed. Yet the one thing that has not changed through all the years and all the family transformations is the need for children to be raised by mothers and fathers. Indeed, in modern, complex societies in which children need an enormous amount of education and psychological security to succeed, active and nurturing relationships with adults may be more critical for children than ever.

Unfortunately, the amount of time children spend with adults, especially their parents, has been dropping dramatically. Absent fathers, working mothers, distant grandparents, anonymous schools, and transient communities have become hallmarks of our era. Associated with this trend in many families, and in society as a whole, is a weakening of the fundamental assumption that children are to be loved and valued at the highest level of priority.

The Individualism Trend

To understand fully what has happened to the family, we must look at the broader cultural changes that have taken place, especially changes in the values and norms that condition everyday choices. Over recent centuries in industrialized and industrializing societies, a gradual shift has occurred from a "collectivist" culture (I am using this term with a cultural and not a political meaning) toward an individualistic culture. In the former, group goals take precedence over individual ones. "Doing one's duty," for example, is more important than "self-fulfillment," and "social bonds" are more important than "personal choice." In individualistic cultures, the welfare of the group is secondary to the importance of such personal goals as self-expression, independence, and competitiveness.

Not surprisingly, individualistic societies rank higher than collectivist societies in political democracy and individual development. But the shift from collectivism to individualism involves social costs as well as personal gains—especially when it proceeds too far. Along with political democracy and individual development, individualistic societies tend to have high rates of individual deviance, juvenile delinquency, crime, loneliness, depression, suicide, and social alienation. In short, these societies have more free and independent citizens but less social order and probably a lower level of psychological well-being.

"Communitarian" Individualism

The United States has long been known as the world's most individualistic society. Certainly, we place a high value on this aspect of our society, and it is a major reason why so many people from other countries want to come here. Yet for most of our history, this individualism has been balanced, or tempered, by a strong belief in the sanctity of accepted social organizations and institutions, such as the family, religion, voluntary associations, local communities, and even the nation as a whole. While individualistic in spirit, people's identities were rooted in these social units, and their lives were directed toward the social goals that they represented. Thus, the United States has been marked for much of its history, not by a pure form of individualism, but by what could be termed a "communitarian" or balanced individualism.

"Expressive" Individualism

As the individualism trend has advanced, however, a more radical or "expressive" individualism has emerged, one that is largely devoted to "selfindulgence" or "self-fulfillment" at the expense of the group. Today, we see a large number of people who are narcissistic or self-oriented, and who show concern for social institutions only when these directly affect their own well-being. Unfortunately, these people have a tendency to distance themselves from the social and community groupings that have long been the basis for personal security and social order. Since the 1950s, the number of people being married, visiting informally with others, and belonging to voluntary associations has decreased, and the number of people living alone has increased.

In turn, the traditional community groupings have been weakened. More people are viewing our once accepted social institutions with considerable skepticism. As measured by public opinion polls, confidence in such public institutions as medicine, higher education, the law, the press, and organized religion has declined dramatically. As measured by people voting with their feet, trust in the institution of marriage also had declined dramatically. And, as we see almost every night on the news, our sense of cultural solidarity seems to be diminishing.

The highly disturbing actions of inner-city residents that we have witnessed in the urban riots of recent years could be considered less a departure from everyday American cultural reality than a gross intensification of it. Few social and cultural trends found in the inner city are not also present in the rest of the nation. Indeed, with respect to the family, the characteristics of the African American family pronounced by President Lyndon Johnson in 1965 to be in a state of "breakdown" are very similar to the family characteristics of America as a whole in 1994!

In summary, for the good of both the individual and society, the individualism trend in the United States has advanced too far. The family holds the key. People need strong families to provide them with the identity, belonging, discipline, and values that are essential for full individual development. The social institutions of the surrounding community depend on strong families to teach those "civic" values—honesty, trust, self-sacrifice, personal responsibility, respect for others—that enable them to thrive. But let us not forget that strong families depend heavily on cultural and social supports. Family life in an unsupportive community is always precarious and the social stresses can be overwhelming.

Not to Forget the Gains

While I have presented a fairly grim picture in describing these cultural changes, it is important to add that not every aspect of our society has deteriorated. In several key areas, this nation has seen significant social progress. For instance, we are a much more inclusive society today—segregation and racism have diminished, and we now accept more African Americans, Hispanics, and other minority groups into the mainstream. The legal, sexual, and financial emancipation of women has become a reality as never before in history. With advances in medicine, we have greater longevity and, on the whole, better physical health. And our average material standard of living, especially in the possession of consumer durables, has increased significantly.

The Nuclear Family and Marriage

Given our nation's past ability to accept positive social change, we can have some confidence in our capacity to solve the problem of family decline. In seeking solutions, we should first consider what family structure is best able to raise children who are autonomous and socially responsible, and also able to meet adult needs for intimacy and personal attachment. Considering the available evidence, as well as the lessons of recent human experience, unquestionably the family structure that works best is the nuclear family. I am not referring to the traditional nuclear family, but rather to the nuclear family that consists of a male and a female who marry and live together and share responsibility for their children and for each other.

Let us look, for a moment, at other family forms. No advanced, Western society exists where the three-generation extended family is very important and where it is not also on the wane. Some scholars suggest that a new extended family has emerged with the trend toward "step" and "blended" families. "Isn't it nice," they say, "that we now have so many new relatives!" The final verdict is not yet in on stepfamilies, but preliminary evidence from the few empirical studies that have been done sends quite the opposite message, and it is a chilling one. For example, a recent British study of 17,000 children born in 1958 concluded that "the chances of stepchildren suffering social deprivation before reaching twenty-one are even greater than those left living after divorce with a lone parent." Similar findings are turning up in the United States.

How are the single-parent families doing? Accumulating evidence on the personal and social consequences of this family type paints an equally grim picture. A 1988 survey by the National Center for Health Statistics found, for example, that children from single-parent families are two to three times more likely to have emotional and behavioral problems than children from intact families, and reduced family income is by no means the only factor involved. In their new book *Growing Up With a Single Parent,* Sara McLanahan and Gary Sandefur, after examining six nationally representative data sets containing over 25,000 children from a variety of racial and social class backgrounds, conclude that "children who grow up with only one of their biological parents are disadvantaged across a broad array of outcomes . . . they are twice as likely to drop out of high school, 2.5 times as likely to become teen mothers, and 1.4 times as likely to be idle—out of school and out of work—as children who grow up with both parents." The loss of economic resources, they report, accounts for only about 50 percent of the disadvantages associated with single parenthood.

Toward Solutions

Of course, many people have no other choice than to live in step- and single-parent families. These families can be successful, and their members deserve our continuing support. Nevertheless, the benefits that strong nuclear families bring to a high-achieving, individualistic, and democratic society are absolutely clear. For example, a committed marriage, which is the basis of the strong nuclear family, brings enormous benefits to adults. It is ironic in this age of self-fulfillment, when people are being pulled away from marriage, that a happy marriage seems to provide the best source of self-fulfillment. By virtually every measure, married individuals are better off than single individuals.

Another reason for supporting strong nuclear families is that society gains enormously when a high percentage of men are married. While unmarried women take relatively good care of themselves, unmarried men often have difficulty in this regard. In general, every society must be wary of the unattached male, for he is universally the cause of numerous social ills. Healthy societies are heavily dependent on men being attached to a strong moral order, which is centered in families, both to discipline sexual behavior and to reduce competitive aggression. Men need the moral and emotional instruction of women more than vice versa. Family life, especially having children, is for men a civilizing force of no mean proportions.

We should be seriously concerned, therefore, that men currently spend more time living apart from families than at probably any other time in American history. About a quarter of all men aged twenty-five to thirty-four live in nonfamily households, either alone or with an unrelated individual. In 1960, average Americans spent 62 percent of their adult lives with spouse and children, which was the highest in our history; by 1980, they spent 43 percent, the lowest in our history. This trend alone may help to account for the high and rising crime rates over the past three decades. During this period, the number of reported violent crimes per capita, largely committed by unattached males, increased by 355 percent.

Today, a growing portion of American men are highly involved in child care, providing more help with the children than their own fathers did. Yet, because they did not stay with or marry the mothers of their children, or because of divorce, a large number of men have abandoned their children entirely.

Between 1960 and 1990 the percentage of children living apart from their biological fathers more than doubled, from 17 percent to 36 percent. In general, childrearing women have become increasingly isolated from men. This is one of the main reasons why nothing would benefit the nation more than a national drive to promote strong marriages.

The New Familism: A Hopeful Trend

One bright spot in this picture is what some of us have called "the new familism," a growing realization in America that, "yes, the family really is in trouble and needs help." Public opinion polls indicate that nearly two-thirds of

Americans believe "family values have gotten weaker in the United States." Both major political parties and our President now seem to be in agreement.

Two primary groups are involved in this cultural mini-shift: the maturing baby boomers, now at the family stage of their life cycle, and the "babyboom echo" children of the divorce revolution. The middle-aged baby boomers, spurred by growing evidence that children have been hurt by recent family changes, have been instrumental in shifting the media in a profamily direction. And many of the echo children of the 1970s, with their troubled childhoods, are coming into adulthood with a resolve not to repeat their parents' mistakes. They tend to put a high premium on marital permanence, perhaps because they have been unable to take the family for granted as many of their parents—the children of the familistic 1950s—did. But one concern is this: will they have the psychological stability to sustain an intimate relationship, or will their insecure childhoods make it impossible for them to fulfill their commitment to a lasting marriage?

Unfortunately, studies of the long-term effects of divorce on children and adolescents provide no optimism in this regard.

A couple of other factors seem to be working in a profamily direction. One is AIDS, which has now noticeably slowed the sexual revolution. As one entertainment figure recently said (with obvious dismay), "dating in Hollywood just isn't what it used to be." Neither, I must add, is dating what it used to be on the college campus, but the changes so far have not been very remarkable. Another factor is that cultural change is often reflected in cycles, and some cycles of change are patterned in generational terms. We know that not all cultural values can be maximized simultaneously. What one generation comes to value because they have less of it, their parents' generation rejected. This factor leads us to believe that the nation as a whole may be primed in the 1990s to run away from the values of radical individualism and more fully embrace the ideals of family and other social bonds.

Conclusion

In thinking about how to solve America's family crisis, we should keep the following considerations uppermost in mind:

- As a society, we cannot return to the era of the traditional nuclear family. But, we must do everything possible to strengthen the husband-wife nuclear family that stays together and takes responsibility for its children. Every child both wants—and needs—a mother and a father.
- Fundamental to strengthening the nuclear family is a renewed emphasis on the importance of marriage, which is the social institution designed primarily to hold men to the mother-child unit. It is extremely important for our children, and for our society, that men are attached to childrearing families.
- With even the strongest of marriages, parents have great difficulty raising children in an unsupportive and hostile environment. We must seek to renew the sinews of community life that can support families, main-

tain social order, and promote the common good. We should give as much attention to recreating a "family culture" as we are now giving to strengthening a "work culture."

- As an overall approach to promoting family life, nothing is more important than trying to diminish and even turn back the trend toward radical individualism. Social bonds, rather than personal choice, and community needs, rather than individual autonomy, must be accorded a higher priority in our culture—and in our lives.

NO

Frank Furstenberg

Can Marriage Be Saved?

A growing number of social scientists fear that marriage may be on the rocks and few doubt that matrimony, as we have known it, has undergone a wrenching period of change in the past several decades. Andrew Cherlin, a leading sociologist of the family, speaks of "the de-institutionalization of marriage," conceding a point to conservative commentators who have argued that marriage and the family have been in a state of free-fall since the 1960s.

Western Europe has experienced many of the same trends—declining rates of marriage, widespread cohabitation, and rising levels of nonmarital childbearing—but has largely shrugged them off. By contrast, concern about the state of marriage in the United States has touched a raw, political nerve. What ails marriage and what, if anything, can be done to restore this time-honored social arrangement to its former status as a cultural invention for assigning the rights and responsibilities of reproduction, including sponsorship and inheritance?

On the left side of the political spectrum, observers believe that the institutional breakdown of marriage has its roots in economic and social changes brought about by shifts in home-based production, structural changes in the economy, and the breakdown of the gender-based division of labor—trends unlikely to be reversed. The other position, championed by most conservatives, is that people have lost faith in marriage because of changes in cultural values that could be reversed or restored through shifts in the law, changes in administrative policies and practices, and public rhetoric to alter beliefs and expectations.

The Bush administration is trying to put into place a set of policies aimed at reversing the symptoms of retreat from marriage: high rates of pre-marital sex, nonmarital childbearing, cohabitation, and divorce. Do their policies make sense and do they have a reasonable prospect of success? To answer this question, I want to begin with the trends that Americans, including many social scientists, have found so alarming and then turn to the question of how much public policy and what kinds of policies could help to strengthen marriage.

Demographic Changes and Political Interpretations

When compared to the 1950s, the institution of marriage seems to be profoundly changed, but is the middle of the twentieth century an appropriate point of comparison? It has been widely known since the baby boom era that the period after the Second World War was unusual demographically: the very early onset of adult transitions; unprecedented rates of marriage; high fertility; an economy that permitted a single wage earner to support a family reasonably well; and the flow of federal funding for education, housing, and jobs distinguished the 1950s and early 1960s as a particular historical moment different from any previous period and certainly different from the decades after the Vietnam War era. For a brief time, the nuclear family in the United States and throughout much of Europe reigned supreme.

If we use the middle of the twentieth century as a comparison point, it might appear that we have been witnessing a deconstruction of the two-parent biological family en masse. But such a view is historically shortsighted and simplistic. The nuclear family, though long the bourgeois ideal, had never been universally practiced, at least as it was in the middle of the last century. Only in the 1950s—and then for a very brief time—did it become the gold standard for what constitutes a healthy family. Indeed, sociologists at that time fiercely debated whether this family model represented a decline from the "traditional" extended family. Even those who argued against this proposition could not agree whether this family form was desirable ("functional" in the language of the day) or contained fatal flaws that would be its undoing.

During the 1960s and 1970s, anthropological evidence indicated that family diversity is universal, and findings from the new field of historical demography revealed that families in both the East and the West had always been changing in response to economic, political, demographic, and social conditions. In short, the nuclear family was cross-culturally and historically not "the natural unit," that many wrongly presume today.

Although it was widely known that the family had undergone considerable changes from ancient times and during the industrial revolution, that family systems varied across culture, and that social-class differences created varied forms of the family within the same society, it was not until the 1960s, when historians began to use computers to analyze census data, that the extent of this variation came into clearer focus. For the first time, family scholars from several disciplines could see the broad outlines of a new picture of how family forms and functions are intimately related to the social, cultural, and perhaps especially the economic contexts in which household and kinship systems are embedded.

From this evidence, students of the family can assert three points. First, no universal form of the family constitutes the appropriate or normative arrangement for reproduction, nurturance, socialization, and economic support. Both across and within societies, family forms, patterns, and practices vary enormously. Second, change is endemic to all family systems, and at least in the West, where we have the best evidence to date, family systems have always been in flux. Typically, these changes create tensions and often ignite public concern.

Since colonial times, the family has been changing and provoking public reaction from moralists, scientists, and, of course, public authorities. Finally, family systems do not evolve in a linear fashion but become more or less complex and more elemental in different eras or among different strata of society depending on the economic and social conditions to which families must adapt.

Does this mean that we are seeing a continuation of what has always been or something different than has ever occurred in human history—the withering of kinship as an organizing feature of human society? The decline of marriage suggests to some that this round of change is unique in human history or that its consequences for children will be uniquely unsettling to society.

Many scholars weighed in on these questions. It is fair to say that there are two main camps: (1) those who have decided that the family is imperiled as a result of changes in the marriage system, a position held by such respectable social scientists as Linda Waite, Norvel Glenn, and Judith Wallerstein; and (2) those who remain skeptical and critical of those sounding the alarm, a position held by the majority of social scientists. Many in this second camp take seriously the concerns of the "alarmists" that children's welfare may be at risk if the current family regime continues. Still, they doubt that the family can be coaxed back into its 1950s form and favor adaptations in government policy to assist new forms of the family—an approach followed by most European nations.

꧁⊙꧂

Some portion of those skeptics are not so alarmed by changes in the family, believing that children's circumstances have not been seriously compromised by family change. They contend that children's well-being has less to do with the family form in which they reside than the resources possessed to form viable family arrangements. Lacking these resources (material and cultural), it matters little whether the children are born into a marriage, cohabitation, or a single-parent household, because they are likely not to fare as well as those whose parents possess the capacity to realize their goals.

I place myself in this latter group. Of course, children will fare better when they have two well-functioning, collaborative parents than one on average, but one well-functioning parent with resources is better than two married parents who lack the resources or skills to manage parenthood. Moreover, parents with limited cultural and material resources are unlikely to remain together in a stable marriage. Because the possession of such psychological, human, and material capital is highly related to marital stability, it is easy to confuse the effects of stable marriage with the effects of competent parenting. Finally, I believe that the best way to foster marriage stability is to support children with an array of services that assist parents and children, regardless of the family form in which they reside.

Marriage and Good Outcomes for Children

A huge number of studies have shown that children fare better in two-biological-parent families than they do in single-biological-parent families, leading most family researchers to conclude that the nuclear family is a more effective unit for reproduction and socialization. Yet this literature reveals some troubling features that have not been adequately examined by social scientists. The most obvious of these is that such findings rule out social selection.

If parents with limited resources and low skills are less likely to enter marriage with a biological parent and remain wed when they do (which we know to be true), then it follows that children will do worse in such single-parent households than in stable marriages. We have known about this problem for decades, but researchers have not been equipped adequately to rule out selection. The standard method for doing so is by statistically controlling for prior differences, but this method is inadequate for ruling out differences because it leaves so many sources of selection unmeasured, such as sexual compatibility, substance abuse, and so on. Newer statistical methods have been employed to correct for unmeasured differences, but strong evidence exists that none of these techniques is up to the challenge. Nevertheless, it is *theoretically* possible to examine social experiments such as those being mounted in the marriage-promotion campaign and assess their long-term effects on children.

Another useful approach is to examine macro-level differences at the state or national level that would be less correlated with social selection and hence more revealing of the impact of marriage arrangements on children's well-being. To date, there is little evidence supporting a correlation between family form and children's welfare at the national level. Consider first the historical data showing that children who grew up in the 1950s (baby boomers) were not notably free of problem behavior. After all, they were the cohort who raised such hell in the 1960s and 1970s. From 1955 to 1975, indicators of social problems among children (test scores, suicide, homicide, controlled-substance use, crime) that can be tracked by vital statistics all rose. These indicators accompanied, and in some cases preceded rather than followed, change in the rates of divorce, the decline of marriage, and the rise of nonmarital childbearing during this period. Conversely, there is no evidence that the cohort of children who came of age in the 1990s and early part of this century is doing worse than previous cohorts because these children are more likely to have grown up in single-parent families. Of course, compensatory public policies or other demographic changes such as small family size, higher parental education, or lower rates of poverty may have offset the deleterious effects of family form, but such an explanation concedes that family form is not as potent a source of children's well-being as many observers seem to believe.

We might also gain some purchase on this issue by comparing the success of children under different family regimes. Do the countries with high rates of cohabitation, low marriage, high divorce, and high nonmarital fertility have the worst outcomes for children? We don't know the answer to this question, but we do know that various indicators of child well-being—health, mental health, educational attainment—do show higher scores in Northern than in Southern Europe. They appear to be linked to the level of investment in children, not the family form (which is certainly more intact in Southern Europe). Still, this question deserves more attention than it has received.

Significantly, many of the countries that continue to adhere to the nuclear model have some of the world's lowest rates of fertility—a problem that seems worse in countries with very low rates of nonmarital childbearing.

I am not claiming that nonmarital childbearing is necessarily desirable as a social arrangement for propping up fertility, but it is a plausible hypothesis that nonmarital childbearing helps to keep the birth rate up in countries that would otherwise be experiencing a dangerously low level of reproduction.

Finally, it is important to recognize that family change in the United States (and in most Western countries, it appears) has not occurred evenly among all educational groups. In this country, marriage, divorce, and non-marital childbearing have jumped since the 1960s among the bottom two-thirds of the educational distribution but have not changed much at all among the top third, consisting, today, of college graduates and postgraduates. Though marriage comes later to this group, they are barely more likely to have children out of wedlock, have high levels of marriage, and, if anything, lower levels of divorce than were experienced several decades ago. In other words, almost all the change has occurred among the segment of the population that has either not gained economically or has lost ground over the past several decades. Among the most socially disadvantaged and most marginalized segments of American society, marriage has become imperiled and family conditions have generally deteriorated, resulting in extremely high rates of union instability. The growing inequality in the United States may provide some clues for why the family, and marriage in particular, is not faring well and what to do about it.

Marriage and Public Policy

The logic of the Bush administration's approach to welfare is that by promoting and strengthening marriage, children's well-being, particularly in lower-income families will be enhanced. At first blush, this approach seems to make good sense. Economies of scale are produced when two adults live together. Two parents create healthy redundancies and perhaps help build social capital both within the household and by creating more connections to the community. The prevalence of marriage and marital stability is substantially higher among well-educated and more stably employed individuals than among those with less than a college education and lower incomes. Wouldn't it be reasonable to help the less educated enjoy the benefits of the nuclear family?

There are several reasons to be skeptical of this policy direction. First, we have the experience of the 1950s, when marriages did occur in abundance among low-income families. Divorce rates were extremely high during this era, and many of these families dissolved their unions when they had an opportunity to divorce because of chronic problems of conflict, disenchantment, and scarcity. In my own study of marriages of teen parents in the 1960s, I discovered that four out of every five women who married the father of their children got divorced before the child reached age eighteen; the rate of marital instability among those who married a stepfather was even higher. Certainly, encouraging marriage among young couples facing a choice of nonmarital childbearing or wedlock is not an easy choice when we know the outcome of the union is so precarious. If divorce is a likely outcome, it is not clear whether children are better off if their parents marry and divorce than remain unmarried, knowing as we do that family conflict and flux have adverse effects on children's welfare.

What about offering help to such couples before or after they enter marriage? This is a good idea, but don't expect any miracles from the current policies. Strong opposition exists to funding sustained and intensive premarital and postmarital counseling among many proponents of marriage-promotion programs. Conservative constituencies largely believe that education, especially under the aegis of religious or quasi-religious sponsorship is the best prescription for shoring up marriage. Yet, the evidence overwhelmingly shows that short-term programs that are largely didactic will not be effective in preserving marriages. Instead, many couples need repeated bouts of help both before and during marriage when they run into difficult straits. Most of these couples have little or no access to professional counseling.

The federal government has funded several large-scale experiments combining into a single program marital education or counseling *and* social services including job training or placement. These experiments, being conducted by the Manpower Research Demonstration Corporation, will use random assignment and have the best hope of producing some demonstrable outcomes. Yet, it is not clear at this point that even comprehensive programs with sustained services will be effective in increasing partner collaboration and reducing union instability.

There is another approach that I believe has a better prospect of improving both children's chances and probably at least an equal chance of increasing the viability of marriages or marriage-like arrangements. By directing more resources to low-income children regardless of the family form they live in, through such mechanisms as access to quality child care, health care, schooling, and income in the form of tax credits, it may be possible to increase the level of human, social, and psychological capital that children receive. And, by increasing services, work support, and especially tuition aid for adolescents and young adults to attend higher education, Americans may be able to protect children from the limitations imposed by low parental resources. Lending this type of assistance means that young adults are more likely to move into higher paying jobs and acquire through education the kinds of communication and problem-solving skills that are so useful to making marriage-like relationships last.

When we invest in children, we are not only likely to reap the direct benefits of increasing human capital but also the indirect benefits that will help preserve union stability in the next generation. This approach is more likely to increase the odds of success for children when they grow up. If I am correct, it probably follows that direct investment in children and youth has a better prospect of strengthening marriage and marriage-like relationships in the next generation by improving the skills and providing the resources to make parental relationships more rewarding and enduring.

So it comes down to a choice in strategy: invest in strengthening marriage and hope that children will benefit or invest in children and hope that marriages will benefit. I place my bet on the second approach.

POSTSCRIPT

Is the Decline of the Traditional Family a National Crisis?

Popenoe admits that there are many positive aspects to the recent changes that have affected families, but he sees the negative consequences, especially for children, as necessitating actions to counter them. He recommends a return to family values and speaks out against the individualistic ethos. Coontz contends that the traditional family form that people like Popenoe are nostalgic for was atypical in American history and cannot be re-created. Nor is there one right universal form of the family. Furthermore, a closer look at the data indicates that the institution of the family is not in crisis.

Support for Furstenberg's point of view can be found in E. L. Kain, *The Myth of Family Decline* (D. C. Heath, 1990); J. F. Gubrium and J. A. Holstein, *What Is a Family?* (Mayfield, 1990); Stephanie Coontz, *The Way We Really Are* (Basic Books, 1997); and Rosalind C. Barnett and Caryl Rivers, *She Works/He Works: How Two-Income Families Are Happier, Healthier, and Better Off* (Harper-Collins, 1997). Recent works describing the weakening of the family and marriage include Richard T. Gill, *Posterity Lost: Progress, Ideology, and the Decline of the American Family* (Rowman & Littlefield, 1997); Dana Mack, *The Assault on Parenthood: How Our Culture Undermines the Family* (Simon & Schuster, 1997); Maggie Gallagher, *The Abolition of Marriage: How We Destroy Lasting Love* (Regnery, 1996); Barbara Dafoe Whitehead, *The Divorce Culture: How Divorce Became an Entitlement and How It Is Blighting the Lives of Our Children* (Alfred A. Knopf, 1997); and James Q. Wilson, *The Marriage Problem: How Our Culture Has Weakened Families* (HarperCollins, 2002). The work dealing with divorce and its consequences that is currently in the spotlight is Judith Wallerstein, *The Unexpected Legacy of Divorce* (Hyperion, 2000). In contrast E. Mavis Hetherington and John Kelly argue that most children in divorced families adjust well in the long run in *For Better or for Worse: Divorce Reconsidered* (W.W. Norton, 2002). David Popenoe and Jean Bethke Elshtain's book *Promises to Keep: Decline and Renewal of Marriage in America* (Rowman & Littlefield, 1996) discusses the decline but also signs of renewal of marriage. Popenoe's latest book is *War Over the Family* (Transaction, 2005)

Works that analyze changes in marriage and the family include; Betty Farrell's *Family: The Making of an Idea, an Institution, and a Controversy in American Culture* (Westview Press, 1999); Karla B. Hackstaff's *Marriage in a Culture of Divorce* (Temple University Press, 1999); Jessica Weiss's *To Have and to Hold: Marriage, the Baby Boom, and Social Change* (University of Chicago Press, 2000); Barbara J. Risman's *Gender Vertigo: American Families in Transition* (Yale University Press, 1998); Ronald D. Taylor and Margaret C. Wang, eds., *Resilience Across Contexts: Family, Work, Culture, and Community* (Lawrence Erlbaum,

2000); Linda J. Waite and Maggie Gallagher, *The Case for Marriage: Why Married People Are Happier, Healthier, and Better Off Financially* (Doubleday, 2000); Daniel P. Moynihan, et al., eds., *Future of the Family* (Russell Sage Foundation, 2004); and Lynne M. Casper and Suzanne M. Bianchi, *Continuity and Change in the American Family* (Sage, 2002). For council on how to strengthen marriages, see David P. Gushee, *Getting Marriage Right: Realistic Counsel for Saving and Strengthening Relationships* (Baker Books, 2004).

For three major works on aspects of familial changes, see David Blankenhorn, *Fatherless America: Confronting Our Most Urgent Social Problem* (Basic Books, 1995); Sara McLanahan and Gary Sandefur, *Growing up With a Single Parent: What Hurts and What Helps* (Harvard University Press, 1994); and David Popenoe, *Life without Father: Compelling New Evidence That Fatherhood and Marriage Are Indispensable for the Good of Children and Society* (Harvard University Press, 1999).

ISSUE 5

Should Mothers Stay Home with Their Children?

YES: Claudia Wallis, from "The Case for Staying Home," *Time* (March 22, 2004)

NO: Susan J. Douglas and Meredith W. Michaels, from *The Mommy Myth* (Free Press, 2004)

ISSUE SUMMARY

YES: Journalist Claudia Wallis reports that more and more mothers are choosing to quit work and stay home to care for the children. The work demands on professional women have increased to the point that very few can do both work and family. Forced to choose, growing numbers choose family.

NO: Communication studies professor Susan Douglas and writer Meredith Michaels attack the media for promoting the mommy myth, that "motherhood is eternally fulfilling and rewarding, that it is always the best and most important thing to do, ... and that if you don't love each and every second of it there's something really wrong with you." They object to the subtle moral pressure that the media puts on mothers to stay home with their children.

The fascinating aspect of social life is how many different trends and changes significantly affect our lives and choices. For example, consider married women and their work-family choices. Ever since the 1950s, married women have increasingly participated in the labor force. Why? The reasons are numerous. Women want the money for themselves. Women need the money for the family. Women want the challenge of a career. Women want the social life that work provides. Women want independence. The list of reasons goes on and on. These reasons change, however, as the context changes. For example, since 1965 the median price of the one-family home compared to the average income of private nonagricultural workers has doubled. Thus, the single-earner family is having much more difficulty buying a house. This trend helps explain why married women increasingly enter or stay in the labor force. Attitudes have also changed. In 1968 a large survey asked young people what they expected to be doing at age 35. About 30% of the 20- to 21-year-olds said that they would be working. Seven years later 65% of 20- to 21-year olds said they would be working. That is an astounding change.

Educational changes in the past half century have also been dramatic. As is pointed out in Issue 10 females have overtaken males in most aspects of education. Reversing 350 years of history, women are now outnumbering men in college and currently earn 57% of all bachelor degrees, 58% of all master degrees, and are rapidly closing the M.D. and Ph.D. gaps. Women are also more focused on professional degrees while in college as demonstrated by their selection of majors. In 1966 40% of college women graduates majored in education and 17% majored in English/literature but only 2% majored in business.

Many other changes are associated with these changes and changes in the labor force participation of women. The feminist movement, which surged in the 1960s and 1970s, encouraged women to fully develop their abilities and have careers and it spearheaded a social and political movement for equality for women. The Civil Rights Act of 1964 included gender in its equality protections and years of discrimination law suits and voluntary changes by employers have greatly altered the workplace. Perhaps the most important factor was the invention of the birth control pill, because it gave women control over their fertility and changed the ramifications of engaging in sex. It contributed to the increasing age of marriage, which made educational preparation for careers more feasible. It also contributed to the substantial decline in fertility. Women are having fewer children on average and are increasingly choosing not to have any children.

Another trend affecting choices and behaviors is the increasing time scarcity. Though the average hours that men and women spent working for pay has remained relatively constant for several decades (43 and 37 hours in both 1970 and 2000), nevertheless the dispersion of the time different workers spend on the job has increased. This means that there has been simultaneously an increase in the number of workers that work very long hours and workers who have short work-weeks. The percentage of males working more than 50 hours a week increased from 21.0 to 26.5 from 1970 to 2000 and for females from 5.2 to 11.3. Many women with professional careers are in this group and suffer from time scarcity.

This brings us to the debate question: Should mothers stay home with their children? There are good reasons why mothers want to both work and have a family and there are good reasons why mothers are quitting work to raise children. For decades the trend for mothers was to increasingly enter or stay in the labor market. According to Claudia Wallis, a journalist for *Time*, this trend has stopped and started to decline slightly. Then she reports the reasons why mothers are quitting work. She focuses on the professional and managerial classes where the husband's high income facilitates this choice. The implication of their report is that mothers in such situations should stay home for the sake of their children. They would seem to be irresponsible if they do not. Susan J. Douglas and Meredith W. Michaels classify Wallis's article as part of the troublesome media myth making about women. The media are idealizing motherhood and undermining the status of working mothers. Both Douglas and Michaels combine work and child rearing and refuse to feel guilty about doing so.

81

Claudia Wallis

 **YES**

The Case for Staying Home

It's 6:35 in the morning, and Cheryl Nevins, 34, dressed for work in a silky black maternity blouse and skirt, is busily tending to Ryan, 2½, and Brendan, 11 months, at their home in the leafy Edgebrook neighborhood of Chicago. Both boys are sobbing because Reilly, the beefy family dog, knocked Ryan over. In a blur of calm, purposeful activity, Nevins, who is 8 months pregnant, shoves the dog out into the backyard, changes Ryan's diaper on the family-room rug, heats farina in the microwave and feeds Brendan cereal and sliced bananas while crooning *Open, Shut Them* to encourage the baby to chew. Her husband Joe, 35, normally out the door by 5:30 a.m. for his job as a finance manager for Kraft Foods, makes a rare appearance in the morning muddle. "I do want to go outside with you," he tells Ryan, who is clinging to his leg, "but Daddy has to work every day except Saturdays and Sundays. That stinks."

At 7:40, Vera Orozco, the nanny, arrives to begin her 10½-hour shift at the Nevinses'. Cheryl, a labor lawyer for the Chicago board of education, hands over the baby and checks her e-mail from the kitchen table. "I almost feel apprehensive if I leave for work without logging on," she confesses. Between messages, she helps Ryan pull blue Play-Doh from a container, then briefs Orozco on the morning's events: "They woke up early. Ryan had his poop this morning, this guy has not." Throughout the day, Orozco will note every meal and activity on a tattered legal pad on the kitchen counter so Nevins can stay up to speed.

Suddenly it's 8:07, and the calm mom shifts from cruise control into hyperdrive. She must be out the door by 8:10 to make the 8:19 train. Once on the platform, she punches numbers into her cell phone, checks her voice mail and then leaves a message for a co-worker. On the train, she makes more calls and proofreads documents. "Right now, work is crazy," says Nevins, who has been responsible for negotiating and administering seven agreements between the board and labor unions.

Nevins is "truly passionate" about her job, but after seven years, she's about to leave it. When the baby arrives, she will take off at least a year, maybe two, maybe five. "It's hard. I'm giving up a great job that pays well, and I have a lot of respect and authority," she says. The decision to stay home was a tough one, but most of her working-mom friends have made the same choice. She concludes, "I know it's the right thing."

Ten, 15 years ago, it all seemed so doable. Bring home the bacon, fry it up in a pan, split the second shift with some sensitive New Age man. But slowly the snappy, upbeat work-life rhythm has changed for women in high-powered posts like Nevins. The U.S. workweek still averages around 34 hours, thanks in part to a sluggish manufacturing sector. But for those in financial services, it's 55 hours; for top executives in big corporations, it's 60 to 70, says Catalyst, a research and consulting group that focuses on women in business. For dual-career couples with kids under 18, the combined work hours have grown from 81 a week in 1977 to 91 in 2002, according to the Families and Work Institute. E-mail, pagers and cell phones promised to allow execs to work from home. Who knew that would mean that home was no longer a sanctuary? Today BlackBerrys sprout on the sidelines of Little League games. Cell phones vibrate at the school play. And it's back to the e-mail after *Goodnight Moon*. "We are now the workaholism capital of the world, surpassing the Japanese," laments sociologist Arlie Hochschild, author of *The Time Bind: When Work Becomes Home and Home Becomes Work*.

Meanwhile, the pace has quickened on the home front, where a mother's job has expanded to include managing a packed schedule of child-enhancement activities. In their new book *The Mommy Myth*, Susan Douglas, a professor of communication studies at the University of Michigan, and Meredith Michaels, who teaches philosophy at Smith College, label the phenomenon the New Momism. Nowadays, they write, our culture insists that "to be a remotely decent mother, a woman has to devote her entire physical, psychological, emotional, and intellectual being, 24/7, to her children." It's a standard of success that's "impossible to meet," they argue. But that sure doesn't stop women from trying.

For most mothers—and fathers, for that matter—there is little choice but to persevere on both fronts to pay the bills. Indeed, 72% of mothers with children under 18 are in the work force—a figure that is up sharply from 47% in 1975 but has held steady since 1997. And thanks in part to a dodgy economy, there's growth in another category, working women whose husbands are unemployed, which has risen to 6.4% of all married couples.

But in the professional and managerial classes, where higher incomes permit more choices, a reluctant revolt is under way. Today's women execs are less willing to play the juggler's game, especially in its current high-speed mode, and more willing to sacrifice paychecks and prestige for time with their family. Like Cheryl Nevins, most of these women are choosing not so much to drop out as to stop out, often with every intention of returning. Their mantra: You can have it all, just not all at the same time. Their behavior, contrary to some popular reports, is not a June Cleaver-ish embrace of old-fashioned motherhood but a new, nonlinear approach to building a career and an insistence on restoring some kind of sanity. "What this group is staying home from is the 80-hour-a-week job," says Hochschild. "They are committed to work, but many watched their mothers and fathers be ground up by very long hours, and they would like to give their own children more than they got. They want a work-family balance."

Because these women represent a small and privileged sector, the dimensions of the exodus are hard to measure. What some experts are zeroing in on is the first-ever drop-off in workplace participation by married mothers with a child less than

1 year old. That figure fell from 59% in 1997 to 53% in 2000. The drop may sound modest, but, says Howard Hayghe, an economist at the Bureau of Labor Statistics, "that's huge," and the figure was roughly the same in 2002. Significantly, the drop was mostly among women who were white, over 30 and well educated.

Census data reveal an uptick in stay-at-home moms who hold graduate or professional degrees—the very women who seemed destined to blast through the glass ceiling. Now 22% of them are home with their kids. A study by Catalyst found that 1 in 3 women with M.B.A.s are not working full-time (it's 1 in 20 for their male peers). Economist and author Sylvia Ann Hewlett, who teaches at Columbia University, says she sees a brain drain throughout the top 10% of the female labor force (those earning more than $55,000). "What we have discovered in looking at this group over the last five years," she says, "is that many women who have any kind of choice are opting out."

Other experts say the drop-out rate isn't climbing but is merely more visible now that so many women are in high positions. In 1971 just 9% of medical degrees, 7% of law degrees and 4% of M.B.A.s were awarded to women; 30 years later, the respective figures were 43%, 47% and 41%.

The Generation Factor

For an older group of female professionals who came of age listening to Helen Reddy roar, the exodus of younger women can seem disturbingly regressive. Fay Clayton, 58, a partner in a small Chicago law firm, watched in dismay as her 15-person firm lost three younger women who left after having kids, though one has since returned part time. "I fear there is a generational split and possibly a step backwards for younger women," she says.

Others take a more optimistic view. "Younger women have greater expectations about the work-life balance," says Joanne Brundage, 51, founder and executive director of Mothers & More, a mothers' support organization with 7,500 members and 180 chapters in the U.S. While boomer moms have been reluctant to talk about their children at work for fear that "people won't think you're a professional," she observes, younger women "feel more entitled to ask for changes and advocate for themselves." That sense of confidence is reflected in the evolution of her organization's name. When Brundage founded it in Elmhurst, Ill., 17 years ago, it was sheepishly called FEMALE, for Formerly Employed Mothers at Loose Ends.

Brundage may be ignoring that young moms can afford to think flexibly about life and work while pioneering boomers first had to prove they could excel in high-powered jobs. But she's right about the generational difference. A 2001 survey by Catalyst of 1,263 men and women born from 1964 to 1975 found that Gen Xers "didn't want to have to make the kind of trade-offs the previous generation made. They're rejecting the stresses and sacrifices," says Catalyst's Paulette Gerkovich. "Both women and men rated personal and family goals higher than career goals."

A newer and larger survey, conducted late last year by the Boston-area marketing group Reach Advisors, provides more evidence of a shift in attitudes. Gen X (which it defined as those born from 1965 to 1979) moms and dads said they spent more time on child rearing and household tasks than did boomer parents (born from 1945 to 1964). Yet Gen Xers were much more likely than boomers to complain that they wanted more time. "At first we thought, Is this just a generation of whiners?" says Reach Advisors president James Chung. "But they really wish they had more time with their kids." In the highest household-income bracket ($120,000 and up), Reach Advisors found that 51% of Gen X moms were home full time, compared with 33% of boomer moms. But the younger stay-at-home moms were much more likely to say they intended to return to work: 46% of Gen Xers expressed that goal, compared with 34% of boomers.

Chung and others speculate that the attitude differences can be explained in part by forces that shaped each generation. While boomer women sought career opportunities that were unavailable to their mostly stay-at-home moms, Gen Xers were the latchkey kids and the children of divorce. Also, their careers have bumped along in a roller-coaster, boom-bust economy that may have shaken their faith in finding reliable satisfaction at work.

Pam Pala, 35, of Salt Lake City, Utah, is in some ways typical. She spent years building a career in the heavily male construction industry, rising to the position of construction project engineer with a big firm. But after her daughter was born 11 months ago, she decided to stay home to give her child the attention Pala had missed as a kid. "I grew up in a divorced family. My mom couldn't take care of us because she had to work," she says. "We went to baby-sitters or stayed home alone and were scared and hid under the bathroom counter whenever the doorbell rang." Pala wants to return to work when her daughter is in school, and she desperately hopes she won't be penalized for her years at home. "I have a feeling that I'll have to start lower on the totem pole than where I left," she says. "It seems unfair."

Maternal Desire and Doubts

Despite such misgivings, most women who step out of their careers find expected delights on the home front, not to mention the enormous relief of no longer worrying about shortchanging their kids. Annik Miller, 32, of Minneapolis, Minn., decided not to return to her job as a business-systems consultant at Wells Fargo Bank after she checked out day-care options for her son Alex, now 11 months. "I had one woman look at me honestly and say she could promise that my son would get undivided attention eight times each day—four bottles and four diaper changes," says Miller. "I appreciated her honesty, but I knew I couldn't leave him."

Others appreciate a slower pace and being there when a child asks a tough question. In McLean, Va., Oakie Russell's son Dylan, 8, recently inquired, out of the blue, "Mom, who is God's father?" Says Russell, 45, who gave up a dream job at PBS: "So, you're standing at the sink with your hands in the dishwater and you're thinking, 'Gee, that's really complicated. But I'm awfully glad I'm the one you're asking.'"

Psychologist Daphne de Marneffe speaks to these private joys in a new book, *Maternal Desire* (Little Brown). De Marneffe argues that feminists and American society at large have ignored the basic urge that most mothers feel to spend meaningful time with their children. She decries the rushed fragments of quality time doled out by working moms trying to do it all. She writes, "Anyone who has tried to 'fit everything in' can attest to how excruciating the five-minute wait at the supermarket checkout line becomes, let alone a child's slow-motion attempt to tie her own shoes when you're running late getting her to school." The book, which puts an idyllic gloss on staying home, could launch a thousand resignations.

What de Marneffe largely omits is the sense of pride and meaning that women often gain from their work. Women who step out of their careers can find the loss of identity even tougher than the loss of income. "I don't regret leaving, but a huge part of me is gone," says Bronwyn Towle, 41, who surrendered a demanding job as a Washington lobbyist to be with her two sons. Now when she joins her husband Raymond, who works at the U.S. Chamber of Commerce, at work-related dinners, she feels sidelined. "Everyone will be talking about what they're doing," says Towle, "and you say, 'I'm a stay-at-home mom.' It's conference-buzz kill."

Last year, after her youngest child went to kindergarten, Towle eased back into the world of work. She found a part-time job in a forward-thinking architectural firm but hopes to return to her field eventually. "I wish there was more part-time or job-sharing work," she says. It's a wish expressed by countless formerly working moms.

Building On-Ramps

Hunter College sociologist Pamela Stone has spent the past few years interviewing 50 stay-at-home mothers in seven U.S. cities for a book on professional women who have dropped out. "Work is much more of a culprit in this than the more rosy view that it's all about discovering how great your kids are," says Stone. "Not that these mothers don't want to spend time with their kids. But many of the women I talked to have tried to work part time or put forth job-sharing plans, and they're shot down. Despite all the family-friendly rhetoric, the workplace for professionals is extremely, extremely inflexible."

That's what Ruth Marlin, 40, of New York City found even at the family-friendly International Planned Parenthood Federation. After giving birth to her second child, 15 months ago, she was allowed to ease back in part time. But Marlin, an attorney and a senior development officer, was turned down when she asked to make the part-time arrangement permanent. "With the job market contracted so much, the opportunities just aren't there anymore," says Marlin, who hates to see her $100,000 law education go to waste. "Back in the dotcom days, people just wanted employees to stay. There was more flexibility. Who knows? Maybe the market will change."

There are signs that in some corners it is changing. In industries that depend on human assets, serious work is being done to create more part-time and flexible positions. At PricewaterhouseCoopers, 10% of the firm's female partners are on a part-time schedule, according to the accounting firm's chief diversity officer, Toni Riccardi. And, she insists, it's not career suicide: "A three-day week might slow your progress, but it won't prohibit you" from climbing the career ladder. The company has also begun to address the e-mail ball and chain. In December PWC shut down for 11 days over the holidays for the first time ever. "We realize people do need to rejuvenate," says Riccardi. "They don't, if their eye is on the BlackBerry and their hand is on a keyboard."

PWC is hardly alone. Last month economist Hewlett convened a task force of leaders from 14 companies and four law firms, including Goldman Sachs and Pfizer, to discuss what she calls the hidden brain drain of women and minority professionals. "We are talking about how to create off-ramps and on-ramps, slow lanes and acceleration ramps" so that workers can more easily leave, slow down or re-enter the work force, she explains.

"This is a war for talent," says Carolyn Buck Luce, a partner at the accounting firm Ernst & Young, who co-chairs the task force. Over the past 20 years, half of new hires at Ernst & Young have been women, she notes, and the firm is eager not only to keep them but to draw back those who have left to tend their children. This spring Deloitte Touche Tohmatsu will launch a Personal Pursuits program, allowing above-average performers to take up to five years of unpaid leave for personal reasons. Though most benefits will be suspended, the firm will continue to cover professional licensing fees for those on leave and will pay to send them for weeklong annual training sessions to keep their skills in shape. Such efforts have spawned their own goofy jargon. Professionals who return to their ex-employers are known as boomerangs, and the effort to reel them back in is called alumni relations.

One reason businesses are getting serious about the brain drain is demographics. With boomers nearing retirement, a shortfall of perhaps 10 million workers appears likely by 2010. "The labor shortage has a lot to do with it," says Melinda Wolfe, managing director and head of Goldman Sachs' global leadership and diversity.

Will these programs work? Will part-time jobs really be part time, as opposed to full-time jobs paid on a partial basis? Will serious professionals who shift into a slow lane be able to pick up velocity when their kids are grown? More important, will corporate culture evolve to a point where employees feel genuinely encouraged to use these options? Anyone who remembers all the talk about flex time in the 1980s will be tempted to dismiss the latest ideas for making the workplace family-friendly. But this time, perhaps, the numbers may be on the side of working moms—along with many working dads who are looking for options.

On-ramps, slow lanes, flexible options and respect for all such pathways can't come soon enough for mothers eager to set examples and offer choices for the next generation. Terri Laughlin, 38, a stay-at-home mom and former psychology professor at the University of Nebraska at Lincoln, was alarmed a few weeks ago when her daughters Erin, 8, and Molly, 6, announced their intentions to marry men "with enough money so we can stay at home." Says Laughlin: "I want to make sure they realize that although it's wonderful staying at home, that's only one of many options. What I hope to show them is that at some point I can re-create myself and go back to work."

NO

Susan J. Douglas and Meredith W. Michaels

The Mommy Myth

The New Momism

From the moment we get up until the moment we collapse in bed at night, the media are out there, calling to us, yelling, "Hey you! Yeah, you! Are you *really* raising your kids right?" Whether it's the cover of *Redbook* or *Parents* demanding "Are You a Sensitive Mother?" "Is Your Child Eating Enough?" "Is Your Baby Normal?" (and exhorting us to enter it's pages and have great sex at 25, 35, or 85), the nightly news warning us about missing children, a movie trailer hyping a film about a cross-dressing dad who's way more fun than his stinky, careerist wife (*Mrs. Doubtfire*), or Dr. Laura telling some poor mother who works four hours a week that she's neglectful, the siren song blending seduction and accusation is there all the time. Mothers are subjected to an onslaught of beatific imagery, romantic fantasies, self-righteous sermons, psychological warnings, terrifying movies about losing their children, even more terrifying news stories about abducted and abused children, and totally unrealistic advice about how to be the most perfect and revered mom in the neighborhood, maybe even in the whole country. (Even *Working Mother*—which should have known better—had a "Working Mother of the Year Contest." When Jill Kirschenbaum became the editor in 2001, one of the first things she did was dump this feature, noting that motherhood should not be a "competitive sport.") We are urged to be fun-loving, spontaneous, and relaxed, yet, at the same time, scared out of our minds that our kids could be killed at any moment. No wonder 81 percent of women in a recent poll said it's harder to be a mother now than it was twenty or thirty years ago, and 56 percent felt mothers were doing a worse job today than mothers back then. Even mothers who deliberately avoid TV and magazines, or who pride themselves on seeing through them, have trouble escaping the standards of perfection, and the sense of threat, that the media ceaselessly atomize into the air we breathe.

We are both mothers, and we adore our kids—for example, neither one of us has ever locked them up in dog crates in the basement (although we have, of course, been tempted). The smell of a new baby's head, tucking a child in at night, receiving homemade, hand-scrawled birthday cards, heart-to-hearts with a teenager after a date, seeing *them* become parents—these are

From THE MOMMY MYTH: THE IDEALIZATION OF MOTHERHOOD AND HOW IT HAS UNDERMINED ALL WOMEN , February 3, 2004, pp. 3-6, 9-10, 15-16, 22-24. Copyright © 2004 by Susan Douglas and Meredith Michaels. Reprinted by permission.

joys parents treasure. But like increasing numbers of women, we are fed up with the myth—shamelessly hawked by the media—that motherhood is eternally fulfilling and rewarding, that it is *always* the best and most important thing you do, that there is only a narrowly prescribed way to do it right, and that if you don't love each and every second of it there's something really wrong with you. At the same time, the two of us still have been complete suckers, buying those black-and-white mobiles that allegedly turn your baby into Einstein Jr., feeling guilty for sending in store-bought cookies to the class bake sale instead of homemade like the "good" moms, staying up until 2:30 A.M. making our kids' Halloween costumes, driving to the Multiplex 18 at midnight to pick up teenagers so they won't miss the latest outing with their friends. We know that building a scale model of Versailles out of mashed potatoes may not be quite as crucial to good mothering as *Martha Stewart Living* suggests. Yet here we are, cowed by the most tyrannical of our cultural icons, Perfect Mom. So, like millions of women, we buy into these absurd ideals at the same time that we resent them and think they are utterly ridiculous and oppressive. After all, our parents—the group Tom Brokaw has labeled "the greatest generation"—had parents who whooped them on the behind, screamed stuff at them like "I'll tear you limb from limb," told them babies came from cabbage patches, never drove them four hours to a soccer match, and yet they seemed to have nonetheless saved the western world.

This book is about the rise in the media of what we are calling the "new momism": the insistence that no woman is truly complete or fulfilled unless she has kids, that women remain the best primary caretakers of children, and that to be a remotely decent mother, a woman has to devote her entire physical, psychological, emotional, and intellectual being, 24/7, to her children. The new momism is a highly romanticized and yet demanding view of motherhood in which the standards for success are impossible to meet. The term "momism" was initially coined by the journalist Philip Wylie in his highly influencial 1942 bestseller *Generation of Vipers*, and it was a very derogatory term. Drawing from Freud (who else?), Wylie attacked the mothers of America as being so smothering, overprotective, and invested in their kids, especially their sons, that they turned them into dysfunctional, sniveling weaklings, maternal slaves chained to the apron strings, unable to fight for their country or even stand on their own two feet. We seek to reclaim this term, rip it from its misogynistic origins, and apply it to an ideology that has snowballed since the 1980s and seeks to return women to the Stone Age.

The "new momism" is a set of ideals, norms, and practices, most frequently and powerfully represented in the media, that seem on the surface to celebrate motherhood, but which in reality promulgate standards of perfection that are beyond your reach. The new momism is the direct descendant and latest version of what Betty Friedan famously labeled the "feminine mystique" back in the 1960s. The new momism *seems* to be much more hip and progressive than the feminine mystique, because now, of course, mothers can and do work outside the home, have their own ambitions and money, raise kids on their own, or freely choose to stay at home with their kids rather than being forced to. And unlike the feminine mystique, the notion that women should be subservient to men is not an accepted tenet of the new momism. Central to the new momism, in fact, is the feminine insistence that woman have choices, that they are active agents in control of their own destiny, that they have autonomy. But here's where the distortion of feminism occurs. The only truly enlightened choice to make as a woman, the one that proves, first, that you are a "real" woman, and second, that you are a decent, worthy one, is to become a "mom" and to bring to child rearing a combination of selflessness and professionalism that would involve the cross cloning of Mother Teresa with Donna Shalala. Thus the new momism is deeply contradictory: It both draws from and repudiates feminism.

The fulcrum of the new momiasm is the rise of a really pernicious ideal in the late twentieth century that the sociologist Sharon Hays has perfectly labeled "intensive mothering." It is no longer okay, as it was even during the heyday of June Cleaver, to let (or make) your kids walk to school, tell them to stop bugging you and go outside and play, or God forbid, serve them something like Tang, once the preferred beverage of the astronauts, for breakfast. Of course many of our mothers baked us cookies, served as Brownie troop leaders, and chaperoned class trips to Elf Land. But today, the standards of good motherhood are really over the top, and they've gone through the roof at the same time that there has been a real decline in leisure time for most Americans. The yuppie work ethic of the 1980s, which insisted that even when you were off the job you should be working—on your abs, your connections, your portfolio, whatever—absolutely conquered motherhood. As the actress Patricia Heaton jokes in *Motherhood & Hollywood*, now mothers are supposed to "sneak echinacea" into the "freshly squeezed, organically grown orange juice" we've made for our kids and teach them to "download research for their kindergarten report on 'My Family Tree—The Early Roman Years.' "

Intensive mothering insists that mothers acquire professional-level skills such as those of a therapist, pediatrician ("Dr. Mom"), consumer products safety inspector, and teacher, and that they lavish every ounce of physical vitality they have, the monetary equivalent of the gross domestic product of Australia, and, most of all, every single bit of their emotional, mental, and psychic energy on their kids. We must learn to put on the masquerade of the doting, self-sacrificing mother and wear it at all times. With intensive mothering, everyone watches us, we watch ourselves and other mothers, and we watch ourselves watching ourselves. How many of you know someone who swatted her child on the behind in a supermarket because he was, say, opening a pack of razor blades in the toiletries aisle, only to be accosted by someone she never met who threatened to put her up on child-abuse charges? In 1997, one mother was arrested for child neglect because she left a ten-year-old and a four-year-old home for an hour and a half while she went to the supermarket. Motherhood has become a psychological police state....

But make no mistake about it—mothers and motherhood came under unprecedented media surveillance in the 1980s and beyond. And since the media traffic in extremes, in anomalies—the rich, the deviant, the exemplary, the criminal, the gorgeous—they emphasize fear and dread on the one hand and promote impossible ideals on the other. In the process, *Good Housekeeping, People,* E!, Lifetime, *Entertainment Tonight,* and *NBC Nightly News* build an interlocking, cumulative image of the dedicated, doting "mom" versus the delinquent, bad "mother." There have been, since the early 1980s, several overlapping media frameworks that have fueled the new momism. First, the media warned mothers about the external threats to their kids from abductors and the like. Then the "family values" crowd made it clear that supporting the family was not part of the government's responsibility. By the late 1980s, stories about welfare and crack mothers emphasized the internal threats to children from mothers themselves. And finally, the media brouhaha over the "Mommy Track" reaffirmed that businesses could not or would not budge much to accommodate the care of children. Together, and over time, these frameworks produced a prevailing common sense that only you, the individual mother, are responsible for your child's welfare: The buck stops with you, period, and you'd better be a superstar.

Of course there has been a revolution in fatherhood over the past thirty years, and millions of men today tend to the details of child rearing in ways their own fathers rarely did. Feminism prompted women to insist that men change diapers and pack school lunches, but it also gave men permission to become more involved with their kids in ways they have found to be deeply satisfying. And between images of cuddly, New Age dads with babies asleep on their chests (think old Folger's ads), movies about hunky men and a baby (or clueless ones who shrink the kids), and sensational news stories about "deadbeat dads" and men who beat up their sons' hockey coaches, fathers too have been subject to a media "dad patrol." But it pales in comparison to the new momism. After all, a dad who knows the name of his kids' pediatrician and reads them stories at night is still regarded as a saint; a mother who doesn't is a sinner....

There are several reasons why the new momism—talk about the wrong idea for the wrong time—triumphed when it did. Baby boom women who, in the 1970s, sought to enter schools and jobs previously reserved for men knew they couldn't be just as good as the guys—they had to be better, in part to dispel the myths that women were too stupid, irrational, hysterical, weak, flighty, or unpredictable during "that time of the month" to manage a business, report the news, wear a stethoscope, or sell real estate. Being an overachiever simply went with the terrain of breaking down the barriers, so it wouldn't be surprising to find these women bringing that same determination to motherhood. And some of us did get smacked around as kids, or had parents who crushed our confidence, and we did want to do a better job than that. One brick in the wall of the new momism.

Many women, who had started working in the 1970s and postponed having children, decided in the 1980s to have kids. Thus, this was a totally excellent time for the federal government to insist that it was way too expensive to support any programs for families and children (like maternity leave or subsidized, high-quality day care or even decent public schools) because then the U.S. couldn't afford that $320 billion appropriation to the Pentagon, which included money for those $1600 coffee makers and $600 toilet seats the military needed so badly in 1984. (Imagine where we'd be today if the government had launched the equivalent of the G.I. bill for mothers in the 1980s!) Parents of baby boomers had seen money flow into America's schools because of the Sputnik scare that the Russkies were way ahead of the U.S. in science and technology; thus the sudden need to reacquaint American kids with a slide rule. Parents in the 1980s saw public schools hemorrhaging money. So the very institutions our mothers had been able to count on now needed massive CPR, while the prospect of any new ones was, we were told, out of the question. Guess who had to take up the slack? Another brick in the wall of the new momism.

The right wing of the Republican party—which controlled the White House from 1980 to 1992, crucial years in the evolution of motherhood—hated the women's movement and believed all women, with the possible exception of Phyllis Schlafly, should remain in the kitchen on their knees polishing their husband's shoes and golf clubs while teaching their kids that Darwin was a very bad man. (Unless the mothers were poor and black—those moms had to get back to work ASAP, because by staying home they were wrecking the country. But more on that later.) We saw, in the 1980s and beyond, the rise of what the historian Ruth Feldstein has called "mother-blaming," attacks on mothers for failing to raise physically and phychologically fit future citizens. See, no one, not even Ronald Reagan, said explicitly to us, "The future and the destiny of the nation are in your hands, oh mothers of America. And you are screwing up." But that's what he meant. Because not only are mothers supposed to repro-duce the nation biologically, we're also supposed to regenerate it cultur-ally and morally. Even after the women's movement, mothers were still expected to be the primary socializers of children. Not only were our indi-vidual kids' well-being our responsibility, but also the entire fate of the nation supposedly rested on our padded and milk-splotched shoulders. So women's own desires to be good parents, their realization that they now had to make up for collapsing institutions, and all that guild-tripping about "family values" added many more bricks to the wall....

There are already bleacher loads of very good, even excellent books attacking the unattainable ideals surrounding motherhood, and we will rely on many of them here. But while many of these books expose and rail against the cultural myths mothers have had to combat—putting your child in day care proves you are a selfish, careerist bitch, if you don't bond with your baby immediately after birth you'll have Ted Kaczynski on your hands, and so forth—they have not examined in detail, and over time, the enormous role the mass media have played in promulgating and exaggerating these myths.

We want to fill this gap, to examine how the images of motherhood in TV shows, movies, advertising, women's magazines, and the news have evolved since 1970, raising the bar, year by year, of the standards of good motherhood while singling out and condemning those we were supposed to see as dreadful mothers....

To give you an idea, let's look briefly at the news, which has played a much more central role in policing the boundaries of motherhood than you might think.... In the 1970s, with the exception of various welfare reform proposals, there was almost nothing in the network news about motherhood, working mothers, or childcare....

But by the 1980s, the explosion in the number of working mothers, the desperate need for day care, sci-fi level reproductive technologies, the discovery of how widespread child abuse was—all this was newsworthy. At the same time, the network news shows were becoming more flashy and sensationalistic in their efforts to compete with tabloid TV offerings like *A Current Affair* and *America's Most Wanted*. NBC, for example, introduced a story about day care centers in 1984 with a beat-up Raggedy Ann doll lying limp next to a chair with the huge words *Child Abuse* scrawled next to her in what appeared to be Charles Manson's handwriting. So stories that were titillating, that could be really tarted up, that were about children and sex, or children and violence—well, they just got more coverage than why Senator Rope-a-Dope refused to vote for decent day care. From the McMartin day-care scandal and missing children to Susan Smith and murdering nannies, the barrage of kids-in-jeopardy, "innocence corrupted" stories made mothers feel they had to guard their kids with the same intensity as the secret service guys watching POTUS.

Having discovered in the summer of 2001 that one missing Congressional intern and some shark attacks could fill the twenty-four-hour news hole, the cable channels the following year gave us the summer of abducted girls (rather than, say, in-depth probes of widespread corporate wrongdoing that robbed millions of people of millions of dollars). Even though FBI figures showed a *decline* in missing persons and child abductions, such stories were, as *Newsweek's* Jonathan Alter put it, "inexpensive" and got "boffo ratings." It goes without saying that such crimes are horrific and, understandably, bereft parents wanted to use the media to help locate their kidnapped children. But the incessant coverage of the abductions of Samantha Runnion (whose mother, the media repeatedly reminded us, was at work), Elizabeth Smart, Tamara Brooks, Jacqueline Marris, and Danielle van Dam terrified parents across the country all out of proportion to the risks their children faced. (To put things in perspective, in a country of nearly three hundred million people, estimates were that only 115 children were taken by strangers in ways that were dangerous to the child.) Unlike mothers in the 1950s, then, we were never to let our children out of our sight at carnivals, shopping malls, or playgrounds, and it was up to us to protect them from failing schools, environmental pollution, molesters, drugs, priests, Alar, the Internet, amusement parks, air bags, jungle gyms, *South Park*, trampolines, rottweilers, gangs, and HBO specials about lap dancers and masturbation clubs. It's a wonder any women had children and, once they did, ever let them out of their sight....

. . . We speak as mothers who succumb to and defy the new momism. And our main point is this: Media imagery that seems so natural, that seems to embody some common sense, while blaming some mothers, or all mothers, for children and a nation gone wrong, needs to have its veneer of supposed truth ripped away by us, mothers. For example, while there have been "zany" sitcoms about families with "two dads" or a working mom living with her mother and male housekeeper, the white, upper-middle-class, married-with-children nuclear family remains as dominant as a Humvee, barreling through the media and forcing images of other, different, and just as legitimate family arrangements off to the side. We want to ridicule this ideal—or any other household formation—as *the* norm that should bully those who don't conform. After all, as any mother will point out, the correct ratio of adult-to-kid in any household should be at least three-to-one, a standard the nuclear family fails to meet.

The new momism involves more than just impossible ideals about child rearing. It redefines all women, first and foremost, through their relationships to children. Thus, being a citizen, a worker, a governor, an actress, a First Lady, all are supposed to take a backseat to motherhood. (Remember how people questioned whether Hillary Clinton was truly maternal because she had only one child?) By insisting that being a mother—and a perfect one at that—is the most important thing a woman can do, a prerequisite for being thought of as admirable and noble, the new momism insists that if you want to do anything else, you'd better prove first that you're a doting, totally involved mother before proceeding. This is not a requirement for men. The only recourse for women who want careers, or to do anything else besides stay home with the kids all day, is to prove that they can "do it all." As the feminist writer (and pioneer) Letty Cottin Pogrebin put it, "You can go be a CEO, and a good one, but if you're not making a themed birthday party, you're not a good mother," and, thus, you are a failure.

The new momism has evolved over the past few decades, becoming more hostile to mothers who work, and more insistent that all mothers become ever more closely tethered to their kids. The mythology of the new momism now insinuates that, when all is said and done, the enlightened mother chooses to stay home with the kids. Back in the 1950s, mothers stayed home because they had no choice, so the thinking goes (even though by 1955 more mothers were working than ever before). Today, having been to the office, having tried a career, women supposedly have seen the inside of the male working world and found it to be the inferior choice to staying home, especially when their kids' future is at stake. It's not that mothers can't hack it (1950s thinking). It's that progressive mothers refuse to back it. Inexperienced women thought they knew what they wanted, but they got experience and learned they were wrong. Now mothers have seen the error of their ways, and supposedly seen that the June Cleaver model, if taken as a *choice*, as opposed to a requirement, is the truly modern, fulfilling, forward-thinking version of motherhood....

In other words, ladies, the new momism seeks to contain and, where possible, eradicate, all of the social changes brought on by feminism. It is backlash in its most refined, pernicious form because it insinuates itself into women's psyches just where we have been rendered most vulnerable: in our love for our kids. The new momism, then, is deeply and powerfully political. The new momism is the result of the combustible intermixing of right-wing attacks on feminism and women, the media's increasingly finely tuned and incessant target marketing of mothers and children, the collapse of governmental institutions—public schools, child welfare programs—that served families in the past (imperfectly, to be sure), and mothers' own, very real desires to do the best job possible raising their kids in a culture that praises mothers in rhetoric and reviles them in public policy.

POSTSCRIPT

Should Mothers Stay Home with Their Children?

Choices are often difficult and working mothers have tough choices to make about how to balance career and family. I know that I would feel very deprived if I had to quit my professor's job to raise children even though children are a great joy. But I do not have to make this choice. This is what is obviously unfair about this issue. It is mostly a female problem. Men are not expected to quit their jobs and stay home and raise their children. Some, in fact, are doing just this since their wives are making far more money than they are, but this is rare. Perhaps this is what makes Douglas and Michaels so angry (for they are angry in their book). Mothers are being told by the media that they should stay home for the good of the children. Why are fathers not also being told to stay home for the good of the children? Life is not fair, but we should make it as fair as possible.

According to Douglas and Michaels the evidence for the "new mom ism" is all around us. Look for it when you watch TV. Look at a couple of years of *Redbook, Good Housekeeping, People, E!, Us, InStyle, Family Life,* or *Parents.* For analyses of the new momism look at some of the sources Douglas and Michaels drew upon including Ruth Feldstein, *Motherhood in Black and White* (Cornell University Press, 2000); Sharon Hays, *The Cultural Contradictions of Motherhood* (Yale University Press,1996); Susan Faludi, *Backlash: The Undeclared War against American Women* (Random House,1995); Ann Crittenden, *The Price of Motherhood* (Metropolitan Books, 2001); Diane Eyer, *Motherguilt* (Times Book); Susan Chira, *A Mother's Place: Choosing Work and Family Without Guilt or Shame* (Perennial, 1999); and Susan Maushart, *The Mask of Motherhood* (The New Press, 1999).

For some recent discussions of the demands of work and family on women, see Arlie Russell Hochschild, *The Second Shift* (Penguin Books, 2003); Daphne Spain and Suzanne M. Bianchi, *Balancing Act: Motherhood, Marriage, and Employment Among American Women* (Russell Sage Foundation, 1996); Nancy Kaltreider, ed., *Dilemmas of a Double Life: Women Balancing Careers and Relationships* (Jason, Aronson, 1997); and Anna Fels, *Necessary Dreams: Ambition in Women's Changing Lives* (Pantheon Book, 2004). For the facts on the changes in women's participation in the labor force, see The National Bureau of Economic Research, *From the Valley to the Summit: The Quit Revolution That Transformed Women's Work* (NBER Working Paper No. 10335). Mary Eberstadt is the major critic of the working mothers who leave much of the childrearing to others. See her *Home-Alone America: The Hidden Toll of Daycare, Behavioral Drugs, and Other Parent Substitutes* (Penguin, 2004).

On the issue of time scarcity and time use, which factors into the debate on the tension between work and family, see *Fighting for Time: Shifting Boundaries of Work and Social Life* edited by Cynthia Fuchs-Epstein and Arne L. Kalleberg (Russell Sage Foundation, 2004); Phyllis Moen, *It's about Time: Couples and Careers* (Cornell University Press, 2003); Harriet B. Presser *Working in a 24/7 Economy: Challenges for American Families* (Russell Sage Foundation, 2003); John Robinson and Geoffrey Godbey, *Time for Life: The Surprising Ways Americans Use Their Time*, 2nd edition (State University Press, 1999); Juliet Schor, *The Overworked American: The Unexpected Decline of Leisure* (Basic Books, 1991); Jerry A. Jacobs and Kathleen Gerson, *The Time Divide: Work, Family, and Gender Inequality* (Harvard University Press, 2004); and Cynthia Fuchs Epstein et al., *Paradox: Time Norms, Professional Life, Family, and Gender* (Routledge, 1999).

The issue of the tension between family and work is recently receiving much attention. See Jerry A. Jacobs, *The Time Divide: Work, Family, and Gender Inequality* (Harvard University Press, 2004); Harriet B. Presser, *Working in a 24/7 Economy: Challenges for American Families* (Russell Sage Foundation, 2003); Arlie Russell Hochschild, *The Commercialization of Intimate Life* (University of California Press, 2003); and Janet C. Gornick and Marcia K. Meyers, *Families that Work Policies for Reconciling Parenthood and Employment* (Russell Sage Foundation, 2003). Brid Featherstone points out that government policies can reduce this stress in *Family Life and Family Support: A Feminist Analysis* (Palgrave Macmillan, 2004).

ISSUE 6

Should Same-Sex Marriages Be Legally Recognized?

YES: Human Rights Campaign, from "Answers to Questions about Marriage Equality" (HRC's FamilyNet Project, 2004)

NO: Peter Sprigg, from "Questions and Answers: What's Wrong with Letting Same-Sex Couples 'Marry'?" (Family Research Council, 2004)

ISSUE SUMMARY

YES: America's largest lesbian and gay organization, The Human Rights Campaign, presents many arguments for why same-sex couples should be able to marry. The main argument is fairness. Marriage confers many benefits that same-sex couples are deprived of.

NO: Researcher Peter Sprigg presents many arguments for why same-sex couples should not be able to marry. The main argument is that the state has the right and duty to specify who a person, whether straight or gay, can marry so no rights are violated.

In 1979 in Sioux Falls, South Dakota, Randy Rohl and Grady Quinn became the first acknowledged homosexual couple in America to receive permission from their high school principal to attend the senior prom together. The National Gay Task Force hailed the event as a milestone in the progress of human rights. It is unclear what the voters of Sioux Falls thought about it, since it was not put up to a vote. However, if their views were similar to those of voters in Dade County, Florida; Houston, Texas; Wichita, Kansas; and various localities in the state of Oregon, they probably were not pleased. In referenda held in these and other areas, voters have reversed decisions by legislators and local boards that banned discrimination by sexual preference.

Yet the attitude of Americans toward the rights of homosexuals is not easy to pin down. Voters have also defeated resolutions such as the one in California in 1978 that would have banned the hiring of homosexual schoolteachers, or the one on the Oregon ballot in 1992 identifying homosexuality as "abnormal, wrong, unnatural and perverse." In some states, notably Colorado, voters have approved initiatives widely perceived as antihomosexual. But, almost invariably, these resolutions have been carefully worded so as to appear to oppose "special" rights for homosexuals. In general, polls show that a large majority of Americans believe that homosexuals should have equal rights with heterosexuals with regard to job opportunities. On the other hand, many view homosexuality as morally wrong.

Currently, same-sex marriages are not legally recognized by Congress. In the Defense of Marriage Act of 1996, Congress defined marriage as heterosexual. A state does not have to recognize another state's nonheterosexual marriage. The legal situation is constantly changing. Several states have legalized same-sex civil unions, and San Francisco and Massachusetts have legalized same-sex marriages. These developments have prompted President Bush to propose a Constitutional Amendment limiting marriage to the union of a man and a women.

The issue of same-sex marriage fascinates sociologists because it represents a basic change in a major social institution and is being played out on several fields: legal, cultural/moral, and behavioral. The legal debate will be decided by courts and legislatures; the cultural/moral debate is open to all of us; and the behavioral debate will be conducted by the activists on both sides. In the readings that follow, the Human Rights Campaign presents the major arguments for same-sex marriages, and Peter Sprigg argues that marriage must remain heterosexual.

Answers to Questions About Marriage Equality

Why Same-Sex Couples Want to Marry

Many same-sex couples want the right to legally marry because they are in love—either they just met the love of their lives, or more likely, they have spent the last 10, 20 or 50 years with that person—and they want to honor their relationship in the greatest way our society has to offer, by making a public commitment to stand together in good times and bad, through all the joys and challenges family life brings.

Many parents want the right to marry because they know it offers children a vital safety net and guarantees protections that unmarried parents cannot provide.

And still other people—both gay and straight—are fighting for the right of same-sex couples to marry because they recognize that it is simply not fair to deny some families the protections all other families are eligible to enjoy.

Currently in the United States, same-sex couples in long-term, committed relationships pay higher taxes and are denied basic protections and rights granted to married heterosexual couples. Among them:

- **Hospital visitation.** Married couples have the automatic right to visit each other in the hospital and make medical decisions. Same-sex couples can be denied the right to visit a sick or injured loved one in the hospital.
- **Social Security benefits.** Married people receive Social Security payments upon the death of a spouse. Despite paying payroll taxes, gay and lesbian partners receive no Social Security survivor benefits—resulting in an average annual income loss of $5,528 upon the death of a partner.
- **Immigration.** Americans in binational relationships are not permitted to petition for their same-sex partners to immigrate. As a result, they are often forced to separate or move to another country.
- **Health insurance.** Many public and private employers provide medical coverage to the spouses of their employees, but most employers do not provide coverage to the life partners of gay and lesbian

employees. Gay employees who do receive health coverage for their partners must pay federal income taxes on the value of the insurance.

- **Estate taxes.** A married person automatically inherits all the property of his or her deceased spouse without paying estate taxes. A gay or lesbian taxpayer is forced to pay estate taxes on property inherited from a deceased partner.
- **Retirement savings.** While a married person can roll a deceased spouse's 401(k) funds into an IRA without paying taxes, a gay or lesbian American who inherits a 401(k) can end up paying up to 70 percent of it in taxes and penalties.
- **Family leave.** Married workers are legally entitled to unpaid leave from their jobs to care for an ill spouse. Gay and lesbian workers are not entitled to family leave to care for their partners.
- **Nursing homes.** Married couples have a legal right to live together in nursing homes. Because they are not legal spouses, elderly gay or lesbian couples do not have the right to spend their last days living together in nursing homes.
- **Home protection.** Laws protect married seniors from being forced to sell their homes to pay high nursing home bills; gay and lesbian seniors have no such protection.
- **Pensions.** After the death of a worker, most pension plans pay survivor benefits only to a legal spouse of the participant. Gay and lesbian partners are excluded from such pension benefits.

Why Civil Unions Aren't Enough

Comparing marriage to civil unions is a bit like comparing diamonds to rhinestones. One is, quite simply, the real deal; the other is not. Consider:

- Couples eligible to marry may have their marriage performed in any state and have it recognized in every other state in the nation and every country in the world.
- Couples who are joined in a civil union in Vermont (the only state that offers civil unions) have no guarantee that its protections will even travel with them to neighboring New York or New Hampshire—let alone California or any other state.

Moreover, even couples who have a civil union and remain in Vermont receive only second-class protections in comparison to their married friends and neighbors. While they receive state-level protections, they do not receive any of the *more than 1,100 federal benefits and protections of marriage.*

In short, civil unions are not separate but equal—they are separate *and* unequal. And our society has tried separate before. It just doesn't work. . . .

Answers to Questions People Are Asking

"I Believe God Meant Marriage for Men and Women. How Can I Support Marriage for Same-Sex Couples?"

Many people who believe in God—and fairness and justice for all—ask this question. They feel a tension between religious beliefs and democratic values that has been experienced in many different ways throughout our nation's history. That is why the farmers of our Constitution established the principle of separation of church and state. That principle applies no less to the marriage issue than it does to any other.

Indeed, the answer to the apparent dilemma between religious beliefs and support for equal protections for all families lies in recognizing that marriage has a significant religious meaning for many people, but that it is also a legal contract. And it is strictly the legal—not the religious—dimension of marriage that is being debated now.

Granting marriage rights to same-sex couples would *not* require Christianity, Judaism, Islam or any other religion to perform these marriages. It would not require religious institutions to permit these ceremonies to be held on their grounds. It would not even require that religious communities discuss the issue. People of faith would remain free to make their own judgments about what makes a marriage in the eyes of God—just as they are today.

Consider, for example, the difference in how the Catholic Church and the U.S. government view couples who have divorced and remarried. Because church tenets do not sanction divorce, the second marriage is not valid in the church's view. The government, however, recognizes the marriage by extending to the remarried couple the same rights and protections as those granted to every other married couple in America. In this situation—as would be the case in marriage for same-sex couples—the church remains free to establish its own teachings on the religious dimension of marriage while the government upholds equality under law.

It should also be noted that there are a growing number of religious communities that have decided to bless same-sex unions. Among them are Reform Judaism, the Unitarian Universalist Association and the Metropolitan Community Church. The Presbyterian Church (USA) also allows ceremonies to be performed, although they are not considered the same as marriage. The Episcopal Church and United Church of Christ allow individual churches to set their own policies on same-sex unions.

"This Is Different From Interracial Marriage. Sexual Orientation Is a Choice."

. . . Decades of research all point to the fact that sexual orientation is not a choice, and that a person's sexual orientation cannot be changed. Who one is drawn to is a fundamental aspect of who we are.

In this way, the struggle for marriage equality for same-sex couples is just as basic as the fight for interracial marriage was. It recognizes that Americans should not be coerced into false and unhappy marriages but should be free to marry the person the love—thereby building marriage on a true and stable foundation.

"Won't This Create a Free-For-All and Make the Whole Idea of Marriage Meaningless?"

Many people share this concern because opponents of gay and lesbian people have used this argument as a scare tactic. But it is not true. Granting same-sex couples the right to marry would in no way change the number of people who could enter into a marriage (or eliminate restrictions on the age or familial relationships of those who may marry). Marriage would continue to recognize the highest possible commitment that can be made between two adults, plain and simple. . . .

"I Strongly Believe Children Need a Mother and a Father."

Many of us grew up believing that everyone needs a mother and father, regardless of whether we ourselves happened to have two parents, or two *good* parents.

But as families have grown more diverse in recent decades, the researchers have studied how these different family relationships affect children, it has become clear that the *quality* of a family's relationship is more important than the particular *structure* of families that exist today. In other words, the qualities that help children grow into good and responsible adults—learning how to learn, to have compassion for others, to contribute to society and be respectful of others and their differences—do not depend on the sexual orientation of their parents but on their parents' ability to provide a loving, stable and happy home, something no class of Americans has an exclusive hold on.

That is why research studies have consistently shown that children raised by gay and lesbian parents do just as well on all conventional measure of child development, such as academic achievement, psychological well-being and social abilities, as children raised by heterosexual parents.

That is also why the nation's leading child welfare organizations, including the American Academy of Pediatrics, the American Academy of Family Physicians and others, have issued statements that dismiss assertions that only heterosexual couples can be good parents—and declare that the focus should now be on providing greater protections for the 1 million to 9 million children being raised by gay and lesbian parents in the United States today. . . .

"How Could Marriage for Same-Sex Couples Possibly Be Good for the American Family—or Our Country?"

. . . The prospect of a significant change in our laws and customs has often caused people to worry more about dire consequences that could result than about the potential positive outcomes. In fact, precisely the same anxiety arose when some people fought to overturn the laws prohibiting marriage between people of different races in the 1950s and 1960s. (One Virginia judge even declared that "God intended to separate the races.")

But in reality, opening marriage to couples who are so willing to fight for it could only strengthen the institution for all. It would open the doors to more supporters, not opponents. And it would help keep the age-old institution alive.

As history has repeatedly proven, institutions that fail to take account of the changing needs of the population are those that grow weak; those that recognize and accommodate changing needs grow strong. For example, the U.S. military, like American colleges and universities, grew stronger after permitting African Americans and women to join its ranks.

Similarly, granting same-sex couples the right to marry would strengthen the institution of marriage by allowing it to better meet the needs of the true diversity of family structures in America today. . . .

"Can't Same-Sex Couples Go to a Lawyer to Secure All the Rights They Need?"

Not by a long shot. When a gay or lesbian person gets seriously ill, there is no legal document that can make their partner eligible to take leave from work under the federal Family and Medical Leave Act to provide care—because that law applies only to married couples.

When gay or lesbian people grow old and in need of nursing home care, there is no legal document that can give them the right to Medicaid coverage without potentially causing their partner to be forced from their home—because the federal Medicaid law only permits married spouses to keep their home without becoming ineligible for benefits.

And when a gay or lesbian person dies, there is no legal document that can extend Social Security survivor benefits or the right to inherit a retirement plan without severe tax burdens that stem from being "unmarried" in the eyes of the law.

These are only a few examples of the critical protections that are granted through more than 1,100 federal laws that protect only married couples. In the absence of the right to marry, same-sex couples can only put in place a handful of the most basic arrangements, such as naming each other in a will or a power of attorney. And even these documents remain vulnerable to challenges in court by disgruntled family members.

"Won't This Cost Taxpayers Too Much Money?"

No, it wouldn't necessarily cost much at all. In fact, treating same-sex couples as families under law could even save taxpayers money because marriage would require them to assume legal responsibility for their joint living expenses and reduce their dependence on public assistance programs, such as Medicaid, Temporary Assistance to Needy Families, Supplemental Security Income disability payments and food stamps.

Put another way, the money it would cost to extend benefits to same-sex couples could be outweighed by the money that would be saved as these families rely more fully on each other instead of state or federal government assistance.

For example, two studies conducted in 2003 by professors at the University of Massachusetts, Amherst, and the University of California, Los Angeles, found that extending domestic partner benefits to same-sex couples in California and New Jersey would save taxpayers millions of dollars a year.

Specifically, the studies projected that the California state budget would save an estimated $8.1 million to $10.6 million each year by enacting the most comprehensive domestic partner law in the nation. In New Jersey, which passed a new domestic partner law in 2004, the savings were projected to be even higher—more than $61 million each year.

(Sources: "Equal Rights, Fiscal Responsibility: The Impact of A.B. 205 on California's Budget," by M. V. Lee Badgett, Ph.D., IGLSS, Department of Economics, University of Massachusetts, and R. Bradley Sears, J.D., Williams Project, UCLA School of Law, University of California, Los Angeles, May 2003, and "Supporting Families, Saving Funds: A Fiscal Analysis of New Jersey's Domestic Partnership Act," by Badgett and Sears with Suzanne Goldberg, J.D., Rutgers School of Law-Newark, December 2003.)

"Where Can Same-Sex Couples Marry Today?"

In 2001, the Netherlands became the first country to extend marriage rights to same-sex couples. Belgium passed a similar law two years later. The laws in both of these countries, however, have strict citizenship or residency requirements that do not permit American couples to take advantage of the protections provided.

In June 2003, Ontario became the first Canadian province to grant marriage to same-sex couples, and in July 2003, British Columbia followed suit—becoming the first places that American same-sex couples could go to get married.

In November 2003, the Massachusetts Supreme Judicial Court recognized the right of same-sex couples to marry—giving the state six months to begin issuing marriage licenses to same-sex couples. It began issuing licenses May 17, 2004.

In February 2004, the city of San Francisco began issuing marriage licenses to same-sex couples after the mayor declared that the state constitution forbade him to discriminate. The issue is being addressed by California courts, and a number of other cities have either taken or are considering taking steps in the same direction.

Follow the latest developments in California, Oregon, New Jersey, New Mexico, New York and in other communities across the country. . . .

Other nations have also taken steps toward extending equal protections to all couples, though the protections they provide are more limited than marriage. Canada, Denmark, Finland, France, Germany, Iceland, Norway, Portugal and Sweden all have nationwide laws that grant same-sex partners a range of important rights, protections and obligations.

For example, in France, registered same-sex (and opposite-sex) couples can be joined in a civil "solidarity pact" that grants them the right to file joint tax returns, extend social security coverage to each other and receive the same health, employment and welfare benefits as legal spouses. It also commits the couple to assume joint responsibility for household debts.

Other countries, including Switzerland, Scotland and the Czech Republic, also have considered legislation that would legally recognize same-sex unions.

"What Protections Other Than Marriage Are Available to Same-Sex Couples?"

At the federal level, there are no protections at all available to same-sex couples. In fact, a federal law called the "Defense of Marriage Act" says that the federal government will discriminate against same-sex couples who marry by refusing to recognize their marriages or providing them with the federal protections of marriage. Some members of Congress are trying to go even further by attempting to pass a Federal Marriage Amendment that would write discrimination against same-sex couples into the U.S. Constitution.

At the state level, only Vermont offers civil unions, which provide important state benefits but no federal protections, such as Social Security survivor benefits. There is also no guarantee that civil unions will be recognized outside

10 FACTS

7. Same-sex couples live in 99.3 percent of all counties nationwide.
8. There are an estimated 3.1 million people living together in same-sex relationships in the United States.
9. Fifteen percent of these same-sex couples live in rural settings.
10. One out of three lesbian couples is raising children. One out of five gay male couples is raising children.
11. Between 1 million and 9 million children are being raised by gay, lesbian and bisexual parents in the United States today.
12. At least one same-sex couple is raising children in 96 percent of all counties nationwide.
13. The highest percentages of same-sex couples raising children live in the South.
14. Nearly one in four same-sex couples includes a partner 55 years old or older, and nearly one in five same-sex couples is composed of two people 55 or older.
15. More than one in 10 same-sex couples include a partner 65 years old or older, and nearly one in 10 same-sex couples is composed of two people 65 or older.
16. The states with the highest numbers of same-sex senior couples are also the most popular for heterosexual senior couples: California, New York and Florida.

These facts are based on analyses of the 2000 Census conducted by the Urban Institute and the Human Rights Campaign. The estimated number of people in same-sex relationships has been adjusted by 62 percent to compensate for the widely-reported undercount in the Census. (See "Gay and Lesbian Families in the United States: Same-Sex Unmarried Partner Households" on *www.hrc.org*.)

Vermont. Thirty-nine states also have "defense of marriage" laws explicitly prohibiting the recognition of marriages between same-sex partners.

Domestic partner laws have been enacted in California, Connecticut, New Jersey, Hawaii and the District of Columbia. The benefits conferred by these laws vary; some offer access to family health insurance, others confer co-parenting rights. These benefits are limited to residents of the state. A family that moves out of these states immediately loses the protections.

NO

Peter Sprigg

Questions and Answers: What's Wrong With Letting Same-Sex Couples "Marry"?

What's Wrong With Letting Same-Sex Couples Legally "Marry?"
There are two key reasons why the legal rights, benefits, and responsibilities of civil marriage should not be extended to same-sex couples.

The first is that homosexual relationships are not marriage. That is, they simply do not fit the minimum necessary condition for a marriage to exist— namely, the union of a man and a woman.

The second is that homosexual relationships are harmful. Not only do they not provide the same benefits to society as heterosexual marriages, but their consequences are far more negative than positive.

Either argument, standing alone, is sufficient to reject the claim that same-sex unions should be granted the legal status of marriage.

Let's Look at the First Argument. Isn't Marriage Whatever the Law Says It Is?
No. Marriage is not a creation of the law. Marriage is a fundamental human institution that predates the law and the Constitution. At its heart, it is an anthropological and sociological reality, not a legal one. Laws relating to marriage merely recognize and regulate an institution that already exists.

But Isn't Marriage Just a Way of Recognizing People Who Love Each Other and Want to Spend Their Lives Together?
If love and companionship were sufficient to define marriage, then there would be no reason to deny "marriage" to unions of a child and an adult, or an adult child and his or her aging parent, or to roommates who have no sexual relationship, or to groups rather than couples. Love and companionship are usually considered integral to marriage in our culture, but they are not sufficient to define it as an institution. . . .

Why Should Homosexuals Be Denied the Right to Marry Like Anyone Else?
The fundamental "right to marry" is a right that rests with *individuals*, not with *couples*. Homosexual *individuals* already have exactly the same "right" to marry as anyone else. Marriage license applications do not inquire as to a person's "sexual orientation.". . .

However, while every individual person is free to get married, *no* person, whether heterosexual or homosexual, has ever had a legal right to marry simply any willing partner. Every person, whether heterosexual or homosexual, is subject to legal restrictions as to whom they may marry. To be specific, every person, regardless of sexual preference, is legally barred from marrying a child, a close blood relative, a person who is already married, or a person of the same sex. There is no discrimination here, nor does such a policy deny anyone the "equal protection of the laws" (as guaranteed by the Constitution), since these restrictions apply equally to every individual.

Some people may wish to do away with one or more of these longstanding restrictions upon one's choice of marital partner. However, the fact that a tiny but vocal minority of Americans desire to have someone of the same sex as a partner does not mean that they have a "right" to do so, any more than the desires of other tiny (but less vocal) minorities of Americans give them a "right" to choose a child, their own brother or sister, or a group of two or more as their marital partners.

Isn't Prohibiting Homosexual "Marriage" Just as Discriminatory as Prohibiting Interracial Marriage, Like Some States Used to Do?

This analogy is not valid at all. Bridging the divide of the sexes by uniting men and women is both a worthy goal and a part of the fundamental purpose of marriage, common to all human civilizations.

Laws against interracial marriage, on the other hand, served only the purpose of preserving a social system of racial segregation. This was both an unworthy goal and one utterly irrelevant to the fundamental nature of marriage.

Allowing a black woman to marry a white man does not change the definition of marriage, which requires one man and one woman. Allowing two men or two women to marry would change that fundamental definition. Banning the "marriage" of same-sex couples is therefore essential to preserve the nature and purpose of marriage itself. . . .

How Would Allowing Same-Sex Couples to Marry Change Society's Concept of Marriage?

As an example, marriage will open wide the door to homosexual adoption, which will simply lead to more children suffering the negative consequences of growing up without both a mother and a father.

Among homosexual men in particular, casual sex, rather than committed relationships, is the rule and not the exception. And even when they do enter into a more committed relationship, it is usually of relatively short duration. For example, a study of homosexual men in the Netherlands (the first country in the world to legalize "marriage" for same-sex couples), published in the journal *AIDS* in 2003, found that the average length of "steady partnerships" was not more than 2 < years (Maria Xiridou et al., in *AIDS* 2003, 17:1029–1038).

In addition, studies have shown that even homosexual men who are in "committed" relationships are not sexually faithful to each other. While infidelity among heterosexuals is much too common, it does not begin to compare to the rates among homosexual men. The 1994 National Health and Social Life Survey, which remains the most comprehensive study of Americans' sexual practices ever undertaken, found that 75 percent of married men and 90 percent of married women had been sexually faithful to their spouse. On the other hand, a major study of homosexual men in "committed" relationships found that only seven out of 156 had been sexually faithful, or 4.5 percent. The Dutch study cited above found that even homosexual men in "steady partnerships" had an average of eight "casual" sex partners per year.

So if same-sex relationships are legally recognized as "marriage," the idea of marriage as a sexually exclusive and faithful relationship will be dealt a serious blow. Adding monogamy and faithfulness to the other pillars of marriage that have already fallen will have overwhelmingly negative consequences for Americans' physical and mental health. . . .

Don't Homosexuals Need Marriage Rights So That They Will Be Able to Visit Their Partners in the Hospital?

The idea that homosexuals are routinely denied the right to visit their partners in the hospital is nonsense. When this issue was raised during debate over the Defense of Marriage Act in 1996, the Family Research Council did an informal survey of nine hospitals in four states and the District of Columbia. None of the administrators surveyed could recall a single case in which a visitor was barred because of their homosexuality, and they were incredulous that this would even be considered an issue.

Except when a doctor limits visitation for medical reasons, final authority over who may visit an adult patient rests with that patient. This is and should be the case regardless of the sexual orientation or marital status of the patient or the visitor.

The only situation in which there would be a possibility that the blood relatives of a patient might attempt to exclude the patient's homosexual partner is if the patient is unable to express his or her wishes due to unconsciousness or mental incapacity. Homosexual partners concerned about this (remote) possibility can effectively preclude it by granting to one another a health care proxy (the legal right to make medical decisions for the patient) and a power of attorney (the right to make all legal decisions for another person). Marriage is not necessary for this. It is inconceivable that a hospital would exclude someone who holds the health care proxy and power of attorney for a patient from visiting that patient, except for medical reasons.

The hypothetical "hospital visitation hardship" is nothing but an emotional smokescreen to distract people from the more serious implications of radically redefining marriage.

Don't Homosexuals Need the Right to Marry Each Other in Order to Ensure That They Will Be Able to Leave Their Estates to Their Partner When They Die?

As with the hospital visitation issue, the concern over inheritance rights is something that simply does not require marriage to resolve it. Nothing in current law prevents homosexual partners from being joint owners of property such as a home or a car, in which case the survivor would automatically become the owner if the partner dies.

An individual may leave the remainder of his estate to whomever he wishes—again, without regard to sexual orientation or marital status—simply by writing a will. As with the hospital visitation issue, blood relatives would only be able to overrule the surviving homosexual partner in the event that the deceased had failed to record his wishes in a common, inexpensive legal document. Changing the definition of a fundamental social institution like marriage is a rather extreme way of addressing this issue. Preparing a will is a much simpler solution.

Don't Homosexuals Need Marriage Rights So That They Can Get Social Security Survivor Benefits When a Partner Dies?

. . . Social Security survivor benefits were designed to recognize the non-monetary contribution made to a family by the homemaking and child-rearing activities of a wife and mother, and to ensure that a woman and her children would not become destitute if the husband and father were to die.

The Supreme Court ruled in the 1970s that such benefits must be gender-neutral. However, they still are largely based on the premise of a division of roles within a couple between a breadwinner who works to raise money and a homemaker who stays home to raise children.

Very few homosexual couples organize their lives along the lines of such a "traditional" division of labor and roles. They are far more likely to consist of two earners, each of whom can be supported in old age by their own personal Social Security pension.

Furthermore, far fewer homosexual couples than heterosexual ones are raising children at all, for the obvious reason that they are incapable of natural reproduction with each other. This, too, reduces the likelihood of a traditional division of labor among them.

Survivor benefits for the legal (biological or adopted) *children* of homosexual parents (as opposed to their partners) are already available under current law, so "marriage" rights for homosexual couples are unnecessary to protect the interests of these children themselves. . . .

Even If "Marriage" Itself Is Uniquely Heterosexual, Doesn't Fairness Require That the Legal and Financial Benefits of Marriage Be Granted to Same-Sex Couples—Perhaps Through "Civil Unions" or "Domestic Partnerships?"

No. The legal and financial benefits of marriage are not an entitlement to be distributed equally to all (if they were, single people would have as much reason to consider them "discriminatory" as same-sex couples). Society grants benefits to marriage because marriage has benefits for society—including, but not limited to, the reproduction of the species in households with the optimal household structure (i.e., the presence of both a mother and a father).

Homosexual relationships, on the other hand, have no comparable benefit for society, and in fact impose substantial costs on society. The fact that AIDS is at least ten times more common among men who have sex with men than among the general population is but one example. . . .

What About the Argument That Homosexual Relations Are Harmful? What Do You Mean by That?

Homosexual men experience higher rates of many diseases, including:

- Human Papillomavirus (HPV), which causes most cases of cervical cancer in women and anal cancer in men
- Hepatitis A, B, and C
- Gonorrhea
- Syphilis
- "Gay Bowel Syndrome," a set of sexually transmitted gastrointestinal problems such as proctitis, proctocolitis, and enteritis
- HIV/AIDS (One Canadian study found that as a result of HIV alone, "life expectancy for gay and bisexual men is eight to twenty years less than for all men.")

Lesbian women, meanwhile, have a higher prevalence of:

- Bacterial vaginosis
- Hepatitis C
- HIV risk behaviors
- Cancer risk factors such as smoking, alcohol use, poor diet, and being overweight . . .

Do Homosexuals Have More Mental Health Problems as Well?

Yes. Various research studies have found that homosexuals have higher rates of:

- Alcohol abuse
- Drug abuse
- Nicotine dependence
- Depression
- Suicide

Isn't It Possible That These Problems Result From Society's "Discrimination" Against Homosexuals?

This is the argument usually put forward by pro-homosexual activists. However, there is a simple way to test this hypothesis. If "discrimination" were the cause of homosexuals' mental health problems, then one would expect those problems to be much less common in cities or countries, like San Francisco or the Netherlands, where homosexuality has achieved the highest levels of acceptance.

In fact, the opposite is the case. In places where homosexuality is widely accepted, the physical and mental health problems of homosexuals are greater, not less. This suggests that the real problem lies in the homosexual lifestyle itself, not in society's response to it. In fact, it suggests that increasing the level of social support *for* homosexual behavior (by, for instance, allowing same-sex couples to "marry") would only increase these problems, not reduce them. . . .

Haven't Studies Shown That Children Raised by Homosexual Parents Are No Different From Other Children?

No. This claim is often put forward, even by professional organizations. The truth is that most research on "homosexual parents" thus far has been marred by serious methodological problems. However, even pro-homosexual sociologists Judith Stacey and Timothy Biblarz report that the actual data from key studies show the "no differences" claim to be false.

Surveying the research (primarily regarding lesbians) in an *American Sociological Review* article in 2001, they found that:

- Children of lesbians are less likely to conform to traditional gender norms.
- Children of lesbians are more likely to engage in homosexual behavior.
- Daughters of lesbians are "more sexually adventurous and less chaste."
- Lesbian "co-parent relationships" are more likely to end than heterosexual ones.

A 1996 study by an Australian sociologist compared children raised by heterosexual married couples, heterosexual cohabiting couples, and homosexual cohabiting couples. It found that the children of heterosexual married couples did the best, and children of homosexual couples the worst, in nine of the thirteen academic and social categories measured. . . .

Do the American People Want to See "Marriages" Between Same-Sex Couples Recognized by Law?

No—and in the wake of the June 2003 court decisions to legalize such "marriages" in the Canadian province of Ontario and to legalize homosexual sodomy in the United States, the nation's opposition to such a radical social experiment has actually grown.

Five separate national opinion polls taken between June 24 and July 27, 2003 showed opponents of civil "marriage" for same-sex couples outnumbering supporters by not less than fifteen percentage points in every poll. The wording of poll questions can make a significant difference, and in this case, the poll with the most straightforward language (a Harris/CNN/Time poll asking "Do you think marriages between homosexual men or homosexual women should be recognized as legal by the law?") resulted in the strongest opposition, with 60 percent saying "No" and only 33 percent saying "Yes."

POSTSCRIPT

Should Same-Sex Marriages Be Legally Recognized?

The issue of the rights of homosexuals creates a social dilemma. Most people would agree that all members of society should have equal rights. However, the majority may disapprove of the lifestyles of a minority group and pass laws against some of their behaviors. The question is: When do these laws violate civil rights? Are laws against same-sex marriage such a violation?

There is a considerable literature on homosexuality and the social and legal status of homosexuals. Recent works on gay marriage include David Moats, *Civil Wars: A Battle for Gay Marriage* (Harcourt, 2004); Evan Gerstmann, *Same-Sex Marriage and the Constitution* (Cambridge University Press, 2004); *Marriage and Same-Sex Unions: A Debate* edited by Lynn D. Wardle, et al. (Praeger, 2003); Martin Dupuis, *Same-Sex Marriage, Legal Mobilization, and the Politics of Rights* (Peter Lang, 2002); and Kevin Bourassa, *Just Married: Gay Marriage and the Expansion of Human Rights* (University of Wisconsin Press, 2002). Recent works on the history of the gay rights movement include Dudley Clendinen and Adam Nagourney, *Out for Good: The Struggle to Build a Gay Rights Movement in America* (Simon & Schuster, 1999); Ronald J. Hunt, *Historical Dictionary of the Gay Liberation Movement* (Scarecrow Press, 1999); JoAnne Myers, *Historical Dictionary of the Lesbian Liberation Movement: Still the Rage* (Scarecrow Press, 2003); and John Loughery, *The Other Side of Silence: Men's Lives and Gay Identities: A Twentieth-Century History* (Henry Holt, 1998). For broad academic works on homosexuality see Kath Weston, *Long Slow Burn: Sexuality and Social Science* (Routledge, 1998); and Michael Ruse, *Homosexuality: A Philosophical Inquiry* (Blackwell, 1998). Recent works that focus on homosexual rights include David A. J. Richards, *Identity and the Case for Gay Rights* (University of Chicago Press, 1999); Daniel R. Pinello, *Gay Rights and American Law* (Cambridge University Press, 2003); Carlos A. Ball, *The Morality of Gay Rights: An Exploration in Political Philosophy* (Routledge, 2003); Brette McWhorter Sember, *Gay and Lesbian Rights: A Guide for GLBT Singles, Couples, and Families* (Sphinx Publishing, 2003); and Nan D. Hunter, *The Rights of Lesbians, Gay Men, Bisexuals, and Transgender People: The Authoritative ACLU Guide to a Lesbian, Gay, Bisexual, or Transgender Person's Rights,* 4th edition (Southern Illinois University Press, 2004).

On the Internet . . .

Statistical Resources on the Web: Sociology

This Statistical Resources on the Web site provides links to data on poverty in the United States. Included is a link that contains both current and historical poverty data.

http://www.lib.umich.edu/govdocs/stats.html

Institute for Research on Poverty (IRP)

The Institute for Research on Poverty researches the causes and consequences of social inequality and poverty in the United States. This Web site includes frequently asked questions about poverty and links to other Internet resources on the subject.

http://www.ssc.wisc.edu/irp/

About.com: Affirmative Action

About com's Web site on affirmative action contains information about resources and organizations that focus on affirmative action policies and current events. This site also enables you to search other topics related to race relations.

http://www.racerelations.about.com/cs/affirmativeaction

Yahoo! Full Coverage: Affirmative Action

This Web site links you to the Yahoo! search engine for the topic of affirmative action.

http://fullcoverage.yahoo.com/fc/US/AffirmativeAction

PART 3

Stratification and Inequality

*W*hy is there so much poverty in a society as rich as ours? Why has there been such a noticeable increase in inequality over the past quarter century? Although the ideal of equal opportunity for all is strong in the United States, many charge that the American political and economic system is unfair. Does extensive poverty demonstrate that policymakers have failed to live up to United States egalitarian principles? Are American institutions deeply flawed in that they provide fabulous opportunities for the educated and rich and meager opportunities for the uneducated and poor? Is the American stratification system at fault or are the poor themselves at fault? And what about the racial gap? The civil rights movement and the Civil Rights Act have made America more fair than it was, so why does a sizeable racial gap remain? Various affirmative action programs have been implemented to remedy unequal opportunities, but some argue that this is discrimination in reverse. In fact, California passed a referendum banning affirmative action. Where should America go from here? Social scientists debate these questions in this part.

- Is Increasing Economic Inequality a Serious Problem?

- Is the Underclass the Major Threat to American Ideals?

- Has Affirmative Action Outlived Its Usefulness?

- Are Boys and Men Disadvantaged Relative to Girls and Women?

ISSUE 7

Is Increasing Economic Inequality a Serious Problem?

YES: Christopher Jencks, from "Does Inequality Matter?" *Daedalus* (Winter 2002)

NO: Christopher C. DeMuth, from "The New Wealth of Nations," *Commentary* (October 1997)

ISSUE SUMMARY

YES: Christopher Jencks, professor of social policy at the Kennedy School at Harvard University, presents data on how large the income inequality is in the United States and describes the consequences of this inequality.

NO: Christopher C. DeMuth, president of the American Enterprise Institute for Public Policy Research, argues that the "recent increase in income inequality . . . is a very small tick in the massive and unprecedented leveling of material circumstances that has been proceeding now for almost three centuries and in this century has accelerated dramatically."

The cover of the January 29, 1996, issue of *Time* magazine bears a picture of 1996 Republican presidential candidate Steve Forbes and large letters reading: "DOES A FLAT TAX MAKE SENSE?" During his campaign Forbes expressed his willingness to spend $25 million of his own wealth in pursuit of the presidency, with the major focus of his presidential campaign being a flat tax, which would reduce taxes substantially for the rich. It seems reasonable to say that if the rich pay less in taxes, others would have to pay more. Is it acceptable for the tax burden to be shifted away from the rich in America? Forbes believed that the flat tax would benefit the poor as well as the rich. He theorized that the economy would surge ahead because investors would shift their money from relatively nonproductive, but tax-exempt, investments to productive investments. Although Forbes has disappeared from the political scene, his basic argument still thrives today. It is an example of the trickle-down theory, which states that helping the rich stimulates the economy, which helps the poor. In fact, the trickle-down theory is the major rationalization for the view that great economic inequality benefits all of society.

Inequality is not a simple subject. For example, America is commonly viewed as having more social equality than the more hierarchical societies of Europe and Japan, but America has more income inequality than almost all other industrial societies. This apparent contradiction is explained when one recognizes that American equality is not in income but in the opportunity to obtain higher incomes. The issue of economic inequality is further complicated by other categories of equality/inequality, which include political power, social status, and legal rights.

Americans believe that everyone should have an equal opportunity to compete for jobs and awards. This belief is backed up by free public school education, which provides poor children with a ladder to success, and by laws that forbid discrimination. Americans, however, do not agree on many specific issues regarding opportunities or rights. For example, should society compensate for handicaps such as disadvantaged family backgrounds or the legacy of past discrimination? This issue has divided the country. Americans do not agree on programs such as income-based scholarships, quotas, affirmative action, or the Head Start compensatory education program for poor preschoolers.

America's commitment to political equality is strong in principle, though less strong in practice. Everyone over 18 years old gets one vote, and all votes are counted equally. However, the political system tilts in the direction of special interest groups; those who do not belong to such groups are seldom heard. Furthermore, as in the case of Forbes, money plays an increasingly important role in political campaigns.

The final dimension of equality/inequality is status. Inequality of status involves differences in prestige, and it cannot be eliminated by legislation. Ideally, the people who contribute the most to society are the most highly esteemed. To what extent does this principle hold true in the United States?

The Declaration of Independence proclaims that "all men are created equal," and the Founding Fathers who wrote the Declaration of Independence went on to base the laws of the land on the principle of equality. The equality they were referring to was equality of opportunity and legal and political rights for white, property-owning males. In the two centuries following the signing of the Declaration, nonwhites and women struggled for and won considerable equality of opportunity and rights. Meanwhile, income gaps in the United States have been widening.

In the readings that follow, Christopher Jencks points out how extreme the inequality has become and how bad off the lowest fifth of the country is. He is cautious in asserting what the impacts are of extreme inequality because he requires hard data that is difficult to get. Nevertheless, he concludes, "My bottom line is that the social consequences of economic inequality are sometimes negative, sometimes neutral, but seldom—as far as I can discover—positive." Christopher C. DeMuth admits that incomes have become more unequally distributed, but he argues that consumption, a better indicator of living conditions, has become much more equally distributed.

Christopher Jencks  **YES**

Does Inequality Matter?

$\mathbf{T}$he economic gap between rich and poor has grown dramatically in the United States over the past generation and is now considerably wider than in any other affluent nation. This increase in economic inequality has no recent precedent, at least in America. The distribution of family income was remarkably stable from 1947 to 1980. We do not have good data on family incomes before 1947, but the wage gap between skilled and unskilled workers narrowed dramatically between 1910 and 1947, which probably means that family incomes also became more equal. The last protracted increase in economic inequality occurred between 1870 and 1910.

The gap between the rich and the rest of America has widened steadily since 1979. The Census Bureau, which is America's principal source of data on household incomes, does not collect good data from the rich, but the Congressional Budget Office (CBO) has recently combined census data with tax records to track income trends near the top of the distribution. Figure 1 shows that the share of after-tax income going to the top 1 percent of American households almost doubled between 1979 and 1997. The top 1 percent included all households with after-tax incomes above $246,000 in 1997. The estimated purchasing power of the top 1 percent rose by 157 percent between 1979 and 1997, while the median household's purchasing power rose only 10 percent. The gap between the poorest fifth of American households and the median household also widened between 1979 and 1997, but the trend was far less dramatic. . . .

Some of the potential costs and benefits of inequality emerge when we contrast the United States with other rich democracies. One simple way to describe income inequality in different countries is to compute what is called the "90/10 ratio." To calculate this ratio we rank households from richest to poorest. Then we divide the income of the household at the ninetieth percentile by the income of the household at the tenth percentile. (Comparing the ninetieth percentile to the tenth percentile is better than, say, comparing the ninety-ninth percentile to the first percentile, because few countries collect reliable data on the incomes of either the very rich or the very poor.)

Figure 1

Percent of Household Income Going to the Richest One Percent

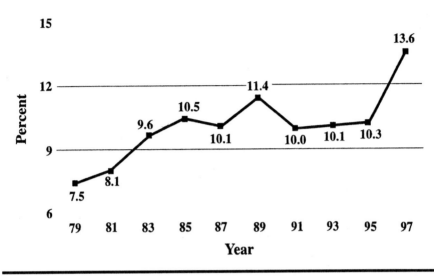

Changes in the percent of household income going to the richest 1 percent of American households, 1979–1977.
Source: Congressional Budget Office, *Historical Effective Tax Rates, 1979–1977.* September 2001, Table G-1C.

The Luxembourg Income Study (LIS), which is the best current source of data on economic inequality in different countries, has calculated 90/10 ratios for fourteen rich democracies in the mid-1990s. Table 1 shows the results. To keep differences between these fourteen countries in perspective I have also included data on two poorer and less democratic countries, Mexico and Russia. If we set aside Mexico and Russia, the big English-speaking democracies are the most unequal, the Scandinavian democracies are the most equal, and Western European democracies fall in the middle. (Italy looks more unequal than the other continental democracies, but the Italian data is somewhat suspect.) Within the English-speaking world the United States is the most unequal of all. The 90/10 ratio in the United States is twice that in Scandinavia. But even the United States is nothing like as unequal as Russia, Mexico, or many other Latin American countries.

America's unusually high level of inequality is not attributable to its unusually diverse labor force. Years of schooling are more equally distributed in the United States than in the European countries for which we have comparable data (Sweden, the Netherlands, and Germany). Adult test scores are more unequally distributed in the United States than Europe, partly because American immigrants score so poorly on tests given in English. But disparities in cognitive skills turn out to play a tiny role in explaining cross-national differences in the distribution of earnings. If one compares American workers with the same test

Table 1

Income Inequality and Economic Output in Various Countries During the 1990s

Country (and year of the ninetieth to the tenth percentile)	Ratio of household income at the 90th to 10th percentile[a]	GDP per capita as a percent of U.S. level in 1998[b]	Life expectancy at birth (1995 est.)[c]
Scandinavia[d]	2.8	75	77.2
Sweden (1995)	2.6	68	78.9
Finland (1995)	2.7	68	76.6
Norway (1995)	2.8	85	77.8
Denmark (1992)	2.9	79	75.4
Western Europe	3.6	73	77.5
Nether. (1994)	3.2	75	77.5
Germany (1994)	3.2	71	76.6
Belgium (1996)	3.2	74	76.4
France (1994)	3.5	66	78.4
Switz. (1992)	3.6	84	78.5
Italy (1995)	4.8	67	77.6
Brit. Com.	4.3	73	77.7
Canada (1994)	4.0	78	78.2
Australia (1994)	4.3	75	78.0
U.K. (1995)	4.6	67	77.0[e]
U.S. (1997)	5.6	100	75.7
Middle-income nations			
Russia (1995)	9.4	21(?)	65.0
Mexico (1998)	11.6	25	NA

[a]From http://lisweb.ceps.lu/key/figures/inqtable.htm.
[b]From U.S. Bureau of the Census *Statistical Abstract of the United States,* 2000, Government Printing Office, Table 1365. GDP is converted to $U.S. using purchasing power parity.
[c]National Center for Health Statistics, *Health, United States,* 2000, Government Printing Office 2000, Table 27.
[d]All area averages are unweighted arithmetic means.
[e]England and Wales.

scores and the same amount of schooling, the Americans' wages vary more than the wages of *all* Swedish, Dutch, or German workers.

Almost everyone who studies the causes of economic inequality agrees that by far the most important reason for the differences between rich democracies is that their governments adopt different economic policies. There is no agreement about *which* policies are crucial, but there is a fairly standard list of suspects. A number of rich countries have centralized wage bargaining, which almost always compresses the distribution of earnings. Many rich democracies also make unionization easy, which also tends to compress the wage distribution. Some rich democracies transfer a lot of money to people who are retired, unemployed, sick, or permanently disabled, while others are far less generous. The United States is unusually unequal partly because it makes little effort to limit wage inequality: the minimum wage is low, and American law makes unionization relatively difficult. In addition, the United States transfers less money to those who are not working than most other rich democracies.

The fact that the American government makes so little effort to reduce economic inequality may seem surprising in a country where social equality is so important. American politicians present themselves to the public as being just like everyone else, and once they step outside their offices, Americans all wear jeans. The way Americans talk and the music they listen to are also affected by egalitarian impulses. But while the tenor of American culture may be democratic, Americans are also far more hostile to government than the citizens of other rich democracies. Since egalitarian economic policies require governmental action, they win far less support in the United States than in most other rich democracies. . . .

Conservatives often blame American poverty on the existence of an "underclass" that rejects mainstream social norms, does little paid work, and has children whom neither parent can support. It is certainly true that poor American households include fewer working adults than affluent American households. This is true in every rich country for which we have data. But when Lars Osberg, an economist at Dalhousie University, compared poor households in the United States, Canada, Britain, Sweden, France, and Germany, he found that the poor American households worked far more hours per year than their counterparts in the other five countries. This finding suggests that what distinguishes the United States from the other rich democracies is not the idleness of the American poor but the anger that idleness inspires in more affluent Americans, which helps explain the stinginess of the American welfare state. . . .

⁂

Up to this point I have been focusing exclusively on what people can afford to buy. While economic goods and services are obviously important, many people believe that inequality also affects human welfare in ways that are independent of any given household's purchasing power. Even if my family income remains constant, the distribution of income in my neighborhood or my nation may influence my children's educational opportunities, my life expectancy, my chance of being robbed, the probability that I will vote, and perhaps even my overall happiness. The remainder of this article tries to summarize what we know about such effects.

Educational opportunities. Increases in economic inequality have raised the value of a college degree in the United States. If all else had remained equal, making a college degree more valuable should increase both teenagers' interest in attending college and their parents' willingness to pay for college. But the growth of economic inequality in America has been accompanied by a change in the way we finance public higher education. Tax subsidies play a smaller role than they once did, and tuition plays a larger role. Since 1979 tuition at America's public colleges and universities has risen faster than most parents' income.

. . . [S]tudents are likely to be far more sensitive to changes in tuition than to a change in the hypothetical lifetime value of a BA. Tuition is easily observed and has to be paid now. The lifetime value of a BA is always uncertain and can-

Table 2

Purchasing Power of Households at the 10th and 90th Percentiles of Each Nation's Distribution Relative to Households at the Same Percentile in the United States in the Same Year, 1992–1997

Country (and year)	Purchasing power as a percent of the U.S. level in the same year		
	10th percentile	90th percentile	Average of all percentiles
Scandinavia	112	57	77
Sweden (1995)	103	49	67
Finland (1995)	105	53	73
Norway (1995)	128	68	88
Denmark (1995)	110	59	80
Western Europe	119	73	88
Neth. (1994)	110	64	76
Germany (1994)	113	67	82
Belgium (1996)	121	73	80
France (1994)	110	71	84
Switz. (1992)	141	89	116
Commonwealth	94	73	80
Canada (1994)	105	80	92
U.K. (1995)	85	68	72
Australia (1994)	87	71	76
U.S. (1997)	100	100	100

Source: Columns 1 and 2 are from Timothy Smeeding and Lee Rainwater, "Comparing Living Standards Across Countries: Real Incomes at the Top, the Bottom, and the Middle" (paper prepared for a conference on "What Has Happened to the Quality of Life in America and Other Advanced Industrial Nations?" Levy Institute, Bard College, Annandale-on-Hudson, N.Y., June 2001). Local currencies were converted to dollars using their estimated purchasing power parity. Area averages are unweighted arithmetic means. Column 3 is calculated from the national means of the logarithms of after-tax household income, using data provided by Rainwater.

not be realized for a long time. Among students who pay their own bills, higher tuition could easily reduce college attendance even when the long-run returns of a college degree are rising.

Table 3 is taken from work by two economists, David Ellwood at Harvard and Thomas Kane at UCLA. It shows changes between 1980–1982 and 1992 in the fraction of high-school graduates from different economic backgrounds entering four-year colleges. Among students from the most affluent families, the proportion entering a four-year college rose substantially. Among students from middle-income families, whose families often help with children's college expenses but seldom pay the whole bill, attendance rose more modestly. Students from the poorest quartile were no more likely to attend a four-year college in 1992 than in 1980–1982. . . .

Life expectancy.   People live longer in rich countries than in poor countries, but the relationship flattens out as national income rises. Indeed, the statistics in Table 1 show that life expectancy and GDP per capita are not strongly related in rich democracies. In particular, life expectancy is lower in the United States than in almost any other rich democracy.

Table 3

Percent of High-School Graduates Enrolling in a 4-year-College or Some Other Form of Postsecondary Education Within 20 months of Graduation, by Income Quartile: 1980–1982 and 1992

Income quar-tile	Entered a 4-year college			Entered some other form of post-secondary education		
	1980–82	1992	Change	1980–82	1992	Change
Lowest	29	28	–1	28	32	4
Second	33	38	5	30	32	2
Third	39	48	9	33	32	–1
Highest	55	66	11	26	24	–2
All	39	45	6	29	30	1

Source: David Ellwood and Thomas Kane, "Who Is Getting a College Education? Family Background and the Growing Gaps in Enrollment," in Sheldon Danziger and Jane Waldfogel, eds., *Securing the Future* (New York: Russell Sage, 2000).

Within any given country people with higher incomes also live longer. This relationship flattens out near the top of the income distribution, but the gap between richer and poorer families does not seem to narrow when everyone's standard of living rises. Despite both rising incomes and the introduction of Medicare and Medicaid, for example, the effects of both income and education on mortality increased in the United States between 1960 and 1986. . . .

In 1992 Richard Wilkinson wrote an influential article arguing that a more equal distribution of income improved life expectancy in rich countries. Subsequent work showed that mortality was also lower in American states and metropolitan areas where incomes were more equal. . . .

Wilkinson and his followers believe that inequality also lowers life expectancy independent of its effect on any given household's income, because it changes the social context in which people live. According to Wilkinson, inequality erodes the social bonds that make people care about one another and accentuates feelings of relative deprivation (the social-science term for what people used to call envy). Other epidemiologists take what they call a "materialist" position, arguing that inequality kills because it affects public policy, altering the distribution of education, health care, environmental protection, and other material resources. . . .

I began this inquiry by arguing that American does less than almost any other rich democracy to limit economic inequality. As a result, the rich can buy a lot more in America than in other affluent democracies, while the poor can buy a little less. If you evaluate this situation by Rawlsian standards, America's policies are clearly inferior to those of most rich European countries. If you evaluate the same situation using a utilitarian calculus, you are likely to conclude that most American consumers do better than their counterparts in other large democracies. Much of this advantage is due to the fact that Americans spend more time working than Europeans do, but that may not be the whole story.

I also looked at evidence on whether economic inequality affects people's lives independent of its effects on their material standard of living. At least in the United States, the growth of inequality appears to have made more people attend college but also made educational opportunities more unequal. Growing inequality may also have lowered life expectancy, but the evidence for such an effect is weak and the effect, if there was one, was probably small. There is some evidence that changes in equality affect happiness in Europe, but not much evidence that this is the case in the United States. If inequality affects violent crime, these effects are swamped by other factors. There is no evidence that changes in economic inequality affect political participation, but declining political participation among the less affluent may help explain why American politicians remained so passive when inequality began to grow after 1980.

My bottom line is that the social consequences of economic inequality are sometimes negative, sometimes neutral, but seldom—as far as I can discover—positive. The case for inequality seems to rest entirely on the claim that it promotes efficiency, and the evidence for that claim is thin. All these judgments are very tentative, however, and they are likely to change as more work is done. Still, it is worthwhile to ask what they would imply about the wisdom of trying to limit economic inequality if they were, in fact, correct.

Readers' answers to that question should, I think, depend on four value judgments. First, readers need to decide how much weight they assign to improving the lot of the least advantaged compared with improving the average level of well-being. Second, they need to decide how much weight they assign to increasing material well-being compared with increasing "family time" or "leisure." Third, they need to decide how much weight they assign to equalizing opportunities for the young as against maximizing the welfare of adults. Fourth, they need to decide how much value they assign to admittingmore people from poor countries such as Mexico to the United States, since this almost inevitably makes the distribution of income more unequal.

If you are a hard-core Rawlsian who thinks that society's sole economic goal should be to improve the position of the least advantaged, European experience suggests that limiting inequality can benefit the poor. If you are a hard-core utilitarian, European experiences suggests—though it certainly does not prove—that limiting inequality lowers consumption. But European experience also suggests that lowering inequality reduces consumption partly by encouraging people to work fewer hours, which many Europeans see as a good thing. If you care more about equal opportunity for children than about consumption among adults, limiting economic inequality among parents probably reduces disparities in the opportunities open to their children.

All things considered, the case for limiting inequality seems to me strong but not overwhelming. That is one reason why most rich societies are deeply divided about the issue. Yet given the centrality of redistribution in modern politics, it is remarkable how little effort rich societies have made to assemble the kinds of evidence they would need to assess the costs and benefits of limiting inequality. Even societies that redistribute a far larger fraction of their GDP than the United States spend almost nothing on answering questions of this kind. Answering such questions would require collecting better evidence, which costs real money. It would also require politicians to run the risk of being proven wrong. Nonetheless, moral sentiments uninformed by evidence have done incalculable damage over the past few centuries, and their malign influence shows no sign of abating. Rich democracies can do better if they try.

NO

Christopher C. DeMuth

The New Wealth of Nations

The Nations of North America, Western Europe, Australia, and Japan are wealthier today than they have ever been, wealthier than any others on the planet, wealthier by far than any societies in human history. Yet their governments appear to be impoverished—saddled with large accumulated debts and facing annual deficits that will grow explosively over the coming decades. As a result, government spending programs, especially the big social-insurance programs like Social Security and Medicare in the United States, are facing drastic cuts in order to avert looming insolvency (and, in France and some other European nations, in order to meet the Maastricht treaty's criteria of fiscal rectitude). American politics has been dominated for several years now by contentious negotiations over deficit reduction between the Clinton administration and the Republican Congress. This past June, first at the European Community summit in Amsterdam and then at the Group of Eight meeting in Denver, most of the talk was of hardship and constraint and the need for governmental austerity ("Economic Unease Looms Over Talks at Denver Summit," read the *New York Times* headline).

These bloodless problems of governmental accounting are said, moreover, to reflect real social ills: growing economic inequality in the United States; high unemployment in Europe; an aging, burdensome, and medically needy population everywhere; and the globalization of commerce, which is destroying jobs and national autonomy and forcing bitter measures to keep up with the bruising demands of international competitiveness.

How can it be that societies so surpassingly wealthy have governments whose core domestic-welfare programs are on the verge of bankruptcy? The answer is as paradoxical as the question. We have become not only the richest but also the freest and most egalitarian societies that have ever existed, and it is our very wealth, freedom, and equality that are causing the welfare state to unravel.

⁕

That we have become very rich is clear enough in the aggregate. That we have become very equal in the enjoyment of our riches is an idea strongly resisted by many. Certainly there has been a profusion of reports in the media and political speeches about increasing income inequality: the rich, it is said, are getting richer, the poor are getting poorer, and the middle and working classes are under the relentless pressure of disappearing jobs in manufacturing and middle management.

Although these claims have been greatly exaggerated, and some have been disproved by events, it is true that, by some measures, there has been a recent increase in income inequality in the United States. But it is a very small tick in the massive and unprecedented leveling of material circumstances that has been proceeding now for almost three centuries and in this century has accelerated dramatically. In fact, the much-noticed increase in measured-income inequality is in part a result of the increase in real social equality. Here are a few pieces of this important but neglected story.

• First, progress in agriculture, construction, manufacturing, and other key sectors of economic production has made the material necessities of life—food, shelter, and clothing—available to essentially everyone. To be sure, many people, including the seriously handicapped and the mentally incompetent, remain dependent on the public purse for their necessities. And many people continue to live in terrible squalor. But the problem of poverty, defined as material scarcity, has been solved. If poverty today remains a serious problem, it is a problem of individual behavior, social organization, and public policy. This was not so 50 years ago, or ever before.

• Second, progress in public health, in nutrition, and in the biological sciences and medical arts has produced dramatic improvements in longevity, health, and physical well-being. Many of these improvements—resulting, for example, from better public sanitation and water supplies, the conquest of dread diseases, and the abundance of nutritious food—have affected entire populations, producing an equalization of real personal welfare more powerful than any government redistribution of income.

The Nobel prize-winning economist Robert Fogel has focused on our improved mastery of the biological environment—leading over the past 300 years to a doubling of the average human life span and to large gains in physical stature, strength, and energy—as the key to what he calls "the egalitarian revolution of the 20th century." He considers this so profound an advance as to constitute a distinct new level of human evolution. Gains in stature, health, and longevity are continuing today and even accelerating. Their outward effects may be observed, in evolutionary fast-forward, in the booming nations of Asia (where, for example, the physical difference between older and younger South Koreans is strikingly evident on the streets of Seoul).

• Third, the critical *source* of social wealth has shifted over the last few hundred years from land (at the end of the 18th century) to physical capital (at the end of the 19th) to, today, human capital—education and cognitive ability. This development is not an unmixed gain from the standpoint of economic equality. The ability to acquire and deploy human capital is a function of intelligence, and intelligence is not only unequally distributed but also, to a significant degree, heritable. As Charles Murray and the late Richard J. Herrnstein argue in *The Bell Curve,* an economy that rewards sheer brainpower replaces one old source of inequality, socioeconomic advantage with a new one, cognitive advantage.

·⸱◉⸱·

But an economy that rewards human capital also tears down far more artificial barriers than it erects. For most people who inhabit the vast middle range of the bell curve, intelligence is much more equally distributed than land or physical capital ever was. Most people, that is, possess ample intelligence to pursue all but a handful of specialized callings. If in the past many were held back by lack of education and closed social institutions, the opportunities to use one's human capital have blossomed with the advent of universal education and the erosion of social barriers.

Furthermore, the material benefits of the knowledge-based economy are by no means limited to those whom Murray and Herrnstein call the cognitive elite. Many of the newest industries, from fast food to finance to communications, have succeeded in part by opening up employment opportunities for those of modest ability and training—occupations much less arduous and physically much less risky than those they have replaced. And these new industries have created enormous, widely shared economic benefits in consumption; I will return to this subject below.

• Fourth, recent decades have seen a dramatic reduction in one of the greatest historical sources of inequality: the social and economic inequality of the sexes. Today, younger cohorts of working men and women with comparable education and job tenure earn essentially the same incomes. The popular view would have it that the entry of women into the workforce has been driven by falling male earnings and the need "to make ends meet" in middle-class families. But the popular view is largely mistaken. Among married women (as the economist Chinhui Juhn has demonstrated), it is wives of men with high incomes who have been responsible for most of the recent growth in employment.

• Fifth, in the wealthy Western democracies, material needs and desires have been so thoroughly fulfilled for so many people that, for the first time in history, we are seeing large-scale voluntary reductions in the amount of time spent at paid employment. This development manifests itself in different forms: longer periods of education and training for the young; earlier retirement despite longer life spans; and, in between, many more hours devoted to leisure, recreation, entertainment, family, community and religious activities, charitable and other nonremunerative pursuits, and so forth. The dramatic growth of the sports, entertainment, and travel industries captures only a small slice of what has happened. In Fogel's estimation, the time devoted to nonwork activities by the average male head of household has grown from 10.5 hours per week in 1880 to 40 hours today, while time per week at work has fallen from 61.6 hours to 33.6 hours. Among women, the reduction in work (including not only outside employment but also household work, food preparation, childbearing and attendant health problems, and child rearing) and the growth in nonwork have been still greater.

There is a tendency to overlook these momentous developments because of the often frenetic pace of modern life. But our busy-ness actually demonstrates the point: time, and not material things, has become the scarce and valued commodity in modern society.

•◎•

One implication of these trends is that in very wealthy societies, income has become a less useful gauge of economic welfare and hence of economic equality. When income becomes to some degree discretionary, and when many peoples' incomes change from year to year for reasons unrelated to their life circumstances, *consumption* becomes a better measure of material welfare. And by this measure, welfare appears much more evenly distributed: people of higher income spend progressively smaller shares on consumption, while in the bottom ranges, annual consumption often exceeds income. (In fact, government statistics suggest that in the bottom 20 percent of the income scale, average annual consumption is about twice annual income—probably a reflection of a substantial underreporting of earnings in this group.) According to the economist Daniel Slesnick, the distribution of consumption, unlike the distribution of reported income, has become measurably *more* equal in recent decades.

If we include leisure-time pursuits as a form of consumption, the distribution of material welfare appears flatter still. Many such activities, being informal by definition, are difficult to track, but Dora Costa of MIT has recently studied one measurable aspect—expenditures on recreation— and found that these have become strikingly more equal as people of lower income have increased the amount of time and money they devote to entertainment, reading, sports, and related enjoyments.

Television, videocassettes, CD's, and home computers have brought musical, theatrical, and other entertainments (both high and low) to everyone, and have enormously narrowed the differences in cultural opportunities between wealthy urban centers and everywhere else. Formerly upper-crust sports like golf, tennis, skiing, and boating have become mass pursuits (boosted by increased public spending on parks and other recreational facilities as well as on environmental quality), and health clubs and full-line book stores have become as plentiful as gas stations. As some of the best things in life become free or nearly so, the price of pursuing them becomes, to that extent, the "opportunity cost" of time itself.

The substitution of leisure activities for income-producing work even appears to have become significant enough to be contributing to the recently much-lamented increase in inequality in measured income. In a new AEI study, Robert Haveman finds that most of the increase in earnings inequality among U.S. males since the mid-1970's can be attributed not to changing labor-market opportunities but to voluntary choice—to the free pursuit of nonwork activities at the expense of income-producing work.

Most of us can see this trend in our own families and communities. A major factor in income inequality in a wealthy knowledge economy is age—

many people whose earnings put them at the top of the income curve in their late fifties were well down the curve in their twenties, when they were just getting out of school and beginning their working careers. Fogel again: today the average household in the top 10 percent might consist of a professor or accountant married to a nurse or secretary, both in their peak years of earning. As for the stratospheric top 1 percent, it includes not only very rich people like Bill Cosby but also people like Cosby's fictional Huxtable family: an obstetrician married to a corporate lawyer. All these individuals would have appeared well down the income distribution as young singles, and that is where their young counterparts appear today.

That more young people are spending more time in college or graduate school, taking time off for travel and "finding themselves," and pursuing interesting but low- or non-paying jobs or apprenticeships before knuckling down to lifelong careers is a significant factor in "income inequality" measured in the aggregate. But this form of economic inequality is in fact the social equality of the modern age. It is progress, not regress, to be cherished and celebrated, not feared and fretted over.

POSTSCRIPT

Is Increasing Economic Inequality a Serious Problem?

This debate can be posed in terms of contradictory statements by the two authors: "The economic gap between rich and poor has grown dramatically in the United States over the past generation and is now considerably wider than in any other affluent nation" (Jencks). "We have become very equal in the enjoyment of our riches" (DeMuth). Both authors support their statements with indicators that measure trends, but they select different indicators. The reader has to decide which set of indicators better describes his or her idea of inequality.

Inequality, stratification, and social mobility are central concerns of sociology, and they are addressed by a large literature. Important discussions of income inequality are Barry Bluestone and Bennett Harrison, *Growing Prosperity: The Battle for Growth With Equity in the Twenty-First Century* (Houghton Mifflin, 2000); D. G. Champernowne and F. A. Cowell, *Economic Inequality and Income Distribution* (Cambridge University Press, 1998); Sheldon Danziger and Peter Gottschalk, *America Unequal* (Harvard University Press, 1995); Richard B. Freeman, *When Earnings Diverge: Causes, Consequences, and Cures for the New Inequality in the U.S.* (National Policy Association, 1997); Andrew Hacker, *Money: Who Has How Much and Why* (Scribner's Reference, 1997); Chuck Collins and Felice Yeskel, *Economic Apartheid in America* (New Press, 2005); Paul Ryscavage, *Income Inequality in America: An Analysis of Trends* (M. E. Sharpe, 1999); Edward N. Wolff, *Top Heavy: The Increasing Inequality of Wealth in America and What Can Be Done about It* (New Press, 2002); *The Causes and Consequences of Increasing Inequality*, edited by Finis Welch (University of Chicago Press, 2001); James Tardner and David Smith (eds.), *Inequality Matters: The Growing Ecomomic Divide in America and Its Poisonous Consequences* (New Press, 2005); and Samuel Bowles, et al. (eds.) *Unequal Chances* (Princeton University Press, 2005). A big part of the inequality picture is the conditions of the working poor, which is analyzed by Lawrence Mishel et al., *The State of Working America, 2002-2003* (Cornell University Press, 2003); *Low-Wage America: How Employers Are Reshaping Opportunity in the Workplace*, edited by Eileen Appelbaum et al. (Russell Sage Foundation, 2003); and David K. Shipler, *The Working Poor: Invisible in America* (Knopf, 2004). For a poignant ethnographic study of the poor and their disadvantages, see Elliot Liebow, *Tell Them Who I Am: The Lives of Homeless Women* (Free Press, 1993).

ISSUE 8

Is the Underclass the Major Threat to American Ideals?

YES: Charles Murray, from "And Now for the Bad News," *Society* (November/December 1999)

NO: Barry Schwartz, from "Capitalism, the Market, the 'Underclass,' and the Future," *Society* (November/December 1999)

ISSUE SUMMARY

YES: Author Charles Murray describes destructive behavior among the underclass. Murray asserts that this type of behavior will result in serious trouble for society even though, according to statistics, the number of crimes committed has decreased.

NO: Psychology professor Barry Schwartz states that the underclass is not the major threat to American ideals. He counters that "the theory and practice of free-market economics have done more to undermine traditional moral values than any other social force."

$\mathbf{T}$ he Declaration of Independence proclaims the right of every human being to "life, liberty, and the pursuit of happiness." It never defines happiness, but Americans tend to agree that happiness includes doing well financially, getting ahead in life, and maintaining a comfortable standard of living.

The fact is that millions of Americans do not do well and do not live comfortably. They are mired in poverty and seem unable to get out. On the face of it, this fact poses no contradiction to America's commitment to the pursuit of happiness. To pursue is not necessarily to catch.

The real difficulty in reconciling the American ideal with American reality is not the problem of income differentials but the *persistence* of poverty from generation to generation. There are two basic explanations for this problem. One largely blames the poor and the other largely blames the circumstances of the poor and, thus, society.

The explanation that blames the poor is most strongly identified with the culture-of-poverty thesis, according to which a large segment of the poor does not really try to get out of poverty. In its more extreme form this view portrays the poor as lazy, stupid, or base. Poverty is not to be blamed on defects of American society but on personal defects. After all, many successful Americans have worked their way up from humble beginnings, and many immigrant groups have made progress in one generation. Therefore, some believe that the United States provides ample opportunities for those who work hard.

According to this view, available opportunities are ignored by the portion of the poor that embraces what is known as the *culture of poverty*. In other words, the poor have a culture all their own that is at variance with middle-class culture and that hinders their success. Although it may keep people locked into what seems to be an intolerable life, some would assert that this culture nevertheless has its own compensations and pleasures. It does not demand that people postpone pleasure, save money, or work hard.

However, the culture of poverty does not play a major role in today's version of the poor-are-to-blame theory. According to recent versions of this theory, having children out of wedlock, teenage pregnancy, divorce, absent fathers, crime, welfare dependency, and child abuse are what contribute to poverty. The culture of poverty contributes to these practices by being permissive or even condoning. This culture, however, is not antithetical to but is rather shared in part by much of the middle class. The difference is that in the middle class its consequences are usually not as extreme.

According to the second explanation of poverty, the poor have few opportunities and many obstacles to overcome to climb out of poverty. Most of the poor will become self-supporting if they are given the chance. Their most important need is for decent jobs that have the potential for advancement. Many poor people cannot find jobs, and when they do, the jobs are degrading or lack further opportunity.

These two perspectives are expressed in the two selections that follow. Charles Murray blames a segment of the poor that he calls the underclass for their poverty and for much of the harm done to society. Barry Schwartz blames the functioning of capitalism and the stock market for creating obstacles to the poor for getting ahead. Values such as sympathy, fairness, and self control, which sustain a productive and humane society, are undermined, according to Schwartz.

And Now for the Bad News

Good news is everywhere. Crime rates are falling; welfare rolls are plunging; unemployment is at rock bottom; teenage births are down. Name an indicator, economic or social, and chances are it has taken a turn in the right direction. This happy story is worth celebrating. It is also a story that begs to be disentangled. For what is happening to the nation as a whole is not happening to the sub-population that we have come to call the underclass.

To make the case, I return to three indicators I first selected in the late 1980s to track the course of the underclass: criminality, dropout from the labor force among young men, and illegitimate births among young women. Then and now, these three seemed to me key outcroppings of what we mean by the underclass: people living outside the mainstream, often preying on the mainstream, in a world where the building blocks of a life—work, family and community—exist in fragmented and corrupt forms. Crime offers the most obvious example of a story that needs disentangling. After seven straight years of decline, the crime rate is at its lowest in a quarter-century. Almost everyone feels safer, especially in big cities. But suppose we ask not how many crimes are committed, but how many Americans demonstrate chronic criminality. That number is larger than ever. We don't notice, because so many of the chronically criminal are in jail.

Off the Street

For the past 20 years the United States has engaged in a massive effort to take criminals off the street. As of 1997, more than 1.8 million people were in prisons, jails and juvenile facilities. It has not been an efficient process—many who should be behind bars aren't and vice versa—but the great majority of prisoners are there because they have been a menace to their fellow citizens. To see how our appraisal of the crime problem depends on the imprisonment binge, suppose that in 1997 we imprisoned at the same rate relative to crime that we did in 1980, the year that the crime rate hit its all-time high. At the 1980 rate, 567,000 people would have been incarcerated in 1997, roughly 1.3 million fewer than the actual number. Now suppose that tomorrow we freed 1.3 million prisoners. Recent scholarly estimates of the average number of crimes prevented per year of incarceration range from 12 to 21. Even if these numbers are too high, it is clear that if we set free 1.3 million people now in prison, we would no longer be bragging about a falling crime rate. The only uncertainty is how sky-high the crime rate would be. It is a major accomplishment that crime has gone down. It has been achieved not by socializing the underclass, but by putting large numbers of its members behind bars.

Unemployment is another success story for the nation as a whole. Unemployment rates have dropped for just about any group of people who have been in the labor market, including blacks, and young black males in particular. Suppose we turn instead to a less-publicized statistic, but one of the most significant in trying to track the course of the underclass, the percentage of young males not in the labor force. When large numbers of young men neither work nor look for work, most are living off the underground economy or are dependent on handouts, perhaps moving into the labor force periodically, getting a job, and then quitting or getting fired a few weeks later, consigning themselves to a life at the margins of the economy.

Sudden and unexpected increases in the labor force dropout rates of young black males in the mid-1960s heralded the deterioration of the inner city. The 1990s have seen a new jump in dropout from the labor force that is just as ominous. The increased dropout has occurred selectively, among a subgroup that should have virtually 100% labor-force participation: young men who are no longer in school. The increase in labor force dropout is largest among young black males. Among 16- to 24-year-old black males not in school, the proportion who are not working or looking for work averaged 17% during the 1980s. It first hit 20% in 1992. As of 1997, it stood at 23%. The magnitude of dropout among white males the same age not in school is smaller, 9% in 1997. But the proportional increase since 1990 is substantial, up 25% overall, and concentrated among white teenagers (up 33% since 1990). That these increases in labor-force dropout have occurred despite a sustained period of high demand for workers at all skill levels is astonishing and troubling.

As for illegitimacy, confusion reigns. Headlines declare that "Illegitimacy is Falling," but the referent is birthrates, illegitimate births per 1,000 unmarried women. The referent for the headlines is also usually blacks, because that's where the dramatic change has occurred: The black illegitimate birth rate for women 15 to 44 fell 18% from 1990 to 1996; the black teenage birth rate fell by even more. But what is happening to the illegitimacy *ratio*—the percentage of babies who are born to unmarried women? The two measures need not track with each other, as the black experience vividly illustrates. Birthrates for unmarried black women and for black teenagers did not begin to drop in 1990. They dropped further and for much longer from 1960 to 1985. But the black illegitimacy ratio rose relentlessly throughout that period. The ratio also rose from 1990 to 1994 as birth rates fell. The good news about the black illegitimacy ratio is that it has since leveled off, even dropping a percentage point—meaning that as of 1997 it stood at a catastrophic 69% instead of a catastrophic 70%.

Most analysts, including me, have focused on the ratio rather than the rate because it is the prevalence of mother-only homes that determines the nature of a neighborhood and the socialization of the next generation. But when we turn from blacks to the national numbers for all races, it doesn't make much difference which measure you think is important. The rate and ratio have both risen substantially over the past few decades. Since 1994 the rate has fallen slightly, while the ratio has been flat at 32%. That is, almost one out of three American babies is now born to an unmarried woman.

The problems associated with illegitimacy have not really leveled off. Because the illegitimacy ratio is so much higher today than 18 years ago, the proportion of American children under 18 who were born to unmarried women will continue to increase. The problems associated with illegitimacy will also continue to increase well into the next century as the babies born in the 1990s grow up. That illegitimacy has stopped rising is a genuinely hopeful sign, but for practical purposes we are at the peak of the problem.

The size of the welfare population was not one of my 1989 indicators for tracking the underclass (it tends to double-count the role of illegitimacy), but recent success on this front has been so dramatic that it should be acknowledged. By "welfare reform" I mean the movement that began in the states in the early 1990s and culminated in the national welfare reform law of 1996. The change has been stunning: In 1993, slightly more than five million families were on welfare. By 1998, that number had dropped to about three million—a 40% drop in five years. The economy gets only a modest part of the credit. During the two preceding booms, welfare soared (in the 1960s) and declined fractionally (in the 1980s).

But once again, disentangling is crucial. For years, liberals defending welfare stressed that half of all women who ever go on welfare exit within a few years (and thus are ordinary women who have hit a rough patch), while conservatives attacking welfare stressed that half the welfare caseload at any point in time consists of women who have been on the rolls for many years (and thus are likely candidates for the underclass). So the crucial question is: How has the 40% reduction in caseload split between the two groups? No one yet knows. Past experience with workfare programs has been that the effect is concentrated on women who fit the profile of the short-term recipient. Answers about the current situation should be forthcoming soon.

The more profound question is what difference it makes if single mothers go to work. Is a community without fathers importantly different just because more mothers are earning a paycheck? One line of argument says yes. Jobs provide regularity, structure and dignity to family life, even if the father is not around. But we know from recent research that the bad effects of single parenting persist for women not on welfare. No counterbalancing body of research demonstrates that it is good for children when a single mother works (rather the opposite). I like to think children who see their mothers working for a living grow up better equipped to make their way in the world than children who watch their mothers live off a welfare check, even if there are no fathers in their lives. But this is a hope, not a finding.

In net, the underclass is as large as or larger than it has ever been. It is probably still growing among males, level or perhaps falling among females. We know for sure that the underclass today is substantially larger than it was at any time in the 1980s when the Reagan administration was being excoriated for ignoring the underclass. Yet the underclass is no longer a political issue. Why? I propose an ignoble explanation. Whatever we might tell ourselves, mainstream Americans used to worry about the underclass primarily insofar as it intruded on our lives. Busing sent children from the wrong side of the tracks into our schools; the homeless infested our public spaces; the pervasive presence of graffiti, street hustlers and clusters of glowering teenagers made us anxious. Most of all, high crime rates twisted urban life into a variety of knots.

It took the better part of three decades, but we dealt with those intrusions. Busing is so far in the past that the word has an archaic ring to it. Revitalized vagrancy laws and shelters took most homeless off the streets. Most of all, we figured out what to do with criminals. Innovations in policing helped, but the key insight was an old one: lock 'em up.

Why is the underclass no longer an issue? Because what bothered us wasn't that the underclass existed, but that it was in our face. Now it is not. So we can forget about it. "For the time being" is the crucial hedge. What about the long term? Can the United States retain its political and social culture in the presence of a permanent underclass? The answer is certainly yes, if an underclass is sufficiently small. As long as it is only a fragment, the disorganization and violence of its culture do not spill over into the mainstream. The answer is certainly no if the underclass is sufficiently large. Trying to decide where the American underclass stands on that continuum raises two questions without clear answers.

First, how much has the culture of the underclass already spilled over into the mainstream? So far, the American underclass has been predominantly urban and black. Urban black culture has been spilling over into mainstream American culture for more than a century now, to America's great advantage. But during the past three decades it has increasingly been infiltrated by an underclass subculture that celebrates a bastardized social code—predatory sex and "getting paid." The violence and misogyny that pervade certain forms of popular music reflect these values. So does the hooker look in fashion, and the flaunting of obscenity and vulgarity in comedy.

Perhaps most disturbing is the widening expression, often approving, of underclass ethics: Take what you want. Respond violently to anyone who antagonizes you. Despise courtesy as weakness. Take pride in cheating (stealing, lying, exploiting) successfully. I do not know how to measure how broadly such principles have spread, but it's hard to deny that they are more openly espoused in television, films and recordings than they used to be. Among the many complicated explanations for this deterioration in culture, cultural spill-over from the underclass is implicated.

Implicated—that's all. There are many culprits behind the coarsening of American life. It should also go without saying that vulgarity, violence and the rest were part of mainstream America before the underclass came along. But these things always used to be universally condemned in public discourse. Now they are not. It is not just that America has been defining deviancy down, slackening old moral codes. Inner-city street life has provided an alternative code and it is attracting converts.

The converts are mainly adolescents, which makes sense. The street ethics of the underclass subculture are not "black." They are the ethics of male adolescents who haven't been taught any better. For that matter, the problem of the underclass itself is, ultimately, a problem of adolescents who haven't been taught any better. There are a lot more white adolescents than black ones, leading to the second question: How fast will the white underclass grow?

National statistics tell us that in the past decade white criminality has not only increased but gotten more violent, that white teenage males are increasingly dropping out of the labor force, and that white illegitimacy has increased rapidly. Anecdotal evidence about changes in white working-class neighborhoods points to increased drug use, worse school performance and a breakdown of neighborhood norms—recalling accounts of black working-class neighborhoods three decades ago. (Systematic documentation of these trends is still lacking.)

Looking ahead, much depends on whether illegitimacy among whites has already reached critical mass—the point at which we can expect accelerated and sustained growth in white crime, labor force dropout and illegitimacy rates. The good news is that the growth in the white illegitimacy ratio has slowed. The bad news is that it stands at 26%-22% for non-Latino whites—which, judging from the black experience in the early 1960s, may be near that point of critical mass. No one knows, of course, whether the subsequent trajectory of events for whites will be the same as it was for blacks, but there is ample cause for worry. European countries with high white illegitimacy ratios offer no comfort. Juvenile crime is increasing rapidly across Europe, along with other indicators of social deterioration in low-income groups.

Jamesian Directions

The most striking aspect of the current situation, and one that makes predictions very dicey, is the degree to which the United States is culturally compartmentalizing itself. America in the 1990s is a place where the local movie theater may play *Sense and Sensibility* next door to *Natural Born Killers*. Brian Lamb (on C-SPAN) is a few channels away from Jerry Springer. Formal balls are in vogue in some circles; mosh pits in others. Name just about any aspect of American life, and a case can be made that the country is going in different directions simultaneously, some of them Jamesian, others Hogarthian.

The Jamesian elements are not confined to a cultured remnant. Broad swaths of American society are becoming more civil and less vulgar, more responsible and less self-indulgent. The good news is truly good, and it extends beyond the statistics. What's more, the bad news may prove manageable. One way to interpret the nation's success in re-establishing public order is that we have learned how to cope with our current underclass. One may then argue that the size of the underclass is stabilizing, meaning that we can keep this up indefinitely. It requires only that we set aside moral considerations and accept that the huge growth of the underclass since 1960 cannot now be reversed.

Welfare reform and the growing school-voucher movement are heartening signs that many are not ready to accept the status quo. But they struggle against a larger movement toward what I have called "custodial democracy," in which the mainstream subsidizes but also walls off the underclass. In effect, custodial democracy takes as its premise that a substantial portion of the population cannot be expected to function as citizens.

At this moment, elated by falling crime rates and shrinking welfare rolls, we haven't had to acknowledge how far we have already traveled on the road to custodial democracy. I assume the next recession will disabuse us. But suppose that our new *modus vivendi* keeps working? We just increase the number of homeless shelters, restore the welfare guarantee, build more prison cells, and life for the rest of us goes on, pleasantly. At some point we will be unable to avoid recognizing that custodial democracy has arrived. This will mark a fundamental change in how we conceive of America. Will anyone mind?

NO

Barry Schwartz

Capitalism, the Market, the "Underclass," and the Future

I share Charles Murray's concern that there is bad news lurking in the shadows of what seems to be unalloyed prosperity in millennial America. I share his concerns about urban crime, employment, the fragility of the family, and the coarseness of the culture. But I am also angry. I am angry at the resolute refusal of conservatives like Murray, William Bennett, and James Q. Wilson to face squarely what their colleague Pat Buchanan is willing to face, when he writes:

> Reaganism and its twin sister, Thatcherism, create fortunes among the highly educated, but in the middle and working classes, they generate anxiety, insecurity and disparities. . . . Tax cuts, the slashing of safety nets and welfare benefits, and global free trade . . . unleash the powerful engines of capitalism that go on a tear. Factories and businesses open and close with startling speed. . . . As companies merge, downsize and disappear, the labor force must always be ready to pick up and move on. . . . The cost is paid in social upheaval and family breakdown. . . . Deserted factories mean gutted neighborhoods, ghost towns, ravaged communities and regions that go from boom to bust . . . Conservatism is being confronted with its own contradictions for unbridled capitalism is an awesome destructive force.

Murray's message is that things have not been working nearly as well as we think they have. Crime is down only because we have locked all the hardened criminals away; the tendency to commit crime has not changed. Unemployment is down, but those who remain unemployed are contemptuous of work. Illegitimate births are down, but legitimate births are down even more, as growing numbers of people seem disdainful of marriage. All these signs of moral decay Murray traces to the underclass, and he is especially worried because the middle class seems increasingly to approve of what he calls "underclass ethics." He says that "among the many complicated explanations for this deterioration in culture, cultural spill-over [from the underclass to the rest of us] is implicated."

But Murray also says this: "There are many culprits behind the coarsening of American life. It should also go without saying that vulgarity, violence and the rest were part of mainstream America before the underclass came along. But these things always used to be universally condemned in public discourse. Now they are not. It is not just that America has been defining deviancy down, slackening old moral codes. Inner-city street life has provided an alternative code and it is attracting converts."

The idea that middle America needs to look at the underclass for examples of coarseness is preposterous. It turns a willful blind eye to what the conservative revolution has brought us. The conservatism that captured America's fancy in the 1980s was actually two distinct conservatisms. It was an *economic* conservatism committed to dismantling the welfare state and turning as many facets of life as possible over to the private sector. And it was a *moral* conservatism committed to strengthening traditional values and the social institutions that foster them. These two conservatisms corresponded to the economic and social agendas that guided the policies of both the Reagan and the Bush administrations. These Presidents and their supporters seemed to share not only the belief that free-market economics and traditional moral values are good, but that they go together.

This has proven to be a serious mistake. The theory and practice of free-market economics have done more to undermine traditional moral values than any other social force. It is not permissive parents, unwed mothers, undisciplined teachers, multicultural curricula, fanatical civil libertarians, feminists, rock musicians, or drug pushers who are the primary sources of the corrosion that moral conservatives are trying to repair. Instead, it is the operation of the market system itself, along with an ideology that justifies the pursuit of economic self-interest as the "American way." And so, I acknowledge that Murray's concerns about the "problem of the underclass" are not being solved by our current prosperity. But I insist that they will never be solved unless we face up squarely to what causes them. And what causes them, I believe, is in large part what is responsible for our current prosperity.

I am not going to argue here that the evils of market capitalism demand that we all gather to storm the barricades and wrest the means of production out of the hands of evil capitalists and turn them over to the state. As everyone says, "the Cold War is over, and we won." State ownership of the means of production is a non-issue. We are all capitalists now. The issues before us really are two. First, what kind of capitalism? Is it the capitalism of Reagan and Thatcher—of unregulated markets and privatization of everything, with government involvement viewed as a cause of waste and inefficiency? Or is it the capitalism of John Maynard Keynes and of Franklin Roosevelt, with significant state regulation of the market and state guarantees of life's necessities? I'm going to argue for the latter—old-fashioned capitalism. The boom we are in the midst of has created perhaps the greatest degree of income inequality in the history of the developed world. What the free market teaches us is that what *anyone* can have not *everyone* can have, often with very painful consequences for the have-nots. And second, if we must live with capitalism, what are we prepared to do to correct the moral corrosion that it brings as a side effect? For in addition to asking what free-market capitalism does *for* people, we must ask what it does *to* people. And I will suggest that it turns people into nasty, self-absorbed, self-interested competitors—that it demands this of people, and celebrates it.

The Market and Inequality

One would think that if the problem is the underclass, the solution—or *a* solution—is to reduce its numbers. What do we know about the great economic "boom" we are living in the midst of? The income of the average wage-earning worker in 1997 was 3.1% lower than it was in 1989. Median family income was $1000 less in 1997 than in 1989. The typical couple worked 250 more hours in 1997 than in 1989. So to the extent that average people have been able to hold their own at all, it is because they worked harder. The median wage of high school graduates fell 6% between 1980 and 1996 while the median wage of college graduates rose 12%.

And this picture looks worse if you include benefits. Benefits used to be the "great equalizer," distributed equally among employees despite huge disparities in salary. For example, the $20,000/year employee and the $500,000/ year employee got the same $4000 medical insurance. But despite IRS efforts to prevent differential benefits based on income (by making such benefits taxable), employers have invented all kinds of tricks. They have introduced lengthy employment "trial periods" with no benefits. They have resorted to hiring temporary workers who get no benefits. The result is that while 80% of workers received paid vacations and holidays in 1996, less than 10% in the bottom tenth of the income distribution did. The result is that while 70% of workers have some sort of employer funded pension, less than 10% of those in the bottom tenth of the income distribution do. The result is that while 90% of high wage employees have health insurance, only 26% of low wage employees do. All told, about 40 million Americans have no health insurance. The picture looks still worse if you consider *wealth* rather than income. The richest 1% of Americans have almost 50% of the nation's wealth. The next 9% have about a third. And the remaining 90% have about a sixth.

America now has the greatest wealth and income inequality in the developed world, and it is getting bigger every day. Efforts to implement even modest increases in the minimum wage are met with intense resistance. Further, as pointed out in a recent analysis in the *Left Business Observer,* the United States has the highest poverty rate of any developed nation, and uses government income transfers to reduce poverty less than any developed nation. Our two main rivals in these categories are Thatcher's England, and postcommunist, gangster-capitalist Russia.

Is this massive inequality an accident—an imperfection in an otherwise wonderful system? I don't think so. Modern capitalism depends on inequality. Modern capitalism is consumer capitalism. People have to buy things. In 1997, $120 billion was spent in the United States on advertising, more than was spent on all forms of education. Consumer debt, excluding home mortgages, exceeded $1 trillion in 1995—more than $10,000 per household. But people also need to save, to accumulate money for investment, especially now, in these days of ferocious global competition. How can you save and spend at the same time? The answer is that some must spend while others save. Income and wealth inequality allow a few to accumulate, and invest, while most of us spend—even more than we earn. And this is not an accident, but a structural necessity. There must be some people who despite society-wide exhortation to spend just cannot spend all they make. These people will provide the capital for investment.

Perhaps this kind of inequality is just the price we pay for prosperity. Concentrating wealth in the hands of the few gives them the opportunity to invest. This investment "trickles down" to improve the lives of all, by improving the products we buy and creating employment opportunities. There is no question that the current political leadership in the U.S.—of both parties—thinks that keeping Wall Street happy is essential to the nation's financial well-being. By encouraging people to buy stocks we put money in the hands of investors who then produce innovation and improvement in economic efficiency. Thus, we reduce capital gains taxes. And we eliminate the deficit to make Wall Street happy, even if it means neglecting the social safety net.

But who gains? It is true that what's good for Wall Street is good for America? On investment, more than 90% of all stock market trades involve just shuffling of paper as shares move from my hands to yours, or vice versa. Almost none of the activity on Wall Street puts capital in the hands of folks who invest in plant and equipment. Similarly, most corporate debt is used to finance mergers and acquisitions, or to buy back stock that later goes to chief executives as performance bonuses.

Why is it that when a company announces major layoffs, its stock goes up? The answer is that layoffs signal higher profits, good news for investors. Why is it that when unemployment rates go down, stock prices go down? The answer is that low unemployment signals potential inflation, bad news for investors. Why is it that banks bailed out a highly speculative hedge fund—for rich folks only— that was able to invest borrowed money (20 times its actual assets) while at the same time lobbying to crack down on personal bankruptcy laws, when the overwhelming majority of those facing personal bankruptcy make less than $20,000/ year? The evidence is clear and compelling: the stock market operates to benefit the few at the expense of the many.

So if, as Murray contends (correctly, I think), the underclass is a social problem for America that is not going away, why isn't Murray demanding a set of policies that make it smaller rather than larger? Why isn't he demanding a minimum wage that is a *living* wage, so that parents can *afford* to take care of their children? And in addition, why isn't he demanding high-quality day care, so that the children of single mothers, or of two worker households, won't be neglected? How is it that a set of economic policies that has made the underclass bigger glides by free of Murray's wrath, as he chooses to condemn instead the nation's growing enthusiasm for underclass values?

The Market and Morality

. . . [R]ecent thinkers have realized that we can't take the bourgeois values that support capitalism for granted. Indeed, as Karl Polanyi, in *The Great*

Transformation, and Fred Hirsch, in *Social Limits to Growth* argue persuasively, not only can we not take these values for granted, but market capitalism—the very thing that so desperately depends on them—actively undermines them. This, I believe, is the lesson that Murray and his cohort refuses to accept. The so-called "underclass" may threaten the comfort and safety of the middle class, but it is the overclass that threatens the stability and the future prospects of society.

One sees this dramatically in James Q. Wilson's . . . book *The Moral Sense.* In that book, Wilson argues for a biologically based moral sense in human beings—a sense that almost guarantees such moral traits as sympathy, duty, self-control, and fairness. . . .

Having made the sweeping claim that the market contributes more to the erosion of our moral sense than any other modern social force, I want to defend that claim with some more specific arguments. In particular, I want to discuss the market's negative effects on some of the moral sentiments that Wilson emphasizes and on some of the social institutions that nurture those sentiments.

One of the moral sentiments that is central to Wilson's argument is sympathy, the ability to feel and understand the misfortune of others and the desire to do something to ameliorate that misfortune. Wilson notes correctly that other-regarding sentiments and actions, including sympathy and altruism, are extremely common human phenomena, notwithstanding the efforts of many cynical social scientists to explain them away as subtle forms of self-interested behavior. What the literature on sympathy and altruism have made clear is that they depend on a person's ability to take the perspective of another (to "walk a mile in her shoes"). This perspective-taking ability in turn depends on a certain general cognitive sophistication, on familiarity with the other, and on proximity to the other. What does the market do to sympathy? Well, the market thrives on anonymity. One of its great virtues is that buyers are interchangeable with other buyers and sellers with other sellers. All that matters is price and quality and the ability to pay. Increasingly, in the modern market, transactions occur over long distances. Indeed, increasingly, they occur over telephone lines, as "e-commerce" joins the lexicon. Thus, the social institution that dominates modern American society is one that fosters, both in principle and in fact, social relations that are distant and impersonal—social relations that are the antithesis of what sympathy seems to require.

A second moral sentiment that attracts Wilson's attention is fairness. He correctly notes (as any parent will confirm) that concern about fairness appears early in human development and that it runs deep. Even four-year-olds have a powerful, if imperfect conception of what is and is not fair. What does fairness look like in adults?

[Professors] Daniel Kahneman, Jack Knetsch, and Richard Thaler asked this question by posing a variety of hypothetical business transactions to randomly chosen informants and asking the informants to judge whether the transactions were fair. What these hypothetical transactions had in common was that they all involved legal, profit-maximizing actions that were of questionable moral character. What these researchers found is that the overwhelming majority of people have a very strong sense of what is fair. While people believe that business people are entitled to make a profit, they do not think it fair for producers to charge what the market will bear (for example, to price gouge during shortages) or to lower wages during periods of slack employment. In short, most people think that concerns for fairness should be a constraint on profit-seeking. So far, so good; this study clearly supports Wilson's contention that fairness is one of our moral sentiments.

But here's the bad news. Another investigator posed these same hypotheticals to students in a nationally prominent MBA program. The overwhelming majority of these informants thought that anything was fair, as long as it was legal. Maximizing profit was the point; fairness was irrelevant. In another study, these same hypotheticals were posed to a group of CEOs. What the authors of the study concluded was that their executive sample was less inclined than those in the original study to find the actions posed in the survey to be unfair. In addition, often when CEOs did rate actions as unfair, they indicated in unsolicited comments that they did not think the actions were unfair so much as they were unwise, that is, bad business practice. . . .

To summarize, people care about fairness, but if they are participants in the market, or are preparing to be participants in the market, they care much less about fairness than others do. Is it the ideology of relativism that is undermining this moral sentiment or the ideology of the market?

Another of the moral sentiments Wilson discusses is self-control. What does the market do to self-control? As many have pointed out, modern corporate management is hardly a paradigm of self-control. The combination of short-termism and me-first management that have saddled large companies with inefficiency and debt are a cautionary tale on the evils of self-indulgence. Short termism is in part structural; managers must answer to shareholders, and in the financial markets, you're only as good as your last quarter. Me-first management seems to be pure greed. Some of the excesses of modern executive compensation have recently been documented by Derek Bok, in his book *The Cost of Talent.* Further, *The Economist,* in a survey of pay published in May of 1999, makes it quite clear that the pay scale of American executives is in another universe from that in any other nation, and heavily loaded with stock options that reward the executive for the company's performance in the stock market rather than the actual markets in goods and services in which the company operates. . . .

The final moral sentiment that Wilson identifies and discusses is duty, "a disposition to honor obligations even without hope of reward or fear of punishment." Wilson is quite right about the importance of duty. If we must rely on threat of punishment to enforce obligations, they become unenforceable. Punishment works only as long as most people will do the right thing most of the time even if they can get away with transgressing. . . .

The enemy of duty is free-riding, taking cost-free advantage of the dutiful actions of others. The more people are willing to be free-riders, the higher the cost to those who remain dutiful, and the higher the cost of enforcement to society as a whole. How does the market affect duty and free-riding? Well, one of the studies of fairness I mentioned above included a report of an investigation of free-riding. Economics students are more likely to be free riders than students in other disciplines. And this should come as no surprise. Free-riding is the "rational, self-interested" thing to do. Indeed, if you are the head of a company, free-riding may even be your fiduciary responsibility. So if free-riding is the enemy of duty, then the market is the enemy of duty.

. . . In my view, this is what market activity does to all the virtues that Wilson, and Murray long for—it submerges them with calculations of personal preference and self-interest.

If Wilson fails to acknowledge the influence of the market on our moral sense, where then does he look? As I said earlier, he thinks a good deal of human morality reflects innate predisposition. But that disposition must be nurtured, and it is nurtured, according to Wilson, in the family, by what might be described as "constrained socialization." The child is not a miniature adult (socialization is required), but nor is she a blank slate (not anything is possible; there are predispositions on the part of both parents and children for socialization to take one of a few "canonical" forms.) One of the primary mechanisms through which socialization occurs is imitation: "There can be little doubt that we learn a lot about how we ought to behave from watching others, especially others to whom we are strongly attached. . . .

So let us accept Wilson's position about socialization and ask what the adults who the young child will be imitating look like. I believe, following the work of [economist] Fred Hirsch, that in the last few decades there has been an enormous upsurge in what might be called the "commercialization of social relations"—that choice has replaced duty and utility maximization replaced fairness in relations among family members. . . .

Wilson seems mindful of all this. He decries the modern emphasis on rights and the neglect of duty. He acknowledges that modern society has posed a real challenge to the family by substituting labor markets for householding. And he deplores the ideology of choice as applied to the family:

> Not even the family has been immune to the ideology of choice. In the 1960s and 1970s (but less so today) books were written advocating "alternative" families and "open" marriages. A couple could choose to have a trial marriage, a regular marriage but without an obligation to sexual fidelity, or a revocable marriage with an easy exit provided by no-fault divorce. A woman could choose to have a child out of wedlock and to raise it alone. Marriage was but one of several "options" by which men and women could manage their intimate needs, an option that ought to be carefully negotiated in order to preserve the rights of each contracting party. The family, in this view, was no longer the cornerstone of human life, it was one of several "relationships" from which individuals could choose so as to maximize their personal goals.

But instead of attributing this ideology of choice to the market, from which I think it clearly arises, Wilson attributes it to the weakening of cultural standards—to relativism. Indeed he even adopts a Becker-like economic analysis of the family himself, apparently unaware that if people actually thought about their families in the way that he and [economist Gary] Becker claim they do, the family would hardly be a source of any of the moral sentiments that are important to him:

> But powerful as they are, the expression of these [familial] instincts has been modified by contemporary circumstances. When children have less economic value, then, at the margin, fewer children will be produced, marriage (and childbearing) will be postponed, and more marriages will end in divorce. And those children who are produced will be raised, at the margin, in ways that reflect their higher opportunity cost. Some will be neglected and others will be cared for in ways that minimize the parental cost in personal freedom, extra income, or career opportunities.

Let me be clear that I think Wilson is right about changes that have occurred in the family, and that he is also right about the unfortunate social consequences of those changes. His mistake is in failing to see the responsibility for these changes that must be borne by the spread of market thinking into the domain of our intimate social relations. As I have said elsewhere, there is an opportunity cost to thinking about one's social relations in terms of opportunity costs. In Wilson's terms, that opportunity cost will be paid in sympathy, fairness, and duty. Sociologist Arlie Hochschild has written that "each marriage bears the footprints of economic and cultural trends which originate far outside marriage." Wilson has emphasized the cultural and overlooked the economic. And so, alas, has Murray.

What Economies Do to People

In Arthur Miller's play, *All My Sons,* much of the drama centers around the belated discovery by a son that his father knowingly shipped defective airplane parts to fulfill a government contract during World War II. The parts were installed, some of the planes crashed, and pilots and their crews were killed. The man responsible, the father, is a good man, a kind man, a man who cares deeply about his family and would do anything to protect them and provide for them. His son simply can't imagine that a man like his father is capable of such an act—but he is. As he explains, he was under enormous pressure to deliver the goods. The military needed the parts right away, and failure to deliver would have destroyed his business. He had a responsibility to take care of his family. And anyway, there was no certainty that the parts would not hold up when in use. As the truth slowly comes out, the audience has the same incredulity as the son. How could it be? If a man like that could do a thing like that, then anyone is capable of doing anything.

This, of course, is one of the play's major points. Almost anyone *is* capable of almost anything. A monstrous system can make a monster of anyone, or perhaps more accurately, can make almost anyone do monstrous things. We see this as drama like Miller's are played out in real life, with horrifyingly tragic consequences.

- All too close to the story of *All My Sons,* military contractors have been caught knowingly making and selling defective brake systems for U.S. jet fighters, defective machine gun parts that cause the guns to jam when used, and defective fire-fighting equipment for navy ships.
- An automobile manufacturer knowingly made and sold a dangerous car, whose gas tank was alarmingly likely to explode in rear end collisions. This defect could have been corrected at a cost of a few dollars per car.
- A chemical company continued operating a chemical plant in Bhopal, India long after it knew the plant was unsafe. A gas leak killed more than 2000 people, and seriously injured more than 30,000. The $5 billion company responded to this tragedy by sending $1 million in disaster relief and a shipment of medicines sufficient for about 400 people.
- Other drug and chemical manufacturers make and sell to the Third World products known to be sufficiently dangerous that their sale is banned in the U.S.
- The asbestos industry knowingly concealed the hazardous nature of their products for years from workers who were exposed to carcinogens on a daily basis.
- Trucking companies put trucks on the road more than 30% of which would fail safety inspections and are thus hazards to their drivers as well as to other motorists.
- And of course, we all know now about the tobacco industry.

And it isn't just about dramatic death and destruction. The death and destruction can be slow and torturous:

- Firms get closed down, people put out of work, and communities destroyed, not because they aren't profitable, but because they aren't *as* profitable as other parts of the business.
- People are put to work in illegal sweatshops, or the work is sent offshore, where the working conditions are even worse, but not illegal.

Why does all this abuse occur? What makes people seek to exploit every advantage over their customers? What makes bosses abuse their employees? Do the people who do these things take pleasure from hurting their unsuspecting customers? Do they relish the opportunity to take advantage of people? It does not seem so. When bosses are challenged about their unscrupulous practices, they typically argue that "everybody does it." Understand, the argument is not that since everybody does it, it is all right. The argument is that since everybody does it, you have to do it also, in self-defense. In competitive situations, it seems inevitable that dishonest, inhumane practices will drive out the honest and humane ones; to be humane becomes a luxury that few business people can afford.

I find it unimaginable as I talk to the talented, ambitious, enthusiastic students with whom I work that any of them aspires to a future in which he or she will oversee the production of cars, drugs, chemicals, foods, military supplies, or anything else that will imperil the lives of thousands of people. I even find it unimaginable that any of them will accept such a future. They are good, decent people, as far removed from those who seek to turn human weakness and vulnerability into profit as anyone could be. And yet, I know that some of my former students already have, and some of my current students surely will accept such positions. They will also marry, have families, and raise wonderful children who won't believe their parents could ever do such things. Surely there is an urgent need to figure out what it is that makes good people do such bad things, and stop it.

The leaders of corporations tell themselves that they have only one mission—to do whatever they can to further the interests of the shareholders, the owners of the company that these leaders have been hired to manage. When the leaders of corporations say these things to themselves, they are telling themselves the truth. They work within a system that asks—even requires—them to be single-minded, no matter how much they wish they could be different. As long as the system has this character, we can expect that only the single-minded will rise to the top. Only rarely will people whose intentions are to change corporate practices go far enough to implement those intentions.

Several years ago United States Catholic Bishops drafted a position paper, a pastoral letter, on the economy. In it they said, "every perspective on economic life that is human, moral, and Christian must be shaped by two questions: What does the economy do *for* people? What does the economy do *to* people?" I have been suggesting that our economy does terrible things *to* people, even to those people who succeed. It makes them into people that they should not and do not want to be, and it encourages them to do things that they should not and do not want to do. No matter what an economy does *for* these people, it cannot be justified if it does these things *to* them. And it seems to me that in the face of massive, antisocial practices like these, blaming the underclass for teaching mainstream America the lessons of incivility is perverse.

POSTSCRIPT

Is the Underclass the Major Threat to American Ideals?

In *Reducing Poverty in America* edited by Michael R. Darby (Sage Publications, 1996), James Q. Wilson summarizes the debate on the causes of poverty as the clash between two views: "The first is incentives or objective factors: jobs, incomes, opportunities. The second is culture: single-parent families, out-of-wedlock births, and a decaying work ethic." Sociologists expect the structural versus individual explanations of poverty to be debated for a long time because both can be seen as at least partially true. The cultural explanation derives from the anthropological studies of Oscar Lewis and was proposed as a major cause of urban poverty in America by Edward Banfield in *The Unheavenly City* (Little, Brown, 1970). More recent proponents of the culture-of-poverty thesis today are Lawrence E. Harrison, who wrote *Who Prospers? How Cultural Values Shape Economic and Political Success* (Basic Books, 1992); and Theodore Dalrymple, *Life at the Bottom: The Worldview that Makes the Underclass* (Ivan R. Dee, 2001). In *The Dream and the Nightmare: The Sixties' Legacy to the Underclass* (William Morrow, 1993), Myron Magnet blames the culture of the underclass for their poverty, but he also blames the upper classes for contributing greatly to the underclass's culture.

The counter to the cultural explanation of poverty is the structural explanation. Its most current version focuses on the loss of unskilled jobs. This is the thrust of William Julius Wilson's analysis of the macroeconomic forces that impact so heavily on the urban poor in *The Truly Disadvantaged* (University of Chicago Press, 1987) and in *When Work Disappears: The World of the New Urban Poor* (Alfred A. Knopf, 1996). If Jeremy Rifkin's analysis in *The End of Work: The Decline of the Global Labor Force and the Dawn of the Post-Market Era* (Putnam, 1995) is correct, then this situation will get worse. A recent treatment of structural factors is Garth L. Mangum, *The Persistence of Poverty in the United States* (Johns Hopkins University Press, 2003).

As the Schwartz reading above points out, capitalism and its culture have serious negative social consequences for America. This position is supported by Joel Bakan, *The Corporation: The Pathological Pursuit of Profit and Power* (Free Press, 2004); and Guy B. Adams, *Unmasking Administrative Evil* (M.E. Sharpe, 2004).

ISSUE 9

Has Affirmative Action Outlived Its Usefulness?

YES: Curtis Crawford, from "Racial Preference Versus Nondiscrimination," *Society* (March/April 2004)

NO: Lawrence D. Bobo, from "Inequalities that Endure?" in Maria Krysan and Amanda E. Lewis, eds., *The Changing Terrain of Race and Ethnicity* (Russell Sage Foundation, 2004)

ISSUE SUMMARY

YES: Curtis Crawford, editor of the Web site http://www.DebatingRacialPreferences.org, explores all possible options for bettering the situation of disadvantaged minorities in a truly just manner. He argues that the right of everyone, including white males, to nondiscrimination is clearly superior to the right of minorities to affirmative action.

NO: Sociologist Lawrence D. Bobo demonstrates that racial prejudice still exists even though it has become a more subtle type of racism, which he calls laissez-faire racism. Though it is harder to identify, it has significant effects that Bobo illustrates. In fact, it plays a big role in current politics.

In America, equality is a principle as basic as liberty. "All men are created equal" is perhaps the most well known phrase in the Declaration of Independence. More than half a century after the signing of the Declaration, the French social philosopher Alexis de Tocqueville examined democracy in America and concluded that its most essential ingredient was the equality of condition. Today we know that the "equality of condition" that Tocqueville perceived did not exist for women, blacks, Native Americans, and other racial minorities, nor for other disadvantaged social classes. Nevertheless, the ideal persisted.

When slavery was abolished after the Civil War, the Constitution's newly ratified Fourteenth Amendment proclaimed, "No State shall . . . deny to any person within its jurisdiction the equal protection of the laws." Equality has been a long time coming. For nearly a century after the abolition of slavery, American blacks were denied equal protection by law in some states and by social practice nearly everywhere. One-third of the states either permitted or forced schools to become racially segregated, and segregation was achieved elsewhere through housing policy and social behavior. In 1954 the Supreme Court reversed a 58-year-old standard that had found "separate but equal" schools compatible with equal protection of the law. A unanimous decision in *Brown v. Board of Education* held that separate is *not* equal for the members of the discriminated-against group when the segregation "generates a feeling of inferiority as to their status in the community that may affect their hearts and minds in a way unlikely ever to be undone." The 1954 ruling on public elementary education has been extended to other areas of both governmental and private conduct, including housing and employment.

Even if judicial decisions and congressional statutes could end all segregationand racial discrimination, would this achieve equality—or simply per-petuate-the status quo? Consider that the unemployment rate for blacks today is much higher than that of whites. Disproportionately higher numbers of blacks experience poverty, brutality, broken homes, physical and mental illness, and early deaths, while disproportionately lower numbers of them reach positions of affluence and prestige. It seems possible that much of this inequality has resulted from 300 years of slavery and segregation. Is termination of this ill treatment enough to end the injustices? No, say the proponents of affirmative action.

Affirmative action—the effort to improve the educational and employment opportunities for minorities—has had an uneven history in U.S. federal courts. In *Regents of the University of California v. Allan Bakke* (1978), which marked the first time the Supreme Court dealt directly with the merits of affirmative action, a 5–4 majority ruled that a white applicant to a medical school had been wrongly excluded in favor of a less qualified black applicant due to the school's affirma-tive action policy. Yet the majority also agreed that "race-conscious" policies may be used in admitting candidates—as long as they do not amount to fixed quotas. The ambivalence of *Bakke* has run through the Court's treatment of the issue since 1978. In 2003 the Supreme Court found the University of Michigan's admissions policy discriminatory but the University of Michigan Law School's admissions policy nondiscriminatory. As a result, race can still be used as one fac-tor among many to create a diverse student body, but the weight of that factor must be far less than some universities had been using.

In the following selections, Curtis Crawford and Lawrence D. Bobo debate the merits of affirmative action. Crawford carefully lays out the options and arguments and balances the various rights and values involved. In the end, he argues, we must hold fast to the principle that the right to not be discriminated against supercedes all other values in this case and will produce the best results. Bobo counters that discrimination against minorities still exists, and affirmative actions—if not egregious—are still needed to bring about greater justice in society.

Curtis Crawford  **YES**

Racial Preference versus Nondiscrimination

After a 25-year silence on the subject, the Supreme Court has pronounced on the constitutionality of race-based affirmative action in university admissions. Those who had hoped that the issues would be wisely clarified and weighed must have been greatly disappointed. The two cases accepted for review, *Grutter v. Bollinger* and *Gratz v. Bollinger,* provided valuable information on how universities actually implement preferential admissions. . . .

The litigation of these two cases revealed large racial inequalities in the treatment of applicants with similar academic credentials. For example, at the trial in federal district court, the Michigan Law School admission grid for 1995 (the year Ms. Grutter was rejected) was offered in evidence. For all applicants, identified by race but not by name, the grid included data on their Undergraduate Grade Point Average (UGPA), Law School Aptitude Test score (LSAT), and admission or rejection. Each cell of the grid combined a small range of grades and scores. . . .

The size of the preference is indicated by the gap between the rates of admission for Favored Minorities and for Other Applicants. In the cell containing the median grade and score for all applicants (UGPA 3.25–3.49, LSAT 161–163), all Favored Minorities were admitted but only 5% of Other Applicants. . . . Down at the 30th percentile (applicants with grades and scores below 70% of their rivals), 83% of Favored Minorities but just 1% of Other Applicants gained admission. . . . In sum, Favored Minorities in the 10th percentile cell had a slightly better chance of admission than Other Applicants in the median cell, while Favored Minorities in the median cell had a slightly better chance than Other Applicants in the top cell. . . .

Racial affirmative action began almost forty years ago with efforts to make sure that people were not being treated unequally because of their race. It soon developed into programs conferring special treatment based on race, especially in higher education and employment. Decisions typically affected have been admission to college and graduate school; and hiring, promotion and training for private and government jobs. The groups now regularly designated for favorable treatment based on race or ethnicity are blacks, Latinos and Native Americans. Asians sometimes receive it; whites, almost never. The advantage is usually conferred by applying a double standard, whereby the requirements for selection are less exacting for members of the favored group.

These programs have been upheld as a remedy for past injustice, yet condemned as an instrument of present injustice. They have been praised for increasing minority access to business and professional careers, and blamed for debasing standards in the process. They are supposed by some to have raised and by others to have undermined the self-esteem of their recipients and the value placed on them by others. The controversy is fierce, partly because people on both sides believe that their position is what justice requires. But contrary views cannot both be right. We must dig deeper than usually occurs in public discussion to uncover and disentangle the relevant standards for moral judgment.

Unequal Treatment in General

At the outset, we need to distinguish between unequal treatment in general, and unequal treatment based on race. The latter may or may not be a special case, with special rules. Unequal treatment is simply treatment that favors one person over another. People are treated unequally for so many reasons, in so many contexts, that the existence of a general moral rule may seem impossible. But I suggest that we have such a rule. Ask yourself if and when you think that treating people unequally is the right thing to do. Is it all right when there is no reason for it? That would be arbitrary. Is it morally permissible if there is a good reason? For example, is it permissible to favor one applicant over another if they differ in ability, character, training, experience, and the like? Of course. Concerning something as important as the opportunity for education or employment, should people ever be treated unequally without good reason? No. But if there is a good reason, is it morally permissible to treat them unequally? It is not only permissible, it may be required.

What if the individual difference on which special treatment is based has nothing to do with an applicant's ability or need? Suppose that a public university gives an admissions preference to in-state residents, or a scholarship preference for veterans. Does the rule still hold, that unequal treatment is morally permissible when it is reasonable? The reasons commonly offered are, in the first case, that a state university is financed by, and owes a primary educational responsibility to, the residents of the state; in the second case, that such scholarships are both reward and incentive for service in the armed forces. The reasons seem good to me, and my sense of right and wrong does not bar the unequal treatment in either example. Others may think the reasons poor and the treatment wrong. In either view, whether unequal treatment is permissible depends on whether there is a good reason for it.

Preferential admission to a private university for the children of alumni is supposed to strengthen the school's relationship with its former students, thereby solidifying their continued interest and financial support, without which the quality and even the survival of the school might be jeopardized.

Whether these are good reasons is disputed, but again the point is that, if one thinks the reasons good, one does not consider the preference immoral.

Supporters of racial preference think that the reasons for it are good: better, indeed, than for many kinds of preference that are generally accepted. Hence they conclude that there is nothing morally wrong with the unequal treatment they advocate. This conclusion is valid, if the rule for unequal treatment based on race is the same as the rule for unequal treatment in general. But are the rules the same?

Does the rule, that unequal treatment is morally permissible when there is good reason, still hold when it is based on race? During the campaign to overthrow American discrimination against blacks and others, it was never suggested that if the discriminators had good reason, their actions would be morally acceptable. The legislatures, schools, professions, businesses and unions that practiced racial discrimination were not asked about their reasons; they were simply told to quit. Any claims that their policies were "reasonable means to legitimate ends" were rejected as rationalizations for racial injustice. The overriding conviction was that racial discrimination was morally out of bounds, no matter what reasons the discriminators might offer.

Based on this moral principle, laws were enacted between 1940 and 1970 at the local, state and national levels, barring unequal treatment in voting, housing, health care, public accommodations, public facilities, education and employment. These statutes established the right not to be discriminated against, and the corresponding duty not to discriminate, on account of "race, color or national origin." Rights are not absolute: they may be overridden by superior rights or by public necessity. But when unequal treatment on a particular basis is barred *as a matter of right*, people are not free to discriminate on that basis simply because they have good reasons. The right not to be racially discriminated against was not reserved for members of particular groups, but ascribed equally to every person in the United States.

Was the moral principle behind this legislation mistaken? For blacks it can be seen as a two-edged sword, banning adverse discrimination to be sure, but also prohibiting any discrimination in their favor. The antidiscrimination statutes left blacks with two important disadvantages. They were still held back by deficiencies in ability, training and motivation attributable at least in part to past discrimination; and they faced the prospect that discrimination against them in the future, though illegal, would often occur. No one doubts that the social and economic condition of American blacks would be better, absent their history of racial oppression. A plausible remedy would be racial preference, until both the effects of past, and the practice of current, anti-black discrimination had dissipated. But such a remedy would require important exceptions to the general ban on racial discrimination.

Any society that decides to end an era of discrimination faces the same moral dilemma. If everyone is granted the right not to be discriminated against on account of race, the possibility of helping the victims of past discrimination through racial preference is lost. If members of the previously excluded groups are favored on the basis of race, the right of others not to suffer racial discrimination is denied.

There is a way to slice through the dilemma, which would assist many disadvantaged individuals. Instead of racial preference, a program could assist those who had suffered specific, oppressive treatment, such as chronic and substantial racial discrimination. Any person, regardless of race, who could demonstrate such treatment in his own case would be eligible for the assistance. Such a program would satisfy the racial nondiscrimination rule, since the basis for assistance would be individual injury, not racial identity. But it would help only a fraction of those who currently benefit from race-based affirmative action.

Are there superior rights or public necessities that might override the right to racial nondiscrimination? The right to racial nondiscrimination, though momentous, is not the only care of the republic. Other (sometimes conflicting) rights and interests must also be protected. The moral dilemma of racial preference for some *versus* racial nondiscrimination for all might be avoided if, in certain circumstances, the right to racial nondiscrimination were superseded by a higher right or by public necessity.

Equity and Compensation

Some argue that there is a right to equal participation for racial groups, which overrides the individual right to nondiscrimination. According to this view, 'equal participation' means equal success in wealth, status, and achievement, not for every individual, but for the average person in each group, as compared with the average American. A belief in this right is often the moral basis for affirmative-action goals, adopted for the purpose of increasing the percentage of "underrepresented" minorities in the higher echelons of education and employment, to match their share of the general population. If such a right exists, it would conflict with the right to nondiscrimination, and might overrule it. . . .

If individuals who have been subjected to racial discrimination can be given compensatory help without running afoul of the nondiscrimination rule, why not an entire racial group? Could we thus escape from our moral dilemma? Is it possible that all we need is a finding by the national legislature that discrimination against certain racial groups has been and continues to be so pervasive that every member of the group is entitled to compensatory preference? Many proponents of affirmative action proceed as if such a finding had occurred, in their own minds if not in the legislative process. This helps them to think of racial preference as compensation, rather than discrimination.

A legislative finding of this sort, though based on evidence of injury to some, would be mere supposition concerning others. But the right of just compensation requires proof of specific injury to the person who invokes it. A legislative decision to compensate an entire racial group could not meet this criterion; it would be discrimination masquerading as compensation. Moreover, a legislature permitted to stereotype racial groups sympathetically would be free to do the contrary. Based on data that discrimination against Blacks is much more frequent than against whites, it would declare every black a victim. Based on statistics that crime by Blacks is much more frequent than by Whites, it could declare every Black a criminal. . . .

A Public Necessity to Achieve Diversity?

Some, giving a broader definition to public necessity, uphold two propositions, (a) that racial diversity in education and employment is a public necessity, and (b) that racial preference is essential to achieve such diversity. If by "diversity" they simply mean difference or variety, proposition (a) may be true, but proposition (b) is manifestly untrue. In a society composed of many different groups, all one needs in order to ensure racial and ethnic variety in colleges and workplaces is not to discriminate. But among supporters of race-based affirmative action, "diversity" often means having a larger number from "underrepresented groups" than would occur without racial preference. Using this definition, proposition (b) is true, but proposition (a) is false. There is no public necessity that racial groups be represented in education or employment in proportions higher than warranted by the fitness of their members, individually and impartially assessed.

A Need to Reduce Bias against Minorities?

Some argue that racial preference helps to prevent racial discrimination. They believe that unlawful discrimination against nonwhites in education and employment is common, since those in power are mostly white; they argue that when decision-makers have to meet goals for increasing minority participation, antiminority discrimination is effectively prevented. Racial goals and quotas are therefore imposed, by institutions over their officials or by courts over institutions, to ensure that people who might discriminate will not do so.

Paradoxically, this policy prevents violations of the right to racial nondiscrimination by making certain that they occur. . . .

The Right to Racial Nondiscrimination

We have found that, if we recognize a general moral right to racial nondiscrimination, racial preference cannot be justified as serving a superior right or a public necessity. The supposed rights and necessities either do not exist, or do not conflict with the right to nondiscrimination. Is there another approach that might clear the way for racial preference?

The moral right to racial nondiscrimination could be expunged or limited. One could (1) scrap the right altogether, (2) define the right more narrowly, (3) exempt education and employment from the nondiscrimination rule, (4) permit discrimination favorable to blacks, or (5) permit discrimination favorable to all "underrepresented" minorities. Should the United States have chosen (or now choose) one of these options?

1. Scrap the Right Entirely?

This option would require us to repeal our antidiscrimination laws and to reject the moral principle on which they are based. No one advocates this. . . .

Wherever practiced, racial discrimination generates racial oppression, hostility and violence. Nondiscrimination is not easy, but it is the only standard to which members of every racial and ethnic group might agree, since it is the only standard that places no one at a disadvantage because of his group membership. . . .

2. Redefine Wrongful Discrimination?

Instead of forbidding all unequal treatment based on race, we might bar such treatment only when it is motivated by racial prejudice or hostility. This would clear the way for "benign" discrimination in behalf of a previously excluded group, without sacrificing anyone's right to be free from "malign" discrimination.

A principal disadvantage to this approach is the extensive harm that it would legalize. A major reason for antidiscrimination laws is to protect people from being deprived of products, services, and opportunities by discriminatory acts. But this deprivation is just as great, whether the discrimination is motivated by prejudice or not. Discrimination is not benign to the person it injures. . . .

3. Exempt Education and Employment?

No one contends that racial discrimination should be outlawed in every kind of decision; to bar it in choosing a friend, a spouse, or a legislative representative would be invasive or unenforceable. Why not, then, withdraw the prohibition from the two areas in which preferential treatment might be most helpful for members of a previously excluded group, by bringing them more quickly into prestigious occupations and encouraging their fellows to aim higher and work harder?

A decision to exempt education and employment from the ban on discrimination would place both society and government in moral contradiction with themselves. The society, having decided that racial discrimination in general is wrong, would nevertheless be treating it in crucial areas as beneficial. The government, in its roles as educator and employer, would freely practice here that which elsewhere it must prosecute and punish. Such broad contradictions are fatal to the public consensus that racial discrimination is ordinarily unjust, a consensus that is necessary for general adherence to antidiscrimination laws. . . .

4. Favor Blacks Only?

This would respond forthrightly to the moral dilemma posed early in this essay, by making Blacks an exception to the nondiscrimination rule. The exception could apply to all areas of life that are covered by the rule, including housing, business, finance, voter registration, shopping, entertainment, criminal and civil justice, *etc.*, as well as education, employment, and government contracting. But an exception this large, which could easily sink the rule, has no champions. What is proposed instead is to limit the exception primarily to employment and higher education.

The exception faces two ways: Blacks would gain the privilege of favorable discrimination, by themselves or in their behalf; while all others would lose the right not to racially discriminated against when blacks are the beneficiaries.

A major argument against this option is the absence of a principled basis for making blacks the only beneficiaries of racial discrimination. If, when the nation decided to ban racial discrimination, blacks were the only group to have suffered it in the past, a basis for this exception would be clear. But Blacks were not alone. American Indians; Mexicans, Puerto Ricans, and other Latinos; Japanese, Chinese, and other Asians; Poles, Italians, Slavs, Arabs, Jews, and other whites could all point to group wounds from past discrimination. . . .

5. Favor "Underrepresented" Minorities?

It may be argued that this, in effect, is the option we have chosen, not by amending the nondiscrimination statutes, but by creating affirmative-action programs. Under them, Blacks, Latinos, and Native Americans receive racial preference and are supposedly not discriminated against; whites do not receive preference and are often discriminated against; Asians are sometimes the beneficiaries, sometimes the victims. That many whites and Asians have lost their right to racial nondiscrimination in these areas is not made explicit. But it is surely implied, by the view that racial preference at their expense is morally permissible when serving a good purpose, and by the argument that they have no more reason to complain when disadvantaged by racial preference, than if the preference had been based on place of residence or family connections. . . .

Supporters of racial preference for black, Hispanic and Native Americans in education and employment typically invoke principles of racial justice, such as the right to compensation for past injury and/or a right to equal racial success. We have argued above that the latter right does not exist and the former right, properly applied, does not require special treatment based on race. We have argued also that the plea of public necessity is unfounded. . . .

Our inquiry began with a moral dilemma. If all have the right not to be subject to racial discrimination, no one may be assisted via racial preference; if racial preference is authorized for some, the right not to suffer racial discrimination is thereby denied to others. Two ways out of the dilemma were examined.

May the right to racial nondiscrimination, especially in education and employment, though belonging to everyone, be overridden by certain higher rights or public necessities? By a right to equal success for racial groups, or to just compensation for past discrimination? Or by a public necessity for racial preference as a means to racial peace, to racial diversity, or to the prevention of discrimination? These supposed rights and necessities were found to be either non-existent, or not in conflict with the right to racial nondiscrimination, and therefore incapable of overriding it.

Should we rescind or limit the right to racial nondiscrimination, in order to make racial preference available? Five options were considered. The nondiscrimination rule could be scrapped altogether, redefined to cover only prejudiced or hostile acts, dropped from education and employment, or modified in these areas to allow preference for blacks only or for all "underrepresented" minorities. The arguments against these limits were in every case preponderant.

We cannot have the individual and social benefits of the nondiscrimination rule if we decline to obey it. We cannot teach our children that racial discrimination is wrong if we persistently discriminate. We cannot preserve the right to nondiscrimination by systematically violating it. But, without breaking or bending the rule, we can respond to many people who need and deserve help. The racial nondiscrimination rule does not preclude compensation for specific injury. It does not bar special assistance, by the public or private sector, to persons who labor under social, cultural, or economic disadvantages, provided that the purpose of the help and the criteria for eligibility are colorblind.

Besides excluding racial preference, there are other important respects in which a desirable assistance program would not imitate current affirmative action. It would help people increase their ability to meet regular standards, instead of lowering standards to accommodate inferior ability. The role of government would be primarily determined by the legislative branch, not the bureaucracy or the judiciary. The participation of the private sector would be voluntary or contractual, not compulsory. The rules and operation of the program would be honestly described and freely accessible to public scrutiny. These guidelines are not mandates of the nondiscrimination rule, just counsels of good sense. They will be easier to meet in a racial policy that we really believe is right.

NO

Lawrence D. Bobo

Inequities That Endure?
Racial Ideology, American Politics,
and the Peculiar Role
of the Social Sciences

As part of research on the intersection of poverty, crime, and race, I conducted two focus groups in a major eastern city in early September 2001, just prior to the tragic events of September 11. The dynamics of the two groups, one with nine white participants and another with nine black participants, drove home for me very powerfully just how deep but also just how sophisticated, elusive, and enduring a race problem the United States still confronts. An example from each group begins to make the point that the very nature of this problem and our vocabularies for discussing it have grown very slippery, very difficult to grasp, and therefore extremely difficult to name and to fight.

First let's consider the white focus group. In response to the moderator's early question, "What's the biggest problem facing your community?" a young working-class white male eagerly and immediately chimed in, "Section 8 housing." "It's a terrible system," he said. The racial implications hung heavy in the room until a middle-aged white bartender tried to leaven things a bit by saying:

> All right. If you have people of a very low economic group who have a low standard of living who cannot properly feed and clothe their children, whose speech patterns are not as good as ours [and] are [therefore] looked down upon as a low class. Where I live most of those people happen to be black. So it's generally perceived that blacks are inferior to whites for that reason.

The bartender went on to explain: "It's not that way at all. It's a class issue, which in many ways is economically driven. From my perspective, it's not a racial issue at all. I'm a bartender. I'll serve anybody if they're a class

[act]." At this, the group erupted in laughter, but the young working-class male was not finished. He asserted, a bit more vigorously:

> Why should somebody get to live in my neighborhood that hasn't earned that right? I'd like to live [in a more affluent area], but I can't afford to live there so I don't. . . . So why should somebody get put in there by the government that didn't earn that right?

And then the underlying hostility and stereotyping came out more directly when he said: "And most of the people on that program are trashy, and they don't know how to behave in a working neighborhood. It's not fair. I call it unfair housing laws."

Toward the end of the session, when discussing why the jails are so disproportionately filled with blacks and Hispanics, this same young man said: "Blacks and Hispanics are more violent than white people. I think they are more likely to shoot somebody over a fender bender than a couple of white guys are. They have shorter fuses, and they are more emotional than white people."

In fairness, some members of the white group criticized antiblack prejudice. Some members of the group tried to point out misdeeds done by whites as well. But even the most liberal of the white participants never pushed the point, rarely moved beyond abstract observations or declarations against prejudice, and sometimes validated the racial stereotypes more overtly embraced by others. In an era when everyone supposedly knows what to say and what not to say and is artful about avoiding overt bigotry, this group discussion still quickly turned to racial topics and quickly elicited unabashed negative stereotyping and antiblack hostility.

When asked the same question about the "biggest problem facing your community," the black group almost in unison said, "Crime and drugs," and a few voices chimed in, "Racism." One middle-aged black woman reported: "I was thinking more so on the lines of myself because my house was burglarized three times. Twice while I was at work and one time when I returned from church, I caught the person in there."

The racial thread to her story became clearer when she later explained exactly what happened in terms of general police behavior in her community:

> The first two robberies that I had, the elderly couple that lived next door to me, they called the police. I was at work when the first two robberies occurred. They called the police two or three times. The police never even showed up. When I came in from work, I had to go . . . file a police report. My neighbors went with me, and they had called the police several times and they never came. Now, on that Sunday when I returned from church and caught him in my house, and the guy that I caught in my house lives around the corner, he has a case history, he has been in trouble since doomsday. When I told [the police] I had knocked him unconscious, oh yeah, they were there in a hurry. Guns drawn. And I didn't have a weapon except for the baseball bat, [and] I wound up face down on my living room floor, and they placed handcuffs on me.

The moderator, incredulous, asked: "Well, excuse me, but they locked you and him up?" "They locked me up and took him to the hospital."

Indeed, the situation was so dire, the woman explained, that had a black police officer who lived in the neighborhood not shown up to help after the patrol car arrived with sirens blaring, she felt certain the two white police officers who arrived, guns drawn, would probably have shot her. As it was, she was arrested for assault, spent two days in jail, and now has a lawsuit pending against the city. Somehow I doubt that a single, middle-aged, churchgoing white woman in an all-white neighborhood who had called the police to report that she apprehended a burglar in her home would end up handcuffed, arrested, and in jail alongside the burglar. At least, I am not uncomfortable assuming that the police would not have entered a home in a white community with the same degree of apprehension, fear, preparedness for violence, and ultimate disregard for a law-abiding citizen as they did in this case. But it can happen in black communities in America today.

To say that the problem of race endures, however, is not to say that it remains fundamentally the same and essentially unchanged. I share the view articulated by historians such as Barbara Fields and Thomas Holt that race is both socially constructed and historically contingent. As such, it is not enough to declare that race matters or that racism endures. *The much more demanding challenge is to account for how and why such a social construction comes to be reconstituted, refreshed, and enacted anew in very different times and places.* How is it that in 2001 we can find a working-class white man who is convinced that many blacks are "trashy people" controlled by emotions and clearly more susceptible to violence? How is it that a black woman defending herself and her home against a burglar ends up apprehended as if she were one of the "usual suspects"? Or cast more broadly, how do we have a milestone like the *Brown* decision and pass a Civil Rights Act, a Voting Rights Act, a Fair Housing Act, and numerous acts of enforcement and amendments to all of these, including the pursuit of affirmative action policies, and yet still continue to face a significant racial divide in America?

The answer I sketch here is but a partial one, focusing on three key observations. First, as I have argued elsewhere and elaborate in important ways here, I believe that we are witnessing the crystallization of a new racial ideology here in the United States. This ideology I refer to as laissez-faire racism. We once confronted a slave labor economy with its inchoate ideology of racism and then watched it evolve in response to war and other social, economic, and cultural trends into an explicit Jim Crow racism of the de jure segregation era. We have more recently seen the biological and openly segregationist thrust of twentieth-century Jim Crow racism change into the more cultural, free-market, and ostensibly color-blind thrust of laissez-faire racism in the new millennium. But make no mistake—the current social structure and attendant ideology reproduce, sustain, and rationalize enormous black-white inequality.

Second, race and racism remain powerful levers in American national politics. These levers can animate the electorate, constrain and shape political discourse and campaigns, and help direct the fate of major social policies. From the persistently contested efforts at affirmative action through a historic expansion of the penal system and the recent dismanding of "welfare as we know it," the racial divide has often decisively prefigured and channeled core features of our domestic politics.

Third, social science has played a peculiar role in the problem of race. And here I wish to identify an intellectual and scholarly failure to come to grips with the interrelated phenomena of white privilege and black agency. This failure may present itself differently depending on the ideological leanings of scholars. I critique one line of analysis on the left and one on the right. On the left, the problem typically presents as a failure of sociological imagination. It manifests itself in arguments that seek to reduce racialized social dynamics to some ontologically more fundamental nonracialized factor. On the right, the problem is typically the failure of explicit victim-blaming. It manifests itself in a rejection of social structural roots or causation of racialized social conditions. I want to suggest that both tactics—the left's search for some structural force more basic than race (such as class or skill levels or child-rearing practices) and the right's search for completely volitional factors (cultural or individual dispositions) as final causes of "race" differences—reflect a deep misunderstanding of the dynamics of race and racism. Race is not just a set of categories, and racism is not just a collection of individual-level anti-minority group attitudes. Race and racism are more fundamentally about sets of intertwined power relations, group interests and identities, and the ideas that justify and make sense out of (or challenge and delegitimate) the organized racial ordering of society. The latter analytic posture and theory of race in society is embodied in the theory of laissez-faire racism.

On Laissez-Faire Racism

There are those who doubt that we should be talking about racism at all. The journalist Jim Sleeper denounces continued talk of racism and racial bias as mainly so much polarizing "liberal racism." The political scientists Paul Sniderman and Edward Carmines write of the small and diminishing effects of racism in white public opinion and call for us to "reach beyond race." And the linguist John McWhorter writes of a terrible "culture of victimology" that afflicts the nation and ultimately works as a form of self-sabotage among black Americans. Even less overtly ideological writers talk of the growing victory of our Myrdalian "American Creed" over the legacy of racism. Some prominent black intellectuals, such as the legal scholar Randall Kennedy, while not as insensitive to the evidence of real and persistent inequality and discrimination, raise profound questions about race-based claims on the polity.

These analysts, I believe, are wrong. They advance a mistaken and counterproductive analysis of where we are today, how we got here, and the paths that we as a nation might best follow in the future. In many respects, these analysts are so patently wrong that it is easy to dismiss them.

Let's be clear first on what I mean by "racism." Attempts at definition abound in the scholarly literature. William Julius Wilson offers a particularly cogent specification when he argues that racism is an "an ideology of racial domination or exploitation that (1) incorporates belief in a particular race's cultural and/or inherent biological inferiority and (2) uses such beliefs to justify and prescribe inferior or unequal treatment for that group." I show here that there remains a profound tendency in the United States to blame racial inequality on the group culture and active choices of African Americans. This is abundantly clear in public opinion data, and it is exemplified by more than a few intellectual tracts, including McWhorter's *Losing the Race.* Closely attendant to this pattern is the profound tendency to downplay, ignore, or minimize the contemporary potency of racial discrimination. Again, this tendency is clear in public opinion and finds expression in the scholarly realm in the Thernstroms' book *America in Black and White.* These building blocks become part of the foundation for rejecting social policy that is race-targeted and aims to reduce or eliminate racial inequality. In effect, these attitudes facilitate and rationalize continued African American disadvantage and subordinated status. Our current circumstances, then, both as social structure and ideology, warrant description and analysis as a racist regime. Yet it is a different, less rigid, more delimited, and more permeable regime as well.

Laissez-faire racism involves persistent negative stereotyping of African Americans, a tendency to blame blacks themselves for the black-white gap in socioeconomic status, and resistance to meaningful policy efforts to ameliorate U.S. racist social conditions and institutions. It represents a critical new stage in American racism. As structures of racial oppression became less formal, as the power resources available to black communities grew and were effectively deployed, as other cultural trends paved the way for an assault on notions of biologically ranked "races," the stage was set for displacing Jim Crow racism and erecting something different in its place.

I have taken up a more complete development of the historical argument and the contemporary structural argument elsewhere. What is worth emphasizing here is, first, the explicit social groundedness and historical foundation of our theoretical logic—something that sets this theory of racial attitudes apart from notions like symbolic racism. Although not directly inspired by his work, our theoretical logic is a direct reflection of ideas articulated by the historian Thomas Holt. As he explains: "Racial phenomena and their meaning do change with time, with history, and with the conceptual and institutional spaces that history unfolds. More specifically they are responsive to major shifts in a political economy and to the cultural systems allied with that political economy."

The second point to emphasize here is that this is an argument about general patterns of group relations and ideology—not merely about variation in views among individuals from a single racial or ethnic category. As such, our primary concern is with the central tendency of attitudes and beliefs within and between racial groups and the social system as such, not within and between individuals. It is the collective dimensions of social experience that I most intend to convey with the notion of laissez-faire racism—not a singular attitude held to a greater or lesser degree by particular individuals. The intellectual case for such a perspective has been most forcefully articulated by the sociologist Mary R. Jackman. We should focus an analysis of attitudes and ideology on group-level comparisons, she writes, because doing so

> draws attention to the structural conditions that encase an intergroup relationship and it underscores the point that individual actors are not free agents but caught in an aggregate relationship. Unless we assume that the individual is socially atomized, her personal experiences constitute only one source of information that is evaluated against the backdrop of her manifold observations of the aggregated experiences (both historical and contemporaneous) of the group as a whole.

The focus is thus more on the larger and enduring patterns and tendencies that distinguish groups than on the individual sources of variation.

With this in mind, I want to focus on three pieces of data, the first of which concerns the persistence of negative stereotypes of African Americans [in a survey he conducted]. . . . Several patterns stand out. It is easier for both blacks and whites to endorse the positive traits when expressing views about the characteristics of blacks than the negative traits. However, African Americans are always more favorable and less negative in their views than whites. Some of the differences are quite large. For instance, there is a thirty-percentage-point difference between white and black perceptions on the trait of intelligence and a thirty-three-percentage-point difference on the "hardworking" trait. . . .

Negative stereotypes of African Americans are common, though not uniform, and to a distressing degree they exist among both blacks and whites and presumably influence perceptions and behaviors for both groups. However, there is a sharp difference in central tendency within each group, in predictable directions. One cannot escape the conclusion that most whites have different and decidedly lesser views of the basic behavioral characteristics of blacks than do blacks themselves. And that generally these patterns indicate that African Americans remain a culturally dishonored and debased group in the American psyche. . . .

On American Politics

As a historic fact and experience as well as a contemporary political condition, racial prejudice has profoundly affected American politics. A wide body of evidence is accumulating to show that racial prejudice still affects politics. Black candidates for office typically encounter severe degree of difficulties securing white votes, partly owing to racial prejudice. There is some evidence, to be sure, that the potency of racial prejudice varies with the racial composition of electoral districts and the salience of race issues in the immediate political context.

Moreover, political candidates can use covert racial appeals to mobilize a segment of the white voting public under some circumstances. For example, the deployment of the infamous Willie Horton political ad during the 1988 presidential campaign heightened the voting public's concern over race issues. It also accentuated the impact of racial prejudice on electoral choices and did so in a way that did not increase concern with crime per se. That is, what appears to give a figure like Willie Horton such efficacy as a political symbol is not his violent criminal behavior per se, but rather his being a violent black man whose actions upset a racial order that should privilege and protect whites.

Major social policy decisions may also be driven by substantially racial considerations. The political psychologists David Sears and Jack Citrin make a strong case that antiblack prejudice proved to be a powerful source of voting in favor of California's historic property tax reduction initiative (Proposition 13), a change in law that fundamentally altered the resources available to government agencies.

On an even larger stage, the very design and early implementation of core features of the American welfare state were heavily shaped by racial considerations. Robert Lieberman has shown that the programs that became Social Security, Aid to Families with Dependent Children (AFDC), and unemployment insurance were initially designed to either exclude the great bulk of the black population or leave the judgment of qualification and delivery of benefits to local officials. The latter design feature of AFDC (originally ADC) had the effect in most southern states of drastically curtailing the share of social provision that went to African Americans. . . .

There are good reasons to believe that the push to "end welfare as we know it"—which began as a liberal reform effort but was hijacked by the political right and became, literally, the end of welfare as we had known it—was just as surely impelled by heavily racial considerations. The political sociologist Martin Gilens (1999) has carefully analyzed white opinion on the welfare state in the United States. Some features of the welfare state, he finds, lack an overtone of black dependency (such as Social Security) and enjoy high consensus support. Other programs (AFDC, food stamps, general relief) are heavily racialized, with much of the white voting public regarding these programs as helping lazy and undeserving blacks.

Indeed, the fundamental alignment of the U.S. national political panics has been centrally driven by a racial dynamic. Over the past thirty-five years we have witnessed a fundamental transformation in the Democratic and Republican party system, a transformation that political scientists call realignment. The more the Democratic Party was seen as advancing a civil rights agenda and black interests—in a manner that clearly set them apart from the Republican Party—the more race issues and race itself became central to party affiliations, political thinking, and voting in the mass white public. What was once a solid white Democrat-controlled South has thus shifted to a substantially white Republican-controlled South.

The end result of all of these patterns, simply put, is that African Americans do not enjoy a full range of voice, representation, and participation in politics. Black candidates, particularly if they are identified with the black community, are unlikely to be viable in majority white electoral districts. Even white candidates who come to be strongly associated with black interests run the risk of losing many white voters. As a consequence, party leaders on both sides have worked to organize the agenda and claims of African Americans out of national politics. In particular, the national Democratic Party, which should arguably reward its most loyal constituents in the black community, instead has often led the way in pushing black issues off the stage. As the political scientist Paul Frymer has explained, party leaders do so because they are at risk of losing coveted white "swing voters" in national elections if they come to be perceived as catering to black interests. Thus is the elite discourse around many domestic social policies, and their ultimate fate, bound up in racial considerations.

Against this backdrop it becomes difficult, if not counterproductive, to accept the widely shared view that American democracy is on an inexorable path toward ever-greater inclusivity and fuller realization of its democratic potential. In the context of such enduring and powerful racialization of American politics, such an assumption is naive at best.

There is an even more incisive point to be made. The presumption of ever-expanding American liberalism is mistaken. For example, the Pulitzer Prize winning–historian Joseph Ellis writes of the terrible "silence" on the subject of slavery and race that the "founding fathers" *deliberately* adopted. They waged a Revolutionary War for freedom, declared themselves the founders of a new nation, and in very nearly the same moment *knowingly* wedded democracy to slave-based racism. The philosopher Charles Mills extends the reach of this observation by showing the deep bias of Enlightenment thinkers toward a view of those on the European continent—whites—as the only real signatories to the "social contract." Others, particularly blacks, were never genuinely envisioned or embraced as fully human and thus were never intended to be covered by the reach of the social contract.

Considerations of this kind led the political theorist Rogers Smith to suggest that the United States has not one but rather multiple political traditions. One tradition is indeed more democratic, universalistic, egalitarian, and expansive. But this tradition competes with and sometimes decisively loses out to a sharply hierarchical, patriarchal, and racist civic tradition. The ultimate collapse of Reconstruction following the Civil War and the subsequent gradual development of de jure segregation and the Jim Crow racist regime provide one powerful case in point.

POSTSCRIPT

Has Affirmative Action Outlived Its Usefulness?

Crawford and Bobo approach the issue of affirmative action from different directions. Bobo starts with the end or goal of fairness to disadvantaged minorities and argues that affirmative action is a necessary means to that end. Crawford starts with the means and argues that affirmative action as morally unjustifiable. On the other hand, compensation for individuals who have been discriminated against is morally justifiable, but most of the people who benefit from affirmative action programs are not in this category. This argument would not persuade anyone who is passionate about justice for disadvantaged minorities, because our laws already allow discrimination victims to seek redress in the courts and that has not stopped or compensated for discrimination. Many believe that something more is needed, and affirmative action properly conducted is the best means.

The writings on this subject are diverse and numerous. For an in-depth discussion of the legal standing of affirmative action, see Girardeau A. Spann, *The Law of Affirmative Action: Twenty-Five Years of Supreme Court Decisions on Race and Remedies* (New York University Press, 2000). For a review of affirmative action programs, see M. Ali Raza et al., *The Ups and Downs of Affirmative Action Preferences* (Greenwood, 1999). William G. Bowen and Derek Bok review affirmative action in college admissions in *The Shape of the River: Long-Term Consequences of Considering Race in College and University Admissions* (Princeton University Press, 1998). Robert K. Fullinwider and Judith Lichtenberg provide a more recent assessment in *Leveling the Playing Field: Justice, Politics, and College Admissions* (Rowman & Littlefield, 2004) and Patricia Gurin et al. defend affirmative action at the University of Michigan in *Defending Diversity: Affirmative Action at the University of Michigan* (University of Michigan Press, 2004). For a history of affirmative action, see Philip F. Rubio, *A History of Affirmative Action* (University Press of Mississippi, 2001). The need for affirmative action or another effective means to address racial and gender inequality is provided in *Problem of the Century: Racial Stratification in the United States,* edited by Elijah Anderson and Douglas S. Massey (Russell Sage Foundation); Andrew Hacker, *Mismatch: The Growing Gulf between Women and Men* (Scribner, 2003); and David Neumark, *Sex Differences in Labor Markets* (Routledge, 2004). The debate on affirmative action is covered by Carl Cohen and James P. Sterba in *Affirmative Action and Racial Preference: A Debate* (Oxford University Press, 2003). Recently an anti-affirmative action movement has mobilized. Three works that try to counter this movement are Fred L. Pincus, *Reverse Discrimination: Dismantling the Myth* (Lynne Rienner, 2003); Faye J. Crosby, *Affirmative Action Is Dead: Long Live Affirmative Action* (Yale University

Press, 2004); and Lee Cokorinos, *The Assault on Diversity: An Organized Challenge to Racial and Gender Justice* (Rowman & Littlefield, 2003). Andrew Hacker argues that affirmative action has relatively minor adverse consequences for whites in *Two Nations: Black and White, Separate, Hostile, Unequal* (Charles Scribner's Sons, 1992). Dinesh D'Souza, in *The End of Racism* (Free Press, 1995), argues that white racism has pretty much disappeared in the United States. The opposite is argued by Joe R. Feagin and Hernan Vera in *White Racism: The Basics* (Routledge, 1995) and by Stephen Steinberg in *Turning Back* (Beacon Press, 1995). For international comparisons see Thomas Sowell, *Affirmative Action around the World: An Empirical Study* (Yale University Press, 2004).

ISSUE 10

Are Boys and Men Disadvantaged Relative to Girls and Women?

YES: Michelle Conlin, from "The New Gender Gap," *Business Week Online* (May 26, 2003)

NO: Joel Wendland, from "Reversing the 'Gender Gap'," *Political Affairs* (March 2004)

ISSUE SUMMARY

YES: Journalist Michelle Conlin reviews the many disadvantages of boys and men in school from kindergarten to grad school. Since education is the route to success, men will be less able to compete in the marketplace.

NO: Joel Wendland acknowledges the edge that females have over males today in education but argues that females are still disadvantaged in the marketplace.

America has always boasted of being the land of opportunity and there are many facts that support this claim. For centuries poor immigrants have come here and prospered or had their children prosper. Widespread public education enabled upward mobility for many in the lower classes. Merit plays a large role in hiring and pay. But America has also failed to give equal opportunity to women and selected minorities. As a result America failed to utilize all of the talent that was available to it, and therefore, developed slower than it could have. The black movement, the women's movement, the Civil Rights Act of 1964, and affirmative action policies have greatly improved the life chances of blacks and women. The changes have been great enough to lead some white males to now feel that they are being discriminated against. Of course, they focus on a single event where a women or black gets a position or a salary that they have good reasons to believe they themselves deserved. But they fail to take into account the many thousands of advantages their race and gender have given to them over their lifetime. If all those advantages were added up, they would greatly outweigh the disadvantage they experienced because of some affirmative action outcome. This issue can be brought into focus by asking "would males trade places with females and would whites trade places with blacks?"

There is one area where males have definitely lost their advantage and that is in education. This change can best be illustrated by looking at the gender distribution of college degrees over time. As recently as 1960 male college graduates outnumbered female by five to three. By 1980 they were equal and today women earn 57% of bachelor degrees. Obviously this radical a change needs to be explained. Is it because women are more intelligent and have been held back in the past by factors that have changed such as discrimination, differential treatment by teachers and parents, lower expectations, less ambition, and low career goals? Most scholars do not think that gender differences in intelligence are large enough to support this explanation. Is it because males are now being discriminated against in school? No way. Is it due to changing attitudes of both males and females toward education and careers? Perhaps. In the selection that follows Michelle Conlin provides a full explanation of this question.

The radical reversal in educational outcomes for males and females has caused some writers, such as Michelle Conlin in the first selection, to write about a new gender gap with males being disadvantaged. This implies that women's fight for equal rights has completely succeeded. In the second selection Joel Wendland argues that this is not the case. There is still the old gender gap with women disadvantaged in many ways.

Michelle Conlin  **YES**

The New Gender Gap

From kindergarten to grad school, boys are becoming the second sex.

Lawrence High is the usual fortress of manila-brick blandness and boxy 1960s architecture. At lunch, the metalheads saunter out to the smokers' park, while the AP types get pizzas at Marinara's, where they talk about—what else?—other people. The hallways are filled with lip-glossed divas in designer clothes and packs of girls in midriff-baring track tops. The guys run the gamut, too: skate punks, rich boys in Armani, and saggy-panted crews with their Eminem swaggers. In other words, they look pretty much as you'd expect.

But when the leaders of the Class of 2003 assemble in the Long Island high school's fluorescent-lit meeting rooms, most of these boys are nowhere to be seen. The senior class president? A girl. The vice-president? Girl. Head of student government? Girl. Captain of the math team, chief of the year-book, and editor of the newspaper? Girls.

It's not that the girls of the Class of 2003 aren't willing to give the guys a chance. Last year, the juniors elected a boy as class president. But after taking office, he swiftly instructed his all-female slate that they were his cabinet and that he was going to be calling all the shots. The girls looked around and realized they had the votes, says Tufts University-bound Casey Vaughn, an Intel finalist and one of the alpha femmes of the graduating class. "So they impeached him and took over."

The female lock on power at Lawrence is emblematic of a stunning gender reversal in American education. From kindergarten to graduate school, boys are fast becoming the second sex. "Girls are on a tear through the educational system," says Thomas G. Mortenson, a senior scholar at the Pell Institute for the Study of Opportunity in Higher Education in Washington. "In the past 30 years, nearly every inch of educational progress has gone to them."

Just a century ago, the president of Harvard University, Charles W. Eliot, refused to admit women because he feared they would waste the precious resources of his school. Today, across the country, it seems as if girls have built a kind of scholastic Roman Empire alongside boys' languishing Greece. Although Lawrence High has its share of boy superstars—like this year's valedictorian—the gender takeover at some schools is nearly complete. "Every time I turn around, if something good is happening, there's a female in charge," says Terrill O. Stammler, principal of Rising Sun High School in Rising Sun, Md. Boys are missing from nearly every leadership position, academic honors slot, and student-activity post at the school. Even Rising Sun's girls' sports teams do better than the boys'.

At one exclusive private day school in the Midwest, administrators have even gone so far as to mandate that all awards and student-government positions be divvied equally between the sexes. "It's not just that boys are falling behind girls," says William S. Pollock, author of *Real Boys: Rescuing Our Sons from the Myths of Boyhood* and a professor of psychiatry at Harvard Medical School. "It's that boys themselves are falling behind their own functioning and doing worse than they did before."

It may still be a man's world. But it is no longer, in any way, a boy's. From his first days in school, an average boy is already developmentally two years behind the girls in reading and writing. Yet he's often expected to learn the same things in the same way in the same amount of time. While every nerve in his body tells him to run, he has to sit still and listen for almost eight hours a day. Biologically, he needs about four recesses a day, but he's lucky if he gets one, since some lawsuit-leery schools have banned them altogether. Hug a girl, and he could be labeled a "toucher" and swiftly suspended—a result of what some say is an increasingly anti-boy culture that pathologizes their behavior.

If he falls behind, he's apt to be shipped off to special ed, where he'll find that more than 70% of his classmates are also boys. Squirm, clown, or interrupt, and he is four times as likely to be diagnosed with attention deficit hyperactivity disorder. That often leads to being forced to take Ritalin or risk being expelled, sent to special ed, or having parents accused of negligence. One study of public schools in Fairfax County, Va., found that more than 20% of upper-middle-class white boys were taking Ritalin-like drugs by fifth grade.

Once a boy makes it to freshman year of high school, he's at greater risk of falling even further behind in grades, extracurricular activities, and advanced placement. Not even science and math remain his bastions. And while the girls are busy working on sweeping the honor roll at graduation, a boy is more likely to be bulking up in the weight room to enhance his steroid-fed Adonis complex, playing Grand Theft Auto: Vice City on his PlayStation2, or downloading rapper 50 Cent on his iPod. All the while, he's 30% more likely to drop out, 85% more likely to commit murder, and four to six times more likely to kill himself, with boy suicides tripling since 1970. "We get a bad rap," says Steven Covington, a sophomore at Ottumwa High School in Ottumwa, Iowa. "Society says we can't be trusted."

As for college—well, let's just say this: At least it's easier for the guys who get there to find a date. For 350 years, men outnumbered women on college campuses. Now, in every state, every income bracket, every racial and ethnic group, and most industrialized Western nations, women reign, earning an average 57% of all BAs and 58% of all master's degrees in the U.S. alone. There are 133 girls getting BAS for every 100 guys—a number that's projected to grow to 142 women per 100 men by 2010, according to the U.S. Education Dept. If current trends continue, demographers say, there will be 156 women per 100 men earning degrees by 2020.

Overall, more boys and girls are in college than a generation ago. But when adjusted for population growth, the percentage of boys entering college, master's programs, and most doctoral programs—except for PhDs in fields like engineering and computer science—has mostly stalled out, whereas for women it has continued to rise across the board. The trend is most pronounced among Hispanics, African Americans, and those from low-income families.

The female-to-male ratio is already 60–40 at the University of North Carolina, Boston University, and New York University. To keep their gender ratios 50–50, many Ivy League and other elite schools are secretly employing a kind of stealth affirmative action for boys. "Girls present better qualifications in the application process—better grades, tougher classes, and more thought in their essays," says Michael S. McPherson, president of Macalester College in St. Paul, Minn., where 57% of enrollees are women. "Boys get off to a slower start."

The trouble isn't limited to school. Once a young man is out of the house, he's more likely than his sister to boomerang back home and sponge off his mom and dad. It all adds up to the fact that before he reaches adulthood, a young man is more likely than he was 30 years ago to end up in the new and growing class of underachiever—what the British call the "sink group."

For a decade, British educators have waged successful classroom programs to ameliorate "laddism" (boys turning off to school) by focusing on teaching techniques that re-engage them. But in the U.S., boys' fall from alpha to omega status doesn't even have a name, let alone the public's attention. "No one wants to speak out on behalf of boys," says Andrew Sum, director of the Northeastern University Center for Labor Market Studies. As a social-policy or educational issue, "it's near nonexistent."

On the one hand, the education grab by girls is amazing news, which could make the 21st the first female century. Already, women are rapidly closing the M.D. and PhD gap and are on the verge of making up the majority of law students, according to the American Bar Assn. MBA programs, with just 29% females, remain among the few old-boy domains.

Still, it's hardly as if the world has been equalized: Ninety percent of the world's billionaires are men. Among the super rich, only one woman, Gap Inc. co-founder Doris F. Fisher, made, rather than inherited, her wealth. Men continue to dominate in the highest-paying jobs in such leading-edge industries as engineering, investment banking, and high tech—the sectors that still power the economy and build the biggest fortunes. And women still face sizable obstacles in the pay gap, the glass ceiling, and the still-Sisyphean struggle to juggle work and child-rearing.

But attaining a decisive educational edge may finally enable females to narrow the earnings gap, punch through more of the glass ceiling, and gain an equal hand in rewriting the rules of corporations, government, and society. "Girls are better able to deliver in terms of what modern society requires of people—paying attention, abiding by rules, being verbally competent, and dealing with interpersonal relationships in offices," says James Garbarino, a professor of human development at Cornell University and author of *Lost Boys: Why Our Sons Turn Violent and How We Can Save Them*.

Righting boys' problems needn't end up leading to reversals for girls. But some feminists say the danger in exploring what's happening to boys would be to mistakenly see any expansion of opportunities for women as inherently disadvantageous to boys. "It isn't a zero-sum game," says Susan M. Bailey, executive director of the Wellesley Centers for Women. Adds Macalester's McPherson: "It would be dangerous to even out the gender ratio by treating women worse. I don't think we've reached a point in this country where we are fully providing equal opportunities to women."

Still, if the creeping pattern of male disengagement and economic dependency continues, more men could end up becoming losers in a global economy that values mental powers over might—not to mention the loss of their talent and potential. The growing educational and economic imbalances could also create societal upheavals, altering family finances, social policies, and work-family practices. Men are already dropping out of the labor force, walking out on fatherhood, and disconnecting from civic life in greater numbers. Since 1964, for example, the voting rate in Presidential elections among men has fallen from 72% to 53%—twice the rate of decline among women, according to Pell's Mortenson. In a turnaround from the 1960s, more women now vote than men.

Boys' slide also threatens to erode male earnings, spark labor shortages for skilled workers, and create the same kind of marriage squeeze among white women that already exists for blacks. Among African Americans, 30% of 40- to 44-year-old women have never married, owing in part to the lack of men with the same academic credentials and earning potential. Currently, the never-married rate is 9% for white women of the same age. "Women are going to pull further and further ahead of men, and at some point, when they want to form families, they are going to look around and say, 'Where are the guys?'" says Mortenson.

Corporations should worry, too. During the boom, the most acute labor shortages occurred among educated workers—a problem companies often solved by hiring immigrants. When the economy reenergizes, a skills shortage in the U.S. could undermine employers' productivity and growth.

Better-educated men are also, on average, a much happier lot. They are more likely to marry, stick by their children, and pay more in taxes. From the ages of 18 to 65, the average male college grad earns $2.5 million over his lifetime, 90% more than his high school counterpart. That's up from 40% more in 1979, the peak year for U.S. manufacturing. The average college diploma holder also contributes four times more in net taxes over his career than a high school grad, according to Northeastern's Sum. Meanwhile, the typical high school dropout will usually get $40,000 more from the government than he pays in, a net drain on society.

Certainly, many boys continue to conquer scholastic summits, especially boys from high-income families with educated parents. Overall, boys continue to do better on standardized tests such as the scholastic aptitude test, though more low-income girls than low-income boys take it, thus depressing girls' scores. Many educators also believe that standardized testing's multiple-choice format favors boys because girls tend to think in broader, more complex terms. But that advantage is eroding as many colleges now weigh grades—where girls excel—more heavily than test scores.

Still, it's not as if girls don't face a slew of vexing issues, which are often harder to detect because girls are likelier to internalize low self-esteem through depression or the desire to starve themselves into perfection. And while boys may act out with their fists, girls, given their superior verbal skills, often do so with their mouths in the form of vicious gossip and female bullying. "They yell and cuss," says 15-year-old Keith Gates, an Ottumwa student. "But we always get in trouble. They never do."

Before educators, corporations, and policymakers can narrow the new gender gap, they will have to understand its myriad causes. Everything from absentee
parenting to the lack of male teachers to corporate takeovers of lunch rooms with
sugar-and-fat-filled food, which can make kids hyperactive and distractable, plays a
role. So can TV violence, which hundreds of studies—including recent ones by Stanford University and the University of Michigan—have linked to aggressive behavior
in kids. Some believe boys are responding to cultural signals—downsized dads cast
adrift in the New Economy, a dumb-and-dumber dude culture that demeans academic achievement, and the glamorization of all things gangster that makes
school seem so uncool. What can compare with the allure of a gun-wielding,
model-dating hip hopper? Boys, who mature more slowly than girls, are also
often less able to delay gratification or take a long-range view.

Schools have inadvertently played a big role, too, losing sight of boys—taking for granted that they were doing well, even though data began to show the
opposite. Some educators believed it was a blip that would change or feared take-
backs on girls' gains. Others were just in denial. Indeed, many administrators saw
boys, rather than the way schools were treating them, as the problem.

Thirty years ago, educational experts launched what's known as the "Girl
Project." The movement's noble objective was to help girls wipe out their
weaknesses in math and science, build self-esteem, and give them the undis-
puted message: The opportunities are yours; take them. Schools focused on
making the classroom more girl-friendly by including teaching styles that
catered to them. Girls were also powerfully influenced by the women's movement, as well as by Title IX and the Gender & Equity Act, all of which created a
legal environment in which discrimination against girls—from classrooms to
the sports field—carried heavy penalties. Once the chains were off, girls soared.

Yet even as boys' educational development was flat-lining in the 1990s—with
boys dropping out in greater numbers and failing to bridge the gap in reading and
writing—the spotlight remained firmly fixed on girls. Part of the reason was that
the issue had become politically charged and girls had powerful advocates. The
American Association of University Women, for example, published research
cementing into pedagogy the idea that girls had deep problems with self-esteem in
school as a result of teachers' patterns, which included calling on girls less and lav-
ishing attention on boys. Newspapers and TV newsmagazines lapped up the news,
decrying a new confidence crisis among American girls. Universities and research
centers sponsored scores of teacher symposiums centered on girls. "All the focus
was on girls, all the grant monies, all the university programs—to get girls interested in science and math," says Steve Hanson, principal of Ottumwa High School
in Iowa. "There wasn't a similar thing for reading and writing for boys."

Some boy champions go so far as to contend that schools have become boy-
bashing laboratories. Christina Hoff Sommers, author of *The War Against Boys*, says
the AAUW report, coupled with zero-tolerance sexual harassment laws, have hijacked
schools by overly feminizing classrooms and attempting to engineer androgyny.

The "earliness" push, in which schools are pressured to show kids achieving the same standards by the same age or risk losing funding, is also far more
damaging to boys, according to Lilian G. Katz, co-director of ERIC Clearing-
house on Elementary and Early Childhood Education. Even the nerves on boys'

fingers develop later than girls', making it difficult to hold a pencil and push out perfect cursive. These developmental differences often unfairly sideline boys as slow or dumb, planting a distaste for school as early as the first grade.

Instead of catering to boys' learning styles, Pollock and others argue, many schools are force-fitting them into an unnatural mold. The reigning sit-still-and-listen paradigm isn't ideal for either sex. But it's one girls often tolerate better than boys. Girls have more intricate sensory capacities and biosocial aptitudes to decipher exactly what the teacher wants, whereas boys tend to be more anti-authoritarian, competitive, and risk-taking. They often don't bother with such details as writing their names in the exact place instructed by the teacher.

Experts say educators also haven't done nearly enough to keep up with the recent findings in brain research about developmental differences. "Ninety-nine-point-nine percent of teachers are not trained in this," says Michael Gurian, author of *Boys and Girls Learn Differently*. "They were taught 20 years ago that gender is just a social function."

In fact, brain research over the past decade has revealed how differently boys' and girls' brains can function. Early on, boys are usually superior spatial thinkers and possess the ability to see things in three dimensions. They are often drawn to play that involves intense movement and an element of make-believe violence. Instead of straitjacketing boys by attempting to restructure this behavior out of them, it would be better to teach them how to harness this energy effectively and healthily, Pollock says.

As it stands, the result is that too many boys are diagnosed with attention-deficit disorder or its companion, attention-deficit hyperactivity disorder. The U.S.—mostly its boys—now consumes 80% of the world's supply of methylphenidate (the generic name for Ritalin). That use has increased 500% over the past decade, leading some to call it the new K–12 management tool. There are school districts where 20% to 25% of the boys are on the drug, says Paul R. Wolpe, a psychiatry professor at the University of Pennsylvania and the senior fellow at the school's Center for Bioethics: "Ritalin is a response to an artificial social context that we've created for children."

Instead of recommending medication—something four states have recently banned school administrators from doing—experts say educators should focus on helping boys feel less like misfits. Experts are designing new developmentally appropriate, child-initiated learning that concentrates on problem-solving, not just test-taking. This approach benefits both sexes but especially boys, given that they tend to learn best through action, not just talk. Activities are geared toward the child's interest level and temperament. Boys, for example, can learn math through counting pinecones, biology through mucking around in a pond. They can read *Harry Potter* instead of *Little House on the Prairie*, and write about aliens attacking a hospital rather than about how to care for people in the hospital. If they get antsy, they can leave a teacher's lecture and go to an activity center replete with computers and manipulable objects that support the lesson plan.

Paying attention to boys' emotional lives also delivers dividends. Over the course of her longitudinal research project in Washington (D.C.) schools, University of Northern Florida researcher Rebecca Marcon found that boys who attend kindergartens that focus on social and emotional skills—as opposed to only academic learning—perform better, across the board, by the time they reach junior high.

Indeed, brain research shows that boys are actually more empathic, expressive, and emotive at birth than girls. But Pollock says the boy code, which bathes them in a culture of stoicism and reticence, often socializes those aptitudes out of them by the second grade. "We now have executives paying $10,000 a week to learn emotional intelligence," says Pollock. "These are actually the skills boys are born with."

The gender gap also has roots in the expectation gap. In the 1970s, boys were far more likely to anticipate getting a college degree—with girls firmly entrenched in the cheerleader role. Today, girls' expectations are ballooning, while boys' are plummeting. There's even a sense, including among the most privileged families, that today's boys are a sort of payback generation—the one that has to compensate for the advantages given to males in the past. In fact, the new equality is often perceived as a loss by many boys who expected to be on top. "My friends in high school, they just didn't see the value of college, they just didn't care enough," says New York University sophomore Joe Clabby. Only half his friends from his high school group in New Jersey went on to college.

They will face a far different world than their dads did. Without college diplomas, it will be harder for them to find good-paying jobs. And more and more, the positions available to them will be in industries long thought of as female. The services sector, where women make up 60% of employees, has ballooned by 260% since the 1970s. During the same period, manufacturing, where men hold 70% of jobs, has shrunk by 14%.

These men will also be more likely to marry women who outearn them. Even in this jobless recovery, women's wages have continued to grow, with the pay gap the smallest on record, while men's earnings haven't managed to keep up with the low rate of inflation. Given that the recession hit male-centric industries such as technology and manufacturing the hardest, native-born men experienced more than twice as much job loss as native-born women between 2000 and 2002.

Some feminists who fought hard for girl equality in schools in the early 1980s and '90s say this: So what if girls have gotten 10, 20 years of attention—does that make up for centuries of subjugation? Moreover, what's wrong with women gliding into first place, especially if they deserve it? "Just because girls aren't shooting 7-Eleven clerks doesn't mean they should be ignored," says Cornell's Garbarino. "Once you stop oppressing girls, it stands to reason they will thrive up to their potential."

Moreover, girls say much of their drive stems from parents and teachers pushing them to get a college degree because they have to be better to be equal—to make the same money and get the same respect as a guy. "Girls are more willing to take the initiative... they're not afraid to do the work," says Tara Prout, the Georgetown-bound senior class president at Lawrence High. "A lot of boys in my school are looking for credit to get into college to look good, but they don't really want to do the grunt work."

A new world has opened up for girls, but unless a symmetrical effort is made to help boys find their footing, it may turn out that it's a lonely place to be. After all, it takes more than one gender to have a gender revolution.

NO

Joel Wendland

Reversing The "Gender Gap"

"**B**oys are becoming the second sex" proclaimed *Business Week* last May in a cover story titled "The New Gender Gap." *Business Week's* article appeared as part of a spate of articles and television news segments on the subject of increased educational opportunities for women. The basics of the story are that in the education system, teachers have become so conscious of catering to the needs of girls and young women that boys are being left behind. Boys, they say, are being punished for "boyish" behavior. They are being put more often into special education programs or disciplinary classes, and the outcome is that boys have a negative educational experience. This trend translates into poorer high school performances and perhaps college as well.

According to statistics offered by *Business Week*, 57 percent of all new bachelor's degrees and 58 percent of master's degrees are awarded to women. This "education grab," according to the article, was the source of the "new gender gap." Though, the article did hint that even with the new trend in the numbers, women still had some ways to go in order to catch up after 350 years of being almost entirely excluded from the university.

Most observers of this situation will find such an article perplexing. Certainly most women will likely be skeptical of its major argument. That this "reverse gender gap" argument exists, however, is not surprising. Like its cousins in other areas of social life (reverse discrimination or reverse class warfare), it is being generated primarily by the ultra-right. The purpose is to stifle the struggle for equality by implying (or stating directly) that the gains made by women through struggle over the last 40 years have gone too far and have detrimentally affected society.

Some in this camp go so far as to suggest that women who demand equality are out to hurt men. At worst, it demonstrates that the right wants to twist the outcome of social progress to divide us. They say that a struggle between men and women for social goods is the fundamental source of social conflict and that women are winning—a situation that, for some, means reversed gender inequality and for others goes against natural laws of male supremacy invoked by God.

Any way you look at it, however, this picture is a distortion of reality. So what does the real gender gap look like?

Barbara Gault, director of research at the Institute for Women's Policy Research, recently told *Women'sWallStreet.com* that there are several explanations for and holes in the current data on the educational experiences of men and women. First, high-paying occupations that do not require college degrees, such as skilled trades, are still male dominated. Second, women need a college degree in order to earn roughly hat men do with only high school diplomas, giving them stronger motives to make a special effort to obtain financial security. Third, among African Americans, where the difference between women and men earning college degrees is the widest among all racial or ethnic groups, it is clear that institutional racism directed at African American men plays a large role in keeping them out of college. Fourth, in the crucial field of information technology, women continue to earn only about one-third of the degrees awarded and get only about one-third of the jobs available. Finally, men continue to outpace women in completing doctoral and professional degrees (81 women for every 100 men), resulting in continued male dominance in corporate board rooms, the seats of political power, the highest positions in universities, etc.

The successes of the women's equality movement, progressive changes in attitudes about roles women can have and the implementation of affirmative action policies (which benefited women as a whole most) have had a tremendous positive impact on the access women have had in education. Just 30 years ago, women earned advanced or professional degrees at a rate of only 23 women per 100 men. In other arenas, such as the workforce or the political field, the gender gap, in sheer numbers, has largely narrowed. But the numbers still don't paint the whole picture.

While higher education is a major factor in gaining financial security, it is something that is only available to about one-fifth of the adult population. So for the vast majority of women, this supposed "new gender gap" means absolutely nothing. Other data on the condition of women's economic security paint another picture altogether. About eight of ten retired women are not eligible for pension benefits. When retired women do get a pension, it is typically far less than retired men get. Fifty percent of women who receive pension benefits get only about 60 cents for every dollar of male pensioners. On the average, retired women depend on Social Security for 71 percent of their income, and about 25 percent of retired women rely solely on Social Security for their income.

In the work force, women's pay averages only 76 percent of men's pay (at a cost of about $200 billion for working families annually). A report produced by the General Accounting Office last October shows that since 1983, the wage differential has actually increased. 60 percent of all women earn less than $25,000 annually. Women are one-third more likely to live below the poverty level. Black women and Latinas are between two and three times more likely to live below the poverty line than men are. For women of color, facing the double oppression of racism and sexism, pay losses are even greater: 64 cents on the dollar at a loss of about $210 a week. The average woman, according to the AFL-CIO, will lose $523,000 in her lifetime due to unequal pay.

Even more costly to women, is the "price of motherhood," as journalist Ann Crittenden argues in her recent book of that title. In almost every case, women lose income, jobs, job experience and retirement income (while work hours increase) when they decide to have children. With some slight improvements, women remain the primary caregiver in nearly every family. For many mothers, single or married, the economic inequalities described above are exacerbated. For married women, dependence on men is heightened and the threat of economic hardship enforces interpersonal inequality and conflict. Divorced mothers and their children have among the highest rates of poverty of any demographic.

Crittenden argues that unless other sources of financial support for motherhood are made available institutionalized inequality will persist. She suggests retirement benefits for mothers, public funding for day care and health care for children and their caregivers, salaries for primary caregivers, expanded public education for pre-school children, equalized social security for spouses, increased financial contributions from husbands and fathers, increased educational and support resources for parents and equalization of living standards for divorced parents.

As for the fallacy of female supremacy, the gains made by women through struggle and implementation of policies such as affirmative action point to the necessity of broader systematic change. But if female supremacy is a fallacy, does this mean that men go unhurt by gender inequalities? No. Men and boys are hurt when their families suffer because pay inequity causes their mothers, grandmothers, sisters and aunts to lose income, get fired, face hiring discrimination, are refused pensions, don't have equal Social Security benefits, lose out on promotions or have limited access to higher education. Additionally, if the average woman loses $523,000 in income in her life, does this mean that the average man is enriched by $523,000 in his lifetime? If pay inequity costs women $200 billion yearly, does this mean that men are enriched by $200 billion? The answer is no. These billions are savings in labor costs to employers. Employers enjoy the profits of male supremacy and gendered divisions among working people. So it makes sense that the right tries to portray the benefits of progressive social change toward equality as bad. It cuts into their bottom line.

POSTSCRIPT

Are Boys and Men Disadvantaged Relative to Girls and Women?

Michelle Conlin establishes the fact that males are not doing as well in the education system as females and offers some plausible explanations why. The foremost reason offered is that K to 12 schools today are ill suited to boys. Upon entrance boys are developmentally behind girls but must handle tasks that they are not ready for. More importantly, boys are not biologically programmed for school life. As Conlin says "While every nerve in his body tells him to run, he has to sit still and listen for almost eight hours a day." The strong version of this argument is that today's schools have "an increasingly anti-boy culture that pathologizes their behavior." Others of the myriad of causes that she cites are the following: "Everything from absentee parenting to the lack of male teachers to corporate takeovers of lunch rooms with sugar-and-fat-filled food, which can make kids hyperactive and distractible, plays a role. So can TV violence, which hundreds of studies . . . have linked to aggressive behavior in kids. Some believe boys are responding to cultural signals—downsized dads cast adrift in the New Economy, a dumb-and-dumber dude culture that demeans academic achievement, and the glamorization of all things gangster that makes school seem so uncool. . . Boys who mature more slowly than girls, are also often less able to delay gratification or take a long-range view."

The gender gap debate is not over the differential educational outcomes for boys and girls, but over whether education and life is unfair to males and advantages females. If so, then the schools and other institutions should be altered to suit males as much as females. But first society would have to find a way to replace the dumb dude culture with a pro education and achievement culture for boys. The argument on the other side does not deny the superior educational achievement of females over males, but challenges the degree of unfairness in the educational system that needs to be corrected. If boys mature later than girls and tend to have a dumb dude culture, it is not the schools fault that they do badly and a pro boy reform may not be necessary. More importantly the female side of the argument points out that females are so much more disadvantaged in the rest of life, especially in employment, that having an advantage in education helps level the playing field. Perhaps it is fair to keep this one advantage.

There is considerable literature on inequality and discrimination against women in the workplace and very little on discrimination against men. The works that address discrimination against women include Nancy Maclean, *Freedom Is Not Enough: The Opening of the American Workplace* (Russell Sage Foundation, 2006); Martha Burke, *Cult of Power: Sex Discrimination in Corporate America and What Can Be Done about It* (Scribner, 2005); Heidi Gottfried and Laura Reese, eds., *Equity in the Workplace: Gendering Workplace Policy Analysis* (Lexington Books, 2004); David Neumark, *Sex Differences in Labor Markets* (Routledge, 2004); Sandy Ruxton, ed., *Gender Equality and Men: Learning from Practice* (Oxfam, 2004); Evelyn F. Murphy, *Getting Even: Why Women Don't Get Paid Like Men—and What to Do about It* (Simon & Schuster, 2005); Judith Lorber, *Breaking the Bowls: Degendering and Feminist Change* (W.W. Norton, 2005) and *Gender Inequality: Feminist Theories and Politics,* 2nd ed. (Roxbury Pub., 2001); Phyllis Moen and Patricia Roehling, *The Career Mystique: Cracks in the American Dream* (Rowman and Littlefield, 2005); Jerry A. Jacobs and Kathleen Gerson, *The Time Divide: Work, Family, and Gender Inequality* (Harvard University Press, 2004); Linda Lavine and Charles V. Dale, *The Male-Female Wage Gap* (Novinka Books, 2003); and Michael S. Kimmel, *The Gendered Society* (Oxford University Press, 2000). For inequality in academia, see Susan K. Dyer, ed., *Tenure Denied: Cases of Sex Discrimination in Academia* (AAUW Educational Foundation, 2004). For worldwide sex discrimination, see Maria Charles, *Occupational Ghettoes: The Worldwide Segregation of Women and Men* (Stanford University Press, 2004) and Trudie M. Eklund, *Sisters around the World: The Global Struggle for Female Equality* (Hamilton Books, 2004).

Economic Report of the President

The Economic Report of the President Web site includes current and anticipated trends in the United States and annual numerical goals concerning topics such as employment, production, real income, and federal budget outlays. The database notes employment objectives for significant groups of the labor force, annual numeric goals, and a plan for carrying out program objectives.

http://www.library.nwu.edu/gpo/help/econr.html

National Center for Policy Analysis

Through the National Center for Policy Analysis site you can read discussions that are of major interest in the study of American politics and government from a sociological perspective.

http://www.ncpa.org

Speakout.com

The Speakout.com Web site contains a library of online information and links related to public policy issues, primarily those in the United States. The issues are organized into topics and subtopics for easy searching.

http://www.speakout.com/activism/issues

Policy.com

Visit Policy.com, the site of the "policy community," to examine major issues related to social welfare, welfare reform, social work, and many other topics. The site includes substantial resources for researching issues online.

http://www.policy.com

PART 4

Political Economy and Institutions

*A*re political power and economic power merged within a "power elite" that dominates the U.S. political system? The first issue in this part explores that debate. The second issue concerns the proper role of government in the economy. Some believe that the government must correct for the many failures of the market, while others think that the government usually complicates the workings of the free market and reduces its effectiveness. The next debate concerns public policy: What is the impact of the end of the Federal AFDC program? The fourth issue examines alternative educational policies for significantly improving public education. Finally, the last issue in this part looks at the use of biotechnology to alter and enhance humans.

- Is Government Dominated by Big Business?
- Should Government Intervene in a Capitalist Economy?
- Has Welfare Reform Benefited the Poor?
- Is Competition the Solution to the Ills of Public Education?
- Should Biotechnology Be Used to Alter and Enhance Humans?

ISSUE 11

Is Government Dominated by Big Business?

YES: Bill Moyers, from "This Is the Fight of Our Lives," *Timeline* (September/October 2004)

NO: Jeffrey M. Berry, from "Citizen Groups and the Changing Nature of Interest Group Politics in America," *The Annals of the American Academy of Political and Social Science* (July 1993)

ISSUE SUMMARY

YES: Television journalist Bill Moyers describes the harmful consequences of the influence and power of businessess and the rich over government. To him, the stories and evidence that he presents are "something to get mad about."

NO: Jeffrey M. Berry, a professor of political science, contends that public interest pressure groups that have entered the political arena since the end of the 1960s have effectively challenged the political power of big business.

Since the framing of the U.S. Constitution in 1787, there have been periodic charges that America is unduly influenced by wealthy financial interests. Richard Henry Lee, a signer of the Declaration of Independence, spoke for many Anti-Federalists (those who opposed ratification of the Constitution) when he warned that the proposed charter shifted power away from the people and into the hands of the "aristocrats" and "moneyites."

Before the Civil War, Jacksonian Democrats denounced the eastern merchants and bankers who, they charged, were usurping the power of the people. After the Civil War, a number of radical parties and movements revived this theme of antielitism. The ferment—which was brought about by the rise of industrial monopolies, government corruption, and economic hardship for western farmers—culminated in the founding of the People's Party at the beginning of the 1890s. The Populists, as they were more commonly called, wanted economic and political reforms aimed at transferring power away from the rich and back to "the plain people."

By the early 1900s the People's Party had disintegrated, but many writers and activists have continued to echo the Populists' central thesis: that the U.S. democratic political system is in fact dominated by business elites. Yet the thesis has not gone unchallenged. During the 1950s and the early 1960s, many social scientists subscribed to the *pluralist* view of America.

Pluralists argue that because there are many influential elites in America, each group is limited to some extent by the others. There are some groups, like the business elites, that are more powerful than their opponents, but even the more powerful groups are denied their objectives at times. Labor groups are often opposed to business groups; conservative interests challenge liberal interests, and vice versa; and organized civil libertarians sometimes fight with groups that seek government-imposed bans on pornography or groups that demand tougher criminal laws. No single group, the pluralists argue, can dominate the political system.

Pluralists readily acknowledge that American government is not democratic in the full sense of the word; it is not driven by the majority. But neither, they insist, is it run by a conspiratorial "power elite." In the pluralist view, the closest description of the American form of government would be neither majority rule nor minority rule but *minorities* rule. (Note that in this context, "minorities" does not necessarily refer to race or ethnicity but to any organized group of people with something in common—including race, religion, or economic interests—not constituting a majority of the population.) Each organized minority enjoys some degree of power in the making of public policy. In extreme cases, when a minority feels threatened, its power may take a negative form: the power to derail policy. When the majority—or, more accurately, a coalition of other minorities—attempts to pass a measure that threatens the vital interests of an organized minority, that group may use its power to obstruct their efforts. (Often cited in this connection is the use of the Senate filibuster, which is the practice of using tactics during the legislative process that cause extreme delays or prevent action, thus enabling a group to "talk to death" a bill that threatens its vital interests.) But in the pluralist view negative power is not the only driving force: when minorities work together and reach consensus on certain issues, they can institute new laws and policy initiatives that enjoy broad public support. Pluralism, though capable of producing temporary gridlock, ultimately leads to compromise, consensus, and moderation.

Critics of pluralism argue that pluralism is an idealized depiction of a political system that is in the grip of powerful elite groups. Critics fault pluralist theory for failing to recognize the extent to which big business dominates the policy-making process. In the selections that follow, Bill Moyers supports this view and spells out the painful consequences for real people, especially the working poor. Jeffrey M. Berry, in opposition, argues that, thanks to new consumer, environmental, and other citizen groups, big business no longer enjoys the cozy relationship it once had with Washington policymakers.

Bill Moyers

 **YES**

This Is the Fight of Our Lives

Earlier this year, Bill Moyers, the noted author and television journalist, delivered a keynote speech at New York University. When we read a copy of his address, we felt that Moyers' message was so insightful, powerful, and relevant to the critical issues the world is facing that we had to reprint it in *Timeline*. After reading it, we hope that you, in turn, will want to share it with others. —The Editors

It is important from time to time to remember that some things are worth getting mad about.

Here's one: On March 10 of this year, on page B8, with a headline that stretched across all six columns, *The New York Times* reported that tuition in the city's elite private schools would hit $26,000 for the coming school year—for kindergarten as well as high school. On the same page, under a two-column headline, Michael Wineraub wrote about a school in nearby Mount Vernon, the first stop out of the Bronx, with a student body that is 97 percent black. It is the poorest school in the town: nine out of ten children qualify for free lunches; one out of ten lives in a homeless shelter. During black history month this past February, a sixth grader wanted to write a report on Langston Hughes. There were no books on Langston Hughes in the library—no books about the great poet, nor any of his poems. There is only one book in the library on Frederick Douglass. None on Rosa Parks, Josephine Baker, Leontyne Price, or other giants like them in the modern era. In fact, except for a few Newberry Award books the librarian bought with her own money, the library is mostly old books—largely from the 1950s and '60s when the school was all white. A 1960 child's primer on work begins with a youngster learning how to be a telegraph delivery boy. All the workers in the book—the dry cleaner, the deliveryman, the cleaning lady—are white. There's a 1967 book about telephones which says: "When you phone you usually dial the number. But on some new phones you can push buttons." The newest encyclopedia dates from 1991, with two volumes—"B" and "R"—missing. There is no card catalog in the library—no index cards or computer.

Here's something else to get mad about. Two weeks ago, the House of Representatives, the body of Congress owned and operated by the corporate, political, and religious right, approved new tax credits for children. Not for poor children, mind you. But for families earning as much as $309,000 a year—families that already enjoy significant benefits from earlier tax cuts. The editorial page of *The*

From *Timeline*, September/October 2004, pp. 2–11. Copyright © 2004 by Bill Moyers. Reprinted by permission of Bill Moyers/Public Affairs Television.

Washington Post called this "bad social policy, bad tax policy, and bad fiscal policy. You'd think they'd be embarrassed," said the *Post*, "but they're not."

And this, too, is something to get mad about. Nothing seems to embarrass the political class in Washington today. Not the fact that more children are growing up in poverty in America than in any other industrial nation; not the fact that millions of workers are actually making less money today in real dollars than they did twenty years ago; not the fact that working people are putting in longer and longer hours and still falling behind; not the fact that while we have the most advanced medical care in the world, nearly 44 million Americans—eight out of ten of them in working families—are uninsured and cannot get the basic care they need.

Astonishing as it seems, no one in official Washington seems embarrassed by the fact that the gap between rich and poor is greater than it's been in 50 years—the worst inequality among all western nations. Or that we are experiencing a shift in poverty. For years it was said those people down there at the bottom were single, jobless mothers. For years they were told work, education, and marriage is how they move up the economic ladder. But poverty is showing up where we didn't expect it—among families that include two parents, a worker, and a head of the household with more than a high school education. These are the newly poor. Our political, financial, and business class expects them to climb out of poverty on an escalator moving downward.

For years now a small fraction of American households have been garnering an extreme concentration of wealth and income while large corporations and financial institutions have obtained unprecedented levels of economic and political power over daily life. In 1960, the gap in terms of wealth between the top 20% and the bottom 20% was 30 fold. Four decades later it is more than 75 fold.

·◦ⓞ⤜·

Such concentrations of wealth would be far less of an issue if the rest of society were benefiting proportionately. But that's not the case. As the economist Jeff Madrick reminds us, the pressures of inequality on middle and working class Americans are now quite severe. "The strain on working people and on family life, as spouses have gone to work in dramatic numbers, has become significant. VCRs and television sets are cheap, but higher education, health care, public transportation, drugs, housing and cars have risen faster in price than typical family incomes. And life has grown neither calm nor secure for most Americans, by any means." You can find many sources to support this conclusion. I like the language of a small outfit here in New York called the Commonwealth Foundation/Center for the Renewal of American Democracy. They conclude that working families and the poor "are losing ground under economic pressures that deeply affect household stability, family dynamics, social mobility, political participation, and civic life."

In my time we went to public schools. My brother made it to college on the GI bill. When I bought my first car for $450, I drove to a subsidized university on free public highways and stopped to rest in state-maintained public parks. This is what I mean by the commonwealth. Rudely recognized in its formative years, always subject to struggle, constantly vulnerable to reactionary counterattacks, the notion of America as a shared project has been the central engine of our national experience.

Until now. I don't have to tell you that a profound transformation is occurring in America: the balance between wealth and the commonwealth is being upended. By design. Deliberately. We have been subjected to what the Commonwealth Foundation calls "a fanatical drive to dismantle the political institutions, the legal and statutory canons, and the intellectual and cultural frameworks that have shaped public responsibility for social harms arising from the excesses of private power." From land, water, and other natural resources, to media and the broadcast and digital spectrums, to scientific discovery and medical breakthroughs, and to politics itself, a broad range of the American commons is undergoing a powerful shift toward private and corporate control. And with little public debate. Indeed, what passes for "political debate" in this country has become a cynical charade behind which the real business goes on—the not-so-scrupulous business of getting and keeping power in order to divide up the spoils.

We could have seen this coming if we had followed the money. The veteran Washington reporter, Elizabeth Drew, says "the greatest change in Washington over the past 25 years—in its culture, in the way it does business and the ever-burgeoning amount of business transactions that go on here—has been in the preoccupation with money." Jeffrey Birnbaum, who covered Washington for nearly twenty years for the *Wall Street Journal*, put it more strongly: "[Campaign cash] has flooded over the gunwales of the ship of state and threatens to sink the entire vessel. Political donations determine the course and speed of many government actions that deeply affect our daily lives." Politics is suffocating from the stranglehold of money. During his brief campaign in 2000, before he was ambushed by the dirty tricks of the religious right in South Carolina and big money from George W. Bush's wealthy elites, John McCain said elections today are nothing less than an "influence peddling scheme in which both parties compete to stay in office by selling the country to the highest bidder."

Small wonder that with the exception of people like John McCain and Russ Feingold, official Washington no longer finds anything wrong with a democracy dominated by the people with money. Hit the pause button here, and recall Roger Tamraz. He's the wealthy oilman who paid $300,000 to get a private meeting in the White House with President Clinton; he wanted help in securing a big pipeline in central Asia. This got him called before congressional hearings on the financial excesses of the 1996 campaign. If you watched the hearings on C-Span, you heard him say he didn't think he had done anything out of the ordinary. When they pressed him he told the senators: "Look, when it comes to money and politics, you make the rules. I'm just playing by your rules." One senator then asked if Tamraz had registered and voted. And he was blunt in his reply: "No, senator, I think money's a bit more (important) than the vote."

So what does this come down to, practically?

Here is one accounting:

When powerful interests shower Washington with millions in campaign contributions, they often get what they want. But it's ordinary citizens and firms that pay the price, and most of them never see it coming. This is what happens if you don't contribute to their campaigns or spend generously on lobbying. You pick up a disproportionate share of America's tax bill. You pay higher prices for a broad range of products from peanuts to prescriptions. You pay taxes that others in a similar situation have been excused from paying. You're compelled to abide by laws while others are granted immunity from them. You must pay debts that you incur while others do not. You're barred from writing off on your tax returns some of the money spent on necessities while others deduct the cost of their entertainment. You must run your business by one set of rules, while the government creates another set for your competitors.

In contrast, the fortunate few who contribute to the right politicians and hire the right lobbyists enjoy all the benefits of their special status. Make a bad business deal; the government bails them out. If they want to hire workers at below market wages, the government provides the means to do so. If they want more time to pay their debts, the government gives them an extension. If they want immunity from certain laws, the government gives it. If they want to ignore rules their competition must comply with, the government gives its approval. If they want to kill legislation that is intended for the public, it gets killed.

I'm not quoting from Karl Marx's *Das Kapital* or Mao's *Little Red Book*. I'm quoting *Time* magazine. *Time's* premier investigative journalists—Donald Bartlett and James Steele—concluded in a series last year that America now has "government for the few at the expense of the many." Economic inequality begets political inequality, and vice versa.

That's why . . . we're losing the balance between wealth and the commonwealth. It's why we can't put things right. And it is the single most destructive force tearing at the soul of democracy. Hear the great justice Learned Hand on this: "If we are to keep our democracy, there must be one commandment: 'Thou shalt not ration justice.'" Learned Hand was a prophet of democracy. The rich have the right to buy more homes than anyone else. They have the right to buy more cars than anyone else, more gizmos than anyone else, more clothes and vacations than anyone else. But they do not have the right to buy more democracy than anyone else.

I know, I know: this sounds very much like a call for class war. But the class war was declared a generation ago, in a powerful paperback polemic by William Simon, who was soon to be Secretary of the Treasury. He called on the financial and business class, in effect, to take back the power and privileges they had lost in the depression and the New Deal. They got the message, and soon they began a stealthy class war against the rest of society and the principles of our democracy. They set out to trash the social contract, to cut their workforces and wages, to scour the globe in search of cheap labor, and to shred the social safety net that was supposed to protect people from hardships beyond their control. *Business Week* put it bluntly at the time: "Some people will obviously have to do with less.... It will be a bitter pill for many Americans to swallow the idea of doing with less so that big business can have more."

The middle class and working poor are told that what's happening to them is the consequence of Adam Smith's "Invisible Hand." This is a lie. What's happening to them is the direct consequence of corporate activism, intellectual propaganda, the rise of a religious orthodoxy that in its hunger for government subsidies has made an idol of power, and a string of political decisions favoring the powerful and the privileged who bought the political system right out from under us.

To create the intellectual framework for this takeover of public policy, they funded conservative think tanks—The Heritage Foundation, the Hoover Institution, and the American Enterprise Institute—that churned out study after study advocating their agenda.

To put political muscle behind these ideas they created a formidable political machine. One of the few journalists to cover the issues of class—Thomas Edsall of *The Washington Post*—wrote: "During the 1970s, business refined its ability to act as a class, submerging competitive instincts in favor of joint, cooperative action in the legislative area." Big business political action committees flooded the political arena with a deluge of dollars. And they built alliances with the religious right—Jerry Falwell's Moral Majority and Pat Robertson's Christian Coalition—who mounted a cultural war providing a smokescreen for the class war, hiding the economic plunder of the very people who were enlisted as foot soldiers in the cause of privilege.

In a book to be published this summer, Daniel Altman describes what he calls the "neo-economy—a place without taxes, without a social safety net, where rich and poor live in different financial worlds—and [said Altman] it's coming to America." He's a little late. It's here. Says Warren Buffett, the savviest investor of them all: "My class won."

Look at the spoils of victory:

Over the past three years, they've pushed through $2 trillion dollars in tax cuts—almost all tilted towards the wealthiest people in the country.

Cuts in taxes on the largest incomes.
Cuts in taxes on investment income.
And cuts in taxes on huge inheritances.

More than half of the benefits are going to the wealthiest one percent. You could call it trickle-down economics, except that the only thing that trickled down was a sea of red ink in our state and local governments, forcing them to cut services for and raise taxes on middle class working America.

Now the Congressional Budget Office forecasts deficits totaling $2.75 trillion over the next ten years.

These deficits have been part of their strategy. Some of you will remember that Senator Daniel Patrick Moynihan tried to warn us 20 years ago, when he predicted that President Ronald Reagan's real strategy was to force the government to cut domestic social programs by fostering federal deficits of historic dimensions. Reagan's own budget director, David Stockman, admitted as much. Now the leading rightwing political strategist, Grover Norquist,

says the goal is to "starve the beast"—with trillions of dollars in deficits resulting from trillions of dollars in tax cuts, until the United States Government is
so anemic and anorexic it can be drowned in the bathtub.

⋅◈⋅

There's no question about it: The corporate conservatives and their allies in
the political and religious right are achieving a vast transformation of American life that only they understand because they are its advocates, its archi-
tects, and its beneficiaries. In creating the greatest economic inequality in the
advanced world, they have saddled our nation, our states, and our cities and
counties with structural deficits that will last until our children's children are
ready for retirement, and they are systematically stripping government of all
its functions except rewarding the rich and waging war.

And they are proud of what they have done to our economy and our
society. If instead of practicing journalism I was writing for Saturday Night
Live, I couldn't have made up the things that this crew have been saying. The
president's chief economic adviser says shipping technical and professional
jobs overseas is good for the economy. The president's Council of Economic
Advisers report that hamburger chefs in fast-food restaurants can be considered manufacturing workers. The president's Federal Reserve Chairman says
that the tax cuts may force cutbacks in social security—but hey, we should
make the tax cuts permanent anyway. The president's Labor Secretary says it
doesn't matter if job growth has stalled because "the stock market is the ultimate arbiter."

You just can't make this stuff up. You have to hear it to believe it. This
may be the first class war in history where the victims will die laughing.

But what they are doing to middle class and working Americans—and to
the workings of American democracy—is no laughing matter. Go online and
read the transcripts of Enron traders in the energy crisis four years ago, discussing how they were manipulating the California power market in telephone calls in which they gloat about ripping off "those poor
grandmothers." Read how they talk about political contributions to politicians like "Kenny Boy" Lay's best friend George W. Bush. Go online and read
how Citigroup has been fined $70 million for abuses in loans to low-income,
high-risk borrowers—the largest penalty ever imposed by the Federal Reserve.
A few clicks later, you can find the story of how a subsidiary of the corporate
computer giant NEC has been fined over $20 million after pleading guilty to
corruption in a federal plan to bring Internet access to poor schools and
libraries. And this, the story says, is just one piece of a nationwide scheme to
rip off the government and the poor.

Let's face the reality: If ripping off the public trust; if distributing tax
breaks to the wealthy at the expense of the poor; if driving the country into
deficits deliberately to starve social benefits; if requiring states to balance their
budgets on the backs of the poor; if squeezing the wages of workers until the
labor force resembles a nation of serfs—if this isn't class war, what is?

It's un-American. It's unpatriotic. And it's wrong.

NO

Jeffrey M. Berry

Citizen Groups and the Changing Nature of Interest Group Politics in America

ABSTRACT: The rise of liberal citizen groups that began in the 1960s has had a strong impact on the evolution of interest group advocacy. The success of these liberal organizations was critical in catalyzing the broader explosion in the numbers of interest groups and in causing the collapse of many subgovernments. New means of resolving policy conflicts had to be established to allow for the participation of broader, more diverse policy communities. Citizen groups have been particularly important in pushing policymakers to create new means of structuring negotiations between large numbers of interest group actors. The greater participation of citizen groups, the increased numbers of all kinds of interest groups, and change in the way policy is made may be making the policymaking process more democratic.

Many protest movements have arisen in the course of American history, each affecting the political system in its own way. The social movements that took hold in the 1960s had their own unique set of roots but seemed to follow a conventional life span. The civil rights and antiwar groups that arose to protest the injustices they saw were classic social movements. Their views were eventually absorbed by one of the political parties, and, after achieving their immediate goals, their vitality was sapped. The antiwar movement disappeared, and black civil rights organizations declined in power. The most enduring and vital citizen groups born in this era of protest were never protest oriented. Consumer groups, environmental groups, and many other kinds of citizen lobbies have enjoyed unprecedented prosperity in the last 25 years. Never before have citizen groups been so prevalent in American politics, and never before have they been so firmly institutionalized into the policymaking process.

The rise of citizen groups has not only empowered many important constituencies, but it has altered the policymaking process as well. This article focuses on how citizen groups have affected interest group politics in general and how these organizations have contributed to the changing nature of public policymaking. A first step is to examine the initial success of liberal advocacy organizations as well as the conservative response to this challenge. Next, I will look at the impact of this growth of citizen group politics on the policymaking process. Then I will turn to how Congress and the executive branch have tried to

From THE ANNALS OF THE AMERICAN ACADEMY OF POLITICAL AND SOCIAL SCIENCE, July 2003. Copyright © 2003 by Sage Publications, Inc. Reprinted by permission.

cope with a dense population of citizen groups and the complex policymaking environment that now envelops government.

Finally, I will speculate as to how all of this has affected policymaking in terms of how democratic it is. The popular perception is that the rise of interest groups along with the decline of political parties has had a very negative impact on American politics. Analysis of the decline of parties will be left to others, but a central point here is that the growth in the numbers of citizen groups and of other lobbying organizations has not endangered the political system. There are some unfortunate developments, such as the increasing role of political action committees in campaign financing, but the rise of citizen groups in particular has had a beneficial impact on the way policy is formulated. The overall argument may be stated succinctly: the rise of liberal citizen groups was largely responsible for catalyzing an explosion in the growth of all types of interest groups. Efforts to limit the impact of liberal citizen groups failed, and the policymaking process became more open and more participatory. Expanded access and the growth in the numbers of competing interest groups created the potential for gridlock, if not chaos. The government responded, in turn, with institutional changes that have helped to rationalize policymaking in environments with a large number of independent actors.

The Rise of Citizen Groups

The lobbying organizations that emerged out of the era of protest in the 1960s are tied to the civil rights and antiwar movements in two basic ways. First, activism was stimulated by the same broad ideological dissatisfaction with government and the two-party system. There was the same feeling that government was unresponsive, that it was unconcerned about important issues, and that business was far too dominant a force in policymaking. Second, the rise of liberal citizen groups was facilitated by success of the civil rights and antiwar movements. More specifically, future organizers learned from these social movements. They learned that aggressive behavior could get results, and they saw that government could be influenced by liberal advocacy organizations. Some activists who later led Washington-based citizen lobbies cut their teeth as volunteers in these earlier movements.

For liberal consumer and environmental groups, an important lesson of this era was that they should not follow the protest-oriented behavior of the civil rights and antiwar movements. There was a collective realization that lasting influence would come from more conventional lobbying inside the political system. For consumer and environmental organizers, "power to the people" was rejected in favor of staff-run organizations that placed little emphasis on participatory democracy. This is not to say that these new organizations were simply copies of business lobbies; leaders of these groups like Ralph Nader and John Gardner placed themselves above politics-as-usual with their moralistic rhetoric and their attacks against the established political order.

While there was significant support for these groups from middle-class liberals, a major impetus behind their success was financial backing from large philanthropic foundations. The foundations wanted to support social change during a time of political upheaval, but at the same time they wanted responsible activism. This early support, most notably from the Ford Foundation's program in public interest law, was largely directed at supporting groups relying on litigation and administrative lobbying. The seed money for these organizations enabled them to flourish and provided them with time to establish a track record so that they could appeal to individual donors when the foundation money ran out. Other groups emerged without the help of foundations, drawing on a combination of large donors, dues-paying memberships, and government grants. Citizen lobbies proved remarkably effective at raising money and at shifting funding strategies as the times warranted.

Citizen groups emerged in a variety of areas. In addition to consumer and environmental groups, there were organizations interested in hunger and poverty, governmental reform, corporate responsibility, and many other issues. A number of new women's organizations soon followed in the wake of the success of the first wave of citizen groups, and new civil rights groups arose to defend other groups such as Hispanics and gays. As has been well documented, the rise of citizen groups was the beginning of an era of explosive growth in interest groups in national politics. No precise baseline exists, so exact measurement of this growth is impossible. Yet the mobilization of interests is unmistakable. One analysis of organizations represented in Washington in 1980 found that 40 percent of the groups had been started since 1960, and 25 percent had begun after 1970.

The liberal citizen groups that were established in the 1960s and 1970s were not simply the first ripples of a new wave of interest groups; rather, they played a primary role in catalyzing the formation of many of the groups that followed. New business groups, which were by far the most numerous of all the groups started since 1960, were directly stimulated to organize by the success of consumer and environmental groups. There were other reasons why business mobilized, but much of their hostility toward the expanded regulatory state was directed at agencies strongly supported by liberal citizen groups. These organizations had seemingly seized control of the political agenda, and the new social regulation demanded increased business mobilization. New conservative citizen lobbies, many focusing on family issues such as abortion and the Equal Rights Amendment, were also begun to counter the perceived success of the liberal groups.

The swing of the ideological pendulum that led to a conservative takeover of the White House in 1980 led subsequently to efforts to limit the impact of liberal citizen groups. The Reagan administration believed that the election of 1980 was a mandate to eliminate impediments to economic growth. Environmental and consumer groups were seen as organizations that cared little about the faltering American economy; President Reagan referred to liberal public interest lawyers as "a bunch of ideological ambulance chasers." Wherever possible, liberal citizen groups were to be removed from the governmental process. . . .

The Reagan administration certainly succeeded in reducing the liberal groups' access to the executive branch. On a broader level, however, the conservative counterattack against the liberal groups was a failure. The reasons go far beyond the more accommodating stance of the Bush administration or the attitude of any conservative administrations that may follow. These organizations have proved to be remarkably resilient, and they are a strong and stable force in American politics. Most fundamentally, though, the Reagan attempt failed because the transformation of interest group politics led to large-scale structural changes in the public policymaking process.

Consequences

The rise of citizen groups and the rapid expansion of interest group advocacy in general have had many important long-term consequences for the way policy is formulated by the national government. Most important, policymaking moved away from closed subgovernments, each involving a relatively stable and restricted group of lobbyists and key government officials, to much broader policymaking communities. Policymaking in earlier years is typically described as the product of consensual negotiations between a small number of back-scratching participants.

Policymaking is now best described as taking place within issue networks rather than in subgovernments. An issue network is a set of organizations that share expertise in a policy area and interact with each other over time as relevant issues are debated. As sociologist Barry Wellman states, "The world is composed of networks, not groups." This is certainly descriptive of Washington policymaking. Policy formulation cannot be portrayed in terms of what a particular group wanted and how officials responded to those demands. The coalitions within networks, often involving scores of groups, define the divisions over issues and drive the policymaking process forward. Alliances are composed of both old friends and strange bedfellows; relationships are built on immediate need as well as on familiarity and trust. Organizations that do not normally work in a particular issue network can easily move into a policymaking community to work on a single issue. The only thing constant in issue networks is the changing nature of the coalitions.

The result of issue network politics is that policymaking has become more open, more conflictual, and more broadly participatory. What is crucial about the role of citizen groups is that they were instrumental in breaking down the barriers to participation in subgovernments. Building upon their own constituency support and working with allies in Congress, citizen groups made themselves players. They have not been outsiders, left to protest policies and a system that excluded them. Rather, they built opposition right into the policymaking communities that had previously operated with some commonality of interest. Even conservative administrators who would prefer to exclude these liberal advocacy groups have recognized that they have to deal with their opponents in one arena or another. The Nuclear Regulatory Commission, the epitome of an agency hostile to liberal advocacy groups, cannot get away with ignoring groups like the Union of Concerned Scientists. The consensus over nuclear power has long been broken. Critics and advocacy groups like the Union of Concerned Scientists have the technical expertise to involve themselves in agency proceedings, and they have the political know-how to get themselves heard on Capitol Hill and in the news media.

Issue networks are not simply divided between citizen groups on one side and business groups on another. Organizations representing business usually encompass a variety of interests, many of which are opposed to each other. As various business markets have undergone rapid change and become increasingly competitive, issue networks have found themselves divided by efforts of one sector of groups to use the policymaking process to try to gain market share from another sector of the network. Citizen groups, rather than simply being the enemy of business, are potential coalition partners for different business sectors. A characteristic of the culture of interest group politics in Washington is that there are no permanent allies and no permanent enemies.

Citizen groups are especially attractive as coalition partners because they have such a high level of credibility with the public and the news media. All groups claim to represent the public interest because they sincerely believe that the course of action they are advocating would be the most beneficial to the country. Since they do not represent any vocational or business interest, citizen groups may be perceived by some to be less biased—though certainly not unbiased—in their approach to public policy problems. This credibility is also built around the high-quality research that many citizen groups produce and distribute to journalists and policymakers in Washington. Reports from advocacy organizations such as Citizens for Tax Justice or the Center for Budget and Policy Priorities are quickly picked up by the media and disseminated across the country. Most business groups would love to have the respect that these citizen groups command in the press. For all the financial strength at the disposal of oil lobbyists, no representative of the oil industry has as much credibility with the public as a lobbyist for the Natural Resources Defense Council.

Despite the growth and stability of citizen groups in national politics, their reach does not extend into every significant policymaking domain. In the broad area of financial services, for example, citizen groups have played a minor role at best. There are some consumer groups that have been marginally active when specific issues involving banks, insurance companies, and securities firms arise, but they have demonstrated little influence or staying power. There is, however, a vital consumer interest at stake as public policymakers grapple with the crumbling walls that have traditionally divided different segments of the financial services market. Defense policy is another area where citizen groups have been relatively minor actors. But if citizen groups are conspicuous by their absence in some important areas, their overall reach is surprisingly broad. They have become major actors in policy areas where they previously had no presence at all. In negotiations over a free trade agreement with Mexico, for example, environmental groups became central players in the bargaining. These groups were concerned that increased U.S. investment in Mexico would result in increased pollution there from unregulated manufacturing, depleted groundwater supplies, and other forms of environmental degradation. To its dismay, the Bush White House found that the only practical course was to negotiate with the groups.

The increasing prominence of citizen groups and the expanding size of issue networks change our conception of the policymaking process. The basic structural attribute of a subgovernment was that it was relatively bounded with a stable set of participants. Even if there was some conflict in that subgovernment, there were predictable divisions and relatively clear expectations of what kind of conciliation between interest groups was possible. In contrast, issue networks seem like free-for-alls. In the health care field alone, 741 organizations have offices in Washington or employ a representative there. Where subgovernments suggested control over public policy by a limited number of participants, issue networks suggest no control whatsoever. Citizen groups make policymaking all the more difficult because they frequently sharpen the ideological debate; they have different organizational incentive systems from those of the corporations and trade groups with which they are often in conflict; and they place little emphasis on the need for economic growth, an assumption shared by most other actors.

This picture of contemporary interest group politics may make it seem impossible to accomplish anything in Washington. Indeed, it is a popular perception that Congress has become unproductive and that we are subject to some sort of national gridlock. Yet the policymaking system is adaptable, and the relationship between citizen groups and other actors in issue networks suggests that there are a number of productive paths for resolving complicated policy issues.

Complex Policymaking

The growth of issue networks is not, of course, the only reason why the policymaking process has become more complex. The increasingly technical nature of policy problems has obviously put an ever higher premium on expertise. Structural changes are critical, too. The decentralization of the House of Representatives that took place in the mid-1970s dispersed power and reduced the autonomy of leaders. Today, in the House, jurisdictions between committees frequently overlap and multiple referrals of bills are common. When an omnibus trade bill passed by both houses in 1987 was sent to conference, the House and the Senate appointed 200 conferees, who broke up into 17 subconferences. The growth of the executive branch has produced a similar problem of overlapping jurisdictions. In recent deliberations on proposed changes in wetlands policy, executive branch participants included the Soil Conservation Service in the Agriculture Department, the Fish and Wildlife Service in Interior, the Army Corps of Engineers, the Environmental Protection Agency (EPA), the Office of Management and Budget, the Council on Competitiveness, and the President's Domestic Policy Council.

Nevertheless, even though the roots of complex policymaking are multifaceted, the rise of citizen groups has been a critical factor in forcing the Congress and the executive branch to focus more closely on developing procedures to negotiate settlements of policy disputes. The quiet bargaining of traditional subgovernment politics was not an adequate mechanism for handling negotiations between scores of interest groups, congressional committees, and executive branch agencies.

Citizen groups have been particularly important in prompting more structured negotiations for a number of reasons. First, in many policy areas, citizen groups upset long-standing working arrangements between policymakers and other interest groups. Citizen groups were often the reason subgovernments crumbled; under pressure from congressional allies and public opinion, they were included in the bargaining and negotiating at some stage in the policymaking process.

Second, citizen groups could not be easily accommodated in basic negotiating patterns. It was not a matter of simply placing a few more chairs at the table. These groups' entrance into a policymaking community usually created a new dividing line between participants. The basic ideological cleavage that exists between consumer and environmental interests and business is not easy to bridge, and, consequently, considerable effort has been expended to devise ways of getting mutual antagonists to negotiate over an extended period. As argued above, once accepted at the bargaining table, citizen groups could be attractive coalition partners for business organizations.

Third, . . . citizen groups typically have a great deal of credibility with the press. Thus, in negotiating, they often have had more to gain by going public to gain leverage with other bargainers. This adds increased uncertainty and instability to the structure of negotiations.

Fourth, citizen groups are often more unified than their business adversaries. The business interests in an issue network may consist of large producers, small producers, foreign producers, and companies from other industries trying to expand into new markets. All these business interests may be fiercely divided as each tries to defend or encroach upon established market patterns. The environmentalists in the same network, while each may have its own niche in terms of issue specialization, are likely to present a united front on major policy disputes. In a perverse way, then, the position of citizen groups has been aided by the proliferation of business groups. (Even without the intrusion of citizen lobbies, this sharp rise in the number of business groups would have irretrievably changed the nature of subgovernments.) . . .

Conclusion

Citizen groups have changed the policymaking process in valuable and enduring ways. Most important, they have broadened representation in our political system. Many previously unrepresented or underrepresented constituencies now have a powerful voice in Washington politics. The expanding numbers of liberal citizen groups and their apparent success helped to stimulate a broad mobilization on the part of business. The skyrocketing increase in the numbers of interest groups worked to break down subgovernments and led to the rise of issue networks.

Issue networks are more fragmented, less predictable policymaking environments. Both Congress and the executive branch have taken steps to bring about greater centralized control and coherence to policymaking. Some of these institutional changes seem aimed directly at citizen groups. Negotiated regulations, for example, are seen as a way of getting around the impasse that often develops between liberal citizen groups and business organizations. Centralized regulatory review has been used by Republican administrations as a means of ensuring that business interests are given primacy; regulators are seen as too sympathetic to the citizen groups that are clients of their agencies.

Although government has established these and other institutional mechanisms for coping with complex policymaking environments, the American public does not seem to feel that the government copes very well at all. Congress has been portrayed as unproductive and spineless, unwilling to tackle the tough problems that require discipline or sacrifice. At the core of this criticism is that interest groups are the culprit. Washington lobbies, representing every conceivable interest and showering legislators with the political action committee donations they crave, are said to be responsible for this country's inability to solve its problems.

Although it is counterintuitive, it may be that the increasing number of interest groups coupled with the rise of citizen groups has actually improved the policymaking system in some important ways. More specifically, our policymaking process may be more democratic today because of these developments. Expanded interest group participation has helped to make the policymaking process more open and visible. The closed nature of subgovernment politics meant not only that participation was restricted but that public scrutiny was minimal. The proliferation of interest groups, Washington media that are more aggressive, and the willingness and ability of citizen groups in particular to go public as part of their advocacy strategy have worked to open up policymaking to the public eye.

The end result of expanded citizen group advocacy is policy communities that are highly participatory and more broadly representative of the public. One can argue that this more democratic policymaking process is also one that is less capable of concerted action; yet there is no reliable evidence that American government is any more or less responsive to pressing policy problems than it has ever been. There are, of course, difficult problems that remain unresolved, but that is surely true of every era. Democracy requires adequate representation of interests as well as institutions capable of addressing difficult policy problems. For policymakers who must balance the demand for representation with the need for results, the key is thinking creatively about how to build coalitions and structure negotiations between large groups of actors.

POSTSCRIPT

Is Government Dominated
by Big Business?

One of the problems for any pluralist is the danger that many people may not be properly represented. Suppose, for example, that business and environmental groups in Washington compromise their differences by supporting environmental legislation but passing the costs along to consumers. The legislation may be good, even necessary, but have the consumer's interests been taken into account? There are, of course, self-styled consumer groups, but it is hard to determine whether or not they really speak for the average consumer. The challenge for pluralists is to make their system as inclusive as possible.

The key issue is how dominant is corporate power in influencing government policies and their administration on issues that concern them. The dominant view is that neither the public nor mobilized non-corporate interests can effectively counterpose corporate interests. Two political scientists who have advocated this view in a lifetime of publications are G. William Domhoff and Thomas R. Dye. Domhoff's latest power elite work offers hope that fighting against corporate power may not be futile. See his *Changing the Powers that Be: How the Left Can Stop Losing and Win* (Rowman and Littlefield, 2003). Two of Dye's recent books are *Who's Running America?: The Bush Restoration* (Prentice Hall, 2003) and *Top Down Policymaking* (Chatham House, 2001). Other works supporting this view are Charles Perrow, *Organizing America: Wealth, Power, and the Origins of Corporate America* (Princeton University Press, 2002); Peter Kobrak, *Cozy Politics: Political Parties, Campaign Finance, and Compromised Governance* (Lynne Rienner, 2002); Arianna Stassinopoulos Huffington, *Pigs at the Trough: How Corporate Greed and Political Corruption Are Undermining America* (Crown, 2003); Ted Nace, *Gangs of America: The Rise of Corporate Power and the Disabling of Democracy* (Berrett-Koehler, 2003); Dan Clawson et al., *Dollars and Votes: How Business Campaign Contributions Subvert Democracy* (Temple University Press, 1998); John B. Parrott, *Being Like God: How American Elites Abuse Politics and Power* (University Press of America, 2003). Steve Fraser and Gary Gerstle (eds.), *Ruling American: A History of Wealth and Power in America* (Harvard University Press, 2005); Russell Mokhiber and Robert Weissman, *On the Rampage: Corporate Power and the Destruction of Democracy* (Common Courage Press, 2005); Paul Kivel, *You Call this Democracy?: Who Benefits, Who Pays and Who Really Decides?* (Apex Press, 2004); and Charles Derber, *Hidden Power: What You Need to Know to Save Our Democracy* (Berret-Koehler, 2005). Several authors advance the thesis that American corporations also to some degree rule the world including David C. Korten, *When Corporations Rule the World*, 2nd edition (Kumarian

Press, 2001); Milessa L. Rossi, *What Every American Should Know about Who's Really Running the World* (Plume, 2005); and Peter Alexis Gourevich and James J. Shinn, *Political Power and Corporate Control: The New Global Politics of Corporate Governance* (Princeton University Press, 2005). According to David C. Korten in *When Corporations Rule the World,* 2nd edition (Kumarian Press, 2001), American corporations also rule the world.

For some pluralist arguments, see David Vogel, *Fluctuating Fortunes: The Political Power of Business in America* (Basic Books, 1989) and *Kindred Strangers: The Uneasy Relationship Between Politics and Business in America* (Princeton University Press, 1996); John P. Heinz, Edward O. Laumann, Robert L. Nelson, and Robert H. Salisbury, *The Hollow Core: Private Interests in National Policy Making* (Harvard University Press, 1993); Susan Herbst, *Numbered Voices: How Opinion Polls Shape American Politics* (University of Chicago Press, 1993); Kevin Danaher, *Insurrection: Citizen Challenges to Corporate Power* (Routledge, 2003); David S. Meyers et al. (eds.), *Routing the Opposition: Social Movements, Public Policy, and Democracy* (University of Minnesota Press, 2005); and *Battling Big Business: Countering Greenwash, Infiltration, and Other Forms of Corporate Bullying* (Common Courage Press, 2002). Recently the pluralist view is being reworked into political process theory. See Andrew S. McFarland, *Neopluralism: The Evolution of Political Process Theory* (University Press of Kansas, 2004) and Andrew S. McFarland, *Neopluralism: The Evolution of Political Process Theory* (University Press of Kansas, 2004).

ISSUE 12

Should Government Intervene in a Capitalist Economy?

YES: Eliot Spitzer and Andrew G. Celli Jr., from "Bull Run: Capitalism with a Democratic Face," *The New Republic* (March 22, 2004)

NO: John Stossel, from "The Real Cost of Regulation," *Imprimis* (May 2001)

ISSUE SUMMARY

YES: Attorneys Eliot Spitzer and Andrew G. Celli Jr. argue that the government plays an essential role in enabling the market to work right. Capitalism runs amuck if it is not regulated to protect against abuse and ensure fairness.

NO: John Stossel, a TV news reporter and producer of one-hour news specials, argues that regulations have done immense damage and do not protect us as well as market forces.

T he expression "That government is best which governs least" sums up a deeply rooted attitude of many Americans. From early presidents Thomas Jefferson and Andrew Jackson to America's most recent leaders, George Bush, Bill Clinton, and George W. Bush, American politicians have often echoed the popular view that there are certain areas of life best left to the private actions of citizens.

One such area is the economic sphere, where people make their living by buying, selling, and producing goods and services. The tendency of most Americans is to regard direct government involvement in the economic sphere as both unnecessary and dangerous. The purest expression of this view is the economic theory of *laissez-faire*, a French term meaning "let be" or "let alone." The seminal formulation of *laissez-faire* theory was the work of eighteenth-century Scottish philosopher Adam Smith, whose treatise *The Wealth of Nations* appeared in 1776. Smith's thesis was that each individual, pursuing his or her own selfish interests in a competitive market, will be "led by an invisible hand to promote an end which was no part of his intention." In other words, when people singlemindedly seek profit, they actually serve the community because sellers must keep prices down and quality up if they are to meet the competition of other sellers.

Laissez-faire economics was much honored (in theory, if not always in practice) during the nineteenth and early twentieth centuries. But as the nineteenth century drew to a close, the Populist Party sprang up. The Populists denounced eastern bankers, Wall Street stock manipulators, and rich "moneyed interests," and they called for government ownership of railroads, a progressive income tax, and other forms of state intervention. The Populist Party died out early in the twentieth century, but the Populist message was not forgotten. In fact, it was given new life after 1929, when the stock market collapsed and the United States was plunged into the worst economic depression in its history.

By 1932 a quarter of the nation's workforce was unemployed, and most Americans were finding it hard to believe that the "invisible hand" would set things right. Some Americans totally repudiated the idea of a free market and embraced socialism, the belief that the state (or "the community") should run all major industries. Most stopped short of supporting socialism, but they were now prepared to welcome some forms of state intervention in the economy. President Franklin D. Roosevelt, elected in 1932, spoke to this mood when he pledged a "New Deal" to the American people. "New Deal" has come to stand for a variety of programs that were enacted during the first eight years of Roosevelt's presidency, including business and banking regulations, government pension programs, federal aid to the disabled, unemployment compensation, and government-sponsored work programs. Side by side with the "invisible hand" of the marketplace was now the very visible hand of an activist government.

Government intervention in the economic sphere increased during World War II as the government fixed prices, rationed goods, and put millions to work in government-subsidized war industries. Activist government continued during the 1950s, but the biggest leap forward occurred during the late 1960s and early 1970s, when the federal government launched a variety of new welfare and regulatory programs: the multibillion-dollar War on Poverty, new civil rights and affirmative action mandates, and new laws protecting consumers, workers, disabled people, and the environment. These, in turn, led to a proliferation of new government agencies and bureaus, as well as shelves and shelves of published regulations. Proponents of the new activism conceded that it was expensive, but they insisted that activist government was necessary to protect Americans against pollution, discrimination, dangerous products, and other effects of the modern marketplace. Critics of government involvement called attention not only to its direct costs but also to its effect on business activity and individual freedom.

In the following selections, Eliot Spitzer and Andrew Calli Jr. are is aware that regulations can go too far, but over two decades of privatization, deregulation, and government downsizing has swung the pendulum too far, and tighter regulations or government interventions are needed for the public good and to make the market work right. John Stossel can only imagine greater harm coming from an expanded role of government if the past is our guide.

Eliot Spitzer
Andrew G. Celli Jr.

 **YES**

Bull Run: Capitalism
with a Democratic Face

We are told we live in the New Economy, an economy of computers and fiber-optic cables, capital without borders, and competition on a global scale. This is mature market capitalism, and its promise for human advancement—when combined with democracy and individual freedom—is rightly touted at every turn. But, if our economy is a creature of the twenty-first century, our thinking about government's role in the economy is mired in the nineteenth.

Two essentially opposite viewpoints dominate today's debate. On one side are those who see market capitalism, loosely regulated and unencumbered by the artificial interventions of government, as perfection itself. They argue: Leave the markets alone, let them work, and efficiency, choice, and progress will follow. On the other side are those who argue that, as miraculous as the capitalist experiment has proved to be, free markets cannot be left unchecked. To maintain a just and equitable society, they say, markets must be protected from their natural tendency toward excesses that lead to monopolies and unfairness. In this scheme, government's role is to put the brakes on capitalism and to protect the public from market forces through its power to tax and regulate.

This conflict has often been reduced to caricature—heartless laissez-faire capitalists versus meddling government bureaucrats. But this characterization presents a false choice. If there is one lesson that can be gleaned from the New Economy, it is that the government's proper role is neither that of passive spectator nor lion tamer. The proper role of government is as market facilitator. Government should act to ensure that markets run cleanly as well as smoothly. It should prevent market failures and right them when they occur. And it should ensure that markets uphold the broad values of our culture rather than debase them. In this vision, government action is necessary for free markets to work as they are intended—in an open, competitive, and fair manner. In this vision, government helps to create, maintain, and expand competition, so the system as a whole can do what it does best: generate and broadly distribute wealth.

Where government has retreated from these core responsibilities, economic dislocation and decay have followed. Three recent examples make the point. We have chosen them not because they are the only or even the best available but because they reflect our practical experience over the past five years in New York state and because they illustrate three distinct rationales for market intervention: to enforce the rules to deal with market failures, and to uphold core American values. They show that the Bush administration's economic approach, while veiled in the rhetoric of free markets, actually subverts them. True free-marketers understand that free markets operate according to principles that must be enforced. But President George W. Bush has abdicated his responsibility to protect our markets, leaving a vacuum in which market failures are ignored or chalked up to "natural force" and the economy suffers shocks that could have been avoided or corrected by careful government intervention. By advocating smart government action and shifting the rhetorical paradigm, Democrats can provide voters with a coherent, pro-market justification for the policy objectives we share. It's good policy and good politics at the same time.

⋅❀⋅

Government has been effective and well received when it has acted to preserve (or restore) confidence in the fairness of the market itself. At a basic level, for a market to be truly free and efficient and have the full confidence of its participants, two things are required: integrity and transparency.

Integrity, in this context, is the idea that actors in the marketplace are what they purport to be: that those who claim to offer independent advice and analysis are not tainted by conflicts of interest; that those who are entrusted with protecting shareholders do so, rather than enriching themselves at shareholders' expenses; and that those who, by virtue of their wealth, power, or access, may be positioned to violate the rules do not. In a system where there is not, and cannot be, a cop on every metaphorical street corner, we rely on this integrity to give us confidence that the system is fair and genuinely competitive.

Just as actors must be what they claim to be, information in a free market must be accurate and truthful, freely flowing, disseminated in a timely way, and available to all. Transparency—implemented through disclosure requirements, institutional barriers to abuse, or widely accepted rules of conduct—is what makes meaningful choice possible. And choice by all actors in a rational market—be they investors or consumers, CEOs or shopkeepers—is what creates the competitive pressures that make the market more efficient and create wealth for us all.

Government is the institution best-suited to protect against corruption and abuse and to ensure that the economic playing field is level. But, in the 1990s, Wall Street experienced what can only be described as the "perfect storm" of government failure. It began with the consolidation of the financial-services sector—permitted by the repeal of the Glass-Steagall Act, a Depression-era statute requiring that commercial and investment banking be separated. The result was the formation of vast full-service enterprises that brought together many potentially conflicting lines of business, including commercial banking, investment banking, stock analysis, and retail brokerage. At the same time, we democratized the marketplace by (wisely) encouraging the American public at large to invest in the capital markets. The interface between mega-institutions and small investors was fraught with risk—risk met by a regulatory void. Indeed, Harvey Pitt, the first Securities and Exchange Commission (SEC) chair appointed by Bush, is a former industry lobbyist who promised the financial sector a "kinder, gentler SEC," an approach that led to a total breakdown in market enforcement. From Tyco to Enron to mutual funds to analyst compensation, the SEC simply was not attentive to the structural failures that were widely known to industry insiders.

With protections against conflicts of interest severely hobbled, integrity and transparency were soon sacrificed. As a result, research analysts whose compensation and career prospects depended upon the fortunes of their investment-banking partners pushed information about companies that was not just "imperfect," but false. In one infamous example, Merrill Lynch analyst Henry Blodget simultaneously helped pitch banking business to InfoSpace, a Web search company, and hyped the stock to investors, all the while telling his co-workers that the stock was a "piece of junk." In relying on corrupted advice like this, investors invested, corporate executives and investment bankers got rich, and companies that should have been market losers actually "succeeded."

But that success, which took the form of skyrocketing stock prices, options values, and compensation packages for corporate executives, was necessarily short-lived. The market had its revenge, as artificially pumped-up companies were unable to compete over the long term. Their business models failed and their stock prices plummeted. And yet abuses continued. Despite WorldCom's sinking fortunes, Citigroup analyst Jack Grubman kept promoting the stock, all the while receiving compensation that resulted from WorldCom's banking business with Citigroup. But, ultimately, he couldn't keep reality from catching up to WorldCom: Its share price dropped from $60 to 20 cents, wiping out $100 billion in market value.

The real victims were the companies' employees, the investing public, and the market itself. Not only had the public confidence essential to market performance been squandered, but the companies into which huge amounts of capital had been funneled were, from a long-term perspective, the wrong ones. Inefficient, unsound, and simply undeserving, these businesses failed to create meaningful jobs, growth, or lasting wealth. Couple these structural failures with the impact of other corporate scandals—such as Enron, Tyco, and Adelphia—and the result was grim. When the bubble burst in the late '90s, and the truth about overhyped companies came to light, stunned investors experienced the biggest drop in the S&P Index since the 1987 market crash—a drop with profound ripple effects throughout the national economy. A recession that was perhaps inevitable was deepened, and individuals who had set aside assets for education or retirement suddenly found these assets diminished or wiped out entirely.

So much had gone wrong in so short a time that government's ability to right the economy was limited. That said, the forceful reassertion of government's role as facilitator of the twin values of integrity and transparency has contributed powerfully to a sense that we are beginning to put our national economic house in order. With the acceptance of industry-wide codes of conduct by financial-services companies, new and more stringent disclosure and certification requirements under the Sarbanes-Oxley Act, and the aggressive policing of segments of the marketplace, the decline in investor confidence has been halted and perhaps even reversed.

⁕

Government can also help facilitate the smooth functioning of markets when they are unable to appropriately distribute costs. The burdens of pollution provide a classic example. Where the market finds itself unable to allocate pollution costs efficiently and fairly, and where the federal government refuses to act, the intervention of others, including state governments like New York's, has become necessary.

Take air pollution in the Northeast caused by coal burning power plants in the Midwest. Corporate players, acting in their rational self-interest, have failed to bear or equitably spread the costs associated with their activity. Instead, they have shifted those costs to others, for whom there is no market recourse. In this case, the costs were acid rain and airborne pollutants, and their devastating effects on the environment and human health—not in the Midwest, where the plants generate and sell their energy, but hundreds of miles downwind, in the Northeast. Plant owners had purposely built smokestacks tall enough that pollutants would fall not on their consumers or those nearby but, quite literally, into someone else's backyard. The costs have been dear. Thousands of New York children suffer from asthma that is at least partially attributable to pollution sent East from power plants in states like Kentucky, Ohio, and West Virginia. And even the Bush administration's Environmental Protection Agency admits that, in New York's Adirondack Mountains, hundreds of lakes have acidity levels that could kill off certain aquatic species.

In a perfectly functioning market, the costs imposed by this conduct would be borne either by the producer in the form of reduced profits or by the consumer in the form of higher prices. Such costs would not be dumped on the doorstep of those who don't benefit from cheap Midwestern energy. But that is precisely what is happening: Northeasterners have been left holding the bag, and the market alone offers them no way to respond. They are stuck—unless and until government intervenes.

Alas, the Bush administration has refused to do that. Even as it spouts the rhetoric of free-market efficiency, the White House has allowed the polluters to avoid bearing the economic and health-related costs they have imposed. It has tried to reverse a long-standing interpretation of Clean Air Act regulations, which require power plants and other industrial facilities to install modern pollution controls when they are upgraded. This shift in environmental policy represents an abandonment of the market principle that costs should be borne by those who consume or pay for the product—an abandonment driven by a desire to benefit the energy industry. Indeed, the connection between administration policy and interest-group politics is direct and explicit: The shift in the Clean Air Act's interpretation—undertaken to protect Midwestern polluters from having to make expensive upgrades—grew directly out of Vice President Dick Cheney's industry-dominated Energy Task Force, through which energy producers effectively dictated the very policies that are supposed to regulate them.

Left with no other choice, the states and citizens suffering from Midwest-generated pollution have gone to court and successfully stopped the administration's attempted policy change. The point of this effort is neither to limit the availability of cheap energy to Midwest consumers, nor to shift the costs to them simply for the sake of doing so. Rather, it is to ensure, as an efficient market must, that the costs are borne by the parties responsible. Only by placing the costs where they belong can the market system as a whole assess whether the product is being efficiently created and appropriately priced vis-á-vis potential competitors. That is when the market, freed from its own failures, really works.

⁕⁕⁕

Lastly, our commitment to market capitalism cannot obscure one glaring and immutable fact: that, in a number of important ways, an unregulated market does not safeguard certain core American values. That's why our government—with broad bipartisan support—has instituted child-labor laws, minimum wage laws, anti-discrimination laws, and certain safety net protections designed to ensure that people do not fall below a basic level of sustenance. There is little debate today about the value of these measures. They are, in essence, what we are all about. Child labor is not forbidden in this country because it is inefficient (although it is): it is forbidden because it is wrong.

Unfortunately, our belief in the importance of equal opportunity and nondiscrimination is too often forgotten when it comes to the debate over whether and how to police the market for home mortgages. In poor and working-class communities across the nation, predatory mortgage lending has become a new scourge. Predatory lending is the practice of imposing inflated interest rates, fees, charges, and other onerous terms on home mortgage loans—not because the imperatives of the market require them, but because the lender has found a way to get away with them. These loans (which are often sold as refinance or home-improvement mechanisms) are foisted on borrowers who have no realistic ability to repay them and who face the loss of their hard-won home equity when the all-but-inevitable default and foreclosure occurs. When lenders systematically target certain low-income communities for loans of this sort, as they often do, the result is more insidious. Costs are imposed and burdens inflicted in a manner and to a degree that is discriminatory by race.

On the surface, predatory lenders are doing nothing more than seizing a "market opportunity" for refinancing or home-improvement loans in lower-income communities. To be sure, such communities desperately need credit. And it stands to reason that the prices and terms will be less favorable to borrowers whose financial circumstances are troubled or limited. In this sense, predatory loans are the natural outcome of a competitive market. In a policy debate bereft of values, this market rationale becomes a value unto itself—and values like equal opportunity disappear.

But, in our system, the market is there to serve our values, not the other way around. As study after study has shown, the overwhelming majority of people who fall prey to predatory loans would be better off with no loan at all. Moreover, borrowers in this category often bear the same or similar financial characteristics—income levels, credit-worthiness, ability and willingness to repay—as their counterparts in the prime market. As a matter of economics, they actually qualify for good loans at good rates. What distinguishes them from borrowers who get credit at the right price, on the right terms, is their actual and perceived lack of options, their limited financial savvy, and, too often, the color of their skin—and sometimes their age or gender.

For a society devoted to fairness and nondiscrimination—as well as the quintessentially American goal of homeownership—the prices, terms, and overall economic impact that we see in predatory home mortgage loans cannot be justified. They are just plain wrong. And, quite apart from the values issue, it is difficult to imagine a less rational, less efficient economic practice than lending of this sort. At the micro-level, it results in a gross misallocation of costs—imposing higher costs than the market requires on those least able to bear them. At the macro-level, it denies lower-cost capital to whole classes of persons who would otherwise qualify for it and to neighborhoods whose economic vitality depends on it.

In these circumstances, government must step in to curb predatory lending and encourage the flow of fairly priced capital to sectors where it is needed and will be well-used. Filling a gap left by federal inaction, state enforcement efforts in this arena have centered on identifying the valid economic criteria considered in mortgage underwriting and compelling lenders to focus on those factors—not on preconceptions, prejudices, or predatory instincts—in determining how to price home mortgage loans. The point is not to protect people from their own bad decisions or, conversely, to guarantee that mortgages be granted to specific persons or groups on specific terms—that would violate the principle of market freedom. The point is to support equal opportunity and to ensure that borrowers are charged rates and fees based upon their status and qualifications as economic actors in the mortgage market, not upon their diminished access or market savvy or their race. In taking action of this sort, state government regulators have upheld core national values and facilitated a fair and open market at the same time.

The Bush administration's reaction has been swift, predictable, and negative. The Treasury Department's Office of the Comptroller of the Currency has issued regulations stripping states of authority to stop predatory lending. It claims that continued state enforcement and regulatory authority will interfere with federal efforts to "regulate" national banks and, of course, with the free market in credit. In truth, the yawning gap between federal rhetoric and federal action in this area suggests a different rationale. Far from seeking to preserve federal prerogatives to regulate or to protect the market from state meddling, these efforts smack of a surrender to banking interests at the expense of market efficiency and the people capitalism is intended to serve.

⋆⊙⋆

In a period of severe budget constraints, complex and shifting global entanglements, and a failure of political will, one of our most difficult choices concerns what role government should play in an economy that on the whole has proved astonishingly durable, efficient, and successful. It is a choice we must make as members of a democratic polity, as citizens of a global economy, and as Democrats for whom the old answers no longer satisfy.

President Bush has helped frame that choice. By pursuing policies that are cloaked in free-market rhetoric but fail to facilitate fair markets, he has surrendered to corporate constituencies. He has shown that his party's rhetorical attachment to free markets is just that—a rhetorical attachment and nothing more. And he has done so at a time when it is clear that government nonintervention leads not to market freedom and a rising of all boats but to unrestrained corporatism, gross market distortions, inequitable accumulation of wealth, and economic stasis.

In trying to articulate a more constructive vision—one that is both fiscally and economically sound and that makes sense to the average American voter—Democrats should promote government as a supporter of free markets, not simply a check on them. Government action must be justified by its ability to define, catalyze, and facilitate the market's core mechanisms; to prevent it from faltering under the weight of its own imperfections; and to uphold the underlying values to which the system is, or ought to be, dedicated. It is a vision consistent with trust-busting and other progressive market measures first enunciated early in the last century by Theodore Roosevelt, who said, "We grudge no man a fortune which represents his own power and sagacity, when exercised with entire regard to the welfare of his fellows."

By taking up the mantle of efficient, forward-looking, and market-oriented government action, Democrats can move from being a party that simply opposes Bush's tainted version of laissez-faire to one that advocates for the progress that comes with real market freedom. It is a powerful argument, a true argument, and it is ours for the making.

NO

John Stossel

The Real Cost of Regulation

The following is an abridged version of Mr. Stossel's speech delivered on February 20, 2001, in Fort Myers, Florida, at a Hillsdale College seminar.

When I started 30 years ago as a consumer reporter, I took the approach that most young reporters take today. My attitude was that capitalism is essentially cruel and unfair, and that the job of government, with the help of lawyers and the press, is to protect people from it. For years I did stories along those lines—stories about Coffee Association ads claiming that coffee "picks you up while it calms you down," or Libby-Owens-Ford Glass Company ads touting the clarity of its product by showing cars with their windows rolled down. I and other consumer activists said, "We've got to have regulation. We've got to police these ads. We've got to have a Federal Trade Commission." And I'm embarrassed at how long it took me to realize that these regulations make things worse, not better, for ordinary people.

The damage done by regulation is so vast, it's often hard to see. The money wasted consists not only of the taxes taken directly from us to pay for bureaucrats, but also of the indirect cost of all the lost energy that goes into filling out the forms. Then there's the distraction of creative power. Listen to Jack Faris, president of the National Federation of Independent Business: "If you're a small businessman, you have to get involved in government or government will wreck your business." And that's what happens. You have all this energy going into lobbying the politicians, forming the trade associations and PACs, and trying to manipulate the leviathan that's grown up in Washington, D.C. and the state capitals. You have many of the smartest people in the country today going into law, rather than into engineering or science. This doesn't create a richer, freer society. Nor do regulations only depress the economy. They depress the spirit. Visitors to Moscow before the fall of communism noticed a dead-eyed look in the people. What was that about? I don't think it was about fear of the KGB. Most Muscovites didn't have intervention by the secret police in their daily lives. I think it was the look that people get when they live in an all-bureaucratic state. If you go to Washington, to the Environmental Protection Agency, I think you'll see the same thing.

One thing I noticed that started me toward seeing the folly of regulation was that it didn't even punish the obvious crooks. The people selling the breast-enlargers and the burn-fat-while-you-sleep pills got away with it. The Attorney

General would come at them after five years, they would hire lawyers to gain another five, and then they would change the name of their product or move to a different state. But regulation *did* punish *legitimate* businesses.

When I started reporting, all the aspirin companies were saying they were the best, when in fact aspirin is simply aspirin. So the FTC sued and demanded corrective advertising. Corrective ads would have been something like, "Contrary to our prior ads, Excedrin does not relieve twice as much pain." Of course these ads never ran. Instead, nine years of costly litigation finally led to a consent order. The aspirin companies said, "We don't admit doing anything wrong, but we won't do it again." So who won? Unquestionably the lawyers did. But did the public? Aspirin ads are more honest now. They say things like, "Nothing works better than Bayer"—which, if you think about it, simply means, "We're all the same." But I came to see that the same thing would have happened without nearly a decade of litigation, because markets police themselves. I can't say for certain *how* it would have happened. I think it's a fatal conceit to predict how markets will work. Maybe Better Business Bureaus would have gotten involved. Maybe the aspirin companies would have sued each other. Maybe the press would have embarrassed them. But the truth would have gotten out. The more I watched the market, the more impressed I was by how flexible and reasonable it is compared to government-imposed solutions.

Market forces protect us even where we tend most to think we need government. Consider the greedy, profit-driven companies that have employed me. CBS, NBC, and ABC make their money from advertisers, and they've paid me for 20 years to bite the hand that feeds them. Bristol-Myers sued CBS and me for $23 million when I did the story on aspirin. You'd think CBS would have said, "Stossel ain't worth that." But they didn't. Sometimes advertisers would pull their accounts, but still I wasn't fired. Ralph Nader once said that this would never happen except on public television. In fact the opposite is true: Unlike PBS, almost every local TV station has a consumer reporter. The reason is capitalism: More people watch stations that give honest information about their sponsors' products. So although a station might lose some advertisers, it can charge the others more. Markets protect us in unexpected ways.

Alternatives to the Nanny State

People often say to me, "That's okay for advertising. But when it comes to health and safety, we've got to have OSHA, the FDA, the CPSC" and the whole alphabet soup of regulatory agencies that have been created over the past several decades. At first glance this might seem to make sense. But by interfering with free markets, regulations almost invariably have nasty side effects. Take the FDA, which saved us from thalidomide—the drug to prevent morning sickness in pregnant women that was discovered to cause birth defects. To be accurate, it wasn't so much that the FDA saved us, as that it was so slow in studying thalidomide that by the end of the approval process, the drug's awful effects were being seen in Europe. I'm glad for this. But since the thalidomide scare, the FDA has grown ten-fold in size, and I believe it now does more harm than good. If you want to get a new drug approved today, it costs about $500 million and takes about ten years. This means that there are drugs currently in existence that would improve or even save lives, but that are being withheld from us because of a tiny chance they contain carcinogens. Some years ago, the FDA held a press conference to announce its long-awaited approval of a new beta-blocker, and predicted it would save 14,000 American lives per year. Why didn't anybody stand up at the time and say, "Excuse me, doesn't that mean you killed 14,000 people last year by not approving it?" The answer is, reporters don't think that way.

Why, in a free society, do we allow government to perform this kind of nanny-state function? A reasonable alternative would be for government to serve as an information agency. Drug companies wanting to submit their products to a ten-year process could do so. Those of us who choose to be cautious could take only FDA-approved drugs. But others, including people with terminal illnesses, could try non-approved drugs without sneaking off to Mexico or breaking the law. As an added benefit, all of us would learn something valuable by their doing so. I'd argue further that we don't need the FDA to perform this research. As a rule, government agencies are inefficient. If we abolished the FDA, private groups like the publisher of *Consumer Reports* would step in and do the job better, cheaper, and faster. In any case, wouldn't that be more compatible with what America is about? Patrick Henry never said, "Give me absolute safety or give me death!"

Lawyers and Liability

If we embrace the idea of free markets, we have to accept the fact that trial lawyers have a place. Private lawsuits could be seen as a supplement to Adam Smith's invisible hand: the invisible fist. In theory they should deter bad behavior. But because of how our laws have evolved, this process has gone horribly wrong. It takes years for victims to get their money, and most of the money goes to lawyers. Additionally, the wrong people get sued. A Harvard study of medical malpractice suits found that most of those getting money don't deserve it, and that most people injured by negligence don't sue. The system is a mess. Even the cases the trial lawyers are most proud of don't really make us safer. They brag about their lawsuit over football helmets, which were thin enough that some kids were getting head injuries. But now the helmets are so thick that kids are butting each other and getting other kinds of injuries. Worst of all, they cost over $100 each. School districts on the margin can't afford them, and as a result some are dropping their football programs. Are the kids from these schools safer playing on the streets? No.

An even clearer example concerns vaccines. Trial lawyers sued over the Diphtheria-Pertussis-Tetanus Vaccine, claiming that it wasn't as safe as it might have been. Although I suspect this case rested on junk science, I don't know what the truth is. But assuming these lawyers were right, and that they've made the DPT vaccine a little safer, are we safer? When they sued, there were twenty companies in America researching and making vaccines. Now there are four. Many got out of the business because they said, "We don't make that much on vaccines. Who needs this huge liability?" Is America better off with four vaccine makers instead of twenty? No way.

These lawsuits also disrupt the flow of information that helps free people protect themselves. For example, we ought to read labels. We should read the label on tetracycline, which says that it won't work if taken with milk. But who reads labels anymore? I sure don't. There are 21 warning labels on stepladders—"Don't dance on stepladders wearing wet shoes," etc.—because of the threat of liability. Drug labels are even crazier. If anyone were actually to read the two pages of fine print that come with birth control pills, they wouldn't need to take the drug. My point is that government and lawyers don't make us safer. Freedom makes us safer. It allows us to protect *ourselves*. Some say, "That's fine for us. We're educated. But the poor and the ignorant need government regulations to protect them." Not so. I sure don't know what makes one car run better or safer than another. Few of us are automotive engineers. But it's hard to get totally ripped off buying a car in America. The worst car you can find here is safer than the best cars produced in planned economies. In a free society, not everyone has to be an expert in order for markets to protect us. In the case of cars, we just need a few car buffs who read car magazines. Information gets around through word-of-mouth. Good companies thrive and bad ones atrophy. Freedom protects the ignorant, too.

Admittedly there are exceptions to this argument. I think we need some environmental regulation, because now and then we lack a market incentive to behave well in that area. Where is the incentive for me to keep my waste-treatment plant from contaminating your drinking water? So we need some rules, and some have done a lot of good. Our air and water are cleaner thanks to catalytic converters. But how much regulation is enough? President Clinton set a record as he left office, adding 500,000 new pages to the Federal Register—a whole new spiderweb of little rules for us to obey. How big should government be? For most of America's history, when we grew the fastest, government accounted for five percent or less of GDP. The figure is now 40 percent. This is still less than Europe. But shouldn't we at least have an intelligent debate about how much government should do? The problem is that to have such a debate, we need an informed public. And here I'm embarrassed, because people in my business are not helping that cause.

Fear-Mongering: A Risky Business

A turning point came in my career when a producer came into my office excited because he had been given a story by a trial lawyer—the lazy reporter's best friend—about Bic lighters spontaneously catching fire in people's pockets. These lighters, he told me, had killed four Americans in four years. By this time I'd done some homework, so I said, "Fine. I'll do the exploding lighter story after I do stories on plastic bags, which kill 40 Americans every four years, and five-gallon buckets, which kill 200 Americans (mostly children) every four years." This is a big country, with 280 million people. Bad things happen to some of them. But if we frighten all the rest about ant-sized dangers, they won't be prepared when an elephant comes along. The producer stalked off angrily and got Bob Brown to do the story. But several years later, when ABC gave me three hour-long specials a year in order to keep me, I insisted the first one be called, "Are We Scaring Ourselves to Death?" In it, I ranked some of these risks and made fun of the press for its silliness in reporting them.

Risk specialists compare risks not according to how many people they kill, but according to how many days they reduce the average life. The press goes nuts over airplane crashes, but airplane crashes have caused fewer than 200 deaths per year over the past 20 years. That's less than one day off the average life. There is no proof that toxic-waste sites like Love Canal or Times Beach have hurt anybody at all, despite widely reported claims that they cause 1,000 cases of cancer a year. (Even assuming they do, and assuming further that all these cancer victims die, that would still be less than four days off the average life.) House fires account for about 4,500 American deaths per year—18 days off the average life. And murder, which leads the news in most towns, takes about 100 days off the average life. But to bring these risks into proper perspective, we need to compare them to far greater risks like driving, which knocks 182 days off the average life. I am often asked to do scare stories about flying—"The Ten Most Dangerous Airports" or "The Three Most Dangerous Airlines"—and I refuse because it's morally irresponsible. When we scare people about flying, more people drive to Grandma's house, and more are killed as a result. This is statistical murder, perpetuated by regulators and the media.

Even more dramatic is the fact that Americans below the poverty line live seven to ten fewer years than the rest of us. Some of this difference is self-induced: poor people smoke and drink more. But most of it results from the fact that they can't afford some of the good things that keep the rest of us alive. They drive older cars with older tires; they can't afford the same medical care; and so on. This means that when bureaucrats get obsessed about flying or toxic-waste sites, and create new regulations and drive up the cost of living in order to reduce these risks, they shorten people's lives by making them poorer. Bangladesh has floods that kill 100,000 people. America has comparable floods and no one dies. The difference is wealth. Here we have TVs and radios to hear about floods, and cars to drive off in. Wealthier is healthier, and regulations make the country poorer. Maybe the motto of OSHA should be: "To save four, kill ten."

Largely due to the prevalence of misleading scare stories in the press, we see in society an increasing fear of innovation. Natural gas in the home kills 200 Americans a year, but we accept it because it's old. It happened before we got crazy. We accept coal, which is awful stuff, but we're terrified of nuclear power, which is probably cleaner and safer. Swimming pools kill over 1,000 Americans every year, and I think it's safe to say that the government wouldn't allow them today if they didn't already exist. What about vehicles that weigh a ton and are driven within inches of pedestrians by 16-year-olds, all while spewing noxious exhaust? Cars, I fear, would never make it off the drawing board in 2001.

What's happened to America? Why do we allow government to make decisions for us as if we were children? In a free society we should be allowed to take risks, and to learn from them. The press carps and whines about our exposure to dangerous new things—invisible chemicals, food additives, radiation, etc. But what's the result? We're living longer than ever. A century ago, most people my age were already dead. If we were better informed, we'd realize that what's behind this longevity is the spirit of enterprise, and that what gives us this spirit—what makes America thrive—isn't regulation. It's freedom.

POSTSCRIPT

Should Government Intervene in a Capitalist Economy?

As with most good debates, the issue of the rightness of government intervention is difficult to decide. Part of the difficulty is that it involves the trade-off of values that are in conflict in real situations, and part of the difficulty is that it involves uncertain estimations of the future consequences of policy changes. Both experts and interested parties can differ greatly on value trade-offs and estimations of impacts. Government regulations and other interventions cost money for both administration and compliance. Nevertheless, Spitzer and Celli argue that certain government actions will provide benefits that greatly exceed the costs, and Stossel argues the contrary view that the costs will be far greater than Spitzer and Celli expect and probably will have net negative results. Part of the strength of Stossel's argument is that regulations often fail to do what they are designed to do. Part of the strength of Spitzer and Celli argument is that there are many observable problems that need to be addressed, and for some of these government action seems to be the only viable option.

One aspect of the issue is the morality of businesses. Most commentators have a low opinion of business ethics and the way corporations use their power, and point to the recent corporate scandals as confirmation. Thus it is easy to conclude that since they will not do what is right, they must be made to do what is right. For support of this view see Joel Bakan, *The Corporation: The Pathological Pursuit of Profit and Power* (Free Press, 2004); Justin O"Brien, *Wall Street on Trial: A Corrupted State?* (Wiley, 2003); Steve Tombs and Dave Whyte, *Unmasking the Crimes of the Powerful: Scrutinizing States and Corporations* (P. Lang, 2003); Jamie Court, *Corporateering: How Corporate Power Steals Your Personal Freedom—and What You Can Do about It* (Jeremy P. Tarcher/Putnam, 2003); Kenneth R. Gray et al., *Corporate Scandels: The Many Faces of Greed: The Great Heist, Financial Bubbles, and the Absence of Virtue* (Paragon House, 2005); and Victor Perlo, *Superprofits and Crisis: Modern U.S. Capitalism* (International Publishers, 1988). Some commentators, however, defend businesses in a competitive capitalistic market.

Philosopher Michael Novak contends that the ethic of capitalism transcends mere moneymaking and is (or can be made) compatible with Judeo-Christian morality. See *The Spirit of Democratic Capitalism* (Madison Books, 1991) and *The Catholic Ethic and the Spirit of Capitalism* (Free Press, 1993). Another broad-based defense of capitalism is Peter L. Berger's *The Capitalist Revolution: Fifty Propositions About Prosperity, Equality and Liberty* (Basic Books, 1988). For a feminist critique of capitalism, see J. K. Gibson-Graham, *The End of Capitalism (As We Know It): A Feminist Critique of Political Economy* (Blackwell, 1996). For a mixed view of capitalism, see Charles Wolf, Jr., *Markets or Governments: Choosing*

Between Imperfect Alternatives (MIT Press, 1993). A strong attack on government interventions in the market is Jonathan Rauch, *Demosclerosis: The Silent Killer of American Government* (Times Books, 1994).

For an in-depth understanding of the way that markets work and the role that institutions maintained by the state, including property rights, function to maintain markets, see Neil Fligstein, *The Architecture of Markets: An Economic Sociology of Twenty-First Century Capitalist Societies* (Princeton University Press, 2001). An interesting role of government is its bailing-out failed corporations. See *Too Big to Fail: Policies and Practices in Government Bailouts* edited by Benton E. Gup (Praeger, 2004) and David G. Mayes et al. *Who Pays for Bank Insolvency?* (Palgrave Macmillan, 2004). Often self-regulation is better than government regulation. See Virgina Haufler, *A Public Role for the Private Sector: Industry Self-Regulation in a Global Economy* (Carnegie Endowment for International Peace, 2001).

ISSUE 13

Has Welfare Reform Benefited the Poor?

YES: Scott Winship and Christopher Jencks, from "Understanding Welfare Reform," *Harvard Magazine* (November/December 2004)

NO: Sharon Hayes, from "Off the Rolls: The Ground-Level Results of Welfare Reform," *Dissent Magazine* (Fall 2003)

ISSUE SUMMARY

YES: Sociologists Scott Winship and Christopher Jencks show that welfare reform and a good economy reduced welfare rolls by more than half and reduced poverty at the same time. They argue that the critics of welfare reform were wrong.

NO: Sharon Hayes, professor of sociology at the University of Virginia, got to know many welfare mothers and learned what happened to them since the welfare reform. Her article points out that while quite a few mothers have left welfare since the reform, many cannot hold on to a job and are now worse off than before.

In his 1984 book *Losing Ground: American Social Policy, 1950–1980* (Basic Books), policy analyst Charles Murray recommends abolishing Aid to Families with Dependent Children (AFDC), the program at the heart of the welfare debate. At the time of the book's publication this suggestion struck many as simply a dramatic way for Murray to make some of his points. However, 14 years later this idea became the dominant idea in Congress. In 1996 President Bill Clinton signed into law the Work Opportunity Reconciliation Act and fulfilled his 1992 campaign pledge to "end welfare as we know it." Murray's thesis that welfare hurt the poor had become widely accepted. In "What to Do About Welfare," *Commentary* (December 1994), Murray argues that welfare contributes to dependency, illegitimacy, and the number of absent fathers, which in turn can have terrible effects on the children involved. He states that workfare, enforced child support, and the abolition of welfare would greatly reduce these problems.

One reason why Congress ended AFDC was the emergence of a widespread backlash against welfare recipients. Much of the backlash, however, was misguided. It often rested on the assumptions that welfare is generous and that most people on welfare are professional loafers. In fact, over the previous two decades payments to families with dependent children eroded considerably relative to the cost of living. Furthermore, most women with dependent children on welfare had intermittent periods of work, were elderly, or were disabled. Petty fraud may be common since welfare payments are insufficient to live on in many cities, but "welfare queens" who cheat the system for spectacular sums are so rare that they should not be part of any serious debate on welfare issues. The majority of people on welfare are those whose condition would become desperate if payments were cut off. Although many believe that women on welfare commonly bear children in order to increase their benefits, there is no conclusive evidence to support this conclusion.

Not all objections to AFDC can be easily dismissed, however. There does seem to be evidence that in some cases AFDC reduces work incentives and increases the likelihood of family breakups. But there is also a positive side to AFDC—it helped many needy people get back on their feet. When all things are considered together, therefore, it is not clear that welfare, meaning AFDC, was bad enough to be abolished. But it was abolished on July 1, 1997, when the Work Opportunity Reconciliation Act went into effect. Now the question is whether the new policy is better than the old policy.

It is too soon to obtain an accurate assessment of the long-term impacts of the act. Nevertheless, AFDC rolls have declined since the act was passed, so many conclude that it is a success rather than a failure. Of course, the early leavers are the ones with the best prospects of succeeding in the work world; the welfare-towork transition gets harder as the program works with the more difficult cases. The crucial question is whether or not the reform will benefit those it affects. Already many working former welfare recipients are better off. But what about the average or more vulnerable recipient?

In the readings that follow, Scott Winship and Christopher Jencks claim that welfare reform was a great success because employment statistics went up dramatically for welfare mothers and welfare rolls went down dramatically. In the second selection, Sharon Hayes acknowledges that welfare rolls have declined but challenges, with stories of ex welfare mothers, the assumption that most lives have improved as a result. The lives of many vulnerable women have become much more unmanageable. Thus the consequences of the welfare reform are mixed.

**Scott Winship and
Christopher Jencks**

 **YES**

Understanding Welfare Reform

One million children pushed into poverty: That was the prediction of a widely cited study on the likely effect of welfare reform, released just before Congress passed the landmark legislation in August 1996. The "Personal Responsibility and Work Opportunity Reconciliation Act" gave states unprecedented discretion in setting eligibility standards, established more stringent work requirements for those receiving federally funded benefits, and imposed a five-year lifetime limit on federal benefits for most recipients. When President Clinton signed the bill into law, in the middle of the presidential campaign, several members of his administration resigned in protest. Liberals, advocates for the poor, and poverty researchers were nearly unanimous in their opposition. Even most conservatives, with their talk of group homes and private charities, implicitly conceded that the benefits of welfare reform lay in the long-run behavioral changes that they expected it to produce. In the short run, all agreed, things would have to get worse before they got better.

Fast-forward to 2002, when the welfare legislation was set to expire. That year the welfare rolls were less than half their size in 1996. Female-headed families with children were less likely to receive welfare benefits than at any point in at least 40 years. The magnitude of the change surpassed everyone's predictions. Even more remarkably, however, the official poverty rate among female-headed families with children—based on $14,500 for a woman with two children in 2002—had fallen from 42 percent to 34 percent during this period. At no time between 1959 (when the Census Bureau first began tabulating such data) and 1996 had this figure dropped below 40 percent. Welfare reform is now widely viewed as one of the greatest successes of contemporary social policy.

Nonetheless, social scientists who study anti-poverty policy disagree about whether welfare reform really improved living standards among female-headed families with children. Analyses that we recently conducted shed new light on this question. Our research leads us to conclude that welfare reform did not increase material hardship among single mothers and their children and may well have helped reduce it. That was because the reform was part of a larger package of policy changes including a more generous Earned Income Tax Credit (EITC), a higher minimum wage, and

From *Harvard Magazine*, November/December 2004, pp. 34-35, 97-98. Copyright © 2004 by Scott Winship and Christopher Jencks. Reprinted by permission of the authors.

expanded childcare subsidies. These policy changes were politically dependent on one another. Congress expanded the EITC in order to help single mothers make ends meet when they took low-wage jobs, and it raised the minimum wage within days of passing welfare reform for the same reason. Likewise, the money that states saved by reducing their welfare caseloads was often used to expand childcare subsidies. Taken together, these changes constitute what we will call the "welfare-reform package." This was a major policy shift, which simultaneously imposed more stringent work requirements on single mothers and provided more government assistance to those who found low-wage jobs.

Even so, the experience of the 1990s allows policymakers to draw only limited inferences about future reforms. Although welfare reform has succeeded in its current form, in our view legislators should now leave it alone, rather than trying to fix what is not broken.

Did Hardship among Single Mothers and Their Children Decline?

If official poverty rates among female-headed families with children declined in the years following welfare reform, why might social scientists question whether hardship declined? One reason is that official poverty rates ignore noncash benefits such as food stamps and Medicaid, the major healthcare program for low-income families. In fact, unmarried female heads were *less* likely to get food stamps and Medicaid in the late 1990s than in either the 1980s or the early 1990s, even though they often remained eligible. (As we shall see, however, other federal and state programs to help these families became more generous during the late 1990s.)

Another reason for not taking changes in the official poverty rate at face value is that poverty estimates are based solely on income and family composition, and are not adjusted for work-related *expenses*. The social-policy reforms of the 1990s dramatically increased the proportion of single mothers who worked. Working usually increased these mothers' income, but in most cases it also increased their expenses for childcare, transportation, and clothes. Greater participation in the formal labor market is also likely to have reduced welfare recipients' earnings from off-the-books jobs, as well as the amount of financial help they got from family members and boyfriends. One might therefore expect the shift from welfare to regular employment to increase unmarried mothers' reported income more than it increased their standard of living.

To get around the limitations of income and poverty statistics, we examined changes in material hardship among all families headed by a single mother, using the Food Security Survey, which the Census Bureau conducts every year for the Department of Agriculture. This survey measures families' ability to feed themselves adequately. It asks about problems that range from relatively common (having to "stretch" the food supply) to the very rare (a child went hungry for an entire day).

Our analysis of nearly 50 such measures revealed that food problems among single mothers and their children declined consistently between 1995 and 2000, when the economy was expanding. In April 1995, for instance, 57 percent of single mothers reported having to stretch their food supply at some point during the previous year because their monthly budget came up short. By April 2001, this figure had fallen to 46 percent. The share of single mothers reporting that a child was not eating enough fell from 11 to 8 percent. In short, while insecurity among mother-only families remained remarkably high in April 2001—given that the national unemployment rate was only 4.5 percent that month—the improvement since 1995 was sizable.

Also consistent with official poverty rates, most measures of food problems increased as unemployment rose between 2000 and 2002. But these increases were almost always much smaller than the declines between 1995 and 2000, so mother-only families still reported significantly fewer problems at the end of 2002 than they had in 1995. Official poverty statistics, then, appear to predict recent trends in hardship among female-headed families with children quite accurately.

Did the Welfare-Reform Package Reduce Hardship among Female-Headed Families?

The fact that hardship declined during the period in which the federal welfare-reform package was being implemented does not mean that the reforms were responsible for the improvement. These were also years of sustained economic growth. Unemployment fell from 1995 to 2000, and real wages among the worst-paid workers rose. Some scholars think that these changes fully account for the gains that mother-only families experienced. Indeed, it is even conceivable that single mothers and their children might have experienced even bigger declines in poverty and hardship had welfare reform not pushed so many unskilled recipients off the rolls.

To distinguish the effects of social-policy changes from the effects of the economic boom of the 1990s, we first examined whether falling unemployment had had comparable effects on poverty rates among single mothers during earlier business cycles. From the early 1960s to the mid 1990s, economic expansions reduced poverty more among two-parent families than among single-mother families, and recessions harmed two-parent families more. This pattern was widely cited both as evidence that welfare was a poverty trap and as evidence that it was a safety net. Both claims may be correct. It is conceivable that during booms, single mothers did not benefit from economic growth as much as they might have, but during busts they were shielded from rising unemployment. At any rate, this pattern is exactly the opposite of the one we observe during the most recent business cycle, when single mothers *gained more* than married couples during the boom and *lost more* during the bust. The implication of this change is that, in the absence of the welfare reform package, falling unemployment would have had less impact on poverty among single mothers and their children in the late 1990s.

The economic boom of the late 1990s was unusual, however, because the wages of America's worst-paid workers rose faster than prices for the first time in a generation. Real hourly wage rates among the bottom 20 percent of workers rose about 11 percent between 1995 and 2000. Mean family income among single mothers in the bottom half of the earnings distribution for all single mothers grew 16 percent during this period. Because single mothers' earnings are only one component of their family incomes, and because not all single mothers work, we estimate that the growth in wages for the worst-paid single mothers can account for only one-fourth of the income gains their families experienced. The difference was largely attributable to increases in employment and hours worked. Social-policy reforms, in conjunction with rising wages paid to low-skilled workers, strengthened single mothers' attachment to the labor force to a greater extent than in previous economic booms.

Why Did the Sky Not Fall?

Predictions of widespread destitution turned out to be wrong for three reasons. First, some of the law's provisions were not as severe as critics assumed. States were supposed to require a rising fraction of their caseloads to participate in work-oriented activities, but any reduction in a state's welfare rolls below the 1995 level counted toward the required target. In 2002, 50 percent of welfare recipients were to be engaged in work activities, but if a state's caseload had fallen by 50 percent since 1995—as was commonly the case—then the work requirement was fulfilled. The dramatic decline in welfare receipt greatly eased pressure on states to force the least-able women toward work. Another example is what happened with the seemingly draconian five-year lifetime limit on welfare receipt, which states were allowed to shorten even further. Many did so. But states have considerable flexibility in determining who is subject to time limits: they may exempt 20 percent of their caseload from time limits on federal funding. Furthermore, time limits may be waived in practice for the vast majority of recipients assisted by state funds. As a result, states can substitute federal and state funds as needed to retain longer-term recipients. (Of course, not all states choose to take advantage of this option.)

Those who predicted disaster may also have underestimated the magnitude of the increase in government support for low-income workers. President Clinton's talk of "ending welfare as we know it" referred not just to negative incentives for single mothers to avoid or exit welfare, but also to positive incentives to join the workforce. The welfare-reform legislation included some of these incentives, such as greater childcare spending and stricter enforcement of child-support responsibilities. Expansion of the EITC, the State Children's Health Insurance Program (SCHIP), and a minimum-wage increase were enacted separately, but they were still linked to welfare reform politically.

The EITC, a tax credit that goes to working parents with low earnings, is refundable, so it is essentially a cash benefit for those with no income-tax liability. For a minimum-wage worker with two children, the EITC has the same effect as a 40 percent increase in annual earnings. It is a bigger program in real terms than welfare ever was. SCHIP provides health coverage to children from low-income families who are not poor enough to qualify for Medicaid. Because Medicaid eligibility also expanded over the course of the late 1980s and 1990s, all children in families with incomes less than 185 percent of the poverty line—roughly $34,500 for a married couple with two children in 2003—are eligible today for health coverage through Medicaid or SCHIP (although many eligible children remain uninsured).

Because federal block grants to states were based on the size of their caseloads prior to welfare reform, the dramatic decline in welfare rolls also freed substantial sums that states could spend on work supports. When combined with time limits and work requirements, these policy changes made working advantageous for more single mothers and enabled them to take advantage of the 1990s boom. Without the work supports, welfare reform almost certainly would have hurt more mother-only families economically than it helped.

Finally, welfare reform occurred in an environment in which demand for low-skilled workers was quite strong. Had welfare reform been implemented during a recession, recipients would have faced pressure to leave the rolls, but few jobs would have been available. Had it been implemented during the late 1980s, when unskilled workers' real wages were *falling*, minimum-wage jobs would have been somewhat easier to find than they are now, but surviving on what they paid would have been harder. In some sense it was the *interaction* of welfare reform, expanded work supports, and the economic boom that produced such unexpected outcomes among female-headed families with children.

Where Do We Go from Here?

Despite the bipartisan consensus that welfare reform has been a great success, Congress has yet to reauthorize the legislation, which expired in September 2002. As this is written in mid September, hardly anyone expects congressional reauthorization before the presidential election. Instead, Congress-watchers predict still another temporary extension. The political stalemate has almost nothing to do with disagreement about the impact of the last round of reform. Instead, there is bitter disagreement over the merits of adopting even tougher work requirements.

The leading proposals before Congress would increase the share of welfare recipients expected to work and require them to work more hours. Given the absence of job growth since 2000, this seems like the wrong time to toughen work requirements. Furthermore, the most employable women have already left the welfare rolls. Those who remain on the rolls tend to have low skill levels, poor mental and physical health, sick children, or other barriers to work. Finally, more welfare recipients will be reaching their time limits. In future economic downturns, there may be no safety net to speak of unless states are willing to take on the responsibility.

Tougher work requirements will require greater spending on work supports if policymakers are to avoid exacerbating hardship among single mothers. In particular, legislators will need to ensure that adequate funds are allocated for childcare. Adequate federal funding for work supports is particularly important right now, because states are no longer flush with cash, as they were in the late 1990s. Indeed, a number of states have completely spent down the reserves they built up then.

In the long run, funding for work supports needs to keep growing as it did in the 1990s. After all, even at the peak of the economic boom, one-third of single mothers were still below the official poverty line, even though nearly three out of four single mothers worked at least part time. Expanding the EITC and simplifying the application process for Medicaid and SCHIP would be straightforward steps toward helping single mothers and their children. Policymakers could also expand federal housing subsidies for female-headed families in which the mother works by excluding, say, the first $200 a month of earnings when calculating rents. Of course, making single motherhood more economically attractive increases the risk that it will become more common, but with work requirements and time limits, welfare today is a far less attractive option than it was in earlier decades. If policymakers wish to discourage single motherhood, their best strategy is to extend work supports to poor two-parent families.

The last round of welfare reform shows that, contrary to the fears of liberals, a policy that combines "sticks" with "carrots" can simultaneously promote work and improve the living standards of single mothers and their children. But it did not teach us much about what we should do about single mothers who cannot find work. Nor do we yet know how mother-only families will fare under this new regime if high unemployment persists. The latest estimates show, for example, that the poverty rate for single mothers increased more between 2002 and 2003, when unemployment was high but flat, than between 2000 and 2002, when unemployment was rising. Welfare reform was the product of a compromise between Democrats and Republicans. It has succeeded. This is not the time to unravel the compromise and try an experiment of doubtful wisdom.

Off the Rolls: The Ground-Level Results of Welfare Reform

It's hard to date it precisely, but I think my severe case of cognitive dissonance set in on a summer evening in 1999. As part of my research on welfare reform, I'd spent the afternoon playing on the floor with Sammy, the four-year-old son of a welfare recipient. I was struck by his intelligence and creativity and imagined that if his mom were middle-class, she'd soon be having him tested and charting the gifted and talented programs he'd attend.

But Sammy's mom, Celia, had other things on her mind. Cradling her infant daughter, she told me that she had been recently diagnosed with cancer. Her doctor wanted her to start treatments immediately. Although she'd been working at a local Fotomart for three months, the welfare office still helped her with the costs of child care—costs she couldn't otherwise manage on her $6 per hour pay. When she asked her boss about flexible hours to manage the cancer treatments, he told her she was just too easily replaced. She'd also checked with her welfare caseworkers; they told her that if she lost her job she'd have to quickly find another or risk being cut off the welfare rolls. I talked to her about the Social Security Disability program, even though I knew that she had only a slim chance of getting help there. Celia had an eighth-grade education, no financial assets, few job skills, and no extended family members with sufficient resources to see her through. And she needed those cancer treatments now.

Under the old welfare system, she could have simply returned to full welfare benefits. Yet, knowing what I did from my research into the worlds of low-wage work, welfare, and disability, I was sure there was now virtually nowhere for her to turn, save all those local charities that were already incredibly overburdened. I didn't have the heart to tell her.

When I went home that night, the local television news was interviewing a smiling former welfare mother recently employed at a supermarket chain. It was a story of redemption—the triumph of individual willpower and American know-how—and the newscaster cheerfully pronounced it a marker of the "success" of welfare reform. That's when the dissonance set in. I've been suffering from it ever since.

From *Dissent Magazine*, Fall 2003, pp. 48–53. Copyright © 2003 by Dissent Magazine. Reprinted with permission.

From one point of view, it makes perfect sense that so many have celebrated the results of the 1996 Personal Responsibility Act. The welfare rolls have been cut by more than half—from twelve million recipients in 1996 to five million today. Among those who have left welfare, the majority (60 percent to 65 percent) are employed. Add to this the fact that public opinion polls show that almost no one liked the old system of welfare and most people (including most welfare recipients) agree that the principles behind reform—independence, self-sufficiency, strong families, a concern for the common good—are worthy ideals.

The problem is that there is a wide gap between the more worthy goals behind reform and the ground-level realities I found in the welfare office. There is also a tremendous amount of diversity hidden in those large-scale statistical accountings of the results of reform—and much of it is a great deal more disheartening than it first appears. After three years of ethnographic research inside two (distant and distinct) welfare offices, after interviewing more than 50 caseworkers and about 130 welfare mothers, and after five years of poring over policy reports on reform, it is clear to me that the majority of the nation's most desperately poor citizens are in worse shape now than they would have been had the Personal Responsibility Act never been passed.

Between Success and Failure

Political speeches, policy reports, and the popular media all cite the declining rolls and the employment of former recipients as the central evidence of the success of welfare reform. By these standards, Celia and her children would count as a success.

Of course there are genuine success stories. Take Sally. With a good job at the phone company, medical benefits, sick leave and vacation leave, a nine-to-five schedule, possibilities for advancement, and enough income to place her and her two kids above the poverty line, she was better off than she'd ever been on welfare benefits or in any of the (many) low-wage, no-benefit jobs she'd had in the past. And there was no question that the supportive services that came with reform had helped her to achieve that success. She got her job through a welfare-sponsored training program offered by the phone company. Welfare caseworkers had helped her out with clothing for work, bus vouchers, and a child care subsidy that got her through the training. "I think welfare's better now," she told me. "They've got programs there to help you. They're actually giving you an opportunity. I'm working and I feel like I can make it on my own." . . .

About one-half of the welfare mothers I met experienced at least temporary successes like these. Yet under the terms of reform, the long-term outlook for the majority is not so positive. And in many cases it is difficult to distinguish the successes from the failures.

Proponents of reform would mark Andrea, for instance, as "successful." When I met her, she was earning $5.75 an hour, working thirty-five hours a week at a Sunbelt City convenience store. After paying rent, utility bills, and food costs for her family of three, she was left with $50 a month to cover the costs of child care, transportation, clothing, medical bills, laundry, school costs, furniture, appliances, and cleaning supplies. Just four months off the welfare rolls. Andrea was already in trouble. Her phone had been turned off the month before, and she was unsure how she'd pay this month's rent. Her oldest daughter was asking for new school clothes, her youngest had a birthday coming soon, and Andrea couldn't take her mind off the upcoming winter utility bills. If she were single, she told me, she would manage somehow. But with children to worry about, she knew she couldn't make it much longer.

National-level accountings of reform would also place Teresa and her three children in the plus column. When I met her, she had a temporary (three-month) job at a collection agency. Thanks to public housing and the time-limited child care subsidy offered by the welfare office, she was making ends meet. Teresa was smart and capable, but had only a high school diploma and almost no work experience. She'd spent most of her adult life outside the mainstream economy—first married to a drug dealer, then working as a street-level prostitute, and finally, drug free, on welfare. As much as Teresa thought she was doing better than ever and spoke of how happy she was to be getting dressed up every morning and going out to work, she was still concerned about the future. The child care costs for her three kids would amount to nearly three-quarters of her paycheck if she had to cover them herself. And her job, like that child care subsidy, was only temporary. Given her résumé, I wondered just what career ladder she might find to offer her sufficient income and stability to stay off the welfare rolls and successfully juggle her duties as both primary caregiver and sole breadwinner for those three kids.

The cycle of work and welfare implied by these cases is the most common pattern among the welfare-level poor. It is a cycle of moving from welfare to low-wage jobs to mounting debts and problems with child care, husbands, boyfriends, employers, landlords, overdue utility bills, broken-down cars, inadequate public transportation, unstable living arrangements, job layoffs, sick children, disabled parents, and the innumerable everyday contingencies of low-income life—any and all of which can lead a poor family back to the welfare office to repeat the cycle again. Most of the people caught up in this cycle face a number of social disadvantages from the start. Welfare recipients are overwhelmingly mothers (90 percent), they are disproportionately non-white (38 percent are black, 25 percent Latino, and 30 percent white), nearly half are without high-school diplomas (47 percent), the majority have experience in only unskilled jobs, about half suffer from physical or mental health disabilities, almost as many have a history of domestic violence, and all have children to care for. At the same time, most welfare recipients have work experience (83 percent), and most want to work. This was true long before welfare reform. Yet given their circumstances, and given the structure of low-wage work, it is not surprising that many have found it difficult to achieve long-term financial and familial stability.

Of those who have left the rolls since reform, a full 40 percent are without work or welfare at any given time. Of the 60 percent who do have jobs, their average wage is approximately $7 per hour. But most former recipients do not find full-time or year-round work, leaving their average annual wage estimated at just over $10,000 a year. Following this same pattern, about three-quarters of the families who left welfare are in jobs without medical insurance, retirement benefits, sick days, or vacation leave; and one-quarter work night or evening shifts. It is true that their average annual wages amount to more income than welfare, food stamps, and Medicaid combined. Yet, as Kathryn Edin and Laura Lein demonstrated in *Making Ends Meet,* taking into account the additional costs associated with employment (such as child care, transportation, clothing), working poor families like these actually suffer more material hardship than their counterparts on welfare.

The reality behind the declining welfare rolls is millions of former welfare families moving in and out of low-wage jobs. Some achieve success, most do not. Approximately one-third have found themselves back on welfare at least once since reform. Overall, two-thirds of those who have left welfare are either unemployed or working for wages that do not lift their families out of poverty. And there are still millions of families on welfare, coming in anew, coming back again, or as yet unable to find a way off the rolls.

The Personal Responsibility Act itself produced two primary changes in the lives of the working/welfare poor. On the one hand, welfare reform offered sufficient positive employment supports to allow poor families to leave welfare more quickly, and in some cases it offered just the boost that was needed to allow those families to achieve genuine long-term financial stability. On the other hand, welfare reform instituted a system of rules, punishments, and time limits that has effectively pressured the poor to steer clear of the welfare office.

A central result of welfare reform, in other words, is that a large proportion of desperately poor mothers and children are now too discouraged, too angry, too ashamed, or too exhausted to go to the welfare office. Nationwide, as the welfare rolls were declining by more than half, the rate of dire (welfare-level) poverty declined by only 15 percent. To put it another way: whereas the vast majority of desperately poor families received welfare support prior to reform (84 percent), today less than half of them do. Why are all these mothers and children now avoiding welfare? To make sense of this part of the story, one needs to understand the complicated changes that have taken place inside welfare offices across the nation. I can here offer only a glimpse.

Punishment and the Push to Work

Upon arrival at the Arbordale welfare office, the first thing one sees is a large red sign, two feet high, twelve feet long, inquiring, "HOW MANY MONTHS DO YOU HAVE LEFT?" This message is driven home by caseworkers' incessant reminders of the "ticking clock," in the ubiquity of employment brochures and job postings, and, above all, by a carefully sequenced set of demanding rules and regulations.

The pressure is intense. It includes the job search that all new clients must start immediately (forty verifiable job contacts in thirty days), the "job readiness" and "lifeskills" workshops they are required to attend, the (time-consuming and difficult) child support enforcement process in which they must agree to participate, and the constant monitoring of their eligibility for welfare and their progress toward employment. Welfare mothers who are not employed within a specified period (thirty days in Arbordale, forty-five in Sunbelt City), are required to enroll in full-time training programs or take full-time unpaid workfare placements until they can find a job. Throughout, these working, training, and job-searching welfare mothers are expected to find somewhere to place their children. Although welfare recipients are all technically eligible for federal child care subsidies, only about one-third receive them. With only a $350 welfare check (the average monthly benefit for a family of three), child care arrangements can be very difficult to manage.

In Sunbelt City the pressure to get off the welfare rolls is introduced even more directly and forcefully. As is true in about half the states nationwide, Sunbelt City has a "diversionary" program designed to keep poor mothers and children from applying for welfare in the first place. Before they even begin the application process, potential welfare clients are required to attend the diversion workshop. The three workshops I went to all focused on the importance of "self sufficiency," the demanding nature of welfare requirements, and the advantages of work—and left most of the poor mothers in attendance weary and confused.

For those who persisted through the application process, their compliance to the rules of reform was assured not just by the long-term threat of time limits, but by the more immediate threat of sanctions. Any welfare mother who fails to follow through with her job search, workfare placement, training program, child support proceedings, reporting requirements, or the myriad of other regulations of the welfare office is sanctioned. To be sanctioned means that all or part of a family's welfare benefits are cut, while the "clock" keeps ticking toward that lifetime limit. National statistics suggest that about one-quarter of welfare recipients lose their benefits as a result of sanctions.

Inside the welfare offices of Arbordale and Sunbelt City many of the women I met became so disheartened that they simply gave up and left the rolls. This included women who made it through some portion of the job search, or the employment workshops, or even took a workfare placement, but just couldn't manage the pressure. Some were sanctioned, others left on their own. Connected to these, but harder to count, were all those poor mothers who gave up before they got started. Eligibility workers in Arbordale estimated that as many as one-quarter of those who started the application process did not complete it. Caseworkers in Sunbelt City guessed that about one-third of the mothers who attended their diversion workshops were ("successfully") diverted from applying for benefits. In Arbordale, about one-quarter gave up before completing the application process.

Sarah was one example of a "diverted" potential welfare client. She was the full-time caregiver for her grandchild on a lung machine, her terminally ill father, and her own two young children. She'd been managing with the help of her father's Social Security checks and her boyfriend's help. But her boyfriend had left her, and medical bills were eating up all her father's income. Sarah discovered at her initial Arbordale welfare interview that in order to receive benefits she would need to begin a job search immediately. Because no one else was available to care for her father or grandchild, she said, it just didn't make sense for her to get a job. I met her as she conveyed this story to her friends in the Arbordale waiting room, fluctuating between tones of anger and sadness. "I have to swallow my pride, and come in here, and these people just don't want to help you no more," she told us. Leaving the office, she vowed never to return. As was true of so many others, it was unclear to me what she would do. . . .

All these women and their children have contributed to the decline of the welfare rolls. They are a central basis for the celebration of reform. They are also a central basis for my case of cognitive dissonance.

The Costs

In focusing on the hardships wrought by reform, I do not mean to suggest that the successes of welfare reform are trivial or inconsequential. Those successes matter. I also don't mean to imply that all welfare mothers are saints and victims. They aren't. But there are many other issues at stake in the reform of welfare.

Reading the daily news these days, one can't help but notice that the topic of poverty has lost its prominence, especially relative to the early days of reform. One reason for this neglect, it seems to me, has been the highly effective campaign pronouncing the triumph of the Personal Responsibility Act. Like all the information that was invisible in popular accounts of the invasion of Iraq, the ground-level hardship and human costs of reform are largely hidden from view. Yet the price tag on welfare reform is real.

By 2002, the National Governors' Association found itself begging Congress not to follow through on plans to increase the pressure on welfare offices and welfare recipients across the nation—the costs, they explained, would be far too high for already stretched state budgets to bear. The U.S. Conference of Mayors found itself pleading with the Bush administration for more financial help to manage the rising populations of the hungry and homeless in American cities. Food banks were running short on food, homeless shelters were closing their doors to new customers, and local charities were raising their eligibility requirements to contend with rising numbers of people in need. The Medicaid system was in crisis, and large numbers of poor families were no longer receiving the food stamps for which they were eligible. Half of the families who left welfare had no money to buy food; one-third have had to cut the size of meals, and nearly half have had trouble paying their rent or utility bills.

In the meantime, only a fraction of welfare families have actually hit their federal lifetime limits on welfare benefits: just 120,000 welfare mothers and children had reached their limits by 2001. Given the work/welfare cycling process, and given that many families can survive at least temporarily on below-poverty wages and pieced-together alternative resources, it will take many more years for the full impact of reform to emerge. But, over the long haul, we can expect to see rising rates of hunger, homelessness, drug abuse, and crime. More children will wind up in foster care, in substandard child care, or left to fend for themselves. More disabled family members will be left without caregivers. Mental health facilities and domestic violence shelters will also feel the impact of this law, as will all the poor men who are called upon to provide additional support for their children.

Of course, this story is not apocalyptic. The poor will manage as they have always managed, magically and mysteriously, to make do on far less than poverty-level income. Many of the most desperate among them will simply disappear, off the radar screen, off to places unknown.

In any case, assessing the results of welfare reform is not just a question of its impact on the poor. It is also a question of what this law says about our collective willingness to support the nation's most disadvantaged and about the extent to which welfare reform actually lives up to the more worthy goals it purports to champion.

POSTSCRIPT

Has Welfare Reform Benefited the Poor?

There was considerable national agreement that the old welfare system had to be changed so that it would assist people in finding jobs and achieving self-sufficiency. Much success has been gained regarding this goal so far, but some state that numerous problems still remain. Hayes focuses on these problems, especially the inadequate supports for welfare-to-workmothers. The main problem, however, is the large number of poor-paying jobs for the bottom quarter of the labor force. If that problem were solved, the welfare-to-work program would be a great success. In fact, few would need welfare in the first place.

Michael B. Katz, in *The Undeserving Poor: From the War on Poverty to the War on Welfare* (Pantheon Books, 1989), traces the evolution of welfare policies in the United States from the 1960s through the 1980s. Charles Noble traces the evolution of welfare policies into the late 1990s and argues that the structure of the political economy has greatly limited the welfare state in *Welfare as We Knew It: A Political History of the American Welfare State* (Oxford University Press, 1997). Bruce S. Johnson criticizes welfare policies in the United States since the 1930s in *The Sixteen-Trillion-Dollar Mistake: How the U.S. Bungled Its National Priorities From the New Deal to the Present* (Columbia University Press, 2001). For discussions of welfare reform Jeff Groggen and Lynn A. Karoly, *Welfare Reform: Effects of a Decade of Change* (Harvard University Press, 2005); Harrell R. Rodgers, Jr., *American Poverty in a New Era of Reform* (M.E. Sharpe, 2006); Sharon Hayes, *Flat Broke with Children: Women in the Age of Welfare Reform* (Oxford University Press, 2003); and *Work, Welfare and Politics: Confronting Poverty in the Wake of Welfare,* edited by Frances Fox Piven et al. (University of Oregon Press, 2002). A great deal of information can be obtained from the reauthorization hearings in the House Committee on Education and the Workforce, *Welfare Reform: Reauthorization of Work and Child Care* (March 15, 2005). A new emphasis in current welfare policy involves faith-based programs, which are discussed in Mary Jo Bane and Lawrence M. Mead, *Lifting Up the Poor: A Dialogue on Religion, Poverty, and Welfare Reform* (Brookings Institution Press, 2003) and John P. Bartkowski, *Charitable Choices: Religion, Race, and Poverty in the Post-Welfare Era* (New York University, 2003). Many recognize that the key to reducing welfare rolls is to make work profitable. To understand welfare from this perspective, see *Making Work Pay: America after Welfare: A Reader,* edited by Robert Kuttner (New York Press, 2002) and Dave Hage, *Reforming Welfare by Rewarding Work: One State's Successful Experiment* (University of Minnesota Press, 2004). Two books that offer explanations as to why welfare provision is so minimal in the United States are Linda Gordon, *Pitied but Not Entitled: Single Mothers and the History of Welfare* (Free Press, 1994) and Joel F. Handler and Yeheskel Hasenfeld, *The Moral Construction of Poverty: Welfare Reform in America* (Sage Publications, 1991).

ISSUE 14

Is Competition the Reform That Will Fix Education?

YES: Clint Bolick, from "The Key to Closing the Minority Schooling Gap: School Choice," *The American Enterprise* (April/May 2003)

NO: Ron Wolk, from "Think the Unthinkable," *Educational Horizons* (Summer 2004)

ISSUE SUMMARY

YES: Clint Bolick, vice president of the Institute for Justice, presents the argument for school choice that competition leads to improvements and makes the case that minorities especially need school choice to improve their educational performance.

NO: Educator and businessman Ron Wolk argues that school choice and most other educational reforms can only be marginally effective because they do not get at the heart of the educational problem, which is the way students learn. Too much attention is directed to the way teachers teach when the attention should be placed on how to stimulate students to learn more. Wolk advocates giving students more responsibility for their education.

The quality of American public schooling has been criticized for several decades. Secretary of Education Richard Riley said in 1994 that some American schools are so bad that they "should never be called schools at all." The average school year in the United States is 180 days, while Japanese children attend school 240 days of the year. American schoolchildren score lower than the children of many other Western countries on certain standardized achievement tests. In 1983 the National Commission on Excellence in Education published *A Nation at Risk,* which argued that American education was a failure. Critics of *A Nation at Risk* maintain that the report produced very little evidence to support its thesis, but the public accepted it anyway. Currently, much of the public still thinks that the American school system is failing and needs to be fixed. The solution most frequently proposed today is some form of competition from charter schools to a voucher system.

Today 99 percent of children ages 6 to 13 are in school. In 1900 only about 7 percent of the appropriate age group graduated from high school, but in 1990, 86 percent did. Another success is the extraordinary improvement in the graduation rates for blacks since 1964, when it was 45 percent, to 1987, when it was 83 percent. Now this rate is almost at parity with white graduation rates. And over two-thirds of the present American population has a high school degree. No other nation comes close to these accomplishments. Nevertheless, most voices are very critical of American education.

American education reforms of the past 40 years have focused on quality and on what is taught. In the late 1950s the Soviet Union's launch of the first space satellite convinced the public of the need for more math and science in the curriculum. In the late 1960s and 1970s schools were criticized for rigid authoritarian teaching styles, and schools were made less structured. They became more open, participatory, and individualized in order to stimulate student involvement, creativity, and emotional growth. In the 1980s a crusade for the return to basics was triggered by the announcement that SAT scores had declined since the early 1960s. In the 1990s the continued problems of public schools led many to call for their restructuring by means of school choice, that is, competition.

The debate today is whether or not competition will finally make American schools succeed. The answer depends on whether or not the current structure of schools is the main reason why schools seem to be failing. Many other trends have also affected school performance, so the structure of the school system may not be the key to the problem. For example, many argue that curricula changes away from basics, new unstructured teaching techniques, and the decline of discipline in the classroom have contributed to perceived problems. Perhaps the quality of teachers needs to be raised. There is evidence that those who go into teaching score far lower on SATs than the average college student. In addition, societal trends outside the school may significantly impact school performance. Increasing breakdown of the family, more permissive childrearing, the substantial decline in the amount of time that parents spend with children, and the increased exposure of children to television are trends that many believe are adversely affecting school performance.

In the selections that follow, the costs and the benefits of school choice are debated. Clint Bolick argues that school choice applies to college education and U.S. higher education is the envy of the world. The role of competition in producing excellence in business, sports, and elsewhere is well-known. And from the moral point of view, the parents should have the right to choose. Wolk argues that most educational reforms, including school choice, do not get at the heart of the educational problem, which is the way students are taught. Too much emphasis is placed on better teaching and not where it belongs, which is on students' learning. Wolk advocates shifting considerable responsibility from teachers to the students for their education.

Clint Bolick  **YES**

The Key to Closing the Minority Schooling Gap: School Choice

In a nation supposedly committed to free enterprise, consumer choice, and equal educational opportunities, school choice should be routine. That it is not demonstrates the clout of those dedicated to preserving the government's monopoly over public education. To listen to the education establishment, one would think that school choice is a radical, scary, alien concept. Indeed, the defenders of the status quo have convinced many voters that school choice is a threat to American society.

But school choice is not threatening, and it is not new. To the contrary, it is the norm in most modern nations. . . . Even in the U.S., non-government schools have long played a key educational role, often using public funds. America's college system—the world's envy—is built on school choice: Students can use the G.I. Bill, Pell Grants, and other forms of government aid to attend either public or private schools, including religious institutions. At the other end of the age spectrum, parents of preschoolers can use child care vouchers in private and religious settings. And under federal law, tens of thousands of disabled elementary and high school age children receive schooling in private schools at public expense. It is only mainstream K-12 schools in which the government commands a monopoly over public funds.

Thomas Paine, the most prescient of our founding fathers, is credited with first suggesting a voucher system in the United States. He wanted an educated, enlightened citizenry, but the idea that the government should operate schools was an alien concept to him and his generation. Instead, Paine proposed providing citizens with financial support that they could use to purchase education in private schools.

The great portion of early American "public" education took place in private schools. Even when states started creating government schools, the teachers often were ministers. The concept of "separation of church and state" is not in the U.S. Constitution, and was certainly never applied to education.

In 1869, Vermont adopted a school choice program for communities that did not build their own public schools, and Maine followed suit in 1873. To this day, both states will pay tuition for children to attend private schools, or public schools in neighboring communities. In Vermont, 6,500 children from 90 towns attend private schools at government expense; in Maine, 5,600 children from 55 towns do so. Those programs, in existence for more than a century and a quarter, have not destroyed the local public schools; to the contrary, both states boast a well-educated population.

But the goal of universal common schooling, fueled by the ideas of Horace Mann, helped make government schools the norm in the late nineteenth century. Thereafter, private schools typically served two groups: the elite, and those seeking a religious immersion different from the Protestant theology that dominated public schools. The latter, of course, were primarily Catholic immigrants.

The rise of Catholic schools bitterly annoyed Protestant public school advocates like Senator James Blaine (R-ME). Blaine struck back in 1876. His proposed amendment to the U.S. Constitution to prohibit any government aid to religious schools came just short of securing passage in Congress. His allies, however, lobbied state legislatures and succeeded in attaching "Blaine amendments" to approximately 37 state constitutions which prohibited expenditure of public funds in "support" of sectarian (i.e., Catholic) schools. Anti-Catholic bigotry crested in an Oregon law, secured by the Ku Klux Klan, which *required* all children to attend government schools.

In the landmark 1925 decision *Pierce v. Society of Sisters,* the U.S. Supreme Court struck down that Oregon law, declaring that "The fundamental theory of liberty upon which all governments in this Union repose excludes any general power of the State to standardize its children by forcing them to accept instruction from public teachers only. The child is not the mere creature of the State; those who nurture him and direct his destiny have the right, coupled with the high duty, to recognize and prepare him for additional obligations." This principle of parental sovereignty remains a cornerstone of American law today. Though it remains constantly under attack, it continues to keep private educational options (among other rights) open to parents.

The modern case for school vouchers was first made by the Nobel laureate economist Milton Friedman in 1955. Instead of providing education as a monopoly supplier, Friedman suggested, government should just finance it. Every child would be given a voucher redeemable at a school of the parent's choice, public or private. Schools would compete to attract the vouchers. Friedman's proposal contained two insights that formed the intellectual foundations of the contemporary school choice movement: that parents, rather than government, should decide where children attend school, and that the economic rules which yield good services and products are not suspended at the schoolhouse door.

Support for school choice began to expand and diversify in the 1970s, when two liberal Berkeley law professors, Jack Coons and Steven Sugarman, began to consider school choice as a means of delivering educational equity. If forced busing plans had failed, Coons and Sugarman argued, why not give vouchers to poor and minority parents so they could choose the best education for their children? Coons and Sugarman adapted Friedman's proposal to their own ends: While Friedman advocated universal vouchers, Coons and Sugarman wanted to target them to disadvantaged populations. Friedman preferred a lightly regulated system, while Coons and Sugarman called for substantial government oversight. Still, there was the beginning of an alliance between freedom-seeking conservatives on the one hand and equality-seeking liberals on the other. That alliance eventually made the school choice programs of the 1990s a reality.

The main force generating support for vouchers, however, was the alarming decline in urban public schools. During the 1960s and 1970s, most urban public schools were ruined. Whites and middle-class blacks fled to the suburbs, leaving poor and mostly minority populations in rapidly worsening city public schools.

The problems of urban public schools were connected to a broader decline in public education. The 1983 study A *Nation at Risk* warned that large doses of mediocrity and failure had crept into American public schools. Meanwhile, starting in the 1980s, social scientists like James Coleman began showing that private and religious schools were succeeding in educating the very same poor, minority schoolchildren that government schools were failing. Many corroborating studies followed.

Also helping set the stage for a school choice movement was the 1990 Brookings Institution study by John Chubb and Terry Moe, *Politics, Markets & America's Schools.* Chubb and Moe set out to discover why suburban public schools and inner-city private schools generally produced good academic outcomes, while inner-city public schools were disasters. They found that whereas the first two types of schools were characterized by strong leaders with a clear mission and a high degree of responsiveness to parents, inner-city schools were not. Instead, urban public school districts were run by bloated bureaucracies whose principal constituencies were not parents, but politicians and unions.

A crucial factor distinguishing the successful and unsuccessful schools was the element of choice: Suburban parents could send their children to private schools, or move to different communities, if they were dissatisfied with their public schools. Private schools, obviously, were entirely dependent on satisfied parents. But inner-city public school parents were captives: They had no choice except to send their children to whatever the local government school offered. In school districts with tens or hundreds of thousands of students, they were powerless to do anything about the system.

Introducing choice in inner-city public schools, Chubb and Moe concluded—particularly giving parents the power to exit the public system altogether—would force the bureaucracy to respond to its customers rather than to politicians and special-interest groups. These findings created a scholarly foundation for school choice as a way not merely of helping children in failing government schools, but also as an essential prerequisite for reforming public school systems.

When the current school choice movement started to come together a decade or two ago, its leading protagonists could have met comfortably in a telephone booth. In an amazingly short period, it has grown into a sophisticated, passionate, and ecumenical movement. There are philanthropists, activists, public officials, clergy, lawyers, and parents, all willing to put aside ideological differences in pursuit of a common cause.

The movement's core argument is that parents, not government, should have the primary responsibility and power to determine where and how their children are educated. That this basic principle should require a vicious fight is testimony to the strength, determination, and ferocity of the reactionary forces defending today's educational status quo. Teacher unions, which form the cornerstone of our education establishment, are the most powerful special-interest group in America today. At the national level, they essentially own the Democratic Party. At the state level, they wield enormous influence over elected officials in both parties. At the local level, they frequently control school boards. They and their education allies dedicated all the resources at their disposal to defeat meaningful school choice anywhere it has presented itself.

For the education establishment, this battle is about preserving their monopolistic vise grip on American schooling. For parents—and our society—the stakes are much higher. Nearly 50 years after *Brown v. Board of Education,* vast numbers of black and Hispanic children do not graduate from high school. Many of those who do still lack the most basic skills needed for even entry-level jobs. As a result, many children in inner-city schools wind up on welfare or in jail. Children who most need the compensations of a quality education are instead regulated to dysfunctional schools. In climbing out of this morass we should not worry about whether a particular reform is too radical; we should worry about whether it is radical enough.

The school choice movement is not only a crusade to improve American education. It is also a true civil rights struggle. It is critical to the real lives of real people. The system has written off many of the people who most need choice—both the parents and their children. Minority citizens may be offered welfare payments, or racial preferences, but little is done to help them become productive, self-supporting citizens. Government schools and their liberal patrons implicitly assume that low-income children are incapable of learning. With little expected of these children, that becomes a self-fulfilling prophecy.

Meanwhile, conditions are different in most inner-city private schools. Not because they have greater resources than their public school counterparts (they typically have far fewer), or because they are selective (they usually accept all applicants), but rather because the operating philosophy is markedly different. At nongovernment schools, parents are not discouraged from involvement, they are *required* to play a role in the school and in their children's education. The children are expected to behave. They are expected to achieve. And research shows that they do.

Ultimately, we want school choice programs that are large and accessible enough to give government schools a serious run for their money. But initially, even a small program—publicly or privately funded—can begin to introduce inner-city parents to the previously unknown concept that there is an alternative to failure. That creates a constituency for a larger program.

Any functioning program, no matter how small, will change the debate from one about hypotheticals to one about realities. When we can show that competition helps public schools, and that families are choosing good schools rather than, say, witch-craft schools, we can begin to debunk the myths of choice adversaries. In Milwaukee, where school choice has been pioneered, public opinion polls show that support for choice is stronger the closer one is to the program. Not only inner-city parents but also suburban parents now support school choice there.

Actual experience has shown that school choice programs do not "skim the cream" of students, as our detractors like to say, leaving only hard cases in the public schools. Instead (not surprisingly), school choice programs usually attract children who are experiencing academic or disciplinary problems in government schools. Many such children are on a downward trajectory. Just arresting that trajectory is an accomplishment, even if it doesn't show up immediately in improved test scores.

Academic research by Harvard's Paul Peterson and others shows that academic gains are modest in the first year or two of a school choice program, and begin to accelerate afterward. Longitudinal studies tracking choice students over many years seem likely to find higher high school graduation and college enrollment rates, plus other measures of success. If that happens, the debate over the desirability of school choice will be over. The pioneers of school choice will have shown how to rescue individuals from otherwise dark futures, as well as how to force our larger system of public education to improve itself for the good of all students.

NO

Ron Wolk

Think the Unthinkable

For more than two decades, the United States has been struggling to improve public education. In April 1983 the federal report *A Nation at Risk* stunned the nation with its dire warning that "a rising tide of mediocrity" was swamping our schools. A spate of articles and editorials on the occasion of its twentieth anniversary last spring concluded that the schools today are not much better than they were then.

Five years after *A Nation at Risk,* in 1988, the first President Bush and the nation's governors, with much fanfare, set lofty education goals to be met by the year 2000, including the goals that every child would be ready for school and that the U.S. would be first in the world in math and science by the dawn of the new millennium. We didn't even come close to meeting any of the goals.

Now we have "No Child Left Behind," the sweeping and intrusive new federal law that more than doubles the amount of standardized testing. It promises, among other things, that a highly qualified teacher will be in every classroom by 2006 and that all children will be proficient in a dozen years. It, too, will inevitably fall well short of its noble objectives.

How could a country with such knowledge, wealth, and power and such stellar accomplishments in every other field of human endeavor try so hard and still be so far behind in education that it ranks among Third World nations?

The Wrong Questions Encourage the Wrong Answers

After pondering that conundrum for many years, I've come to believe it is because we are seeking answers to the wrong questions. In the current school-reform movement—and in every previous one—we have asked:

- How do we fix our broken public schools?
- How do we raise student achievement (meaning test scores)?

Not surprisingly, the answers to those questions nearly always focus on the school. We always accept the school as a given, which means we are essentially stuck with all the conventions and sacred cows of the traditional school. It almost guarantees that we will not be able, as they say, to "think outside the box."

The questions we should be asking are:

- How do we guide our kids through their very challenging formative years so that they emerge as responsible young adults with the skills and attitudes they need to function and thrive in a rapidly changing world?
- What do we want every child to achieve?

The answers to those questions must focus on a lot more than just school. Three short sketches from where I live—Providence, Rhode Island— make the point.

Jesse the Janitor.   Sixteen-year-old Jesse lived with his widowed mother and attended Coventry High School in Rhode Island. Bored to death and "fed up" with school, Jesse told the principal he intended to drop out. Although Jesse had been labeled "troubled," the principal knew Jesse liked to work and considered him to be a bright, mature young man. So he offered Jesse a deal: if Jesse would attend classes in the morning, he could work as a janitor in the afternoons for five dollars an hour.

Jesse accepted, and in the following months the school was never cleaner. Jesse got grass to grow where it hadn't grown before and even inspired his classmates to cease littering almost completely. Jesse now wants to go on to community college to study computer programming. Says his principal: "This kid is going to be a productive citizen someday, and I would not have been able to say that months ago."

Following Footsteps.   Michelle and Tiffany were sophomores at the Met school in Providence, perhaps the most unconventional high school in the nation. Students at the Met spend a couple of days a week out of school, working with mentors on term projects in the community. Each student has a personalized curriculum worked out in consultation with the parent, teacher (known as "adviser"), and mentor. Michelle and Tiffany decided that for their term project they would join a group of adults and retrace Martin Luther King Jr.'s Alabama Freedom March from Selma to Montgomery.

They read biographies of King, studied contemporary accounts of the march in newspapers and magazines, and plotted their day-by-day itinerary. Then, with their adviser's help, they arranged to stay with families along the route. The girls traveled for three weeks, interviewing civil rights leaders and participants in the march.

When the girls returned to school, they wrote a detailed account of their adventure. Michelle said she had never understood before all the fuss about voting, but she learned during that trip that people died so she could vote, and she vowed that her vote would never be wasted.

Learning Leadership. To be admitted to Classical High School (arguably Providence's best), students must pass an examination. On her first day as a freshman, Maria, nervous and scared, sat in the auditorium as the principal told students to look to their left and right. One of those kids would not be there at graduation, he warned. As the months passed, Maria found school boring and irrelevant. She wondered if she might be one of the absent ones four years later.

Then Maria heard about a community organization called "Youth in Action" and joined. Suddenly she was immersed in meaningful and interesting work—designing an AIDS curriculum, gathering data for a local environmental-justice campaign, working with troubled children, speaking to groups, planning events, raising money. Maria became an officer and a member of the board of Youth in Action.

After graduating from high school and beginning college, Maria returned to Providence to speak at a meeting on educational opportunities for American adolescents. Poised, passionate, and articulate, she talked more about her work in the community than her high school experience. When she finished, she was complimented on her accomplishments and asked how much of her success she attributed to attending Classical and how much to participating in Youth in Action. Without hesitation, she said that the youth group was responsible for 95 percent of her growth.

Jesse was fortunate that his principal was perceptive enough and flexible enough to adapt to his needs and skills. Michelle and Tiffany learned about history and the meaning of citizenship by following their own interests. Maria blossomed through doing real work in the real world.

America Wasn't Listening

For those youngsters and millions like them, the conventional school with its rigid academic curriculum and inflexible procedures is neither the only way nor the best way to become educated—that is, if we accept Webster's definition of educate, which means "to rear, to develop mentally and morally." If our primary goal is to help children become competent and responsible adults, then the conventional school, at least after grade six, may be counterproductive.

That same message was delivered to the nation by a panel of researchers assembled by the White House Science Advisory Committee almost a decade before *A Nation at Risk.* Led by the noted sociologist James S. Coleman, the panel in 1974 published "Youth: Transition to Adulthood." The report began with this profound observation:

> As the labor of children has become unnecessary to society, school has been extended for them. With every decade, the length of schooling has increased, until a thoughtful person must ask whether society can conceive of no other way for youth to come into adulthood.
>
> If schooling were a complete environment, the answer would probably be that no amount of school is too much, and increased schooling for the young is the best way for the young to spend their increased leisure and society its increased wealth.

Coleman and his colleagues concluded, however, that schooling was far from a complete environment, and called for a "serious examination" of the institutional framework in which young people develop into adults. They argued, "The school is not the world, and is not perceived by students as 'real.'" The panel recommended that high school play a lesser role in the lives of adolescents and that their learning be transferred to a variety of sites in the community where they can develop the skills and attitudes which society expects of responsible young adults.

If that 175-page report had galvanized the nation the way *A Nation at Risk* did, the past twenty-five years of education reform probably would have been much different and, arguably, much more productive.

Two years before Coleman's report appeared, a colleague of his, the sociologist Christopher Jencks, published his landmark study *Inequality: A Reassessment of the Effect of Family and Schooling in America*. Jencks found that not only is school not the complete environment, but he discovered no evidence that "school reform can be expected to bring about significant social changes outside of schools." The research showed that the outcomes of school depend largely on what goes in: i.e., the students. Middle- and upper-class kids tend to perform adequately; poor kids tend to do poorly. The schools that kids from affluent families attend do relatively well; the schools that poor kids attend do poorly.

That remains true today. The quality of a child's education in the United States depends mainly on where he lives, the color of her skin, and the socioeconomic status of the family. . . .

The Good Old Days

There was a time when the responsibility for transforming kids into competent young adults was mainly the job of the family, shared by the church and, for six or eight years of children's lives, the public school. The responsibility was more easily fulfilled in the simpler era of the nineteenth century because the distractions were far fewer than they are in this cacophonous age of mass media. Today, neither the family nor the church wields the kind of influence on the young that it once did. That has left the school as the primary institution charged with shaping our young.

The school might have successfully filled the vacuum left by family and church had it changed as dramatically and continually as the rest of the world, but it didn't. The core of the school remains essentially as it was a century ago, even though the students and the world have changed radically. As a consequence, schools are declining in influence and effectiveness at the very time that kids are facing greater and more demanding challenges. Restoring the family and the church to their long-lost cultural dominance is unlikely. And because the school is in decline, we are leaving much of the social and intellectual development of our children to their peers, the media, and popular culture.

Needed: A New Education Strategy

It is not productive to criticize schools or to blame them for not changing over the decades or for not solving a problem they are not now equipped to solve. The rational course of action is to recognize where we are, what the main task is, and how to accomplish it. Our paramount goal should be to help kids progress successfully into adulthood. To accomplish that, our priorities should include, at least, the following:

- To help youngsters acquire the skills and knowledge they will need to function in a continually changing world. That means nourishing in them the motivation and ability to continue educating themselves.
- To guide them as they develop a system of positive values and ethics that will govern their day-to-day behavior and their relationships with others.
- To assist them in understanding their rights and responsibilities as members of a community and a democratic society.
- To give them the opportunity to explore the world of work and to recognize their obligation to support themselves and their families.

Schools have an important role to play in the development of the young, but it is not their only—or even the dominant—role. If we want children to become responsible adults, we need to forge an alternative or parallel system that offers a range of choices to young people and allows them to make decisions and change directions as they grow into adults.

The elements of such a new system already exist in some schools and communities across the country. Certainly, there are enough models available for states and municipalities to construct a system that addresses the varied needs of young people and offers them choices at critical times in their development. The challenge to policymakers in statehouses and school-district offices is to create some open space in the present system for new educational opportunities.

Here is a glimpse of what that system might look like and how it might come to be.

Proposed: A Parallel System to Educate the Young

On the premise that it is easier to make significant change by starting something new than by trying to reform something old, I would argue that each should charter a nongeographic district that could include institutions anywhere in the state. The charter district would be led by a superintendent a relatively small administrative staff. The superintendent ted by, and accountable to, a board, whose members would the individual schools in the charter district. The state rter district from all regulations governing public ing safety and civil rights.

rict would be largely to coordinate and support innovation in education and youth development. It would offer educational alternatives to the conventional schools. The charter district might be viewed as the research and development arm of the state's educational system. There would be two kinds of learning institutions in the charter district. Children from age five to age thirteen would attend "primary" schools, and children ages thirteen and over would enroll in secondary learning centers.

The primary schools could be new schools established by the state, schools chartered by nonprofit organizations (the way charter schools are today in most states), or existing innovative elementary schools that opt into the new charter district. Like many of the innovative elementary schools, the primary schools in the charter district could be organized around a theme or a particular pedagogy. All primary schools in the charter district would focus significantly on literacy, numeracy, and the arts. Students would be exposed to the disciplines—science, history, literature, biography, geography, and civics—through reading in those disciplines. The emphasis would be on reading and comprehension of concepts and ideas in those disciplines, not on coverage and memorization of enormous amounts of trivia. In addition, the primary school would nourish children's curiosity and inculcate good habits of mind and behavior.

To be admitted to a secondary learning center or school in the charter district, students would have to demonstrate mastery of reading comprehension and basic mathematics. The secondary learning centers would not be schools as such, but rather community-based organizations created by the state or operated under contract with the state by existing organizations. Their primary functions would be supervising young people and helping them manage their education. Secondary learning centers would be limited to about 200 "students."

In addition to the new secondary learning centers, the charter district could include innovative secondary schools that already exist in virtually every state. The Bill and Melinda Gates Foundation funds some of the more innovative schools, such as the New Country School in Minnesota, High Tech High in San Diego, the Met in Providence, and Best Practices High School in Chicago. Schools like those would add strength and diversity to the charter district. In addition, they would find the sanctuary and support that they often lack as outliers in the conventional system. (For additional examples of innovative schools, see Timothy J. Dyer, *Breaking Ranks: Changing an American Institution*, DIANE Publishing, November 1999, ISBN 0788183559, and Thomas Toch, *High Schools on a Human Scale: How Small Schools Can Transform American Education*, Beacon Press, April 2003, ISBN 080703245X.)

New Institutions and New Roles for Teachers and Students.   In the new secondary learning centers, the roles of teachers and students would change. Student would assume much more responsibility for their own education and would assigned to an adult adviser: a teacher in most cases. Although advisers w teach, their primary function would be supervising fifteen to twenty st and helping them manage their learning and their time. The adviser an her students would remain together during the students' stay at the center. In schools practicing that model, students and advisers tend to become "families," forging close and productive relationships.

Personalized Curricula.   In consultation with advisers and parents, students would formulate personalized curricula. Each year they would choose from a menu of opportunities. Periodically, as they progressed, they would be able to change directions if they were so inclined. For example, they could participate in apprenticeships and internships with adult mentors in businesses, hospitals, government agencies, and other employers where they could experience the workplace and see the need for punctuality, attention to detail, and teamwork. They could volunteer to perform social and human services or work for worthy causes where they would observe democratic practices and politics in action.

Educational Travel.   Youngsters would have opportunities for educational travel in the United States and abroad, both individually and in groups. Programs like Americorps could provide opportunities for high- school-age kids. Programs like Outward Bound could help young people test themselves and develop self-confidence. Previous efforts such as the Civilian Conservation Corps of the New Deal era could provide a useful model for such programs.

Extracurricular Activities.   As the role of high schools diminished, extracurricular activities would have to be provided largely through out-of-school clubs, teams, and youth organizations, perhaps coordinated by the secondary learning center. Many graduates attest that their most rewarding experiences in high school were activities such as chorus, band, debate, and athletics. To the extent that those activities met student needs, they would continue to command a significant amount of time and resources. However, because students would be spending much of their time in real-world situations, they might come to rely less on extracurricular activities to develop a sense of self-worth and to learn the values of teamwork, performance, effort, and proficiency.

Just-in-Time Instruction.   All the activities the students chose would be constructed to involve learning at several levels, including academic instruction. Students would have available "just-in-time" instruction: e.g., a student interning in a hospital might need to take a course in biology or anatomy; an intern in a bank might require instruction in math or accounting; a student apprenticing in a restaurant might need chemistry instruction. The secondary learning centers could make such instruction available both in person and online.

Technology.   A modest investment in research and development and a little imagination could produce software programs to provide "just-in-time" instruction. Simulations, computer games, chat rooms, CDs, Internet courses, and the like enable students to do almost everything that they could in a classroom: dissect a frog on the computer, conduct physics experiments, learn languages, study poetry read aloud by the poets themselves, conduct research, and carry on extensive discussions about issues. The infrastructure is already there: most schools in nearly every state already are wired to the Internet. Indeed, following the lead of the University of Phoenix, many of the nation's top universities and nearly seventy charter schools now offer online courses and degrees.

In-person Instruction.   Technology by itself would not encompass the complete environment that students need to learn and grow. Secondary learning centers would offer live instruction either by contracting with a conventional school, arranging for courses in community or four-year colleges, or arranging for tutoring.

Flexible Scheduling.   Whether online or in person, instruction would not necessarily be delivered in semester courses of several classes a week. For example, an adviser and a small group of students might spend every day for two weeks in intense study of the Constitution, an area of mathematics, or the geography of the United States, but the decision to do so would arise from the needs and desires of the students— not from a pre-set curriculum.

The great philosopher and mathematician Alfred North Whitehead described the challenge this way: "The result of teaching small parts of a large number of subjects is the passive reception of disconnected ideas; not illumined with any spark of vitality. Let the main ideas which are introduced into a child's education be few and important and let them be thrown into every combination possible. The child should make them his own, and should understand their application here and now in the circumstances of his actual life."

Students at the Met School in Providence constantly demonstrate how effective and committed kids can be when they are working on something that interests them, which they have chosen. For example:

A play of her own: A young woman in her junior year wrote a play for her term project. When she finished it, she decided to produce it. She selected the cast, designed the set, directed the play, rented the hall, printed and distributed announcements, sold the tickets, and played the lead. She symbolizes the independence and conscientiousness of students who engage in self-education, and she is not unusual.

His father's war: A young man had long been intrigued by the fact that his father had served in Vietnam, but the father always declined to talk about his experience. The boy decided he had to visit Vietnam and he desperately wanted to take his father with him. He studied the history and geography of the country and read widely about the war; then he wrote a proposal that helped him raise enough money to cover travel expenses. He and his father spent several weeks visiting places in Vietnam where his father had been stationed. When they returned, the student wrote a detailed and thoughtful report about the experience and what he had learned about his father and himself.

"This is who I am":   Met students must write a seventy-five-page autobiography to graduate. Many students moan and resist. One student in particular insisted that he couldn't do it, that it was cruel and unusual punishment. When he walked across the stage to collect his diploma, that student's adviser noted that the young man had submitted a 100-page autobiography with the comment, "Until I wrote that paper, I didn't really know who I was."

In such projects, students learn a great deal and it becomes part of them, not just something to regurgitate on a test and forget. Doing real work in the real world—whether interning with a chef, a glassblower, or a hospital technician—requires some knowledge in a number of disciplines. Youngsters pursue that knowledge and assimilate it because they need it to do their work. Equally important, the work helps them to mature, gain confidence, and understand the power of learning. And their success in one endeavor tends to fuel their curiosity and lead to broader learning. . . .

It's the Students' Work, Stupid!   Students' work and accomplishments are at the heart of the new system. Common norm-referenced and criterion-referenced standardized testing would not be used. For diagnostic purposes and to assess value added, the charter district would use computer-adaptive online testing. In all the students' activities, teachers, mentors, and other adults would view the students' work and accomplishments to determine progress. Evaluating the work would be more complicated but far richer than assigning test scores. The evaluations of advisers and mentors would reveal infinitely more about a student's ability, attitude, and effort than simple letter grades.

At age sixteen, each student would have three options: continuing in the system for two more years; leaving to enroll in postsecondary education; or leaving to take a job, which could include the military, the Peace Corps, and other such occupations (which today is usually considered dropping out). If students left school at age sixteen for any reason, they would have the right to return to the system for two years before they turned twenty-one.

Instead of receiving a high school diploma, which tells an employer or a college admission officer virtually nothing about who a student is and what he or she has accomplished, students would receive a certificate of completion and a dossier. The dossier would list the courses they took, the internships they served, their volunteer work, and the organizations to which they belonged, along with the evaluations submitted by their adult supervisors. It would include selected samples of their work. Employers are much more likely to be satisfied with such an evaluation than colleges, suggesting that higher education needs to reassess admission requirements and find more substantive ways to evaluate student ability.

POSTSCRIPT

Is Competition the Reform
That Will Fix Education?

Since school reformers have focused on school choice, the literature on it has mushroomed. The choice proposal first gained public attention in 1955 when Milton Friedman wrote about vouchers in "The Role of Government in Education," in Robert Solo, ed., *Economics and the Public Interest* (Rutgers University Press). More recent school choice advocates include Harry Brighouse, *School Choice and Social Justice* (Oxford University Press, 2000); Mark Schneider, *Choosing Schools: Consumer Choice and the Quality of American Schools* (Princeton University Press, 2000); Philip A. Woods, *School Choice and Competition: Markets in the Public Interest* (Routledge, 1998); Sol Stern, *Breaking Free: Public School Lessons and the Imperative of School Choice* (Encounter Books, 2003); Clint Bolick, *Voucher Wars: Waging the Legal Battle over School Choice* (Cato Institute, 2003); Clive R. Belfield and Henry M. Levin, *Privatizing Educational Choice* (Paradigm Publishers, 2005); James G. Dwyer, *Vouchers within Reason: A Child-Centered Approach to Education Reform* (Cornell University Press, 2002); and Emily Van Dunk, *School Choice and the Question of Accountability: The Milwaukee Experience* (Yale University Press, 2003). School choice is most strongly advocated for inner-city schools. See Frederick M. Hess, *Revolution at the Margins: The Impact of Competition on Urban School Systems* (Brookings Institution Press, 2002) and William G. Howell, *The Education Gap: Vouchers and Urban Schools* (Brookings Institution Press, 2002). For discussions between school choice systems, see *Public School Choice vs. Private School Vouchers,* edited by Richard D. Kahlenberg (Century Foundation, 2003). For a less partisan view see Joseph P. Viteritti, *Choosing Equality: School Choice, the Constitution, and Civil Society* (Brookings Institute Press, 1999). For comparisons of school choice with other reforms, see Margaret C. Wang and Herbert J. Walberg, eds., *School Choice or Best Systems: What Improves Education?* (L. Erlbaum Associates, 2001). Some advocates of choice would limit the choices in major ways. TimothyW. Young and Evans Clinchy, in *Choice in Public Education* (Teachers College Press, 1992), contend that there is already considerable choice in public education so they argue against a voucher system, which they feel will divert badly needed financial resources from the public schools to give further support to parents who can already afford private schools.

Important critiques of school choice include Albert Shanker and Bella Rosenberg, *Politics, Markets, and America's Schools: The Fallacies of Private School Choice* (American Federation of Teachers, 1991); Kevin B. Smith and Kenneth J. Meier, *The Case Against School Choice: Politics, Markets, and Fools* (M. E. Sharpe, 1995); Seymour Bernard Sarason, *Questions You Should Ask about Charter Schools and Vouchers* (Heinemann, 2002); Lois H. André Buchely, *Could It Be Otherwise? Parents and the Inequities of Public School Choice* (Routledge, 2005); Gary Miron and Christopher Nelson, *What's Public about Charter Schools?: Lessons Learned about Choice and Accountability* (Corwin Press, 2002); R. Kenneth Godwin and Frand R. Kemerer, *School Choice Tradeoff: Liberty, Equity, and Diversity* (University of Texas Press, 2002); *School Choice: The Moral Debate,* edited by Alan Wolfe (Princeton University Press, 2003); Ronald G. Corwin and E. Joseph Schneider, *The School Choice Hoax: Fixing American's Schools* (Praeger, 2005).

ISSUE 15

Should Biotechnology Be Used to Alter and Enhance Humans?

YES: President's Council on Bioethics, from *Beyond Therapy* (Regan Books, 2004)

NO: Michael J. Sandel, from "The Case Against Perfection," *The Atlantic Monthly* (April 2004)

ISSUE SUMMARY

YES: The President's Council on Bioethics was commissioned by George Bush to report to him their findings about the ethical issues involved in the uses of biotechnology. Included in this selection are the expected positive benefits from the biotechnologies that are on the horizon.

NO: Political science professor Michael J. Sandel was on the President's Council on Bioethics but presents his private view in this selection, which is very cautionary on the use of biotechnology to alter and enhance humans. Many other uses of biotechnology he praises, but he condemns using biotechnology to alter and enhance humans. In these activities, humans play God and attempt in inappropriate remaking of nature.

$\mathbf{A}$s a sociologist I feel that I am on relatively firm ground discussing the 19 other issues in this book. I am not on firm ground discussing the issue of how biotechnology should or should not be used. And I am not alone. The nation does not know what to think about this issue, at least not in a coherent way. But the discussion must begin because the issue is coming at us like a tornado. Already America is debating the use of drugs to enhance athletic performance. Athletes and body builders want to use them to build muscle, strength, and/or endurance, but much of the public do not approve. It has been outlawed for competitive sports and users have been publicly discredited. Soon, however, parents will be able to pay for genetic engineering to make their children good athletes and perhaps even great athletes. Will that also be illegal? This is only the tip of the iceberg. Thousands of difficult questions will arise as the technology for designing babies will become more and more powerful. Stem cell research is currently a divisive issue. Are we blocking the development of technologies that can save thousands of lives by severely limiting stem cell research?

The classic expression of this issue is in the stories and legends of a very learned sixteenth-century German doctor named Faust. According to legend he sold his soul to the devil in exchange for knowledge and magical power. The first printed version of the legend was by Johann Spiess, which was later used by Christopher Marlow as the basis for his famous play, *Dr. Faustus* (1593). Speiss and Marlow presented Faust as a scoundrel who deserved damnation. Some of the other representations of Faust made him a heroic figure who strived for knowledge and power for good. This theme was continued by the most famous Faust legend of all, written by Johann Wolfgang von Goethe in both a poem and a play. In the beginning Faust's bargain with the Devil was for a moment of perfect happiness or contentment. The Devil, however, could not deliver this to Faust. More elements are added to the story including women's love. In the end Faust finds a moment of perfect contentment and happiness in helping others and dies because of the wager. But Goethe gives the story a Hollywood ending and Faust, the hero, goes to heaven.

Many of the issues in the biotechnology debate are found in the Faust legends. Both are focused on the search for knowledge and its use. Is the knowledge-seeking Faust a scoundrel or saint? Will his knowledge be used for selfish or altruistic purposes? Is mankind better off with it or without it? If powerful new biotechnologies are able to make our babies safe from diseases and defects, certainly we should use them. By the same logic we should also use them when they can enhance our children's physical and mental powers. Continuing the same logic we should also use them to enhance our physical and mental powers as adults. Sooner or later, however, we must face the Faustian myth, which suggests that at some point mankind's reach for knowledge may transcend man's proper role in the universe and be devilish. But this question takes us into realms where I get quickly lost. How do I discuss mankind's proper role in the universe? The wise thing for me to do is not to try and to leave it to you and the readings.

The President's Council on Bioethics presents the reasons for using biotechnology to alter and enhance humans. They are simply the many benefits that biotechnology can produce. The Council also presented the case against using biotechnology for altering and enhancing humans. It is a very evenhanded report. But I have not used that part of the report. Instead I have selected Michael J. Sandel to present the arguments against using biotechnology for altering and enhancing humans. Sandel is not even-handed. He is passionately against going down this road.

Beyond Therapy

Biotechnology and the Pursuit of Happiness: An Introduction

What is biotechnology for? Why is it developed, used, and esteemed? Toward what ends is it taking us? To raise such questions will very likely strike the reader as strange, for the answers seem so obvious: to feed the hungry, to cure the sick, to relieve the suffering—in a word, to improve the lot of humankind, or, in the memorable words of Francis Bacon, "to relieve mans estate." Stated in such general terms, the obvious answers are of course correct. But they do not tell the whole story, and, when carefully considered, they give rise to some challenging questions, questions that compel us to ask in earnest not only, "What is biotechnology for?" but also, "What should it be for?"

Before reaching these questions, we had better specify what we mean by "biotechnology," for it is a new word for our new age. Though others have given it both narrow and broad definitions,* our purpose—for reasons that will become clear—recommends that we work with a very broad meaning: the processes and products (usually of industrial scale) offering the potential to alter and, to a degree, to control the phenomena of life—in plants, in (non-human) animals, and, increasingly, in human beings (the last, our exclusive focus here). Overarching the processes and products it brings forth, biotechnology is also a *conceptual and ethical outlook,* informed by progressive aspirations. In this sense, it appears as a most recent and vibrant expression of the technological spirit, a desire and disposition rationally to understand, order, predict, and (ultimately) control the events and workings of nature, all pursued for the sake of human benefit.

Thus understood, biotechnology is bigger than its processes and products; it is a form of human empowerment. By means of its techniques (for example, recombining genes), instruments (for example, DNA sequencers), and products (for example, new drugs or vaccines), biotechnology empowers us human beings to assume greater control over our lives, diminishing our subjection to disease and misfortune, chance and necessity. The techniques, instruments, and products of biotechnology—like similar technological fruit produced in other technological areas—augment our capacities to act or perform effectively, for many different purposes. Just as the automobile is an instrument that confers enhanced powers of "auto-mobility" (of moving *oneself*), which powers can then be used for innumerable purposes not defined by the machine itself, so DNA sequencing is a technique that confers powers for genetic screening that can be used for various purposes not determined by the technique; and synthetic growth hormone is a product that confers powers to try to increase height in the short or to augment muscle strength in the old. If we are to understand what biotechnology is for, we shall need to keep our eye more on the new abilities it provides than on the technical instruments and products that make the abilities available to us. . . .

There are several questions regarding the overall goal of biotechnology: improving the lot of humankind. What exactly is it about the lot of humankind that needs or invites improvement? Should we think only of specific, as-yet-untreatable diseases that compromise our well-being, such ailments as juvenile diabetes, cancer, or Alzheimer disease? Should we not also include mental illnesses and infirmities, from retardation to major depression, from memory loss to melancholy, from sexual incontinence to self-contempt? And should we consider in addition those more deep-rooted limitations built into our nature, whether of body or mind, including the harsh facts of decline, decay, and death? What exactly is it about "man's estate" that most calls for relief? Just sickness and suffering, or also such things as nastiness, folly, and despair? Must "improvement" be limited to eliminating these and other evils, or should it also encompass augmenting our share of positive goods—beauty, strength, memory, intelligence, longevity, or happiness itself? . . .

As this report will demonstrate, these are not idle or merely academic concerns. Indeed, some are already upon us. We now have techniques to test early human embryos for the presence or absence of many genes: shall we use these techniques only to prevent disease or also to try to get us "better" children? We are acquiring techniques for boosting muscle strength and performance: shall we use them only to treat muscular dystrophy and the weak muscles of the elderly or also to enable athletes to attain superior performance? We are gradually learning how to control the biological processes of aging: should we seek only to diminish the bodily and mental infirmities of old age or also to engineer large increases in the maximum human lifespan? We are gaining new techniques for altering mental life, including memory and mood: should we use them only to prevent or treat mental illness or also to blunt painful memories of shameful behavior, transform a melancholic temperament, or ease the sorrows of mourning? Increasingly, these are exactly the kinds of questions that we shall be forced to face as a consequence of new biotechnical powers now and soon to be at our disposal. Increasingly we must ask, "What is biotechnology for?" "What should it be for?"

The Golden Age: Enthusiasm and Concern

By all accounts, we have entered upon a golden age for biology, medicine, and biotechnology. With the completion of (the DNA sequencing phase of) the Human Genome Project and the emergence of stem cell research, we can look forward to major insights into human development, normal and abnormal, as well as novel and more precisely selected treatments for human diseases. Advances in neuroscience hold out the promise of powerful new understandings of mental processes and behavior, as well as remedies for devastating mental illnesses. Ingenious nanotechnological devices, implantable into the human body and brain, raise hopes for overcoming blindness and deafness, and, more generally, of enhancing native human capacities of awareness and action. Research on the biology of aging and senescence suggests the possibility of slowing down age-related declines in bodies and minds, and perhaps even expanding the maximum human lifespan. In myriad ways, the discoveries of biologists and the inventions of biotechnologists are steadily increasing our power ever more precisely to intervene into the workings of our bodies and minds and to alter them by rational design.

For the most part, there is great excitement over and enthusiasm for these developments. Even before coming to the practical benefits, we look forward to greatly enriched knowledge of how our minds and bodies work. But it is the promised medical benefits that especially excite our admiration. Vast numbers of people and their families ardently await cures for many devastating diseases and eagerly anticipate relief from much human misery. We will surely welcome, as we have in the past, new technological measures that can bring us healthier bodies, decreased pain and suffering, peace of mind, and longer life. . . .

Truth to tell, not everyone who has considered these prospects is worried. On the contrary, some celebrate the perfection-seeking direction in which biotechnology may be taking us. Indeed, some scientists and biotechnologists have not been shy about prophesying a better-than-currently-human world to come, available with the aid of genetic engineering, nanotechnologies, and psychotropic drugs. "At this unique moment in the history of technical achievement," declares a recent report of the National Science Foundation, "improvement of human performance becomes possible," and such improvement, if pursued with vigor, "could achieve a golden age that would be a turning point for human productivity and quality of life." "Future humans—whoever or whatever they may be—will look back on our era as a challenging, difficult, traumatic moment," writes a scientist observing present trends. "They will likely see it as a strange and primitive time when people lived only seventy or eighty years, died of awful diseases, and conceived their children outside a laboratory by a random, unpredictable meeting of sperm and egg."[2] James Watson, co-discoverer of the structure of DNA, put the matter as a simple question: "If we could make better human beings by knowing how to add genes, why shouldn't we?". . .

Genetic Engineering of Desired Traits ("Fixing Up")

With directed genetic change aimed at producing certain desired improvements, we enter the futuristic realm of "designer babies." Proponents have made this prospect look straightforward, and, on a theory of strict genetic determinism, it is. One would first need to identify all (or enough) of the specific variants of genes whose presence (or absence) correlates with certain desired traits: higher intelligence, better memory, perfect pitch, calmer temperament, sunnier disposition, greater ambitiousness, etc. Once identified, the requisite genes could be isolated, replicated or synthesized, and then inserted into the early embryo (or perhaps into the egg or sperm) in ways that would eventually contribute to the desired phenotypic traits. In the limit, there is talk of babies "made to order," embodying a slew of desirable qualities acquired with such genetic engineering. But in our considered judgment, these dreams of fully designed babies, based on directed genetic change, are for the foreseeable future pure fantasies. There are huge obstacles, both to accurate knowing and to effective doing. One of these obstacles—the reality that these traits are heavily influenced by environment—will not be overcome by better technology. . . .

Selecting Embryos for Desired Traits ("Choosing In")

Unlike the prospect for precise genetic engineering through directed genetic change, the possibility of genetic enhancement of children through embryo selection cannot be easily dismissed. This approach, less radical or complete in its power to control, would not introduce new genes but would merely select positively among those that occur naturally. It depends absolutely on IVF, as augmented by the screening of the early embryos for the presence (or absence) of the desired genetic markers, followed by the selective transfer of those embryos that pass muster. This would amount to an "improvement-seeking" extension of the recently developed practice of preimplantation genetic diagnosis (PGD), now in growing use as a way to detect the presence or absence of genetic or chromosomal abnormalities *before* the start of a pregnancy.

As currently practiced, PGD works as follows: Couples at risk for having a child with a chromosomal or genetic disease undertake IVF to permit embryo screening before transfer, obviating the need for later prenatal diagnosis and possible abortion. A dozen or more eggs are fertilized and the embryos are grown to the four-cell or the eight-to-ten-cell stage. One or two of the embryonic cells (blastomeres) are removed for chromosomal analysis and genetic testing. Using a technique called polymerase chain reaction to amplify the tiny amount of DNA in the blastomere, researchers are able to detect the presence of genes responsible for one or more genetic disorders. Only the embryos free of the genetic or chromosomal determinants for the disorders under scrutiny are made eligible for transfer to the woman to initiate a pregnancy.

The use of IVF and PGD to move from disease avoidance to baby improvement is conceptually simple, at least in terms of the techniques of screening, and would require no change in the procedure. Indeed, PGD has already been used to serve two goals unrelated to the health of the child-to-be: to pre-select the sex of a child, and to produce a child who could serve as a compatible bone-marrow or umbilical-cord-blood donor for a desperately ill sibling. (In the former case, chromosomal analysis of the blastomere identifies the embryos sex; in the latter case, genetic analysis identifies which embryos are immunocompatible with the needy recipient.) It is certainly likely that blastomere testing can be adapted to look for specific genetic variants at *any* locus of the human genome. And even without knowing the precise function of specific genes, statistical correlation of the presence of certain genetic variants with certain phenotypic traits (say, with an increase in IQ points or with perfect pitch) could lead to testing for these genetic variants, with selection following on this basis. As Dr. Francis Collins, director of the National Human Genome Research Institute, noted in his presentation to the Council, the time may soon arrive in which PGD is practiced for the purpose of selecting embryos with desired genotypes, even in the absence of elevated risk of particular genetic disorders. Dr. Yury Verlinsky, director of the Reproductive Genetics Institute in Chicago, has recently predicted that soon "there will be no IVF without PGD." Over the years, more and more traits will presumably become identifiable with the aid of PGD, including desirable genetic markers for intelligence, musicality, and so on, as well as undesirable markers for obesity, nearsightedness, color-blindness, etc. . . .

Benefits

There is no question but that assisted reproductive technologies have, over the past few decades, enabled many infertile couples to conceive and bear children, and that the more recent addition of PGD holds the promise of helping couples conceive healthy children when there is a serious risk of heritable disease. The widespread practice of prenatal screening in high-risk pregnancies has enabled numerous couples to terminate pregnancies when severe genetic disorders have been detected. It is the natural aspiration of couples not only to have children, but to have healthy children, and these procedures have in many cases lent crucial assistance to that aspiration. People welcome these technologies for multiple reasons: compassion for the suffering of those afflicted with genetic diseases; the wish to spare families the tragedy and burden of caring for children with deadly and devastating illnesses; sympathy for those couples who might otherwise forego having children, for fear of passing on heritable disorders; an interest in reducing the economic and social costs of caring for the incurable; and hopes for progress in the overall health and fitness of human society. No one would *wish* to be afflicted, or to have one's child afflicted, by a debilitating genetic disorder, and the new technologies hold out the prospect of eliminating or reducing the prevalence of some of the worst conditions.

Should it become feasible, many people would have reason to welcome the use of these technologies to select or produce children with improved natural endowments, above and beyond being free of disease. Parents, after all, hope not only for healthy children, but for children best endowed to live fulfilling lives. At some point, if some of the technical challenges are overcome, PGD is likely to present itself as an attractive way to enhance our children's potential in a variety of ways. Assuming that it became possible to select embryos containing genes that conferred certain generic benefits—for example, greater resistance to fatigue, or lowered distractibility, or better memory, or increased longevity—many parents would be eager to secure these advantages for their children. And they would likely regard it as an extension of their reproductive freedom to be able to do so; they might even regard it as their parental obligation. In a word, parents would enjoy enlarged freedom of choice, greater mastery of fortune, and satisfaction of their desires to have "better children." And, if all went well, both parents and children would enjoy the benefits of the enhancements. . . .

"Beyond Therapy": General Reflections

The four preceding chapters have examined how several prominent and (generally) salutary human pursuits may be aided or altered using a wide variety of biotechnologies that lend themselves to purposes "beyond therapy." . . .In this concluding chapter, we step back from the particular "case studies" to pull together some common threads and to offer some generalizations and conclusions to which the overall inquiry has led.

The Big Picture

The first generalization concerns the wide array of biotechnologies that are, or may conceivably be, useful in pursuing goals beyond therapy. Although not originally developed for such uses, the available and possible techniques we have considered—techniques for screening genes and testing embryos, choosing sex of children, modifying the behavior of children, augmenting muscle size and strength, enhancing athletic performance, slowing senescence, blunting painful memories, and brightening mood—do indeed promise us new powers that can serve age-old human desires. True, in some cases, the likelihood that the new technologies will be successfully applied to those purposes seems, at least for the foreseeable future, far-fetched: genetically engineered "designer babies" are not in the offing. In other cases, as with psychotropic drugs affecting memory, mood, and behavior, some uses beyond therapy are already with us. In still other cases, such as research aimed at retarding senescence, only time will tell what sort of powers may become available for increasing the maximum human lifespan, and by how much. Yet the array of biotechnologies potentially useful in these ventures should not be underestimated, especially when we consider how little we yet know about the human body and mind and how much our knowledge and technique will surely grow in the coming years. Once we acquire technical tools and the potential for their use based on fuller knowledge, we will likely be able to intervene much more knowingly, competently, and comprehensively. . . .

The Council's experience of considering these disparate subjects under this one big idea—"beyond therapy, for the pursuit of happiness"—and our discovery of overlapping ethical implications would seem to vindicate the starting assumption that led us to undertake this project in the first place: *biotechnology beyond therapy deserves to be examined not in fragments, but as a whole.*

Yet, third, the "whole" that offers us the most revealing insights into this subject is not itself technological. For the age of biotechnology is not so much about technology itself as it is about *human beings empowered by biotechnology.* Thus, to understand the human and social meaning of the new age, we must begin not from our tools and products but from where human beings begin, namely, with the very human desires that we have here identified in order to give shape to this report: desires for better children, superior performance, younger and more beautiful bodies, abler minds, happier souls. Looking at the big picture through this lens keeps one crucial fact always in focus: how people exploit the relatively unlimited uses of biotechnical power will be decisively determined by the perhaps still more unlimited desires of human beings, especially—and this is a vital point—as these desires themselves become transformed and inflated by the new technological powers they are all the while acquiring. Our desires to alter our consciousness or preserve our youthful strength, perhaps but modest to begin with, could swell considerably if and when we become more technically able to satisfy them. And as they grow, what would have been last years satisfaction will only fuel this year's greater hunger for more.

NO

Michael J. Sandel

The Case Against Perfection

Breakthroughs in genetics present us with a promise and a predicament. The promise is that we may soon be able to treat and prevent a host of debilitating diseases. The predicament is that our newfound genetic knowledge may also enable us to manipulate our own nature—to enhance our muscles, memories, and moods; to choose the sex, height, and other genetic traits of our children; to make ourselves "better than well." When science moves faster than moral understanding, as it does today, men and women struggle to articulate their unease. In liberal societies they reach first for the language of autonomy, fairness, and individual rights. But this part of our moral vocabulary is ill equipped to address the hardest questions posed by genetic engineering. The genomic revolution has induced a kind of moral vertigo.

Consider cloning. The birth of Dolly the cloned sheep, in 1997, brought a torrent of concern about the prospect of cloned human beings. There are good medical reasons to worry. Most scientists agree that cloning is unsafe, likely to produce offspring with serious abnormalities. (Dolly recently died a premature death.) But suppose technology improved to the point where clones were at no greater risk than naturally conceived offspring. Would human cloning still be objectionable? Should our hesitation be moral as well as medical? What, exactly, is wrong with creating a child who is a genetic twin of one parent, or of an older sibling who has tragically died—or, for that matter, of an admired scientist, sports star, or celebrity? . . .

In order to grapple with the ethics of enhancement, we need to confront questions largely lost from view—questions about the moral status of nature, and about the proper stance of human beings toward the given world. Since these questions verge on theology, modern philosophers and political theorists tend to shrink from them. But our new powers of biotechnology make them unavoidable. To see why this is so, consider four examples already on the horizon: muscle enhancement, memory enhancement, growth-hormone treatment, and reproductive technologies that enable parents to choose the sex and some genetic traits of their children. In each case what began as an attempt to treat a disease or prevent a genetic disorder now beckons as an instrument of improvement and consumer choice.

From *The Atlantic Monthly*, (293:3), April 2004, pp. 51, 54, 56–60, 62. Copyright © 2004 by Michael J. Sandel, Ph. D. Reprinted by permission.

Muscles.   Everyone would welcome a gene therapy to alleviate muscular dystrophy and to reverse the debilitating muscle loss that comes with old age. But what if the same therapy were used to improve athletic performance? Researchers have developed a synthetic gene that, when injected into the muscle cells of mice, prevents and even reverses natural muscle deterioration. The gene not only repairs wasted or injured muscles but also strengthens healthy ones. This success bodes well for human applications. H. Lee Sweeney, of the University of Pennsylvania, who leads the research, hopes his discovery will cure the immobility that afflicts the elderly. But Sweeney's bulked-up mice have already attracted the attention of athletes seeking a competitive edge. Although the therapy is not yet approved for human use, the prospect of genetically enhanced weight lifters, home-run sluggers, linebackers, and sprinters is easy to imagine. The widespread use of steroids and other performance-improving drugs in professional sports suggests that many athletes will be eager to avail themselves of genetic enhancement. . . .

It is commonly said that genetic enhancements undermine our humanity by threatening our capacity to act freely, to succeed by our own efforts, and to consider ourselves responsible—worthy of praise or blame—for the things we do and for the way we are. It is one thing to hit seventy home runs as the result of disciplined training and effort, and something else, something less, to hit them with the help of steroids or genetically enhanced muscles. Of course, the roles of effort and enhancement will be a matter of degree. But as the role of enhancement increases, our admiration for the achievement fades—or, rather, our admiration for the achievement shifts from the player to his pharmacist. This suggests that our moral response to enhancement is a response to the diminished agency of the person whose achievement is enhanced.

Though there is much to be said for this argument, I do not think the main problem with enhancement and genetic engineering is that they undermine effort and erode human agency. The deeper danger is that they represent a kind of hyperagency—a Promethean aspiration to remake nature, including human nature, to serve our purposes and satisfy our desires. The problem is not the drift to mechanism but the drive to mastery. And what the drive to mastery misses and may even destroy is an appreciation of the gifted character of human powers and achievements.

To acknowledge the giftedness of life is to recognize that our talents and powers are not wholly our own doing, despite the effort we expend to develop and to exercise them. It is also to recognize that not everything in the world is open to whatever use we may desire or devise. Appreciating the gifted quality of life constrains the Promethean project and conduces to a certain humility. It is in part a religious sensibility. But its resonance reaches beyond religion. . . .

The real problem with genetically altered athletes is that they corrupt athletic competition as a human activity that honors the cultivation and display of natural talents. From this standpoint, enhancement can be seen as the ultimate expression of the ethic of effort and willfulness—a kind of high-tech striving. The ethic of willfulness and the biotechnological powers it now enlists are arrayed against the claims of giftedness.

◦✦◦

The ethic of giftedness, under siege in sports, persists in the practice of parenting. But here, too, bioengineering and genetic enhancement threaten to dislodge it. To appreciate children as gifts is to accept them as they come, not as objects of our design or products of our will or instruments of our ambition. Parental love is not contingent on the talents and attributes a child happens to have. We choose our friends and spouses at least partly on the basis of qualities we find attractive. But we do not choose our children. Their qualities are unpredictable, and even the most conscientious parents cannot be held wholly responsible for the kind of children they have. That is why parenthood, more than other human relationships, teaches what the theologian William F. May calls an "openness to the unbidden."

May's resonant phrase helps us see that the deepest moral objection to enhancement lies less in the perfection it seeks than in the human disposition it expresses and promotes. The problem is not that parents usurp the autonomy of a child they design. The problem lies in the hubris of the designing parents, in their drive to master the mystery of birth. Even if this disposition did not make parents tyrants to their children, it would disfigure the relation between parent and child, and deprive the parent of the humility and enlarged human sympathies that an openness to the unbidden can cultivate.

To appreciate children as gifts or blessings is not, of course, to be passive in the face of illness or disease. Medical intervention to cure or prevent illness or restore the injured to health does not desecrate nature but honors it. Healing sickness or injury does not override a child's natural capacities but permits them to flourish.

Nor does the sense of life as a gift mean that parents must shrink from shaping and directing the development of their child. Just as athletes and artists have an obligation to cultivate their talents, so parents have an obligation to cultivate their children, to help them discover and develop their talents and gifts. As May points out, parents give their children two kinds of love: accepting love and transforming love. Accepting love affirms the being of the child, whereas transforming love seeks the well-being of the child. Each aspect corrects the excesses of the other, he writes: "Attachment becomes too quietistic if it slackens into mere acceptance of the child as he is." Parents have a duty to promote their children's excellence.

These days, however, overly ambitious parents are prone to get carried away with transforming love—promoting and demanding all manner of accomplishments from their children, seeking perfection. "Parents find it difficult to maintain an equilibrium between the two sides of love," May observes. "Accepting love, without transforming love, slides into indulgence and finally neglect. Transforming love, without accepting love, badgers and finally rejects." May finds in these competing impulses a parallel with modem science: it, too, engages us in beholding the given world, studying and savoring it, and also in molding the world, transforming and perfecting it.

The mandate to mold our children, to cultivate and improve them, complicates the case against enhancement. We usually admire parents who seek the best for their children, who spare no effort to help them achieve happiness and success. Some parents confer advantages on their children by enrolling them in expensive schools, hiring private tutors, sending them to tennis camp, providing them with piano lessons, ballet lessons, swimming lessons, SAT-prep courses, and so on. If it is permissible and even admirable for parents to help their children in these ways, why isn't it equally admirable for parents to use whatever genetic technologies may emerge (provided they are safe) to enhance their children's intelligence, musical ability, or athletic prowess?

The defenders of enhancement are right to this extent: improving children through genetic engineering is similar in spirit to the heavily managed, high-pressure childrearing that is now common. But this similarity does not vindicate genetic enhancement. On the contrary, it highlights a problem with the trend toward hyperparenting. One conspicuous example of this trend is sports-crazed parents bent on making champions of their children. Another is the frenzied drive of overbearing parents to mold and manage their children's academic careers. . . .

However those questions are resolved, the debate reveals the cultural distance we have traveled since the debate over marijuana, LSD, and other drugs a generation ago. Unlike the drugs of the 1960s and 1970s, Ritalin and Adderall are not for checking out but for buckling down, not for beholding the world and taking it in but for molding the world and fitting in. We used to speak of nonmedical drug use as "recreational." That term no longer applies. The steroids and stimulants that figure in the enhancement debate are not a source of recreation but a bid for compliance—a way of answering a competitive society's demand to improve our performance and perfect our nature. This demand for performance and perfection animates the impulse to rail against the given. It is the deepest source of the moral trouble with enhancement.

Some see a clear line between genetic enhancement and other ways that people seek improvement in their children and themselves. Genetic manipulation seems somehow worse—more intrusive, more sinister—than other ways of enhancing performance and seeking success. But morally speaking, the difference is less significant than it seems. Bioengineering gives us reason to question the low-tech, high-pressure child-rearing practices we commonly accept. The hyperparenting familiar in our time represents an anxious excess of mastery and dominion that misses the sense of life as a gift. This draws it disturbingly close to eugenics.

⋅⊙⋅

The shadow of eugenics hangs over today's debates about genetic engineering and enhancement. Critics of genetic engineering argue that human cloning, enhancement, and the quest for designer children are nothing more than "privatized" or "free-market" eugenics. Defenders of enhancement reply that genetic choices freely made are not really eugenic—at least not in the pejorative sense. To remove the coercion, they argue, is to remove the very thing that makes eugenic policies repugnant.

Sorting out the lesson of eugenics is another way of wrestling with the ethics of enhancement. The Nazis gave eugenics a bad name. But what, precisely, was wrong with it? Was the old eugenics objectionable only insofar as it was coercive? Or is there something inherently wrong with the resolve to deliberately design our progeny's traits? . . .

Consider the market in eggs and sperm. The advent of artificial insemination allows prospective parents to shop for gametes with the genetic traits they desire in their offspring. It is a less predictable way to design children than cloning or pre-implantation genetic screening, but it offers a good example of a procreative practice in which the old eugenics meets the new consumerism. A few years ago some Ivy League newspapers ran an ad seeking an egg from a woman who was at least five feet ten inches tall and athletic, had no major family medical problems, and had a combined SAT score of 1400 or above. The ad offered $50,000 for an egg from a donor with these traits. More recently a Web site was launched claiming to auction eggs from fashion models whose photos appeared on the site, at starting bids of $15,000 to $150,000.

On what grounds, if any, is the egg market morally objectionable? Since no one is forced to buy or sell, it cannot be wrong for reasons of coercion. Some might worry that hefty prices would exploit poor women by presenting them with an offer they couldn't refuse. But the designer eggs that fetch the highest prices are likely to be sought from the privileged, not the poor. If the market for premium eggs gives us moral qualms, this, too, shows that concerns about eugenics are not put to rest by freedom of choice. . . .

A number of political philosophers call for a new "liberal eugenics." They argue that a moral distinction can be drawn between the old eugenic policies and genetic enhancements that do not restrict the autonomy of the child. "While old-fashioned authoritarian eugenicists sought to produce citizens out of a single centrally designed mould," writes Nicholas Agar, "the distinguishing mark of the new liberal eugenics is state neutrality." Government may not tell parents what sort of children to design, and parents may engineer in their children only those traits that improve their capacities without biasing their choice of life plans. A recent text on genetics and justice, written by the bioethicists Alien Buchanan, Dan W. Brock, Norman Daniels, and Daniel Wilder, offers a similar view. The "bad reputation of eugenics," they write, is due to practices that "might be avoidable in a future eugenic program." The problem with the old eugenics was that its burdens fell disproportionately on the weak and the poor, who were unjustly sterilized and segregated. But provided that the benefits and burdens of genetic improvement are fairly distributed, these bioethicists argue, eugenic measures are unobjectionable and may even be morally required.

The libertarian philosopher Robert Noziek proposed a "genetic supermarket" that would enable parents to order children by design without imposing a single design on the society as a whole: "This supermarket system has the great virtue that it involves no centralized decision fixing the future human type(s)."

Even the leading philosopher of American liberalism, John Rawls, in his classic *A Theory of Justice* (1971), offered a brief endorsement of noncoercive eugenics. Even in a society that agrees to share the benefits and burdens of the genetic lottery, it is "in the interest of each to have greater natural assets," Rawls wrote. "This enables him to pursue a preferred plan of life." The parties to the social contract "want to insure for their descendants the best genetic endowment (assuming their own to be fixed)." Eugenic policies are therefore not only permissible but required as a matter of justice. "Thus over time a society is to take steps at least to preserve the general level of natural abilities and to prevent the diffusion of serious defects."

⊰◈⊱

But removing the coercion does not vindicate eugenics. The problem with eugenics and genetic engineering is that they represent the one-sided triumph of willfulness over giftedness, of dominion over reverence, of molding over beholding. Why, we may wonder, should we worry about this triumph? Why not shake off our unease about genetic enhancement as so much superstition? What would be lost if biotechnology dissolved our sense of giftedness?

From a religious standpoint the answer is clear: To believe that our talents and powers are wholly our own doing is to misunderstand our place in creation, to confuse our role with God's. Religion is not the only source of reasons to care about giftedness, however. The moral stakes can also be described in secular terms. If bioengineering made the myth of the "self-made man" come true, it would be difficult to view our talents as gifts for which we are indebted, rather than as achievements for which we are responsible. This would transform three key features of our moral landscape: humility, responsibility, and solidarity.

In a social world that prizes mastery and control, parenthood is a school for humility. That we care deeply about our children and yet cannot choose the kind we want teaches parents to be open to the unbidden. Such openness is a disposition worth affirming, not only within families but in the wider world as well. It invites us to abide the unexpected, to live with dissonance, to rein in the impulse to control. A *Gattaca*-like world in which parents became accustomed to specifying the sex and genetic traits of their children would be a world inhospitable to the unbidden, a gated community writ large. The awareness that our talents and abilities are not wholly our own doing restrains our tendency toward hubris.

Though some maintain that genetic enhancement erodes human agency by overriding effort, the real problem is the explosion, not the erosion, of responsibility. As humility gives way, responsibility expands to daunting proportions. We attribute less to chance and more to choice. Parents become responsible for choosing, or failing to choose, the right traits for their children. Athletes become responsible for acquiring, or failing to acquire, the talents that will help their teams win.

One of the blessings of seeing ourselves as creatures of nature, God, or fortune is that we are not wholly responsible for the way we are. The more we become masters of our genetic endowments, the greater the burden we bear for the talents we have and the way we perform. Today when a basketball player misses a rebound, his coach can blame him for being out of position. Tomorrow the coach may blame him for being too short. Even now the use of performance-enhancing drugs in professional sports is subtly transforming the expectations players have for one another, on some teams players who take the field free from amphetamines or other stimulants are criticized for "playing naked."

The more alive we are to the chanced nature of our lot, the more reason we have to share our fate with others. Consider insurance. Since people do not know whether or when various ills will befall them, they pool their risk by buying health insurance and life insurance. As life plays itself out, the healthy wind up subsidizing the unhealthy, and those who live to a ripe old age wind up subsidizing the families of those who die before their time. Even without a sense of mutual obligation, people pool their risks and resources and share one another's fate.

But insurance markets mimic solidarity only insofar as people do not know or control their own risk factors. Suppose genetic testing advanced to the point where it could reliably predict each person's medical future and life expectancy. Those confident of good health and long life would opt out of the pool, causing other people's premiums to skyrocket. The solidarity of insurance would disappear as those with good genes fled the actuarial company of those with bad ones.

The fear that insurance companies would use genetic data to assess risks and set premiums recently led the Senate to vote to prohibit genetic discrimination in health insurance. But the bigger danger, admittedly more speculative, is that genetic enhancement, if routinely practiced, would make it harder to foster the moral sentiments that social solidarity requires.

Why, after all, do the successful owe anything to the least-advantaged members of society? The best answer to this question leans heavily on the notion of giftedness. The natural talents that enable the successful to flourish are not their own doing but, rather, their good fortune—a result of the genetic lottery. If our genetic endowments are gifts, rather than achievements for which we can claim credit, it is a mistake and a conceit to assume that we are entitled to the full measure of the bounty they reap in a market economy. We therefore have an obligation to share this bounty with those who, through no fault of their own, lack comparable gifts.

A lively sense of the contingency of our gifts—a consciousness that none of us is wholly responsible for his or her success—saves a meritocratic society from sliding into the smug assumption that the rich are rich because they are more deserving than the poor. Without this, the successful would become even more likely than they are now to view themselves as self-made and self-sufficient, and hence wholly responsible for their success. Those at the bottom of society would be viewed not as disadvantaged, and thus worthy of a measure of compensation, but as simply unfit, and thus worthy of eugenic repair. The meritocracy, less chastened by chance, would become harder, less forgiving. As perfect genetic knowledge would end the simulacrum of solidarity in insurance markets, so perfect genetic control would erode the actual solidarity that arises when men and women reflect on the contingency of their talents and fortunes.

⁂

Thirty-five years ago Robert L. Sinsheimer, a molecular biologist at the California Institute of Technology, glimpsed the shape of things to come. In an article titled "The Prospect of Designed Genetic Change" he argued that freedom of choice would vindicate the new genetics, and set it apart from the discredited eugenics of old.

> To implement the older eugenics ... would have required a massive social programme carried out over many generations. Such a programme could not have been initiated without the consent and co-operation of a major fraction of the population, and would have been continuously subject to social control. In contrast, the new eugenics could, at least in principle, be implemented on a quite individual basis, in one generation, and subject to no existing restrictions.

According to Sinsheimer, the new eugenics would be voluntary rather than coerced, and also more humane. Rather than segregating and eliminating the unfit, it would improve them. "The old eugenics would have required a continual selection for breeding of the fit, and a culling of the unfit," he wrote. "The new eugenics would permit in principle the conversion of all the unfit to the highest genetic level."

Sinsheimer's paean to genetic engineering caught the heady, Promethean self-image of the age. He wrote hopefully of rescuing "the losers in that chromosomal lottery that so firmly channels our human destinies," including not only those born with genetic defects but also "the 50,000,000 'normal' Americans with an IQ of less than 90." But he also saw that something bigger than improving on nature's "mindless, age-old throw of dice" was at stake. Implicit in technologies of genetic intervention was a more exalted place for human beings in the cosmos. "As we enlarge man's freedom, we diminish his constraints and that which he must accept as given," he wrote. Copernicus and Darwin had "demoted man from his bright glory at the focal point of the universe," but the new biology would restore his central role. In the mirror of our genetic knowledge we would see ourselves as more than a link in the chain of evolution: "We can be the agent of transition to a whole new pitch of evolution. This is a cosmic event."

There is something appealing, even intoxicating, about a vision of human freedom unfettered by the given. It may even be the case that the allure of that vision played a part in summoning the genomic age into being. It is often assumed that the powers of enhancement we now possess arose as an inadvertent by-product of biomedical progress—the genetic revolution came, so to speak, to cure disease, and stayed to tempt us with the prospect of enhancing our performance, designing our children, and perfecting our nature. That may have the story backwards. It is more plausible to view genetic engineering as the ultimate expression of our resolve to see ourselves astride the world, the masters of our nature. But that promise of mastery is flawed. It threatens to banish our appreciation of life as a gift, and to leave us with nothing to affirm or behold outside our own will.

POSTSCRIPT

Should Biotechnology Be Used to Alter and Enhance Humans?

The most often cited arguments in favor of using biotechnologies for altering and enhancing humans are the benefits of protecting children from diseases, preventing handicaps and deficiencies, and enhancing physical and mental abilities. The main arguments against using biotechnology are the fear that something awful will happen and moral arguments against playing God and too mightily interfering in nature. But what about the possibility of making people more moral in the sense of more caring, compassionate, cooperative, trusting, and helpful and less uncooperative, unsympathetic, and easily irritated? A number of scientists believe that these characteristics are fairly closely related to genes so the moral improvement of the human race could be assisted by bioengineering. Furthermore, chemical treatments could help adults become less selfish and aggressive and become more altruistic and cooperative. Thus, the moral argument can be used in favor of biotechnologies.

In some sense this is an old debate as the Faust legend indicates. Nevertheless, it is only recently that science has brought us to the doorstep of the bioengineering of humans. Two books from the mid 1980s serve as classics in this field. Jeremy Rivkin and Nicanor Perlas warn against bioengineering in *Algeny* (Penguin Books, 1984). They argue that biotechnology's destructive power far exceeds its potential benefits. Johnathan Glover reverses the weights for benefits and costs and champions bioengineering in *What Sort of People Should there Be?* (Penguin Books, 1984). More recent works that are opposed to bioengineering include Jeremy Rivkin, *The Biotech Century* (Tarcher/Putnam, 1998); Francis Fukuyama, *Our Posthuman Future* (Farrar, Strauss, and Giroux, 2002); and Bill McKibben, *Enough* (Henry Holt, 2003). More positive views of genetic engineering are found in the following: Ramex Naam, *More than Human: Embracing the Promise of Biological Enhancement* (Broadway Books, 2005); Ronald Bailey, *Liberation Biology: The Scientific and Moral Case for the Biotech Revolution* (Prometheus Books, 2005); Gregory Stock, *Redesigning Humans: Our Inevitable Genetic Future* (Houghton Mifflin, 2002); Allan Buchanan et al., *From Chance to Choice: Genetics and Justice* (Cambridge University Press, 2000); and Emirates Center for Strategic Studies and Research, *Biotechnology and the Future of Society: Challenges and Opportunities* (Emirates Center for Strategic Studies and Research, 2004). For works that present multiple views, see Pete Shanks, *Human Genetic Engineering: A Guide for Activists, Skeptics, and the Very Perplexed* (Nation Books, 2005); Gerald Magill, ed., *Genetics and Ethics: An Interdisciplinary Study* (Saint Louis University Press, 2004); Audrey R. Chapman and Mark S. Frankel eds., *Designing Our Descendants: The Promises and Perils of Genetic Modifications* (Johns Hopkins University Press, 2003); Scott Gilbert et al., *Bioethics and the New Embryology: Springboards for Debate* (W.H. Freeman, 2005); Howard W. Baillie and Timothy K. Casey, eds., *Is Human Nature Obsolete?: Genetics, Bioengineering, and the Future of the Human Condition* (MIT Press, 2005); and Rose M. Morgan, *The Genetic Revolution: History, Fears, and Future of a Life-Altering Science* (Greenwood Press, 2006). For discussions of human cloning, see Martha C. Nusbaum and Cass R. Sunstein, eds., *Clones and Clones: Facts and Fantasies about Human Cloning* (W.W. Norton, 1998) and President's Council on Bioethics, *Human Cloning and Human Dignity: An Ethical Inquiry* (Government Printing Office, 2002).

We leave to Colin Tudge ("The Future of Humanity," *New Statesman*, (April 8, 2002) the final word on this subject. "On present knowledge, or even with what we are likely to know in the next two centuries, it would be as presumptuous to try to improve on the genes of a healthy human baby as it would be to edit sacred verse in medieval Chinese if all we had to go on was a bad dictionary. So all in all, human beings are likely to remain as they are, genetically speaking . . . and there doesn't seem to be much that meddling human beings can do about it. This, surely, is a mercy. We may have been shaped blindly by evolution. We may have been guided on our way by God. Whichever it was, or both, the job has been done a million times better than we are ever likely to do. Natural selection is far more subtle than human invention. "What a piece of work is a man!" said Hamlet. "How beauteous mankind is!" said Miranda. Both of them were absolutely right."

On the Internet . . .

American Society of Criminology

The American Society of Criminology Web site is an excellent starting point for studying all aspects of criminology and criminal justice. This page provides links to sites on criminal justice in general, international criminal justice, juvenile justice, courts, the police, and the government.

http://www.bsos.umd.edu/asc/four.html

Crime Times

This Crime Times site lists research reviews and other information regarding the causes of criminal and violent behavior. It is provided by the nonprofit Wacker Foundation, publishers of Crime Times.

http://www.crime-times.org

Justice Information Center (JIC)

Provided by the National Criminal Justice Reference Service, the Justice Information Center (JIC) site connects to information about corrections, courts, crime prevention, criminal justice, statistics, drugs and crime, law enforcement, and victims, among other topics.

http://www.ncjrs.org

PART 5

Crime and Social Control

*A*ll societies label certain hurtful actions as crimes and punish those who commit them. Other harmful actions, however, are not defined as crimes, and the perpetrators are not punished. Today the definition of crime and the appropriate treatment of criminals is widely debated. Some of the major questions are: Does street crime pose more of a threat to the public's well-being than white-collar crime? Billions of dollars have been spent on the "war on drugs," but who is winning? Would legalizing some drugs free up money that could be directed to other types of social welfare programs, such as the rehabilitation of addicts?

- Is Street Crime More Harmful Than White-Collar Crime?
- Should Drug Use Be Decriminalized?
- Does the Threat of Terrorism Warrant Curtailment of Civil Liberties?

ISSUE 16

Is Street Crime More Harmful Than White-Collar Crime?

YES: David A. Anderson, from "The Aggregate Burden of Crime," *Journal of Law and Economics* XLII (2) (October 1999)

NO: Jeffrey Reiman, from *The Rich Get Richer and the Poor Get Prison: Ideology, Class, and Criminal Justice,* 5th ed. (Allyn & Bacon, 1998)

ISSUE SUMMARY

YES: David A. Anderson estimates the total annual cost of crime including law enforcement and security services. The costs exceed one trillion, with fraud (mostly white collar crime) causing about one-fifth of the total. His calculations of the full costs of the loss of life and injury comes to about half of the total costs. It is right, therefore, to view personal and violent crime as the big crime problem.

NO: Professor of philosophy Jeffrey Reiman argues that the dangers posed by negligent corporations and white-collar criminals are a greater menace to society than are the activities of typical street criminals.

The word *crime* entered the English language (from the Old French) around A.D. 1250, when it was identified with "sinfulness." Later, the meaning of the word was modified: crime became the kind of sinfulness that was rightly punishable by law. Even medieval writers, who did not distinguish very sharply between church and state, recognized that there were some sins for which punishment was best left to God; the laws should punish only those that cause harm to the community. Of course, their concept of harm was a very broad one, embracing such offenses as witchcraft and blasphemy. Modern jurists, even those who deplore such practices, would say that the state has no business punishing the perpetrators of these types of offenses.

What, then, should the laws punish? The answer depends in part on our notion of harm. We usually limit the term to the kind of harm that is tangible and obvious: taking a life, causing bodily injury or psychological trauma, and destroying property. For most Americans today, particularly those who live in cities, the word *crime* is practically synonymous with street crime. Anyone who has ever been robbed or beaten by street criminals will never forget the experience. The harm that these criminals cause is tangible, and the connection between the harm and the perpetrator is very direct.

But suppose the connection is not so direct. Suppose, for example, that A hires B to shoot C. Is that any less a crime? B is the actual shooter, but is A any less guilty? Of course not, we say; he may even be more guilty, since he is the ultimate mover behind the crime. A would be guilty even if the chain of command were much longer, involving A's orders to B, and B's to C, then on to D, E, and F to kill G. Organized crime kingpins go to jail even when they are far removed from the people who carry out their orders. High officials of the Nixon administration, even though they were not directly involved in the burglary attempt at the Democratic National Committee headquarters at the Watergate Hotel complex in 1972, were imprisoned.

This brings us to the topic of white-collar crime. The burglars at the Watergate Hotel were acting on orders that trickled down from the highest reaches of political power in the United States. Other white-collar criminals are as varied as the occupations from which they come. They include stockbrokers who make millions through insider trading, as Ivan Boesky did; members of Congress who take payoffs; and people who cheat on their income taxes, like hotel owner and billionaire Leona Helmsley. Some, like Helmsley, get stiff prison sentences when convicted, though many others (like most of the officials in the Watergate scandal) do little or no time in prison. Do they deserve stiffer punishment, or are their crimes less harmful than the crimes of street criminals?

Although white-collar criminals do not directly cause physical harm or relieve people of their wallets, they can still end up doing considerable harm. The harm done by Nixon's aides threatened the integrity of the U.S. electoral system. Every embezzler, corrupt politician, and tax cheat exacts a toll on our society. Individuals can be hurt in more tangible ways by decisions made in corporate boardrooms: Auto executives, for example, have approved design features that have caused fatalities. Managers of chemical companies have allowed practices that have polluted the environment with cancer-causing agents. And heads of corporations have presided over industries wherein workers have been needlessly killed or maimed.

Whether or not these decisions should be considered crimes is debatable. A crime must always involve "malicious intent," or what the legal system calls *mens rea*. This certainly applies to street crime—the mugger obviously has sinister designs—but does it apply to every decision made in a boardroom that ends up causing harm? And does that harm match or exceed the harm caused by street criminals? In the following selections, David A. Anderson tries to calculate all the costs of all crimes. His message is that crime costs society far more than we realize. But for the debate on the relative costs of street vs. white collar crime, his study shows that street crime costs society more than white collar crime. According to Jeffrey Reiman, white-collar crime does more harm than is commonly recognized. By his count, white-collar crime causes far more deaths, injuries, illnesses, and financial loss than street crime. In light of this, he argues, we must redefine our ideas about what crime is and who the criminals are.

David A. Anderson  **YES**

The Aggregate Burden of Crime

Introduction

Distinct from previous studies that have focused on selected crimes, regions, or outcomes, this study attempts an exhaustively broad estimation of the crime burden. . . .

Overt annual expenditures on crime in the United States include $47 billion for police protection, $36 billion for corrections, and $19 billion for the legal and judicial costs of state and local criminal cases. (Unless otherwise noted, all figures are adjusted to reflect 1997 dollars using the Consumer Price Index.) Crime victims suffer $876 million worth of lost workdays, and guns cost society $25 billion in medical bills and lost productivity in a typical year. Beyond the costs of the legal system, victim losses, and crime prevention agencies, the crime burden includes the costs of deterrence (locks, safety lighting and fencing, alarm systems and munitions), the costs of compliance enforcement (non-gendarme inspectors and regulators), implicit psychic and health costs (fear, agony, and the inability to behave as desired), and the opportunity costs of time spent preventing, carrying out, and serving prison terms for criminal activity.

This study estimates the impact of crime taking a comprehensive list of the repercussions of aberrant behavior into account. While the standard measures of criminal activity count crimes and direct costs, this study measures the impact of crimes and includes indirect costs as well. Further, the available data on which crime cost figures are typically based is imprecise. Problems with crime figures stem from the prevalence of unreported crimes, inconsistencies in recording procedures among law enforcement agencies, policies of recording only the most serious crime in events with multiple offenses, and a lack of distinction between attempted and completed crimes. This research does not eliminate these problems, but it includes critical crime-prevention and opportunity costs that are measured with relative precision, and thus places less emphasis on the imprecise figures used in most other measures of the impact of crime. . . .

Previous Studies

Several studies have estimated the impact of crime; however, none has been thorough in its assessment of the substantial indirect costs of crime and the

Table 1

Previous Study	Focus	Not Included	$ (billions)
Colins (1994)	General	Opportunity Costs, Miscellaneous Indirect Components	728
Cohen, Miller, and Wiersema (1995)	Victim Costs of Violent and Property Crimes	Prevention, Opportunity, and Indirect Costs	472
U.S. News (1974)	General	Opportunity Costs, Miscellaneous Indirect Components	288
Cohen, Miller, Rossman (1994)	Cost of Rape, Robbery, and Assault	Prevention, Opportunity, and Indirect Costs	183
Zedlewski (1985)	Firearms, Guard Dogs, Victim Losses, Commercial Security	Residential Security, Opportunity Costs, Indirect Costs	160
Cohen (1990)	Cost of Personal and Household Crime to Victims	Prevention, Opportunity, and Indirect Costs	113
President's Commission on Law Enforcement (1967)	General	Opportunity Costs, Miscellaneous Indirect Components	107
Klaus (1994)	National Crime and Victimization Survey Crimes	Prevention, Opportunity, and Indirect Costs	19

crucial consideration of private crime prevention expenditures. The FBI Crime Index provides a measure of the level of crime by counting the acts of murder, rape, robbery, aggravated assault, burglary, larceny, motor vehicle theft, and arson each year. The FBI Index is purely a count of crimes and does not attempt to place weights on various criminal acts based on their severity. If the number of acts of burglary, larceny, motor vehicle theft, or arson decreases, society might be better off, but with no measure of the severity of the crimes, such a conclusion is necessarily tentative. From a societal standpoint what matters is the extent of damage inflicted by these crimes, which the FBI Index does not measure.

Over the past three decades, studies of the cost of crime have reported increasing crime burdens, perhaps more as a result of improved understanding and accounting for the broad repercussions of crime than due to the increase in the burden itself. Table 1 summarizes the findings of eight previous studies. . . .

The Effects of Crime

The effects of crime fall into several categories depending on whether they constitute the allocation of resources due to crime that could otherwise be used more productively, the production of ill-favored commodities, transfers from victims to criminals, opportunity costs, or implicit costs associated with risks to life and health. This section examines the meaning and ramifications of each of these categories of crime costs.

Crime-Induced Production

Crime can result in the allocation of resources towards products and activities that do not contribute to society except in their association with crime. Examples include the production of personal protection devices, the trafficking of drugs, and the operation of correctional facilities. In the absence of crime, the time, money, and material resources absorbed by the provision of these goods and services could be used for the creation of benefits rather than the avoidance of harm. The foregone benefits from these alternatives represent a real cost of crime to society. (Twenty dollars spent on a door lock is twenty dollars that cannot be spent on groceries.) Thus, expenditures on crime-related products are treated as a loss to society.

Crimes against property also create unnecessary production due to the destruction and expenditure of resources, and crimes against persons necessitate the use of medical and psychological care resources. In each of these cases, crime-related purchases bid-up prices for the associated items, resulting in higher prices for all consumers of the goods. In the absence of crime, the dollars currently spent to remedy and recover from crime would largely be spent in pursuit of other goals, bidding-up the prices of alternative categories of goods. For this reason, the *net* impact of price effects is assumed to be zero in the present research.

Opportunity Costs

As the number of incarcerated individuals increases steadily, society faces the large and growing loss of these potential workers' productivity. . . . Criminals are risk takers and instigators—characteristics that could make them contributors to society if their entrepreneurial talents were not misguided. Crimes also take time to conceive and carry out, and thus involve the opportunity cost of the criminals' time regardless of detection and incarceration. For many, crime is a full-time occupation. Society is deprived of the goods and services a criminal would have produced in the time consumed by crime and the production of "bads" if he or she were on the level. Additional opportunity costs arise due to victims' lost workdays, and time spent securing assets, looking for keys, purchasing and installing crime prevention devices, and patrolling neighborhood-watch areas.

The Value of Risks to Life and Health

The implicit costs of violent crime include the fear of being injured or killed, the anger associated with the inability to behave as desired, and the agony of being a crime victim. Costs associated with life and health risks are perhaps the most difficult to ascertain, although a considerable literature is devoted to their estimation. The implicit values of lost life and injury are included in the list of crime costs below; those not wishing to consider them can simply subtract these estimates from the aggregate figure.

Transfers

One result of fraud and theft is a transfer of assets from victim to criminal. . . .

Numerical Findings

Crime-Induced Production

... Crime-induced production accounts for about $400 billion in expenditures annually. Table 2 presents the costs of goods and services that would not have to be produced in the absence of crime. Drug trafficking accounts for an estimated $161 billion in expenditure. With the $28 billion cost of prenatal drug exposure and almost $11 billion worth of federal, state, and local drug control efforts (including drug treatment, education, interdiction, research, and intelligence), the combined cost of drug-related activities is about $200 billion. Findings that over half of the arrestees in 24 cities tested positive for recent drug use and about one-third of offenders reported being under the influence of drugs at the time of their offense suggest that significant portions of the other crime-cost categories may result indirectly from drug use.

Table 2

Crime-Induced Production	$ (millions)
Drug Trafficking	160,584
Police Protection	47,129
Corrections	35,879
Prenatal Exposure to Cocaine and Heroin	28,156
Federal Agencies	23,381
Judicial and Legal Services—State & Local	18,901
Guards	17,917
Drug Control	10,951
DUI Costs to Driver	10,302
Medical Care for Victims	8,990
Computer Viruses and Security	8,000
Alarm Systems	6,478
Passes for Business Access	4,659
Locks, Safes, and Vaults	4,359
Vandalism (except Arson)	2,317
Small Arms and Small Arms Ammunition	2,252
Replacements due to Arson	1,902
Surveillance Cameras	1,471
Safety Lighting	1,466
Protective Fences and Gates	1,159
Airport Security	448
Nonlethal weaponry, e.g., Mace	324
Elec. Retail Article Surveillance	149
Theft Insurance (less indemnity)	96
Guard Dogs	49
Mothers Against Drunk Driving	49
Library Theft Detection	28
Total	**397,395**

About 682,000 police and 17,000 federal, state, special (park, transit, or county) and local police agencies account for $47 billion in expenditures annually. Thirty-six billion dollars is dedicated each year to the 895 federal and state prisons, 3,019 jails, and 1,091 state, county, and local juvenile detention centers. Aside from guards in correctional institutions, private expenditure on guards amounts to more than $18 billion annually. Security guard agencies employ 55 percent of the 867,000 guards in the U.S.; the remainder are employed in-house. While guards are expected and identifiable at banks and military complexes, they have a less conspicuous presence at railroads, ports, golf courses, laboratories, factories, hospitals, retail stores, and other places of business. The figures in this paper do not include receptionists, who often play a duel role of monitoring unlawful entry into a building and providing information and assistance. . . .

Opportunity Costs

In their study of the costs of murder, rape, robbery, and aggravated assault, Cohen, Miller, and Rossman estimate that the average incarcerated offender costs society $5,700 in lost productivity per year. Their estimate was based on the observation that many prisoners did not work in the legal market prior to their offense, and the opportunity cost of those prisoners' time can be considered to be zero. The current study uses a higher estimate of the opportunity cost of incarceration because unlike previous studies, it examines the relative savings from a *crime-free* society. It is likely that in the absence of crime including drug use, some criminals who are not presently employed in the legal workforce would be willing and able to find gainful employment. This assumption is supported by the fact that many criminals are, in a way, motivated entrepreneurs whose energy has taken an unfortunate focus. In the absence of more enticing underground activities, some of the same individuals could apply these skills successfully in the legal sector. . . .

The Value of Risks to Life and Health

Table 3 presents estimates of the implicit costs of violent crime. The value of life and injury estimates used here reflect the amounts individuals are willing to accept to enter a work environment in which their health state might change. The labor market estimates do not include losses covered by workers' compensation, namely health care costs (usually provided without dollar or time limits) and lost earnings (within modest bounds, victims or their spouses typically receive about two thirds of lost earnings for life or the duration of the injury).

Table 3

The Value of Risks to Life and Health	$ (millions)
Value of Lost Life	439,880
Value of Injuries	134,515
Total	574,395

The values do capture perceived risks of pain, suffering, and mental distress associated with the health losses. If the risk of involvement in violent crime evokes more mental distress than the risk of occupational injuries and fatalities, the labor market values represent conservative estimates of the corresponding costs of crime. Similar estimates have been used in previous studies of crime costs. . . .

The average of 27 previous estimates of the implicit value of human life as reported by W. Kip Viscusi is 7.1 million. Removing two outlying estimates of just under $20 million about which the authors express reservation, the average of the remaining studies is $6.1 million. Viscusi points out that the majority of the estimates fall between $3.7 and $8.6 million ($3 and $7 million in 1990 dollars), the average of which is again $6.1 million. The $6.1 million figure was multiplied by the 72,111 crime-related deaths to obtain the $440 billion estimate of the value of lives lost to crime. Similarly, the average of 15 studies of the implicit value of non-fatal injuries, $52,637, was multiplied by the 2,555,520 reported injuries resulting from drunk driving and boating, arson, rape, robbery, and assaults to find the $135 billion estimate for the implicit cost of crime-related injuries.

Transfers

More than $603 billion worth of transfers result from crime. After the $204 billion lost to occupational fraud and the $123 billion in unpaid taxes, the $109 billion lost to health insurance fraud represents the greatest transfer by more than a factor of two, and the associated costs amount to almost ten percent of the nations' health care expenditures. Robberies, perhaps the classic crime, ironically generate a smaller volume of transfers ($775 million) than any other category of crime. The transfers of goods and money resulting from fraud and theft do not necessarily impose a net burden on society, and may in fact increase social welfare to the extent that those on the receiving end value the goods more than those losing them. Nonetheless, as Table 4 illustrates, those on the losing side bear a $603 billion annual burden. . . .

There are additional cost categories that are not included here, largely because measures that are included absorb much of their impact. Nonetheless, several are worth noting. Thaler, Hellman and Naroff, and Rizzo estimate the erosion of property values per crime. An average of their figures, $2,024, can be multiplied by the total number of crimes reported in 1994, 13,992, to estimate an aggregate housing devaluation of $28 billion. Although this figure should reflect the inability to behave as desired in the presence of crime, it also includes psychic and monetary costs imposed by criminal behavior that are already included in this [article].

Julie Berry Cullen and Stephen D. Levitt discuss urban flight resulting from crime. They report a nearly one-to-one relationship between serious crimes and individuals parting from major cities. The cost component of this is difficult to assess because higher commuting costs must be measured against lower property costs in rural areas, and the conveniences of city living must be compared with the amenities of suburbia. Several other categories of crime costs receive incomplete representation due to insufficient data, and therefore make the estimates here conservative. These include the costs of unreported crimes (although

Table 4

Transfers	$ (millions)
Occupational Fraud	203,952
Unpaid Taxes	123,108
Health Insurance Fraud	108,610
Financial Institution Fraud	52,901
Mail Fraud	35,986
Property/Casualty Insurance Fraud	20,527
Telemarketing Fraud	16,609
Business Burglary	13,229
Motor Vehicle Theft	8,913
Shoplifting	7,185
Household Burglary	4,527
Personal Theft	3,909
Household Larceny	1,996
Coupon Fraud	912
Robbery	775
Total	**603,140**

the National Crime Victimization Survey provides information beyond that reported to the police), lost taxes due to the underground economy, and restrictions of behavior due to crime.

When criminals' costs are estimated implicitly as the value of the assets they receive through crime, the gross cost of crime (including transfers) is estimated to exceed $2,269 billion each year, and the net cost is an estimated $1,666 billion. When criminals' costs are assumed to equal the value of time spent planning and committing crimes and in prison, the estimated annual gross and net costs of crime are $1,705 and $1,102 billion respectively. Table 5 presents the aggregate costs of crime based on the more conservative, time-based estimation method. The disaggregation of this and the previous tables facilitates the creation of customized estimates based on the reader's preferred assumptions. Each of the general studies summarized in Table 1 included transfers, so the appropriate

Table 5

The Aggregate Burden of Crime	$ (billions)
Crime-Induced Production	397
Opportunity Costs	130
Risks to Life and Health	574
Transfers	603
Gross Burden	**$1,705**
Net of Transfers	**$1,102**
Per Capita (in dollars)	**$4,118**

comparison is to the gross cost estimate in the current study. As the result of a more comprehensive treatment of repercussions, the cost of crime is now seen to be more than twice as large as previously recognized.

Conclusion

Previous studies of the burden of crime have counted crimes or concentrated on direct crime costs. This paper calculates the aggregate burden of crime rather than absolute numbers, includes indirect costs, and recognizes that transfers resulting from theft should not be included in the net burden of crime to society. The accuracy of society's perspective on crime costs will improve with the understanding that these costs extend beyond victims' losses and the cost of law enforcement to include the opportunity costs of criminals' and prisoners' time, our inability to behave as desired, and the private costs of crime deterrence.

As criminals acquire an estimated $603 billion dollars worth of assets from their victims, they generate an additional $1,102 billion worth of lost productivity, crime-related expenses, and diminished quality of life. The net losses represent an annual per capita burden of $4,118. Including transfers, the aggregate burden of crime is $1,705 billion. In the United States, this is of the same order of magnitude as life insurance purchases ($1,680 billion), the outstanding mortgage debt to commercial banks and savings institutions ($1,853 billion), and annual expenditures on health ($1,038 billion).

As the enormity of this negative-sum game comes to light, so, too, will the need for countervailing efforts to redefine legal policy and forge new ethical standards. Periodic estimates of the full cost of crime could speak to the success of national strategies to encourage decorum, including increased expenditures on law enforcement, new community strategic approaches, technological innovations, legal reform, education, and the development of ethics curricula. Economic theory dictates that resources should be devoted to moral enhancement until the benefits from marginal efforts are surpassed by their costs. Programs that decrease the burden of crime by more than the cost of implementation should be continued, while those associated with negligible or positive net increments in the cost of crime should be altered to better serve societal goals.

NO

Jeffrey Reiman

A Crime by Any Other Name . . .

If one individual inflicts a bodily injury upon another which leads to the death of the person attacked we call it manslaughter; on the other hand, if the attacker knows beforehand that the blow will be fatal we call it murder. Murder has also been committed if society places hundreds of workers in such a position that they inevitably come to premature and unnatural ends. Their death is as violent as if they had been stabbed or shot. . . . Murder has been committed if society knows perfectly well that thousands of workers cannot avoid being sacrificed so long as these conditions are allowed to continue. Murder of this sort is just as culpable as the murder committed by an individual.

—Frederick Engels
The Condition of the Working Class in England

What's In a Name?

If it takes you an hour to read this chapter, by the time you reach the last page, three of your fellow citizens will have been murdered. *During that same time, at least four Americans will die as a result of unhealthy or unsafe conditions in the workplace!* Although these work-related deaths could have been prevented, they are not called murders. Why not? Doesn't crime by any other name still cause misery and suffering? What's in a name?

The fact is that the label "crime" is not used in America to name all or the worst of the actions that cause misery and suffering to Americans. It is primarily reserved for the dangerous actions of the poor.

In the February 21, 1993, edition of the *New York Times*, an article appears with the headline: "Company in Mine Deaths Set to Pay Big Fine." It describes an agreement by the owners of a Kentucky mine to pay a fine for safety misconduct that may have led to "the worst American mining accident in nearly a decade." Ten workers died in a methane explosion, and the company pleaded guilty to "a pattern of safety misconduct" that included falsifying reports of methane levels and requiring miners to work under unsupported roofs. The company was fined $3.75 million. The acting foreman at the mine was the only individual charged by the federal government, and for his cooperation with the investigation, prosecutors were recommending that he receive the minimum sentence: probation to six months in prison. The company's president expressed regret for the tragedy that occurred. And the U.S. attorney said he hoped the case "sent a clear message that violations of Federal safety and health regulations that endanger the lives of our citizens will not be tolerated."

Compare this with the story of Colin Ferguson, who prompted an editorial in the *New York Times* of December 10, 1993, with the headline: "Mass Murder on the 5:33." A few days earlier, Colin had boarded a commuter train in Garden City, Long Island, and methodically shot passengers with a 9-millimeter pistol, killing 5 and wounding 18. Colin Ferguson was surely a murderer, maybe a mass murderer. My question is, Why wasn't the death of the miners also murder? Why weren't those responsible for subjecting ten miners to deadly conditions also "mass murderers"?

Why do ten dead miners amount to an "accident," a "tragedy," and five dead commuters a "mass murder"? "Murder" suggests a murderer, whereas "accident" and "tragedy" suggest the work of impersonal forces. But the charge against the company that owned the mine said that they "repeatedly exposed the mine's work crews to danger and that such conditions were frequently concealed from Federal inspectors responsible for enforcing the mine safety act." And the acting foreman admitted to falsifying records of methane levels only two months before the fatal blast. Someone was responsible for the conditions that led to the death of ten miners. Is that person not a murderer, perhaps even a *mass murderer?*

These questions are at this point rhetorical. My aim is not to discuss this case but rather to point to the blinders we wear when we look at such an "accident." There was an investigation. One person, the acting foreman, was held responsible for falsifying records. He is to be sentenced to six months in prison (at most). The company was fined. But no one will be tried for *murder.* No one will be thought of as a murderer. *Why not?. . .*

Didn't those miners have a right to protection from the violence that took their lives? *And if not, why not?*

Once we are ready to ask this question seriously, we are in a position to see that the reality of crime—that is, the acts we label crime, the acts we think of as crime, the actors and actions we treat as criminal—is *created*: It is an image shaped by decisions as to *what* will be called crime and *who* will be treated as a criminal.

The Carnival Mirror

. . .The American criminal justice system is a mirror that shows a distorted image of the dangers that threaten us-an image created more by the shape of the mirror than by the reality reflected. What do we see when we look in the criminal justice mirror? . . .

He is, first of all, a *he.* Out of 2,012,906 persons arrested for FBI Index crimes [which are criminal homicide, forcible rape, robbery, aggravated assault, burglary, larceny, and motor vehicle theft] in 1991, 1,572,591, or 78 percent, were males. Second, he is a *youth*. . . . Third, he is predominantly *urban*. . . . Fourth, he is disproportionately *black*—blacks are arrested for Index crimes at a rate three times that of their percentage in the national population. . . . Finally, he is *poor:* Among state prisoners in 1991, 33 percent were unemployed prior to being arrested—a rate nearly four times that of males in the general population. . . .

This is the Typical Criminal feared by most law-abiding Americans. Poor, young, urban, (disproportionately) black males make up the core of the enemy forces in the war against crime. They are the heart of a vicious, unorganized guerrilla army, threatening the lives, limbs, and possessions of the law-abiding members of society—necessitating recourse to the ultimate weapons of force and detention in our common defense.

. . . The acts of the Typical Criminal are not the only acts that endanger us, nor are they the acts that endanger us the most. As I shall show . . . , we have as great or sometimes even a greater chance of being killed or disabled by an occupational injury or disease, by unnecessary surgery, or by shoddy emergency medical services than by aggravated assault or even homicide! Yet even though these threats to our well-being are graver than those posed by our poor young criminals, they do not show up in the FBI's Index of serious crimes. The individuals responsible for them do not turn up in arrest records or prison statistics. *They never become part of the reality reflected in the criminal justice mirror, although the danger they pose is at least as great and often greater than the danger posed by those who do!*

Similarly, the general public loses more money *by for* . . . from price-fixing and monopolistic practices and from consumer deception and embezzlement than from all the property crimes in the FBI's Index combined. Yet these far more costly acts are either not criminal, or if technically criminal, not prosecuted, or if prosecuted, not punished, or if punished, only mildly . . . *Their faces rarely appear in the criminal justice mirror, although the danger they pose is at least as great and often greater than that of those who do. . . .*

The criminal justice system is like a mirror in which society can see the face of the evil in its midst. Because the system deals with some evil and not with others, because it treats some evils as the gravest and treats some of the gravest evils as minor, the image it throws back is distorted like the image in a carnival mirror. Thus, the image cast back is false not because it is invented out of thin air but because the proportions of the real are distorted. . . .

If criminal justice really gives us a carnival-mirror of "crime," we are doubly deceived. First, we are led to believe that the criminal justice system is protecting us against the gravest threats to our well-being when, in fact, the system is protecting us against only some threats and not necessarily the gravest ones. We are deceived about how much protection we are receiving and thus left vulnerable. The second deception is just the other side of this one. If people believe that the carnival mirror is a true mirror—that is, if they believe the criminal justice system simply *reacts* to the gravest threats to their well-being—they come to believe that whatever is the target of the criminal justice system must be the greatest threat to their well-being. . . .

A Crime by Any Other Name . . .

Think of a crime, any crime. Picture the first "crime" that comes into your mind. What do you see? The odds are you are not imagining a mining company executive sitting at his desk, calculating the costs of proper safety precautions and deciding not to invest in them. Probably what you do see with your mind's eye is one person physically attacking another or robbing something from another via the threat of physical attack. Look more closely. What does the attacker look like? It's a safe bet he (and it is a *he*, of course) is not wearing a suit and tie. In fact, my hunch is that you—like me, like almost anyone else in America—picture a young, tough lower-class male when the thought of crime first pops into your head. You (we) picture someone like the Typical Criminal described above. The crime itself is one in which the Typical Criminal sets out to attack or rob some specific person.

It is important to identify this model of the Typical Crime because it functions like a set of blinders. It keeps us from calling a mine disaster a mass murder even if ten men are killed, even if someone is responsible for the unsafe conditions in which they worked and died. I contend that this particular piece of mental furniture so blocks our view that it keeps us from using the criminal justice system to protect ourselves from the greatest threats to our persons and possessions.

What keeps a mine disaster from being a mass murder in our eyes is that it is not a one-on-one harm. What is important in one-on-one harm is not the numbers but the *desire of someone (or ones) to harm someone (or ones) else.* An attack by a gang on one or more persons or an attack by one individual on several fits the model of one-on-one harm; that is, for each person harmed there is at least one individual who wanted to harm that person. Once he selects his victim, the rapist, the mugger, the murderer all want this person they have selected to suffer. A mine executive, on the other hand, does not want his employees to be harmed. He would truly prefer that there be no accident, no injured or dead miners. What he does want is something legitimate. It is what he has been hired to get: maximum profits at minimum costs. If he cuts corners to save a buck, he is just doing his job. If ten men die because he cut corners on safety, we may think him crude or callous but not a murderer. He is, at most, responsible for an *indirect harm*, not a one-on-one harm. For this, he may even be criminally indictable for violating safety regulations—but not for murder. The ten men are dead as an unwanted consequence of his (perhaps overzealous or undercautious) pursuit of a legitimate goal. So, unlike the Typical Criminal, he has not committed the Typical Crime—or so we generally believe. As a result, ten men are dead who might be alive now if cutting corners of the kind that leads to loss of life, whether suffering is specifically aimed at or not, were treated as murder.

This is my point. Because we accept the belief . . . that the model for crime is one person specifically trying to harm another, we accept a legal system that leaves us unprotected against much greater dangers to our lives and well-being than those threatened by the Typical Criminal. . . .

According to the FBI's *Uniform Crime Reports,* in 1991, there were 24,703 murders and nonnegligent manslaughters, and 1,092,739 aggravated assaults. In 1992, there were 23,760 murders and nonnegligent manslaughters, and 1,126,970 aggravated assaults. . . . Thus, as a measure of the physical harm done by crime in the beginning of the 1990s, we can say that reported crimes lead to roughly 24,000 deaths and 1,000,000 instances of serious bodily injury short of death a year. As a measure of monetary loss due to property crime, we can use $15.1 billion—the total estimated dollar losses due to property crime in 1992 according to the UCR. Whatever the shortcomings of these reported crime statistics, they are the statistics upon which public policy has traditionally been based. Thus, I will consider any actions that lead to loss of life, physical harm, and property loss comparable to the figures in the UCR as actions that pose grave dangers to the community comparable to the threats posed by crimes. . . .

In testimony before the Senate Committee on Labor and Human Resources, Dr. Philip Landrigan, director of the Division of Environmental and Occupational Medicine at the Mount Sinai School of Medicine in New York City, stated that

> [I]t may be calculated that occupational disease is responsible each year in the United States for 50,000 to 70,000 deaths, and for approximately 350,000 new cases of illness.

. . . The BLS estimate of 330,000 job-related illnesses for 1990 roughly matches Dr. Landrigan's estimates. For 1991, BLS estimates 368,000 job-related illnesses. These illnesses are of varying severity. . . . Because I want to compare these occupational harms with those resulting from aggravated assault, I shall stay on the conservative side here too, as with deaths from occupational diseases, and say that there are annually in the United States approximately 150,000 job-related serious illnesses. Taken together with 25,000 deaths from occupational diseases, how does this compare with the threat posed by crime?

Before jumping to any conclusions, note that the risk of occupational disease and death falls only on members of the labor force, whereas the risk of crime falls on the whole population, from infants to the elderly. Because the labor force is about half the total population (124,810,000 in 1990, out of a total population of 249,900,000), to get a true picture of the *relative* threat posed by occupational diseases compared with that posed by crimes, we should *halve* the crime statistics when comparing them with the figures for industrial disease and death. Using the crime figures for the first years of the 1990s, . . . we note that the *comparable* figures would be

	Occupational Hazard	Crime (halved)
Death	25,000	12,000
Other physical harm	150,000	500,000

. . . Note . . . that the estimates in the last chart are *only* for occupational *diseases* and deaths from those diseases. They do not include death and disability from work-related injuries. Here, too, the statistics are gruesome. The National Safety Council reported that in 1991, work-related accidents caused 9,600 deaths and 1.7 million disabling work injuries, a total cost to the economy of $63.3 billion. This brings the number of occupation-related deaths to 34,600 a year and other physical harms to 1,850,000. If, on the basis of these additional figures, we recalculated our chart comparing occupational harms from both disease and accident with criminal harms, it would look like this:

	Occupational Hazard	Crime (halved)
Death	34,600	12,000
Other physical harm	1,850,000	500,000

Can there be any doubt that workers are more likely to stay alive and healthy in the face of the danger from the underworld than in the work-world? . . .

To say that some of these workers died from accidents due to their own carelessness is about as helpful as saying that some of those who died at the hands of murderers asked for it. It overlooks the fact that where workers are careless, it is not because they love to live dangerously. They have production quotas to meet, quotas that they themselves do not set. If quotas were set with an eye to keeping work at a safe pace rather than to keeping the production-to-wages ratio as high as possible, it might be more reasonable to expect workers to take the time to be careful. Beyond this, we should bear in mind that the vast majority of occupational deaths result from disease, not accident, and disease is generally a function of conditions outside a worker's control. Examples of such conditions are the level of coal dust in the air ("260,000 miners receive benefits for [black lung] disease, and perhaps as many as 4,000 retired miners die from the illness or its complications each year"; about 10,000 currently working miners "have X-ray evidence of the beginnings of the crippling and often fatal disease") or textile dust . . . or asbestos fibers . . . or coal tars . . .; (coke oven workers develop cancer of the scrotum at a rate five times that of the general population). Also, some 800,000 people suffer from occupationally related skin disease each year. . . .

To blame the workers for occupational disease and deaths is to ignore the history of governmental attempts to compel industrial firms to meet safety standards that would keep dangers (such as chemicals or fibers or dust particles in the air) that are outside the worker's control down to a safe level. This has been a continual struggle, with firms using everything from their own "independent" research institutes to more direct and often questionable forms of political pressure to influence government in the direction of loose standards and lax enforcement. So far, industry has been winning because OSHA [Occupational Safety and Health Administration] has been given neither the personnel nor the mandate to fulfill its purpose. It is so understaffed that, in 1973, when 1,500 federal sky marshals guarded the nation's airplanes from hijackers, only 500 OSHA inspectors toured the nation's workplaces. By 1980, OSHA employed 1,581 compliance safety and health officers, but this still enabled inspection of only roughly 2 percent of the 2.5 million establishments covered by OSHA. The *New York Times* reports that in 1987 the number of OSHA inspectors was down to 1,044. As might be expected, the agency performs fewer inspections that it did a dozen years ago. . . .

According to a report issued by the AFL-CIO [American Federation of Labor and Congress of Industrial Organizations] in 1992, "The median penalty paid by an employer during the years 1972–1990 following an incident resulting in death or serious injury of a worker was just $480." The same report claims that the federal government spends $1.1 billion a year to protect fish and wildlife and only $300 million a year to protect workers from health and safety hazards on the job. . . .

Is a person who kills another in a bar brawl a greater threat to society than a business executive who refuses to cut into his profits to make his plant a safe place to work? By any measure of death and suffering the latter is by far a greater danger than the former. Because he wishes his workers no harm, because he is only indirectly responsible for death and disability while pursuing legitimate economic goals, his acts are not called "crimes." Once we free our imagination from the blinders of the one-on-one model of crime, can there be any doubt that the criminal justice system does *not* protect us from the gravest threats to life and limb? It seeks to protect us when danger comes from a young, lower-class male in the inner city. When a threat comes from an upper-class business executive in an office, the criminal justice system looks the other way. This is in the face of growing evidence that for every three American citizens murdered by thugs, at least four American workers are killed by the recklessness of their bosses and the indifference of their government.

Health Care May Be Dangerous to Your Health

. . . On July 15, 1975, Dr. Sidney Wolfe of Ralph Nader's Public Interest Health Research Group testified before the House Commerce Oversight and Investigations Subcommittee that there "were 3.2 million cases of unnecessary surgery performed each year in the United States." These unneeded operations, Wolfe added, "cost close to $5 billion a year and kill as many as 16,000 Americans.". . .

In an article on an experimental program by Blue Cross and Blue Shield aimed at curbing unnecessary surgery, *Newsweek* reports that

> a Congressional committee earlier this year [1976] estimated that more than 2 million of the elective operations performed in 1974 were not only unnecessary—but also killed about 12,000 patients and cost nearly $4 billion.

Because the number of surgical operations performed in the United States rose from 16.7 million in 1975 to 22.4 million in 1991, there is reason to believe that at least somewhere between . . . 12,000 and . . . 16,000 people a year still die from unnecessary surgery. In 1991, the FBI reported that 3,405 murders were committed by a "cutting or stabbing instrument." Obviously, the FBI does not include the scalpel as a cutting or stabbing instrument. If they did, they would have had to report that between 15,405 and 19,405 persons were killed by "cutting or stabbing" in 1991. . . . No matter how you slice it, the scalpel may be more dangerous than the switchblade. . . .

Waging Chemical Warfare Against America

One in 4 Americans can expect to contract cancer during their lifetimes. The American Cancer Society estimated that 420,000 Americans would die of cancer in 1981. The National Cancer Institute's estimate for 1993 is 526,000 deaths from cancer. "A 1978 report issued by the President's Council on Environmental Quality (CEQ) unequivocally states that 'most researchers agree that 70 to 90 percent of cancers are caused by environmental influences and are hence theoretically preventable.'" This means that a concerted national effort could result in saving 350,000 or more lives a year and reducing each individual's chances of getting cancer in his or her lifetime from 1 in 4 to 1 in 12 or fewer. If you think this would require a massive effort in terms of money and personnel, you are right. How much of an effort, though, would the nation make to stop a foreign invader who was killing a thousand people and bent on capturing one-quarter of the present population?

In face of this "invasion" that is already under way, the U.S. government has allocated $1.9 billion to the National Cancer Institute (NCI) for fiscal year 1992, and NCI has allocated $219 million to the study of the physical and chemical (i.e., environmental) causes of cancer. Compare this with the (at least) $45 billion spent to fight the Persian Gulf War. The simple truth is that the government that strove so mightily to protect the borders of a small, undemocratic nation 7,000 miles away is doing next to nothing to protect us against the chemical war in our midst. This war is being waged against us on three fronts:

- Pollution
- Cigarette smoking
- Food additives

. . . The evidence linking *air pollution* and cancer, as well as other serious and often fatal diseases, has been rapidly accumulating in recent years. In 1993, the *Journal of the American Medical Association* reported on research that found "'robust' associations between premature mortality and air pollution levels." They estimate that pollutants cause about 2 percent of all cancer deaths (at least 10,000 a year). . . .

A . . . recent study . . . concluded that air pollution at 1988 levels was responsible for 60,000 deaths a year. The Natural Resources Defense Council sued the EPA [Environmental Protection Agency] for its foot-dragging in implementation of the Clean Air Act, charging that "One hundred million people live in areas of unhealthy air."

This chemical war is not limited to the air. The National Cancer Institute has identified as carcinogens or suspected carcinogens 23 of the chemicals commonly found in our drinking water. Moreover, according to one observer, we are now facing a "new plague—toxic exposure.". . .

The evidence linking *cigarette smoking* and cancer is overwhelming and need not be repeated here. The Centers for Disease Control estimates that cigarettes cause 87 percent of lung cancers—approximately 146,000 in 1992. Tobacco continues to kill an estimated 400,000 Americans a year. Cigarettes are widely estimated to cause 30 percent of all cancer deaths. . . .

This is enough to expose the hypocrisy of running a full-scale war against heroin (which produces no degenerative disease) while allowing cigarette sales and advertising to flourish. It also should be enough to underscore the point that once again there are threats to our lives much greater than criminal homicide. The legal order does not protect us against them. Indeed, not only does our government fail to protect us against this threat, it promotes it! . . .

Based on the knowledge we have, there can be no doubt that air pollution, tobacco, and food additives amount to a chemical war that makes the crime wave look like a football scrimmage. Even with the most conservative estimates, it is clear that *the death toll in this war is far higher than the number of people killed by criminal homicide!*

Summary

Once again, our investigations lead to the same result. The criminal justice system does not protect us against the gravest threats to life, limb, or possessions. Its definitions of crime are not simply a reflection of the objective dangers that threaten us. The workplace, the medical profession, the air we breathe, and the poverty we refuse to rectify lead to far more human suffering, far more death and disability, and take far more dollars from our pockets than the murders, aggravated assaults, and thefts reported annually by the FBI. What is more, this human suffering is preventable. A government really intent on protecting our well-being could enforce work safety regulations, police the medical profession, require that clean air standards be met, and funnel sufficient money to the poor to alleviate the major disabilities of poverty—but it does not. Instead we hear a lot of cant about law and order and a lot of rant about crime in the streets. It is as if our leaders were not only refusing to protect us from the major threats to our well-being but trying to cover up this refusal by diverting our attention to crime—as if this were the only real threat.

POSTSCRIPT

Is Street Crime More Harmful Than White-Collar Crime?

It is important to consider both the suffering and the wider ramifications caused by crimes. Anderson captures many of these dimensions and gives a full account of the harms of street crime. Today the public is very concerned about street crime, especially wanton violence. However, it seems relatively unconcerned about white-collar crime. Reiman tries to change that perception. By defining many harmful actions by managers and professionals as crimes, he argues that white-collar crime is worse than street crime. He says that more people are killed and injured by "occupational injury or disease, by unnecessary surgery, and by shoddy emergency medical services than by aggravated assault or even homicide!" But are shoddy medical services a crime? In the end, the questions remain: What is a crime? Who are the criminals?

A set of readings that support Reiman's viewpoint is *Corporate Violence: Injury and Death for Profit* edited by Stuart L. Hills (Rowman & Littlefield, 1987); *Unmasking the Crimes of the Powerful: Scrutinizing States and Corporations,* edited by Steve Tombs and Dave Whyte (P. Lang, 2003); Joel Bakan, *The Corporation: The Pathological Pursuit of Profit and Power* (Free Press, 2004); Hazel Croall, *Understanding White Collar Crime* (Open University Press, 2001); Stephen M. Rosoff et el, *Looting, America: Greed, Corruption, Villians, and Victims* (Prentice Hall, 2003) *Readings in White-Collar Crime,* edited by David Shichor et al. (Waveland Press, 2002); and David Weisburd, *White-Collar Crime and Criminal Career* (Cambridge University Press, 2001). Most works on crime deal mainly with theft, drugs, and violence and the injury and fear that they cause including Leslie Williams Reid, *Crime in the City: A Political and Economic Analysis of Urban Crime* (LFB Scholarly Pub., 2003); Walter S. DeKeseredy, *Under Seige: Poverty and Crime in a Public Housing Community* (Lexington Books, 2003); Alex Alverez and Ronet Bachman, *Murder American Style* (Wadsworth, 2003); Claire Valier, *Crime and Punishment in Contemporary Culture* (Routledge, 2004); Matthew B. Robinson, *Why Crime?: An Integrated Systems Theory of Antisocial Behavior* (Pearson, 2004); Ronald B. Flowers, *Male Crime and Deviance: Exploring Its Causes, Dynamics, and Nature* (C.C. Thomas, 2003); and Meda Chesney-Lind and Lisa Pasko, *The Female Offender: Girls, Women, and Crime*, 2nd edition (Sage, 2004). Two works on gangs, which are often connected with violent street crime, are Martin Sanchez Jankowski, *Islands in the Street: Gangs and American Urban Society* (University of California Press, 1991) and Felix M. Padilla, *The Gang as an American Enterprise* (Rutgers University Press, 1992). William J. Bennett, John J. DiIulio, and John P. Walters, in *Body Count: Moral Poverty—and How to Win America's War Against Crime and Drugs* (Simon & Schuster, 1996), argue that moral poverty is the root cause of crime (meaning street crime). How applicable is this thesis to white-collar crime? One interesting aspect of many corporate, or white-collar, crimes is that they involve crimes of obedience, as discussed in Herman C. Kelman and V. Lee Hamilton, *Crimes of Obedience: Toward a Social Psychology of Authority and Responsibility* (Yale University Press, 1989).

For recent effort to calculate the costs of crime and law enforcement see Mark A. Cohen, *The Costs of Crime and Justice* (Routledge, 2005). Finally, there is a new type of crime that is increasingly troublesome: digital crime and terrorism. This is thoroughly examined by Robert W. Taylor et al., in *Digital Crime and Digital Terrorism* (Pearson/Prentice Hall, 2006).

ISSUE 17

Should Drug Use Be Decriminalized?

YES: Ethan A. Nadelmann, from "Commonsense Drug Policy," *Foreign Affairs* (January/February 1998)

NO: Eric A. Voth, from "America's Longest 'War,'" *The World & I* (February 2000)

ISSUE SUMMARY

YES: Ethan A. Nadelmann, director of the Lindesmith Center, a drug policy research institute, argues that history shows that drug prohibition is costly and futile. Examining the drug policies in other countries, he finds that decriminalization plus sane and humane drug policies and treatment programs can greatly reduce the harms from drugs.

NO: Eric A. Voth, chairman of the International Drug Strategy Institute, contends that drugs are very harmful and that our drug policies have succeeded in substantially reducing drug use.

A century ago, drugs of every kind were freely available to Americans. Laudanum, a mixture of opium and alcohol, was popularly used as a painkiller. One drug company even claimed that it was a very useful substance for calming hyperactive children, and the company called it Mother's Helper. Morphine came into common use during the Civil War. Heroin, developed as a supposedly less addictive substitute for morphine, began to be marketed at the end of the nineteenth century. By that time, drug paraphernalia could be ordered through Sears and Roebuck catalogues, and Coca-Cola, which contained small quantities of cocaine, had become a popular drink.

Public concerns about addiction and dangerous patent medicines, and an active campaign for drug laws waged by Dr. Harvey Wiley, a chemist in the U.S. Department of Agriculture, led Congress to pass the first national drug regulation act in 1906. The Pure Food and Drug Act required that medicines containing certain drugs, such as opium, must say so on their labels.

The Harrison Narcotic Act of 1914 went much further and cut off completely the supply of legal opiates to addicts. Since then, ever-stricter drug laws have been passed by Congress and by state legislatures.

Drug abuse in America again came to the forefront of public discourse during the 1960s, when heroin addiction started growing rapidly in inner-city neighborhoods. Also, by the end of the decade, drug experimentation had spread to the middle-class, affluent baby boomers who were then attending college. Indeed, certain types of drugs began to be celebrated by some of the leaders of the counterculture. Heroin was still taboo, but other drugs, notably marijuana and LSD (a psychedelic drug), were regarded as harmless and even spiritually transforming. At music festivals like Woodstock in 1969, marijuana and LSD were used openly and associated with love, peace, and heightened sensitivity. Much of this enthusiasm cooled over the next 20 years as baby boomers entered the workforce full-time and began their careers. But even among the careerists, certain types of drugs enjoyed high status. Cocaine, noted for its highly stimulating effects, became the drug of choice for many hard-driving young lawyers, television writers, and Wall Street bond traders.

The high price of cocaine put it out of reach for many people, but in the early 1980s, cheap substitutes began to appear on the streets and to overtake poor urban communities. Crack cocaine, a potent, highly addictive, smokable form of cocaine, came into widespread use. By the end of the 1980s, the drug known as "ice," or as it is called on the West Coast, "L.A. glass," a smokable form of amphetamine, had hit the streets. These stimulants tend to produce very violent, disorderly behavior. Moreover, the street gangs who sell them are frequently at war with one another and are well armed. Not only gang members but also many innocent people have become victims of contract killings, street battles, and drive-by shootings.

This new drug epidemic prompted President George Bush to declare a "war on drugs," and in 1989 he asked Congress to appropriate $10.6 billion for the fight. Although most Americans support such measures against illegal drugs, some say that in the years since Bush made his declaration, the drug situation has not showed any signs of improvement. Some believe that legalization would be the best way to fight the drug problem.

The drug decriminalization issue is especially interesting to sociologists because it raises basic questions about what should be socially sanctioned or approved, what is illegal or legal, and what is immoral or moral. An aspect of the basic value system of America is under review. The process of value change may be taking place in front of our eyes. As part of this debate, Ethan A. Nadelmann argues that the present policy does not work and that it is counterproductive. Legalization, he contends, would stop much of the disease, violence, and crime associated with illegal drugs. Although Nadelmann concedes that it may increase the use of lower-potency drugs, he believes that legalization would reduce the use of the worst drugs. Eric A. Voth maintains that legalization would be madness because he asserts that the current drug policies in effect are working.

Ethan A. Nadelmann  **YES**

Commonsense Drug Policy

First, Reduce Harm

In 1988 Congress passed a resolution proclaiming its goal of "a drug-free America by 1995." U.S. drug policy has failed persistently over the decades because it has preferred such rhetoric to reality, and moralism to pragmatism. Politicians confess their youthful indiscretions, then call for tougher drug laws. Drug control officials make assertions with no basis in fact or science. Police officers, generals, politicians, and guardians of public morals qualify as drug czars—but not, to date, a single doctor or public health figure. Independent commissions are appointed to evaluate drug policies, only to see their recommendations ignored as politically risky. And drug policies are designed, implemented, and enforced with virtually no input from the millions of Americans they affect most: drug users. Drug abuse is a serious problem, both for individual citizens and society at large, but the "war on drugs" has made matters worse, not better.

Drug warriors often point to the 1980s as a time in which the drug war really worked. Illicit drug use by teenagers peaked around 1980, then fell more than 50 percent over the next 12 years. During the 1996 presidential campaign, Republican challenger Bob Dole made much of the recent rise in teenagers' use of illicit drugs, contrasting it with the sharp drop during the Reagan and Bush administrations. President Clinton's response was tepid, in part because he accepted the notion that teen drug use is the principal measure of drug policy's success or failure; at best, he could point out that the level was still barely half what it had been in 1980.

In 1980, however, no one had ever heard of the cheap, smokable form of cocaine called crack, or drug-related HIV infection or AIDS. By the 1990s, both had reached epidemic proportions in American cities, largely driven by prohibitionist economics and morals indifferent to the human consequences of the drug war. In 1980, the federal budget for drug control was about $1 billion, and state and local budgets were perhaps two or three times that. By 1997, the federal drug control budget had ballooned to $16 billion, two-thirds of it for law enforcement agencies, and state and local funding to at least that. On any day in 1980, approximately 50,000 people were behind bars for violating a drug law. By 1997, the number had increased eightfold, to

From Ethan A. Nadelmann, "Commonsense Drug Policy," *Foreign Affairs,* vol. 77, no. 1 (January/February 1998). Copyright © 1998 by The Council on Foreign Relations, Inc. Reprinted by permission of *Foreign Affairs.* Notes omitted.

about 400,000. These are the results of a drug policy overreliant on criminal justice "solutions," ideologically wedded to abstinence-only treatment, and insulated from cost-benefit analysis.

Imagine instead a policy that starts by acknowledging that drugs are here to stay, and that we have no choice but to learn how to live with them so that they cause the least possible harm. Imagine a policy that focuses on reducing not illicit drug use per se but the crime and misery caused by both drug abuse and prohibitionist policies. And imagine a drug policy based not on the fear, prejudice, and ignorance that drive America's current approach but rather on common sense, science, public health concerns, and human rights. Such a policy is possible in the United States, especially if Americans are willing to learn from the experiences of other countries where such policies are emerging.

Attitudes Abroad

Americans are not averse to looking abroad for solutions to the nation's drug problems. Unfortunately, they have been looking in the wrong places: Asia and Latin America, where much of the world's heroin and cocaine originates. Decades of U.S. efforts to keep drugs from being produced abroad and exported to American markets have failed. Illicit drug production is bigger business than ever before. The opium poppy, source of morphine and heroin, and *cannabis sativa*, from which marijuana and hashish are prepared, grow readily around the world; the coca plant, from whose leaves cocaine is extracted, can be cultivated far from its native environment in the Andes. Crop substitution programs designed to persuade Third World peasants to grow legal crops cannot compete with the profits that drug prohibition makes inevitable. Crop eradication campaigns occasionally reduce production in one country, but new suppliers pop up elsewhere. International law enforcement efforts can disrupt drug trafficking organizations and routes, but they rarely have much impact on U.S. drug markets. . . .

While looking to Latin America and Asia for supply-reduction solutions to America's drug problems is futile, the harm-reduction approaches spreading throughout Europe and Australia and even into corners of North America show promise. These approaches start by acknowledging that supply-reduction initiatives are inherently limited, that criminal justice responses can be costly and counterproductive, and that single-minded pursuit of a "drug-free society" is dangerously quixotic. Demand-reduction efforts to prevent drug abuse among children and adults are important, but so are harm-reduction efforts to lessen the damage to those unable or unwilling to stop using drugs immediately, and to those around them.

Most proponents of harm reduction do not favor legalization. They recognize that prohibition has failed to curtail drug abuse, that it is responsible for much of the crime, corruption, disease, and death associated with drugs, and that its costs mount every year. But they also see legalization as politically unwise and as risking increased drug use. The challenge is thus making drug prohibition work better, but with a focus on reducing the negative consequences of both drug use and prohibitionist policies. . . .

Harm-reduction innovations include efforts to stem the spread of HIV by making sterile syringes readily available and collecting used syringes; allowing doctors to prescribe oral methadone for heroin addiction treatment, as well as heroin and other drugs for addicts who would otherwise buy them on the black market; establishing "safe injection rooms" so addicts do not congregate in public places or dangerous "shooting galleries"; employing drug analysis units at the large dance parties called raves to test the quality and potency of MDMA, known as Ecstasy, and other drugs that patrons buy and consume there; decriminalizing (but not legalizing) possession and retail sale of cannabis and, in some cases, possession of small amounts of "hard" drugs; and integrating harm-reduction policies and principles into community policing strategies. Some of these measures are under way or under consideration in parts of the United States, but rarely to the extent found in growing numbers of foreign countries.

Stopping HIV With Sterile Syringes

The spread of HIV, the virus that causes AIDS, among people who inject drugs illegally was what prompted governments in Europe and Australia to experiment with harm-reduction policies. During the early 1980s public health officials realized that infected users were spreading HIV by sharing needles. Having already experienced a hepatitis epidemic attributed to the same mode of transmission, the Dutch were the first to tell drug users about the risks of needle sharing and to make sterile syringes available and collect dirty needles through pharmacies, needle exchange and methadone programs, and public health services. Governments elsewhere in Europe and in Australia soon followed suit. The few countries in which a prescription was necessary to obtain a syringe dropped the requirement. Local authorities in Germany, Switzerland, and other European countries authorized needle exchange machines to ensure 24-hour access. In some European cities, addicts can exchange used syringes for clean ones at local police stations without fear of prosecution or harassment. Prisons are instituting similar policies to help discourage the spread of HIV among inmates, recognizing that illegal drug injecting cannot be eliminated even behind bars.

These initiatives were not adopted without controversy. Conservative politicians argued that needle exchange programs condoned illicit and immoral behavior and that government policies should focus on punishing drug users or making them drug-free. But by the late 1980s, the consensus in most of Western Europe, Oceania, and Canada was that while drug abuse was a serious problem, AIDS was worse. Slowing the spread of a fatal disease for which no cure exists was the greater moral imperative. There was also a fiscal imperative. Needle exchange programs' costs are minuscule compared with those of treating people who would otherwise become infected with HIV.

Only in the United States has this logic not prevailed, even though AIDS was the leading killer of Americans ages 25 to 44 for most of the 1990s and is now No. 2. The Centers for Disease Control (CDC) estimates that half of new HIV infections in the country stem from injection drug use. Yet both the White House and Congress block allocation of AIDS or drug-abuse prevention funds for needle exchange, and virtually all state governments retain drug paraphernalia laws, pharmacy regulations, and other restrictions on access to sterile syringes. During the 1980s, AIDS activists engaging in civil disobedience set up more syringe exchange programs than state and local governments. There are now more than 100 such programs in 28 states, Washington, D.C., and Puerto Rico, but they reach only an estimated 10 percent of injection drug users.

Governments at all levels in the United States refuse to fund needle exchange for political reasons, even though dozens of scientific studies, domestic and foreign, have found that needle exchange and other distribution programs reduce needle sharing, bring hard-to-reach drug users into contact with health care systems, and inform addicts about treatment programs, yet do not increase illegal drug use. In 1991 the National AIDS Commission appointed by President Bush called the lack of federal support for such programs "bewildering and tragic." In 1993 a CDC-sponsored review of research on needle exchange recommended federal funding, but top officials in the Clinton administration suppressed a favorable evaluation of the report within the Department of Health and Human Services. In July 1996 President Clinton's Advisory Council on HIV/AIDS criticized the administration for its failure to heed the National Academy of Sciences' recommendation that it authorize the use of federal money to support needle exchange programs. An independent panel convened by the National Institute[s] of Health reached the same conclusion in February 1997. Last summer, the American Medical Association, the American Bar Association, and even the politicized U.S. Conference of Mayors endorsed the concept of needle exchange. In the fall, an endorsement followed from the World Bank.

To date, America's failure in this regard is conservatively estimated to have resulted in the infection of up to 10,000 people with HIV. Mounting scientific evidence and the stark reality of the continuing AIDS crisis have convinced the public, if not politicians, that needle exchange saves lives; polls consistently find that a majority of Americans support needle exchange, with approval highest among those most familiar with the notion. Prejudice and political cowardice are poor excuses for allowing more citizens to suffer from and die of AIDS, especially when effective interventions are cheap, safe, and easy.

Methadone and Other Alternatives

The United States pioneered the use of the synthetic opiate methadone to treat heroin addiction in the 1960s and 1970s, but now lags behind much of Europe and Australia in making methadone accessible and effective. Methadone is the best available treatment in terms of reducing illicit heroin use and associated crime, disease, and death. In the early 1990s the National Academy of Sciences' Institute of Medicine stated that of all forms of drug treatment, "methadone maintenance has been the most rigorously studied modality and has yielded the most incontrovertibly positive results. . . . Consumption of all illicit drugs, especially heroin, declines. Crime is reduced, fewer individuals become HIV positive, and individual functioning is improved." However, the institute went on to declare, "Current policy . . . puts too much emphasis on protecting society from methadone, and not enough on protecting society from the epidemics of addiction, violence, and infectious diseases that methadone can help reduce."

Methadone is to street heroin what nicotine skin patches and chewing gum are to cigarettes—with the added benefit of legality. Taken orally, methadone has little of injected heroin's effect on mood or cognition. It can be consumed for decades with few if any negative health consequences, and its purity and concentration, unlike street heroin's, are assured. Like other opiates, it can create physical dependence if taken regularly, but the "addiction" is more like a diabetic's "addiction" to insulin than a heroin addict's to product brought on the street. Methadone patients can and do drive safely, hold good jobs, and care for their children. When prescribed adequate doses, they can be indistinguishable from people who have never used heroin or methadone.

Popular misconceptions and prejudice, however, have all but prevented any expansion of methadone treatment in the United States. The 115,000 Americans receiving methadone today represent only a small increase over the number 20 years ago. For every ten heroin addicts, there are only one or two methadone treatment slots. Methadone is the most tightly controlled drug in the pharmacopoeia, subject to unique federal and state restrictions. Doctors cannot prescribe it for addiction treatment outside designated programs. Regulations dictate not only security, documentation, and staffing requirements but maximum doses, admission criteria, time spent in the program, and a host of other specifics, none of which has much to do with quality of treatment. Moreover, the regulations do not prevent poor treatment; many clinics provide insufficient doses, prematurely detoxify clients, expel clients for offensive behavior, and engage in other practices that would be regarded as unethical in any other field of medicine. Attempts to open new clinics tend to be blocked by residents who don't want addicts in their neighborhood. . . .

The Swiss government began a nationwide trial in 1994 to determine whether prescribing heroin, morphine, or injectable methadone could reduce crime, disease, and other drug-related ills. Some 1,000 volunteers—only heroin addicts with at least two unsuccessful experiences in methadone or other conventional treatment programs were considered—took part in the experiment. The trial quickly determined that virtually all participants preferred heroin, and doctors subsequently prescribed it for them. Last July the government reported the results so far: criminal offenses and the number of criminal offenders dropped 60 percent, the percentage of income from illegal and semilegal activities fell from 69 to 10 percent, illegal heroin *and* cocaine use declined dramatically (although use of alcohol, cannabis, and tranquilizers like Valium remained fairly constant), stable employment increased from 14 to 32 percent, physical health improved enormously, and most participants greatly reduced their contact with the drug scene. There were no deaths from overdoses, and no prescribed drugs were diverted to the black market. More than half those who dropped out of the study switched to another form of drug treatment, including 83 who began abstinence therapy. A cost-benefit analysis of the program found a net economic benefit of $30 per patient per day, mostly because of reduced criminal justice and health care costs.

The Swiss study has undermined several myths about heroin and its habitual users. The results to date demonstrate that, given relatively unlimited availability, heroin users will voluntarily stabilize or reduce their dosage and some will even choose abstinence; that long-addicted users can lead relatively normal, stable lives if provided legal access to their drug of choice; and that ordinary citizens will support such initiatives. In recent referendums in Zurich, Basel, and Zug, substantial majorities voted to continue funding local arms of the experiment. And last September, a nationwide referendum to end the government's heroin maintenance and other harm-reduction initiatives was rejected by 71 percent of Swiss voters, including majorities in all 26 cantons. . . .

Reefer Sanity

Cannabis, in the form of marijuana and hashish, is by far the most popular illicit drug in the United States. More than a quarter of Americans admit to having tried it. Marijuana's popularity peaked in 1980, dropped steadily until the early 1990s, and is now on the rise again. Although it is not entirely safe, especially when consumed by children, smoked heavily, or used when driving, it is clearly among the least dangerous psychoactive drugs in common use. In 1988 the administrative law judge for the Drug Enforcement Administration, Francis Young, reviewed the evidence and concluded that "marihuana, in its natural form, is one of the safest therapeutically active substances known to man."

As with needle exchange and methadone treatment, American politicians have ignored or spurned the findings of government commissions and scientific organizations concerning marijuana policy. In 1972 the National Commission on Marihuana and Drug Abuse—created by President Nixon and chaired by a former Republican governor, Raymond Shafer—recommended that possession of up to one ounce of marijuana be decriminalized. Nixon rejected the recommendation. In 1982 a panel appointed by the National Academy of Sciences reached the same conclusions as the Shafer Commission.

Between 1973 and 1978, with attitudes changing, 11 states approved decriminalization statutes that reclassified marijuana possession as a misdemeanor, petty offense, or civil violation punishable by no more than a $100 fine. Consumption trends in those states and in states that retained stricter sanctions were indistinguishable. A 1988 scholarly evaluation of the Moscone Act, California's 1976 decriminalization law, estimated that the state had saved half a billion dollars in arrest costs since the law's passage. Nonetheless, public opinion began to shift in 1978. No other states decriminalized marijuana, and some eventually recriminalized it.

Between 1973 and 1989, annual arrests on marijuana charges by state and local police ranged between 360,000 and 460,000. The annual total fell to 283,700 in 1991, but has since more than doubled. In 1996, 641,642 people were arrested for marijuana, 85 percent of them for possession, not sale, of the drug. Prompted by concern over rising marijuana use among adolescents and fears of being labeled soft on drugs, the Clinton administration launched its own anti-marijuana campaign in 1995. But the administration's claims to have identified new risks of marijuana consumption—including a purported link between marijuana and violent behavior—have not withstood scrutiny. Neither Congress nor the White House seems likely to put the issue of marijuana policy before a truly independent advisory commission, given the consistency with which such commissions have reached politically unacceptable conclusions. . . .

Will It Work?

Both at home and abroad, the U.S. government has attempted to block resolutions supporting harm reduction, suppress scientific studies that reached politically inconvenient conclusions, and silence critics of official drug policy. In May 1994, the State Department forced the last-minute cancellation of a World Bank conference on drug trafficking to which critics of U.S. drug policy had been invited. That December the U.S. delegation to an international meeting of the U.N. Drug Control Program refused to sign any statement incorporating the phrase "harm reduction." In early 1995 the State Department successfully pressured the World Health Organization to scuttle the release of a report it had commissioned from a panel that included many of the world's leading experts on cocaine because it included the scientifically incontrovertible observations that traditional use of coca leaf in the Andes causes little harm to users and that most consumers of cocaine use the drug in moderation with few detrimental effects. Hundreds of congressional hearings have addressed multitudinous aspects of the drug problem, but few have inquired into the European harm-reduction policies described above. When former Secretary of State George Shultz, then–Surgeon General M. Joycelyn Elders, and Baltimore Mayor Kurt Schmoke pointed to the failure of current policies and called for new approaches, they were mocked, fired, and ignored, respectively—and thereafter mischaracterized as advocating the outright legalization of drugs.

In Europe, in contrast, informed, public debate about drug policy is increasingly common in government, even at the EU level. In June 1995 the European Parliament issued a report acknowledging that "there will always be a demand for drugs in our societies . . . the policies followed so far have not been able to prevent the illegal drug trade from flourishing." The EU called for serious consideration of the Frankfurt Resolution, a statement of harm-reduction principles supported by a transnational coalition of 31 cities and regions. In October 1996 Emma Bonino, the European commissioner for consumer policy, advocated decriminalizing soft drugs and initiating a broad prescription program for hard drugs. Greece's minister for European affairs, George Papandreou, seconded her. Last February the monarch of Liechtenstein, Prince Hans Adam, spoke out in favor of controlled drug legalization. Even Raymond Kendall, secretary general of Interpol, was quoted in the August 20, 1994, *Guardian* as saying, "The prosecution of thousands of otherwise law-abiding citizens every year is both hypocritical and an affront to individual, civil and human rights. . . . Drug use should no longer be a criminal offense. I am totally against legalization, but in favor of decriminalization for the user." . . .

The lessons from Europe and Australia are compelling. Drug control policies should focus on reducing drug-related crime, disease, and death, not the number of casual drug users. Stopping the spread of HIV by and among drug users by making sterile syringes and methadone readily available must be the first priority. American politicians need to explore, not ignore or automatically condemn, promising policy options such as cannabis decriminalization, heroin prescription, and the integration of harm-reduction principles into community policing strategies. Central governments must back, or at least not hinder, the efforts of municipal officials and citizens to devise pragmatic approaches to local drug problems. Like citizens in Europe, the American public has supported such innovations when they are adequately explained and allowed to prove themselves. As the evidence comes in, what works is increasingly apparent. All that remains is mustering the political courage.

NO

Eric A. Voth

America's Longest "War"

Bashing our drug policy is a popular activity. The advocates of legalization and decriminalization repeatedly contend that restrictive drug policy is failing, in the hope that this becomes a self-fulfilling prophecy. An objective look at the history of drug policy in the United States, especially in comparison to other countries, demonstrates that, indeed, our policies are working. What we also see is the clear presence of a well-organized and well-financed drug culture lobby that seeks to tear down restrictive drug policy and replace it with permissive policies that could seriously jeopardize our country's viability.

To understand our current situation, we must examine the last 25 years. The 1970s were a time of great social turmoil for the United States, and drug use was finding its way into the fabric of society. Policymakers were uncertain how to deal with drugs. As permissive advisers dominated the discussion, drug use climbed. The National Household Survey and the Monitoring the Future Survey both confirm that drug use peaked in the late 1970s. Twenty-five million Americans were current users of drugs in 1979, 37 percent of high school seniors had used marijuana in the prior 30 days, and 10.7 percent of them used marijuana daily. During the same time frame, 13 states embraced the permissive social attitude and legalized or decriminalized marijuana.

In the late 1970s, policymakers, parents, and law enforcement began to realize that our drug situation was leading to Armageddon. As never before, a coordinated war on drugs was set in motion that demanded a no-use message. This was largely driven by parents who were sick of their children falling prey to drugs. The "Just Say No" movement was the centerpiece of antidrug activities during the subsequent years. A solid national antidrug message was coupled with rigorous law enforcement. The results were striking. As perception of the harmfulness of drugs increased, their use dropped drastically. By 1992, marijuana use by high school students in the prior 30 days had dropped to 11.9 percent and daily use to 1.9 percent.

Breakdown in the 1990s

Unfortunately, several major events derailed our policy successes in the early 1990s, resulting in an approximate doubling of drug use since that time.

From a national vantage point, a sense of complacency set in. Satisfied that the drug war was won, we lost national leadership. Federal funding for anti-drug programs became mired in bureaucracy and difficult for small prevention organizations to obtain. A new generation of drug specialists entered the scene. Lacking experience of the ravages of the 1970s, they were willing to accept softening of policy. The Internet exploded as an open forum for the dissemination of inaccurate, deceptive, and manipulative information supporting permissive policy, even discussions of how to obtain and use drugs. The greatest audience has been young people, who are exposed to a plethora of drug-permissive information without filter or validation.

The entertainment media have provided a steady diet of alcohol and drug use for young people to witness. A recent study commissioned by the White House Office of National Drug Control Policy found that alcohol appeared in more than 93 percent of movies and illicit drugs in 22 percent, of which 51 percent depicted marijuana use. Concurrently, the news media have begun to demonstrate bias toward softening of drug policy, having the net effect of changing public opinion.

The single most dramatic influence, however, came in the transformation of the drug culture from a disorganized group of legalization advocates to a well-funded and well-organized machine. With funding from several large donors, drug-culture advocates were able to initiate large-scale attacks on the media and policymakers. The most prominent funder is the billionaire George Soros, who has spent millions toward the initiation of organizations such as the Drug Policy Foundation, Lindesmith Center, medical-marijuana-advocacy and needle-handout groups, to name a few projects.

A slick strategic shift toward compartmentalizing and dissecting restrictive drug policy has resulted in what is termed the "harm reduction" movement. After all, who would oppose the idea of reducing the harm to society caused by drug use? The philosophy of the harm reduction movement is well summarized by Ethan Nadelman of the Lindesmith Center (also funded by Soros), who is considered the godfather of the legalization movement:

> Let's start by dropping the "zero tolerance" rhetoric and policies and the illusory goal of drug-free societies. Accept that drug use is here to stay and that we have no choice but to learn to live with drugs so that they cause the least possible harm. Recognize that many, perhaps most, "drug problems" in the Americas are the results not of drug use per se but of our prohibitionist policies. . . .

The harm reduction movement has attacked the individual components of restrictive drug policy and created strategies to weaken it. Some of these strategies include giving heroin to addicts; handing out needles to addicts; encouraging use of crack cocaine instead of intravenous drugs; reducing drug-related criminal penalties; teaching "responsible" drug use to adolescents instead of working toward prevention of use; the medical marijuana movement; and the expansion of the industrial hemp movement.

Softening Drug Policies

The move toward soft drug policy has created some strange bedfellows. On one hand, supporters of liberal policy such as Gov. Gary Johnson of New Mexico have always taken the misguided view that individuals should have a right to use whatever they want in order to feel good. They often point to their own "survival" of drug use as justification for loosening laws and letting others experiment. Interestingly, the governor's public safety secretary quit as a result of being undermined by Johnson's destructive stand on legalization. Libertarian conservatives such as Milton Friedman and William Buckley have attacked drug policy as an infringement of civil liberties and have incorrectly considered drug use to be a victimless event. Societal problems such as homelessness, domestic abuse, numerous health problems, crimes under the influence, poor job performance, decreased productivity, and declining educational levels have strong connections to drug use and cost our society financially and spiritually.

The notion that decriminalizing or legalizing drugs will drive the criminal element out of the market is flawed and reflects a total lack of understanding of drug use and addiction. Drug use creates its own market, and often the only thing limiting the amount of drugs that an addict uses is the amount of money available. Further, if drugs were legalized, what would the legal scenario be? Would anyone be allowed to sell drugs? Would they be sold by the government? If so, what strengths would be available? If there were any limitations on strength or availability, a black market would immediately develop. Most rational people can easily recognize this slippery slope.

Consistently, drug-culture advocates assert that policy has failed and is extremely costly. This is a calculated strategy to demoralize the population and turn public sentiment against restrictive policy. The real question is, has restrictive policy failed? First we should consider the issues of cost. An effective way to determine cost-effectiveness is to compare the costs to society of legal versus illegal drugs. Estimates from 1990 suggest that the costs of illegal drugs were $70 billion, as compared to that of alcohol alone at $99 billion and tobacco at $72 billion. Estimates from 1992 put the costs of alcohol dependence at $148 billion and all illegal drugs (including the criminal justice system costs) at $98 billion.

Referring to the National Household Survey data from 1998, there were 13.6 million current users of illicit drugs compared to 113 million users of alcohol and 60 million tobacco smokers. There is one difference: legal status of the drugs. The Monitoring the Future Survey of high school seniors suggests that in 1995, some 52.5 percent of seniors had been drunk within the previous year as compared to 34.7 percent who had used marijuana. Yet, alcohol is illegal for teenagers. The only difference is, again, the legal status of the two substances.

Results of Legalization

Permissive drug policy has been tried both in the United States and abroad. In 1985, during the period in which Alaska legalized marijuana, the use of marijuana and cocaine among adolescents was more than twice as high as in other parts of the country. Baltimore has long been heralded as a centerpiece for harm reduction drug policy. Interestingly, the rate of heroin use found among arrestees in Baltimore was higher than in any other city in the United States. Thirty-seven percent of male and 48 percent of female arrestees were positive, compared with 6–23 percent for Washington, D.C., Philadelphia, and Manhattan.

Since liberalizing its marijuana-enforcement policies, the Netherlands has found that marijuana use among 11- to 18-year-olds has increased 142 percent from 1990 to 1995. Crime has risen steadily to the point that aggravated theft and breaking and entering occur three to four times more than in the United States. Along with the staggering increases in marijuana use, the Netherlands has become one of the major suppliers of the drug Ecstacy. Australia is flirting with substantial softening of drug policy. That is already taking a toll. Drug use there among 16- to 29-year-olds is 52 percent as compared with 9 percent in Sweden, a country with a restrictive drug policy. In Vancouver in 1988, HIV prevalence among IV drug addicts was only 1–2 percent. In 1997 it was 23 percent, after wide adoption of harm reduction policies. Vancouver has the largest needle exchange in North America.

Clearly, the last few years have witnessed some very positive changes in policy and our antidrug efforts. A steady national voice opposing drug use is again being heard. Efforts are being made to increase cooperation between the treatment and law enforcement communities to allow greater access to treatment. The primary prevention movement is strong and gaining greater footholds. The increases in drug use witnessed in the early 1990s have slowed.

On the other hand, the drug culture has been successful at some efforts to soften drug policy. Medical marijuana initiatives have successfully passed in several states. These were gross examples of abuse of the ballot initiative process. Large amounts of money purchased slick media campaigns and seduced the public into supporting medical marijuana under the guise of compassion. Industrial hemp initiatives are popping up all over the country in an attempt to hurt anti-marijuana law enforcement and soften public opinion. Needle handouts are being touted as successes, while the evidence is clearly demonstrating failures and increases in HIV, hepatitis B, and hepatitis C. Internationally, our Canadian neighbors are moving down a very destructive road toward drug legalization and harm reduction. The Swiss are experimenting with the lives of addicts by implementing heroin handouts and selective drug legalization. In this international atmosphere, children's attitudes about the harmfulness of drugs teeter in the balance.

Future drug policy must continue to emphasize and fund primary prevention, with the goal of no use of illegal drugs and no illegal use of legal drugs. Treatment availability must be seriously enhanced, but treatment must not be a revolving door. It must be carefully designed and outcomes based. The Rand Drug Policy Research Center concluded that the costs of cocaine use could be reduced by $33.9 billion through the layering of treatment for heavy users on top of our current enforcement efforts.

Drug screening is an extremely effective means for identifying drug use. It should be widely extended into business and industry, other social arenas, and schools. Screening must be coupled with a rehabilitative approach, however, and not simply punishment. The self-serving strategies of the drug culture must be exposed. The public needs to become aware of how drug-culture advocates are manipulating public opinion in the same fashion that the tobacco industry has for so many years.

A compassionate but restrictive drug policy that partners prevention, rehabilitation, and law enforcement will continue to show the greatest chance for success. Drug policy must focus on harm prevention through clear primary prevention messages, and it must focus upon harm elimination through treatment availability and rigorous law enforcement.

POSTSCRIPT

Should Drug Use Be Decriminalized?

The analogy often cited by proponents of drug legalization is the ill-fated attempt to ban the sale of liquor in the United States, which lasted from 1919 to 1933. Prohibition has been called "an experiment noble in purpose," but it was an experiment that greatly contributed to the rise of organized crime. The repeal of Prohibition brought about an increase in liquor consumption and alcoholism, but it also deprived organized crime of an important source of income. Would drug decriminalization similarly strike a blow at the drug dealers? Possibly, and such a prospect is obviously appealing. But would drug decriminalization also exacerbate some of the ills associated with drugs? Would there be more violence, more severe addiction, and more crack babies born to addicted mothers?

There are a variety of publications and theories pertaining to drug use and society. For a comprehensive overview of the history, effects, and prevention of drug use, see Mike Gray, *Drug Crazy: How We Got Into This Mess and How We Can Get Out* (Random House, 1998). For a balanced review of drug policies, see Douglas Husak and Peter de Marneffe, *The Legalization of Drugs* (Cambridge University Press, 2005). Terry Williams describes the goings-on in a crackhouse in *Crackhouse: Notes From the End of the Zone* (Addison-Wesley, 1992). Works that examine the connection of drugs with predatory crime include Charles Bowden, *Down by the River: Drugs, Money, Murder, and Family* (Simon & Schuster, 2002); Philip Bean, *Drugs and Crime* (Willan, 2002); and Pierre Kipp, *Political Economy of Illegal Drugs* (Routledge, 2004). Three works that advocate or debate legalizing drugs are Douglas N. Husak, *Legalize This!: The Case for Decriminalizing Drugs* (Verso, 2002) Jacob Sullum, *Saying Yes: In Defense of Drug Use* (J.P. Tarcher, 2003), and *The Drug Legalization Debate*, edited by James A. Inciardi (Sage, 1999). For a relatively balanced yet innovative set of drug policies, see Elliott Carrie, *Reckoning: Drugs, the Cities, and the American Future* (Hill & Wang, 1993). William O. Walker III, ed., *Drug Control Policy* (Pennsylvania State University Press, 1992) critically evaluates drug policies from historical and comparative perspectives. On the legalization debate, see Eric Goode, *Between Politics and Reason: The Drug Legalization Debate* (St. Martin's Press, 1997). For criticism of the current drug policies, see Dan Baum, *Smoke and Mirrors: The War on Drugs and the Politics of Failure* (Little, Brown, 1996) and Leif Rosenberger, *America's Drug War Debacle* (Avebury, 1996).

ISSUE 18

Does the Threat of Terrorism Warrant Curtailment of Civil Liberties?

YES: Robert H. Bork, from "Liberty and Terrorism: Avoiding a Police State," *Current* (December 2003)

NO: Barbara Dority, from "Your Every Move," *The Humanist* (January/February 2004)

ISSUE SUMMARY

YES: Robert H. Bork, senior fellow at the American Enterprise Institute, recognizes that the values of security and civil rights must be balanced while we war against terrorism, but he is concerned that some commentators would hamstring security forces in order to protect nonessential civil rights. For example, to not use ethnic profiling of Muslim or Arab persons would reduce the effectiveness of security forces, while holding suspected terrorists without filing charges or allowing them council would increase their effectiveness.

NO: Barbara Dority, president of Humanists of Washington, describes some specific provisions of the Patriot Act to show how dangerous they could be to the rights of all dissidents. She argues that provisions of the act could easily be abused.

America was very optimistic at the end of the twentieth century. The cold war had ended, and the 1990s brought the longest economic boom in American history. The only danger on the horizon was the Y2K problem, and that vanished like the mist. September 11, 2001, changed everything. Now Americans live in fear of terrorism, and this fear led the government to launch two wars—the first against the Taliban and Al Qaeda in Afghanistan and the second against Saddam Hussein's regime in Iraq. The United States has also aggressively pursued international terrorists throughout the world and pushed many countries to aid in the capture of known terrorists. All of these efforts have been quite successful in specific strategic objectives but not in reducing our fear of terrorism. The number of terrorists dedicated to mass terrorist events in America have even increased in the past three years, because hatred of America has increased greatly.

The German sociologist and political leader Ralph Dahrendorf, who was a child when Hitler came to power in his country, said that fear is antithetical to democracy. In fearful times the public wants the government to do whatever it must to solve the crisis, whether the crisis is economic failure; social disorder; or danger from criminals, terrorists, or foreign powers. Some civil rights are often the first things sacrificed. During the economic crisis of the 1930s Germany turned to Hitler, and Italy turned to Mussolini. Democracy was sacrificed for the hope of a more prosperous economy.

Fortunately, during the Great Depression the United States turned to President Franklin D. Roosevelt, not to a dictator. But in other dangerous times our history has proven to be less democratic. In the 1860s President Abraham Lincoln suspended habeas corpus and detained hundreds of suspected confederate sympathizers. The chief justice of the Supreme Court ruled Lincoln's suspension of habeas corpus as unconstitutional, but Lincoln ignored the ruling. There were widespread violations of civil liberties during World War I and again during World War II, including the shameful internment of Japanese-American citizens in concentration camps. Civil liberties were diminished again during the McCarthy era in the 1950s, a time when a witch-hunt atmosphere occurred due to anti-communist hysteria. American history caused civil rights advocates to become quite concerned when Attorney General John Ashcroft said after September 11th, "We should strengthen our laws to increase the ability of the Department of Justice and its component agencies to identify, prevent, and punish terrorism." Of course he is right, but the question is whether the government will go too far in policing us and whether the newly authorized powers will be badly abused. Senator Joseph Biden, Jr. remarked that "if we alter our basic freedom, our civil liberties, change the way we function as a democratic society, then we will have lost the war before it has begun in earnest." As of this writing the Patriot Act has been passed in an attempt to give the government the power it needs to better protect citizens from terrorism. Does this act go too far? Will its results be shameful?

One of the great aspects of America is our freedom to debate issues such as this one. This gives us the hope that through passionate and/or reasoned dialogue we will work toward the right balance between the values of security and civil rights. The articles that have been selected to debate this issue are both passionate and well-reasoned. Robert H. Bork discusses many of the provisions of the Patriot Act and explains how useful they are in the war against terrorism. He also argues that the Act contains safeguards such as judicial approval that should adequately protect against abuse. Barbara Dority also discusses specific provisions of the Patriot Act but for the purpose of pointing out how excessive and open to abuse they are. In her view, this act is a "brazen attack" on our civil liberties.

Robert H. Bork  **YES**

Liberty and Terrorism: Avoiding a Police State

When a nation faces deadly attacks on its citizens at home and abroad, it is only reasonable to expect that its leaders will take appropriate measures to increase security. And, since security inevitably means restrictions, it is likewise only reasonable to expect a public debate over the question of how much individual liberty should be sacrificed for how much individual and national safety.

That, however, is not the way our national debate has shaped up. From the public outcry over the Bush administration's measures to combat terrorism, one might suppose that America is well on the way to becoming a police state. A full-page newspaper ad by the American Civil Liberties Union (ACLU), for instance, informs us that the Patriot Act, the administration's major security initiative, goes "far beyond fighting terrorism" and has "allowed government agents to violate our civil liberties—tapping deep into the private lives of innocent Americans." According to Laura W. Murphy, director of the ACLU's Washington office, Attorney General John Ashcroft has "clearly abused his power," "systematically erod[ing] free-speech rights, privacy rights, and due-process rights." From the libertarian Left, Anthony Lewis in the *New York Times Magazine* has charged President Bush with undermining safeguards for the accused in a way that Lewis "did not believe was possible in our country," while from the libertarian Right, William Safire has protested the administration's effort to realize "the supersnoop's dream" of spying on all Americans.

The charge that our civil liberties are being systematically dismantled must be taken seriously. America has, in the past, overreacted to perceived security threats; the Palmer raids after World War I and the internment of Japanese-Americans during World War II are the most notorious examples. Are we once again jeopardizing the liberties of all Americans while also inflicting particular harm on Muslims in our midst? . . .

Security and Ethnic Profiling

According to Ibrahim Hooper, a spokesman for the Council on American-Islamic Relations, American Muslims have already lost many of their civil rights. "All Muslims are now suspects," Hooper has protested bitterly. The

From *Commentary*, July/August 2003, pp. 29–35. Copyright © 2003 by Commentary. Reprinted with permission.

most salient outward sign of this is said to be the ethnic profiling that now occurs routinely in this country, particularly at airports but elsewhere as well—a form of discrimination widely considered to be self-evidently evil.

For most of us, airport security checks are the only first-hand experience we have with counter-measures to terrorism, and their intrusiveness and often seeming pointlessness have, not surprisingly, led many people to question such measures in general. But minor vexations are not the same as an assault on fundamental liberties. As for ethnic profiling, that is another matter, and a serious one. It is serious, however, not because it is rampant but because it does not exist.

That profiling is wicked *per se* is an idea that seems to have originated in connection with police work, when black civil-rights spokesmen began to allege that officers were relying on race as the sole criterion for suspecting someone of criminal activity. Profiling, in other words, equaled racism by definition. Yet, as Heather Mac Donald has demonstrated in *Are Cops Racist?*, the idea rests on a false assumption—namely, that crime rates are constant across every racial and ethnic component of our society. Thus, if blacks, who make up 11 percent of the population, are subject to 20 percent of all police stops on a particular highway, racial bias must be at fault.

But the truth is that (to stick to this particular example) blacks do speed more than whites, a fact that in itself justifies a heightened awareness of skin color as one of several criteria in police work. Of course, there is no excuse for blatant racism; but, as Mac Donald meticulously documents in case after case around the country, there is by and large no evidence that police have relied excessively on ethnic or racial profiling in conducting their normal investigations.

The War on Terror

The stigma attached to profiling where it hardly exists has perversely carried over to an area where it should exist but does not: the war against terrorism. This war, let us remember, pre-dates 9/11. According to Mac Donald, when a commission on aviation security headed by then-Vice President Al Gore was considering a system that would take into account a passenger's national origin and ethnicity—by far the best predictors of terrorism—both the Arab lobby and civil libertarians exploded in indignation. The commission duly capitulated—which is why the final Computer-Assisted Passenger Prescreening System (CAPPS) specified that such criteria as national origin, religion, ethnicity, and even gender were not to be taken into consideration.

This emasculated system did manage, even so, to pinpoint two of the September 11 terrorists on the day of their gruesome flight, but prevented any action beyond searching their luggage. As Mac Donald points out, had the system been allowed to utilize all relevant criteria, followed up by personal searches, the massacres might well have been averted.

Ironically, it is the very randomness of the new security checks that has generated so much skepticism about their efficacy. Old ladies, children, Catholic priests—all have been subject to searches of San Quentin-like thoroughness despite being beyond rational suspicion. According to the authorities, this randomness is itself a virtue, preventing would-be terrorists from easily predicting who or what will draw attention. But it is far more probable that frisking unlikely persons has nothing to do with security and everything to do with political correctness. Frightening as the prospect of terrorism may be, it pales, in the minds of many officials, in comparison with the prospect of being charged with racism.

Ethnic Profiling

Registration, Tracking, and Detention of Visitors

Ethnic Profiling, it is charged, is also responsible for the unjustified harassment and occasional detention of Arab and Muslim visitors to the United States. This is said to be an egregious violation not only of the rights of such persons but of America's traditional hospitality toward foreign visitors.

An irony here is that the procedures being deplored are hardly new, although they are being imposed with greater rigor. The current system has its roots in the 1950's in the first of a series of statutes ordering the Immigration and Naturalization Service (INS) to require aliens from countries listed as state sponsors of terrorism, as well as from countries with a history of breeding terrorists, to register and be fingerprinted, to state where they will be while in the U.S., and to notify the INS when they change address or leave the country.

Historically, however, the INS has been absurdly lax about fulfilling its mandate. When a visitor with illegal status—someone, for example, thought to have overstayed a student visa or committed a crime—is apprehended, the usual practice of immigration judges has been to release him upon the posting of a bond, unless he is designated a "person of interest." In the latter case, he is held for deportation or criminal prosecution and given a handbook detailing his rights, which include access to an attorney. It is a matter of dispute whether the proceedings before an immigration judge can be closed, as authorities prefer, or whether they must be open; the Supreme Court has so far declined to review the practice.

The procedures are now being adhered to more strictly, and this is what has given rise to accusations of ethnic or religious profiling. But such charges are as beside the point as in the case of domestic police work, if not more so. There is indeed a correlation between detention and ethnicity or religion, but that is because most of the countries identified as state sponsors or breeders of terrorism are, in fact, populated by Muslims and Arabs.

Stricter enforcement has also led to backlogs, as the Justice Department has proved unable to deal expeditiously with the hundreds of illegal immigrants rounded up in the aftermath of September 11. A report by the department's inspector general, released in early June, found "significant problems" with the processing of these cases. There is no question that, in an ideal world, many of them would have been handled with greater dispatch, but it is also hardly surprising that problems that have long plagued our criminal justice system should reappear in the context of the fight against terrorism. In any case, the department has already taken steps to ameliorate matters. The only way for the problems to vanish would be for the authorities to cease doing their proper job; we have tried that route, and lived to regret it.

Discovery, Detention, and Prosecution of Suspected Terrorists

According to civil libertarians, the constitutional safeguards that normally protect individuals suspected of criminal activity have been destroyed in the case of persons suspected of links with terrorism. This accusation reflects an ignorance both of the Constitution and of long-established limits on the criminal-justice system.

History

Prior to 1978, and dating back at least to World War II, attorneys general of the United States routinely authorized warrantless FBI surveillance, wire taps, and break-ins for national-security purposes. Such actions were taken pursuant to authority delegated by the President as commander-in-chief of the armed forces and as the officer principally responsible for the conduct of foreign affairs. The practice was justified because obtaining a warrant in each disparate case resulted in inconsistent standards and also posed unacceptable risks. (In one notorious instance, a judge had read aloud in his courtroom from highly classified material submitted to him by the government; even under more conscientious judges, clerks, secretaries, and others were becoming privy to secret materials.)

Attorneys general were never entirely comfortable with these warrantless searches, whose legality had never been confirmed by the Supreme Court. The solution in 1978 was the enactment of the Foreign Intelligence Surveillance Act (FISA). Henceforth, sitting district court judges would conduct secret hearings to approve or disapprove government applications for surveillance.

A further complication arose in the 1980's, however, when, by consensus of the Department of Justice and the FISA court, it was decided that the act authorized the gathering of foreign intelligence only for its own sake ("primary purpose"), and not for the possible criminal prosecution of any foreign agent. The effect was to erect a "wall" between the gathering of intelligence and the enforcement of criminal laws. But last year, the Foreign Intelligence Surveillance Court of Review held that the act did not, in fact, preclude or limit the government's use of that information in such prosecutions. In the opinion of the court, arresting and prosecuting terrorist agents or spies might well be the best way to inhibit their activities, as the threat of prosecution might persuade an agent to cooperate with the government, or enable the government to "turn" him.

When the wall came down, Justice Department prosecutors were able to learn what FBI intelligence officials already knew. This contributed to the arrest of Sami al-Arian, a professor at the University of South Florida, on charges that he raised funds for Palestinian Islamic Jihad and its suicide bombers. Once the evidence could be put at the disposition of prosecutors, al-Arian's longstanding claim that he was being persecuted by the authorities as an innocent victim of anti-Muslim prejudice was shattered.

Treatment of Captured Terrorists

According, by depriving certain captured individuals of access to lawyers, and by holding them without filing charges, the government is violating the Geneva Convention's protections of lawful combatants or prisoners of war. This is nonsense.

Lawful Combatants

Four criteria must be met to qualify a person as a lawful combatant. He must be under the command of a person responsible for his subordinates; wear a fixed distinctive emblem recognizable at a distance; carry arms openly; and conduct operations in accordance with the laws and customs of war. The men the United States has captured and detained so far do not meet these criteria.

The government's policy is as follows: if a captured unlawful enemy combatant is believed to have further information about terrorism, he can be held without access to legal counsel and without charges being filed. Once the government is satisfied that it has all the relevant information it can obtain, the captive can be held until the end of hostilities, or be released, or be brought up on charges before a criminal court. . . .

The Terrorist Information Awareness Program

Among Menaces to American liberty, this has been widely held to be the most sinister of all. Here is William Safire:

Every purchase you make with a credit card, every magazine subscription you buy and medical prescription you fill, every website you visit and e-mail you send or receive, every academic grade you receive, every bank deposit you make, every trip you book and every event you attend—all these transactions and communications will go into what the Defense Department describes as "a virtual, centralized grand database."

To this computerized dossier on your private life from commercial sources, add every piece of information that government has about you—passport application, driver's license and bridge toll records, judicial and divorce records, complaints from nosy neighbors to the F.B.I., your lifetime paper trail plus the latest hidden camera surveillance—and you have the supersnoop's dream.

Information Awareness

What is the reality? The Terrorist Information Awareness program (TIA) is still only in a developmental stage; we do not know whether it can even be made to work. If it can, it might turn out to be one of the most valuable weapons in America's war with terrorists.

In brief, the program would seek to identify patterns of conduct that indicate terrorist activity. This entails separating small sets of transactions from a vast universe of similar transactions. Since terrorists use the same avenues of communication, commerce, and transportation that everybody else uses, the objective is to build a prototype of an intelligence system whose purpose would be to find terrorists' signals in a "sea of noise." Taking advantage of the integrative power of computer technology, the system would allow the government to develop hypotheses about possible terrorist activity, basing itself entirely on data that are *already legally available*.

But we may never find out whether the program's objective can be achieved, since TIA has been effectively gutted in advance. Impressed, no doubt, by the ideological breadth of the opposition to TIA, Congress was led to adopt a vague prohibition, sponsored by Democratic Senator Ron Wyden, draining TIA of much of its value. The amendment specifies that the program's technology may be used for military operations outside the U.S. and for "lawful foreign intelligence activities conducted wholly against non-United States persons." By inference, TIA may therefore *not* be used to gather information about U.S. citizens or resident aliens—despite the clear fact that significant number of persons in these categories have ties to terrorist groups. . . .

Possible Safeguards

Are there techniques that could be devised to prevent TIA from becoming the playground of Safire's hypothetical supersnoop without disabling it altogether? In domestic criminal investigations, courts require warrants for electronic surveillances. As we have seen, the Foreign Intelligence Surveillance Act also requires judicial approval of surveillances for intelligence and counterintelligence purposes. While there would be no need for a warrant-like requirement in initiating a computer search, other safeguards can be imagined for TIA. Among them, according to Taylor, might be "software designs and legal rules that would block human agents from learning the identities of people whose transactions are being 'data-mined' by TIA computers unless the agents can obtain judicial warrants by showing something analogous to the 'probable cause' that the law requires to justify a wiretap." . . .

The benefits of the TIA program are palpable, and potentially invaluable; the hazards are either hyped or imaginary. There is nothing to prevent Congress from replacing the Wyden amendment with oversight provisions, or from requiring reasonable safeguards that would preserve the program's efficacy.

What Remains to Be Done

The fact that opponents of the Bush administration's efforts to protect American security have resorted to often shameless misrepresentation and outright scaremongering does not mean those efforts are invulnerable to criticism. They are indeed vulnerable—for not going far enough.

In addition to the lack of properly targeted security procedures at airports, and the failure to resist the gutting of TIA, a truly gaping deficiency in our arrangements is the openness of our northern and southern borders to illegal entrants. In the south, reportedly, as many as 1,000 illegal aliens *a day* enter through Arizona's Organ Pipe National Monument park. . . .

There is, in short, plenty of work to go around. The war we are in, like no other we have ever faced, may last for decades rather than years. The enemy blends into our population and those of other nations around the world, attacks without warning, and consists of men who are quite willing to die in order to kill us and destroy our civilization. Never before has it been possible to imagine one suicidal individual, inspired by the promise of paradise and armed with a nuclear device, able to murder tens or even hundreds of thousands of Americans in a single attack. Those facts justify what the administration has already done, and urgently require more. . . .

NO

Barbara Dority

Your Every Move

On November 11, 2003, former President Jimmy Carter condemned U.S. leaders' attacks on American civil liberties, particularly the Uniting and Strengthening America by Providing Appropriate Tools Required to Intercept and Obstruct Terrorism Act (USA PATRIOT Act). Speaking at a gathering of Human Rights Defenders on the Front Lines of Freedom at the Carter Center in Washington, D.C., Carter said that post-9/11 policies "work against the spirit of human rights" and are "very serious mistakes." Egyptian human rights activist and sociology professor Saad Eddin Ibrahim added, "Every dictator is using what the United States has done under the Patriot Act to justify human rights abuses in the past, as well as a license to continue human rights abuses."

Since its passage in October 2001, the Patriot Act has decimated many basic American civil liberties. The law gives broad new powers to domestic law enforcement and international intelligence agencies. Perhaps worse still, it eliminates the system of checks and balances that gave courts the responsibility of ensuring that these powers weren't abused. The Electronic Frontier Foundation (EFF), an electronic privacy watchdog group, believes that the opportunities for abuse of these broad new powers are immense.

A particularly egregious part of the Patriot Act gives the government access to "any tangible things." This section grants the Federal Bureau of Investigation (FBI) the authority to request an order "requiring the production of any tangible things (including books, records, papers, documents, and other items)" relevant to an investigation of terrorism or clandestine intelligence activities. Although the section is entitled "Access to Certain Business Records," the scope of its authority is far broader and applies to any records pertaining to an individual. This section, which overrides state library confidentiality laws, permits the FBI to compel production of business records, medical records, educational records, and library records without showing probable cause.

Many aspects of the Patriot Act unfairly target immigrants. The attorney general has the ability to "certify" that the government has "reasonable grounds to believe that an alien is a terrorist or is engaged in other activity that endangers the national security of the United States." Once that certification is made and someone is labeled a potential threat, the government may detain him or her indefinitely—based on secret evidence it isn't required to share with anyone.

Currently over thirteen thousand Arab and Muslim immigrants are being held in deportation proceedings. Not one of them has been charged with terrorism. Most are being deported for routine immigration violations that normally could be rectified in hearings before immigration judges. Families are being separated and lives ruined because of selective enforcement of immigration laws that have been on the books for many years and are now being used to intimidate and deport law-abiding Arab and Muslim Americans. Fear and confusion are pervasive in the Arab-American community today. Many people are too afraid to step forward when they are harassed on the job or fired, when they are denied housing because of their last name, or when a family member is picked up by immigration authorities and detained in another state on evidence that remains undisclosed to both detainees and lawyers alike. According to Karen Rignal's article "Beyond Patriotic" on Alternet.org, some of these people have been detained for as long as eight months, mistreated, and confined twenty-three hours a day. Some Arab immigrants have opted to return to the Middle East because they no longer feel welcome in the United States.

Nearly seven hundred men are being held at "Camp X-Ray" in Guantanamo Bay, Cuba. But it isn't just "foreigners" who are being deemed dangerous and un-American. For example, there is Tom Treece, a teacher who taught a class on "public issues" at a Vermont high school. A uniformed police officer entered Treece's classroom in the middle of the night because a student art project on the wall showed a picture of Bush with duct ape over his mouth and the words, "Put your duct tape to good use. Shut your mouth." Residents refused to pass the school budget if Treece wasn't fired, resulting in his removal.

The American Civil Liberties Union (ACLU) went to court to help a fifteen year-old who faced suspension from school when he refused to take off a T-shirt with the words "International Terrorist" written beneath a picture of Bush. And there was the college student from North Carolina who was visited at home by secret service agents who told her, "Ma'am, we've gotten a report that you have anti-American material." She refused to let them in but eventually showed them what she thought they were after, an anti-death-penalty poster showing Bush and a group of lynched bodies over the epithet "We hang on your every word." The agents then asked her if she had any "pro-Taliban stuff."

Then there's art dealer Doug Stuber, who ran the 2000 North Carolina presidential campaign for Green Party candidate Ralph Nader. Stuber was told he couldn't board a plane to Prague, Czech Republic, because no Greens were allowed to fly that day. He was questioned by police, photographed by two secret service agents, and asked about his family and what the Greens were up to. Stuber reports that he was shown a Justice Department document suggesting that Greens were likely terrorists.

Michael Franti, lead singer of the progressive hip hop band Spearhead, reports that the mother of one of his colleagues, who has a sibling in the Persian Gulf, was visited by "two plain-clothes men from the military" in March 2003. They came in and said, "You have a child who's in the Gulf and you have a child who's in this band Spearhead who's part of the resistance." They had pictures of the band at peace rallies, their flight records for several months, their banking records, and the names of backstage staff.

A report by the ACLU called "Freedom Under Fire" states, "There is a pall over our country. The response to dissent by many government officials so clearly violates the letter and the spirit of the supreme law of the land that they threaten the very underpinnings of democracy itself."

In the face of these cases and many more, Justice Department spokespeople have repeatedly claimed that the Patriot Act doesn't apply to Americans. But this is false. First of all, under the Patriot Act the four tools of surveillance—wiretaps, search warrants, pen/trap orders, and subpoenas—are increased. Second, their counterparts under the Foreign Intelligence Surveillance Act (FISA), which allows spying in the United States by foreign intelligence agencies, are concurrently expanded. New definitions of terrorism also increase the amount of government surveillance permitted. And three expansions of previous terms increase the scope of spying allowed. The Patriot Act provides a FISA detour around limitations on federal domestic surveillance and a domestic detour around FISA limitations. The attorney general can nullify domestic surveillance limits on the Central Intelligence Agency, for example, by obtaining a FISA wiretap where probable cause cannot be shown but the person is a suspected foreign government agent. All this information can be shared with the FBI and vice versa.

In sum, the Patriot Act allows U.S. foreign intelligence agencies to more easily spy on U.S. citizens and FISA now provides for increased information sharing between domestic law enforcement and foreign intelligence officials. This partially repeals the protections implemented in the 1970s after the revelation that the FBI and CIA were conducting investigations on thousands of U.S. citizens during and after the McCarthy era. The Patriot Act allows sharing wiretap results and grand jury information when that constitutes "foreign intelligence information."

In response to other criticisms, Justice Department spokespeople have also claimed that the Patriot Act applies only to "terrorists and spies" and that the FBI can't obtain a person's records without probable cause. As one might expect, all of this is false as well.

The Patriot Act specifically gives the government and the FBI authority to monitor people not engaged in criminal activity or espionage and to do so in complete secrecy. It also imposes a gag order that prohibits an organization that has been forced to turn over records from disclosing the fact of the search to its clients, customers, or anyone else.

Furthermore, in other statements, federal officials contradict themselves by saying that the government is using its expanded authority under the far-reaching law to investigate suspected blackmailers, drug traffickers, money launderers, pornographers, and white-collar criminals. Dan Dodson, speaking to the Associated Press this past September on behalf of the National Association of Criminal Defense Attorneys, reported, "Within six months of passing the Patriot Act, the Justice Department was conducting seminars on how to stretch the new wiretapping provisions to extend them beyond terror cases.

A guidebook used in a 2002 Justice Department employee seminar on financial crimes says: "We all know that the USA Patriot Act provided weapons for the war on terrorism. But do you know how it affects the war on crime as well?" . . .

Publicly, of course, Attorney General John Ashcroft continues to speak almost exclusively of how Patriot Act powers are helping fight terrorism. In his nationwide tour this past fall to bolster support for the act (which has engendered growing discontent), Ashcroft lauded its "success" stories. However, his department also officially labels many cases as terrorism which aren't. A January 2003 study by the General Accounting Office concluded that, of those convictions classified as "international terrorism," fully 75 percent actually dealt with more common nonterrorist crimes. . . .

Perhaps the most frightening thing about the Patriot Act—even putting aside these other impending restrictions on civil liberties—is how similar the act is to legislation enacted in the eighteenth century. The Alien and Sedition Acts are notorious in history for their abuse of basic civil liberties. For example, in 1798, the Alien Friends Act made it lawful for the president of the United States "to order all such aliens, as he shall judge dangerous to the peace and safety of the United States, or shall have reasonable grounds to suspect are concerned in any treasonable or secret machinations against the government thereof, to depart out of the territory of the United States." For years Americans have pointed to legislation like this as a travesty never to be repeated. Yet now it is back!

It seems unimaginable that any presidential administration would impose such brazen attacks as these on the civil liberties of a supposedly free people. Apparently, many Americans were initially so traumatized by 9/11 that they were ready to surrender their most treasured liberties. But pockets of resistance are developing and organizations forming. Three states and more than two hundred cities, counties, and towns around the country have passed resolutions opposing the Patriot Act. Many others are in progress. The language of these resolutions includes statements affirming a commitment to the rights guaranteed in the Constitution and directives to local law enforcement not to cooperate with federal agents involved in investigations deemed unconstitutional. A bill has also been introduced in the House to exclude bookstore and library records from the materials that could be subpoenaed by law enforcement without prior notification of the targeted person.

Some leading organizations, such as the ACLU and EFF, continue to keep the pressure on and are always worthy of support. American citizens who treasure their heritage of freedom should find at least one group to join and support—keeping in mind that the government may one day know the organizations they have checked out.

POSTSCRIPT

Does the Threat of Terrorism Warrant Curtailment of Civil Liberties?

Since September 11th, books and articles on terrorism have increased greatly. Some recent notable general works on terrorism include Clifford E. Simonsen and Jeremy R. Spindlove, *Terrorism Today: The Past, the Players, the Future*, 2d ed. (Prentice Hall, 2004); Cindy C. Combs, *Terrorism in the Twenty-First Century*, 3rd ed. (Prentice Hall, 2003); Pamala Griset and Sue Mahan, *Terrorism in Perspective* (Sage Publications, 2003); Gus Martin, *Understanding Terrorism: Challenges, Perspectives, and Issues* (Sage Publications, 2003); Vincent Burns and Kate Dempsey Peterson, *Terrorism: A Documentary and Reference Guide* (Greenwood Press, 2005); Bard E. O'Neill, *Insurgency and Terrorism: From Revolution to Apocalypse*, 2nd edition (Potomac Books, 2005); James M. and Benda J. Lutz, Terrorism: Origins and Evolution (Palgrave Macmillan, 2005); and Leonard Weinberg, *Global Terrorism: A Beginner's Guide* (Oneworld, 2005). Three works that focus on the motives for terrorism are Robert A. Pape, *Dying to Win: The Strategic Logic of Suicide Terrorism* (Random House, 2005); David M. Rosen, *Armies of the Young: Child Soldiers in War and Terrorism* (Rutgars University Press, 2005); and Bruce Wilshire, *Get 'em All! Kill 'em!: Genocide, Terrorism, Righteous Communities* (Lexington Books, 2005).

Terrorism with weapons of mass destruction has been labeled "the new terrorism," and an extensive literature on it has rapidly formed, including Walter Laqueur, *No End to War: Terrorism in the Twenty-First Century* (Continuum, 2003); Nadine Gurr and Benjamin Cole, *The New Face of Terrorism: Threats From Weapons of Mass Destruction* (St. Martin's Press, 2000); Paul Gilbert, *New Terror, New Wars* (Georgetown University Press, 2003); and Peter Brookes, *A Devil's Triangle: Terrorism, Weapons of Mass Destruction, and Rogue States* (Rowman & Litlefield, 2005). Another threatening aspect of terrorism is the terrorists' willingness to commit suicide. To explore this issue, see Christopher Reuter, *My Life as a Weapon: A Modern History of Suicide Bombing* (Princeton University Press, 2004).

The critical issue is how the United States deals with the terrorist threat. Richard A. Clark provides an insider's revelation of the U.S. response in *Against All Enemies: Inside America's War on Terror* (Free Press, 2004). See also Michael Ignatieff, *The Lesser Evil: Political Ethics in an Age of Terror* (Princeton University Press, 2004); *The Politics of Terror: The U.S. Response to 9/11*, edited by William Crotty (Northwestern University Press, 2004); Lawrence Freedman, ed., *Superterrorism: Policy Responses* (Blackwell Publishers, 2002); Dilip K. Das and Peter C. Kratcoski, eds., *Meeting the Challenges of Global Terrorism: Prevention, Control, and Recovery* (Lexington, 2003); Hayim Granot and Jay Levinson, *Terror Bombing: The*

New Urban Threat: Practical Approaches for Response Agencies and Security (Dekel, 2002); Mark A. Sauter and James Jay Carafano, *Homeland Security: A Complete Guide to Understanding, Preventing, and Surviving Terrorism* (McGraw-Hill, 2005); Russell D. Howard et al. (eds.), *Homeland Security and Terrorism* (McGraw-Hill, 2006); Joel Leson, *New Realities: Assessing and Managing the Terrorism Threat* (U.S. Department of Justice, 2005); John Davis (ed.), *The Global War on Terrorism: Assessing the American Response* (Nova Science Publishers, 2005); Medea Benjamin and Jodie Evans (eds.), *Stop the Next War Now: Effective Responses to Violence and Terrorism* (Inner Ocean Publishers, 2005); and Amy Sterling Casil, *Coping With Terrorism* (Rosen, 2004). Works that discuss the issue of balancing the need for greater police powers and the desire for strong civil rights include *National Security: Opposing Viewpoints*, edited by Helen Cothern (Greenhaven Press, 2004); *American National Security and Civil Liberties in an Age of Terrorism*, edited by David B. Cohen and John W. Wells (Palgrave Macmillan, 2004); Richard Ashby Wilson (ed.), *Human Rights in the 'War on Terror'* (Cambridge University Press, 2005); and Raneta Lawson Mack and Michael J. Kelly, *Equal Justice in the Balance: America's Legal Responses to the Emerging Terrorist Threat* (University of Michigan Press, 2004). Three works that criticize the U.S. legal response are *Lost Liberties: Ashcroft and the Assault on Personal Freedom,* edited by Cynthia Brown (New Press, 2003); Thomas E. Baker and John F. Stack, Jr. (eds.), *At War with Civil Rights and Civil Liberties* (Rowman & Littlefield Publishers, 2006); and Jeffrey Rosen *The Naked Crowd: Reclaiming Security and Freedom in an Anxious Age* (Random House, 2004). Another side of the story is provided by Alan M. Dershowitz in *Why Terrorism Works* (Yale University Press, 2002).

On the Internet . . .

United Nations Environment Program (UNEP)

The United Nations Environment Program (UNEP) Web site offers links to environmental topics of critical concern to sociologists. The site will direct you to useful databases and global resource information.

http://www.unep.ch

Worldwatch Institute Home Page

The Worldwatch Institute is dedicated to fostering the evolution of an environmentally sustainable society in which human needs are met without threatening the health of the natural environment. This site provides access to World Watch Magazine and State of the World 2000.

http://www.worldwatch.org

WWW Virtual Library: Demography and Population Studies

The WWW Virtual Library provides a definitive guide to demography and population studies. A multitude of important links to information about global poverty and hunger can be found at this site.

http://demography.anu.edu.au/VirtualLibrary/

William Davidson Institute

The William Davidson Institute at the University of Michigan Business School is dedicated to the understanding and promotion of economic transition. Consult this site for discussions of topics related to the changing global economy and the effects of globalization on society.

http://www.wdi.bus.umich.edu

World Future Society

The World Future Society is an educational and scientific organization for those interested in how social and technological developments are shaping the future.

http://www.wfs.org

PART 6

The Future: Population/ Environment/Society

*T*he leading issues for the beginning of the twenty-first century include global warming, environmental decline, and globalization. The state of the environment and the effects of globalization produce strong arguments concerning what can be harmful or beneficial. Technology has increased enormously in the last 100 years, as have worldwide population growth, consumption, and new forms of pollution that threaten to undermine the world's fragile ecological support system. Although all nations have a stake in the health of the planet, many believe that none are doing enough to protect its health. Will technology itself be the key to controlling or accommodating the increase of population and consumption, along with the resulting increase in waste production? Perhaps so, but new policies will also be needed. Technology is driving the process of globalization, which can be seen as both good and bad. Those who support globalization theory state that globalization increases competition, production, wealth, and the peaceful integration of nations. However, not everyone agrees. This section explores what is occurring in our environment and in our current global economy.

- Is Mankind Dangerously Harming the Environment?
- Is Globalization Good for Mankind?

ISSUE 19

Is Mankind Dangerously Harming the Environment?

YES: Lester R. Brown, from "Pushing Beyond the Earth's Limits," *The Futurist* (May/June 2005)

NO: Bjorn Lomborg, from "The Truth About the Environment," *The Economist* (August 4, 2001)

ISSUE SUMMARY

YES: Lester R. Brown, founder of the Worldwatch Institute, and now president of the Earth Policy Institute, argues the population growth and economic development are placing increasing harmful demands on the environment for resources and to grow food for improving diets.

NO: Bjorn Lomborg, a statistician at the University of Aarhus, Denmark, presents evidence that population growth is slowing down, natural resources are not running out, species are disappearing very slowly, the environment is improving in some ways, and assertions about environmental decline are exaggerated.

$\mathbf{M}$uch of the literature on socioeconomic development in the 1960s was premised on the assumption of inevitable material progress for all. It largely ignored the impacts of development on the environment and presumed that the availability of raw materials would not be a problem. The belief was that all societies would get richer because all societies were investing in new equipment and technologies that would increase productivity and wealth. Theorists recognized that some poor countries were having trouble developing, but they blamed those problems on the deficiencies of the values and attitudes of those countries and on inefficient organizations.

In the late 1960s and early 1970s an intellectual revolution occurred. Environmentalists had criticized the growth paradigm throughout the 1960s, but they were not taken very seriously at first. By the end of the 1960s, however, marine scientist Rachel Carson's book *Silent Spring* (Alfred A. Knopf, 1962) had worked its way into the public's consciousness. Carson's book traces the noticeable loss of birds to the use of pesticides. Her book made the middle and upper classes in the United States realize that pollution affects complex ecological systems in ways that put even the wealthy at risk.

In 1968 Paul Ehrlich, a professor of population studies, published *The Population Bomb* (Ballantine Books), which states that overpopulation is the major problem facing mankind. This means that population has to be controlled or the human race might cause the collapse of the global ecosystems and the deaths of many humans. Ehrlich explained why he thought the devastation of the world was imminent:

> Because the human population of the planet is about five times too large, and we're managing to support all these people—at today's level of misery—only by spending our capital, burning our fossil fuels, dispersing our mineral resources and turning our fresh water into salt water. We have not only overpopulated but overstretched our environment. We are poisoning the ecological systems of the earth—systems upon which we are ultimately dependent for all of our food, for all of our oxygen and for all of our waste disposal.

In 1973 *The Limits to Growth* (Universe) by Donella H. Meadows et al. was published. It presents a dynamic systems computer model for world economic, demographic, and environmental trends. When the computer model projected trends into the future, it predicted that the world would experience ecological collapse and population die-off unless population growth and economic activity were greatly reduced. This study was both attacked and defended, and the debate about the health of the world has been heated ever since.

Let us examine the population growth rates for the past, present, and future. At about A.D. 1, the world had about one-quarter billion people. It took about 1,650 years to double this number to one-half billion and 200 years to double the world population again to 1 billion by 1850. The next doubling took only about 80 years, and the last doubling took about 45 years (from 2 billion in 1930 to about 4 billion in 1975). The world population may double again to 8 billion sometime between 2015 and 2025. At the same time that population is growing people are trying to get richer, which means consuming more, polluting more, and using more resources. Are all these trends threatening the carrying capacity of the planet and jeopardizing the prospects for future generations?

In the following selections, Lester R. Brown warns that the population growth and the sevenfold expansion of the economy in the past half century is placing demands on the environment that exceeds the earth's natural capacity. As a result we face many environmental problems. The one that Brown focuses on is the difficulty of increasing food production enough to feed growing populations with better diets and with declining natural resources. Bjorn Lomborg counters that the evidence supports optimism—not environmental pessimism. He maintains that resources are becoming more abundant, food per capita is increasing, the extinction of species is at a very slow rate, and environmental problems are transient and will get better.

Lester R. Brown  **YES**

Pushing Beyond the Earth's Limits

During the last half of the twentieth century, the world economy expanded sevenfold. In 2000 alone, its growth exceeded that of the entire nineteenth century. Economic growth, now the goal of governments everywhere, has become the status quo. Stability is considered a departure from the norm.

As the economy grows, its demands are outgrowing the earth, exceeding many of the planet's natural capacities. While the world economy multiplied sevenfold in just 50 years, the earth's natural life-support systems remained essentially the same. Water use tripled, but the capacity of the hydrological system to produce fresh water through evaporation changed little. The demand for seafood increased fivefold, but the sustainable yield of oceanic fisheries was unchanged. Fossil-fuel burning raised carbon dioxide (CO_2) emissions fourfold, but the capacity of nature to absorb it changed little, leading to a buildup of CO_2 in the atmosphere and a rise in the earth's temperature. As human demands surpass the earth's natural capacities, expanding food production becomes more difficult.

Losing Agricultural Momentum

Environmentalists have been saying for years that, if the environmental trends of recent decades continued, the world would one day be in trouble. What was not clear was what form the trouble would take and when it would occur. Now it has become increasingly clear that tightening food supplies will be our greatest trouble and that it will emerge within the next few years. In early 2004, China's forays into the world market to buy 8 million tons of wheat marked what could be the beginning of the global shift from an era of grain surpluses to one of grain scarcity.

World grain production is a basic indicator of dietary adequacy at the individual level and of overall food security at the global level. After nearly tripling from 1950 to 1996, the grain harvest stayed flat for seven years in a row, through 2003, showing no increase at all. And production fell short of consumption in each of the last four of those years. The shortfalls of nearly 100 million tons in 2002 and again in 2003 were the largest on record.

Consumption exceeded production for four years, leading world grain stocks to drop to the lowest level in 30 years. The last time stocks were this low, in 1972–1974, wheat and rice prices doubled. Importing countries competed vigorously for inadequate supplies. A politics of scarcity emerged, and some countries, such as the United States, restricted exports.

In 2004, a combination of stronger grain prices at planting time and the best weather in a decade yielded a substantially larger harvest for the first time in eight years. Yet even with a harvest that was up 124 million tons from that in 2003, the world still consumed all the grain it produced, leaving none to rebuild stocks. If stocks cannot be rebuilt in a year of exceptional weather, when can they?

From 1950 to 1984, world grain production expanded faster than population, raising the grain produced per person per year from 250 kilograms to the historic peak of 339 kilograms—an increase of 34%. This positive development initially reflected recovery from the disruption of World War II, and then later solid technological advances. The rising tide of food production lifted all ships, largely eradicating hunger in some countries and substantially reducing it in many others.

But since 1984, growth in grain harvests has fallen behind growth in population. The amount of grain produced per person fell to 308 kilograms in 2004.

Africa is suffering the most, with a decline in grain produced per person that is unusually steep and taking a heavy human toll. Soils are depleted of nutrients, and the amount of grainland per person has been shrinking steadily due to population growth in recent decades. But in addition, Africa must now contend with the loss of adults to AIDS, which is depleting the rural workforce and undermining agriculture. In two of the last three years, grain production per person in sub-Saharan Africa has been below 120 kilograms—dropping to a level that leaves millions of Africans on the edge of starvation.

Several long-standing environmental trends are contributing to the global loss of agricultural momentum. Among these are the cumulative effects of soil erosion on land productivity, the loss of cropland to desertification, and the accelerating conversion of cropland to nonfarm uses. All are taking a toll, although their relative roles vary among countries.

In addition, farmers are seeing fewer new technologies to dramatically boost production. The high-yielding varieties of wheat, rice, and corn that were developed a generation or so ago doubled and tripled yields, but there have not been any dramatic advances in the genetic yield potential of grains since then.

Similarly, the use of fertilizer has now plateaued or even declined slightly in key food-producing countries. The rapid growth in irrigation that characterized much of the last half century has also slowed. Indeed, in some countries the irrigated area is shrinking.

And now, two newer environmental trends are slowing the growth in world food production: falling water tables and rising temperatures. The bottom line is that it is now more difficult for farmers to keep up with the growing demand for grain. The rise in world grainland productivity, which averaged over 2% a year from 1950 to 1990, fell to scarcely 1% a year in the last decade of the twentieth century. This will likely drop further in the years immediately ahead.

If the rise in land productivity continues to slow and if population continues to grow by 70 million or more per year, governments may begin to define national security in terms of food shortages, rising food prices, and the emerging politics of scarcity. Food insecurity may soon eclipse terrorism as the overriding concern of national governments.

Food Challenges Go from Local to Global

The world economy is making excessive demands on the earth. Evidence of this can be seen in collapsing fisheries, shrinking forests, expanding deserts, rising CO_2 levels, eroding soils, rising temperatures, falling water tables, melting glaciers, deteriorating grasslands, rising seas, rivers that are running dry, and disappearing species.

Nearly all of these environmentally destructive trends contribute to global food insecurity. For example, even a modest rise of 1°F in temperature in mountainous regions can substantially increase rainfall and decrease snowfall. The result is more flooding during the rainy season and less snowmelt to feed rivers during the dry season, when farmers need irrigation water.

Or consider the collapse of fisheries and the associated leveling off of the oceanic fish catch. During the last half century, the fivefold growth in the world fish catch that satisfied much of the growing demand for animal protein pushed oceanic fisheries to their limits and beyond. Now, in this new century, we cannot expect any growth at all in the catch. The Food and Agriculture Organization warns that all future growth in animal protein supplies can only come from that produced on land, not the sea, putting even more pressure on the earth's land and water resources.

Until recently, the economic effects of environmental trends, such as overfishing, overpumping, and overplowing, were largely local. Among the many examples are the collapse of the cod fishery off Newfoundland from overfishing that cost Canada 40,000 jobs, the halving of Saudi Arabia's wheat harvest as a result of aquifer depletion, and the shrinking grain harvest of Kazakhstan as wind erosion claimed half of its cropland.

Now, if world food supplies tighten, we may see the first global economic effect of environmentally destructive trends. Rising food prices could be the first economic indicator to signal serious trouble in the deteriorating relationship between the global economy and the earth's ecosystem. The short-lived 20% rise in world grain prices in early 2004 may turn out to be a warning tremor before the quake.

Two New Challenges

As world demand for food has tripled, so too has the use of water for irrigation. As a result, the world is incurring a vast water deficit. But the trend is largely invisible because the deficit takes the form of aquifer overpumping and falling water tables. Falling water levels are often not discovered until wells go dry.

The world water deficit is a relatively recent phenomenon. Only within the last half century have powerful diesel and electrically driven pumps given us the pumping capacity to deplete aquifers. The worldwide spread of these pumps since the late 1960s and the drilling of millions of wells have in many cases pushed water withdrawal beyond the aquifers' recharge from rainfall. As a result, water tables are now falling in countries that are home to more than half of the world's people, including China, India, and the United States—the three largest grain producers.

Groundwater levels are falling throughout the northern half of China. Under the North China Plain, they are dropping 1–3 meters (3–10 feet) a year. In India, they are falling in most states, including the Punjab, the country's bread-basket. And in the United States, water levels are falling throughout the southern Great Plains and the Southwest. Overpumping creates a false sense of food security: It enables us to satisfy growing food needs today, but it almost guarantees a decline in food production tomorrow when the aquifer is depleted.

It takes a thousand tons of water to produce a single ton of grain, so food security is closely tied to water security. Seventy percent of world water use is for irrigation, 20% is used by industry, and 10% is for residential pur-poses. As urban water use rises while aquifers are being depleted, farmers are faced with a shrinking share of a shrinking water supply.

Meanwhile, temperatures are rising and concern about climate change is intensifying. Scientists have begun to focus on the precise relationship between temperature and crop yields. Crop ecologists at the International Rice Research Institute in the Philippines and at the U.S. Department of Agri-culture (USDA) have jointly concluded that each 1°C rise in temperature dur-ing the growing season cuts 10% off the yields of wheat, rice, and corn.

Over the last three decades, the earth's average temperature has climbed by nearly 0.7°C; the four warmest years on record came during the last six years. In 2002, record-high temperatures and drought shrank grain harvests in both India and the United States. In 2003, Europe bore the brunt of the intense heat. The record-breaking August heat wave claimed 35,000 lives in eight nations and withered grain harvests in virtually every country from France to Ukraine.

In a business-as-usual scenario, the earth's average temperature will rise by 1.4°–5.8°C (2°–10°F) during this century, according to the Intergovernmen-tal Panel on Climate Change. These projections are for the earth's average tem-perature, but the rise is expected to be much greater over land than over the oceans, in the higher latitudes than in the equatorial regions, and in the inte-rior of continents than in the coastal regions. This suggests that increases far in excess of the projected average are likely for regions such as the North Ameri-can breadbasket—the region defined by the Great Plains of the United States and Canada and the U.S. corn belt. Today's farmers face the prospect of tem-peratures higher than any generation of farmers since agriculture began.

The Japan Syndrome

When studying the USDA world grain database more than a decade ago, I noted that, if countries are already densely populated when they begin to industrialize rapidly, three things happen in quick succession to make them heavily dependent on grain imports: Grain consumption climbs as incomes rise, grainland area shrinks, and grain production falls. The rapid industrial-ization that drives up demand simultaneously shrinks the cropland area. The inevitable result is that grain imports soar. Within a few decades, countries can go from being essentially self-sufficient to importing 70% or more of their grain. I call this the "Japan syndrome" because I first recognized this sequence of events in Japan, a country that today imports 70% of its grain.

In a fast-industrializing country, grain consumption rises rapidly. Initially, rising incomes permit more direct consumption of grain, but before long the growth shifts to the greater indirect consumption of grain in the form of grain-intensive livestock products, such as pork, poultry, and eggs.

Once rapid industrialization is under way, the grainland area begins to shrink within a few years. As a country industrializes and modernizes, cropland gets taken over by industrial and residential developments and by roads, highways, and parking lots to accommodate more cars and drivers. When farmers are left with fragments of land that are too small to be cultivated economically, they often simply abandon their plots, seeking employment elsewhere.

As rapid industrialization pulls labor out of the countryside, it often leads to less double cropping, a practice that depends on quickly harvesting one grain crop once it is ripe and immediately preparing the seedbed for the next crop. With the loss of workers as young people migrate to cities, the capacity to do this diminishes.

As incomes rise, diets diversify, generating demand for more fruits and vegetables. This in turn leads farmers to shift land from grain to these more profitable, high-value crops.

Japan was essentially self-sufficient in grain when its grain harvested area peaked in 1955. Since then the grainland area has shrunk by more than half. The multiple-cropping index has dropped from nearly 1.4 crops per hectare per year in 1960 to scarcely one crop today. Some six years after Japan's grain area began to shrink, the shrinkage overrode the rise in land productivity and overall production began to decline. With grain consumption climbing and production falling, grain imports soared. By 1983, imports accounted for 70% of Japan's grain consumption, a level they remain at today.

South Korea and Taiwan are tracing Japan's pattern. In both cases, the decline in grain area was followed roughly a decade later by a decline in production. Perhaps this should not be surprising, since the forces at work in the two countries are exactly the same as in Japan. And, like Japan, both South Korea and Taiwan now import some 70% of their total grain supply.

Based on the sequence of events in these three countries that affected grain production, consumption, and imports—the Japan syndrome—it was easy to anticipate the precipitous decline in China's grain production that began in 1998. The obvious question now is which other countries will enter a period of declining grain production because of the same combination of forces. Among those that come to mind are India, Indonesia, Bangladesh, Pakistan, Egypt, and Mexico.

Of particular concern is India, with a population of nearly 1.1 billion now and growing by 18 million a year. In recent years, India's economic growth has accelerated, averaging 6%-7% a year. This growth, only slightly slower than that of China, is also beginning to consume cropland. In addition to the grainland shrinkage associated with the Japan syndrome, the extensive overpumping of aquifers in India—which will one day deprive farmers of irrigation water—will also reduce grain production.

Exactly when rapid industrialization in a country that is densely populated will translate into a decline in grain production is difficult to anticipate. Once crop production begins to decline, countries often try to reverse the trend. But the difficulty of achieving this can be seen in Japan, where a rice support price that is four times the world market price has failed to expand production.

The China Factor

China—the most-populous country in the world—is now beginning to experience the Japan syndrome. The precipitous fall in China's grain production since 1998 is perhaps the most alarming recent world agricultural event. After an impressive climb from 90 million tons in 1950 to a peak of 392 million tons in 1998, China's grain harvest fell in four of the next five years, dropping to 322 million tons in 2003. For perspective, this decline of 70 million tons exceeds the entire grain harvest of Canada. . . .

If smaller countries like Japan, South Korea, and Taiwan import 70% or more of their grain, the impacts on the global economy are not so dramatic. But if China turns to the outside world to meet even 20% of its grain needs—which would be close to 80 million tons—it will create a huge challenge for grain exporters. The resulting rise in world grain prices could destabilize governments in low-income, grain-importing countries. The entire world thus has a stake in China's efforts to stabilize its agricultural resource base.

The Challenge Ahead

We must not underestimate the challenges that the world faces over the next half century. There will be a projected 3 billion more people to feed, and 5 billion who will want to improve their diets by eating more meat, which requires more grain (as livestock feed) to produce. Meanwhile, the world's farmers will still be fighting soil erosion and the loss of cropland to nonfarm uses, as well as newer challenges, such as falling water tables, the diversion of irrigation water to cities, and rising temperatures. . . .

In a world where the food economy has been shaped by an abundance of cheap oil, tightening world oil supplies will further complicate efforts to eradicate hunger. Modern mechanized agriculture requires large amounts of fuel for tractors, irrigation pumps, and grain drying. Rising oil prices may soon translate into rising food prices.

Feeding the World

If grain imports continue to grow in Asia, where half the world's people live, and if harvests continue to shrink in Africa, the second-most populous continent, we have to ask where tomorrow's grain will come from. The countries that dominated world grain exports for the last half century—the United States, Canada, Australia, and Argentina—may not be able to export much beyond current levels.

The United States has produced as much as 350 million tons of grain a year several times over the last two decades, though never much more than this. The country exported about 100 million tons of grain a year two decades ago, but only an average of 80 million tons in recent years, as demand has increased domestically. The potential for expanding grain production and export in both Canada and Australia is constrained by relatively low rainfall in their grain-growing regions. Argentina's grain production has actually declined over the last several years as land has shifted to soybeans, principally used for feeding livestock rather than people.

By contrast, Russia and Ukraine should be able to expand their grain exports, at least modestly, as population has stabilized or is declining. There is also some unrealized agricultural production potential in these countries. But northern countries heavily dependent on spring wheat typically have lower yields, so Russia is unlikely to become a major grain exporter. Ukraine has a somewhat more promising potential if it can provide farmers with the economic incentives they need to expand production. So, too, do Poland and Romania.

Yet, the likely increases in exports from these countries are small compared with the prospective import needs of China and, potentially, India. It is worth noting that the drop in China's grain harvest of 70 million tons over five years is equal to the grain exports of Canada, Australia, and Argentina combined.

Argentina can expand its already large volume of soybean exports, but its growth potential for grain exports is limited by the availability of arable land. The only country that has the potential to substantially expand the world's grainland area is Brazil, with its vast cerrado—a savannah-like region on the southern edge of the Amazon basin. Because its soils require the heavy use of fertilizer and because transporting grain from Brazil's remote interior to distant world markets is costly, it would likely take substantially higher world grain prices for Brazil to emerge as a major exporter. Beyond this, would a vast expansion of cropland in Brazil's interior be sustainable? Or is its vulnerability to soil erosion likely to prevent it from making a long-term contribution? And what will be the price paid in the irretrievable loss of ecosystems and plant and animal species?

In sum, ensuring future food security is a formidable, multifaceted problem. To solve it, the world will need to:

- Check the HIV epidemic before it so depletes Africa's adult population that starvation stalks the land.
- Arrest the steady shrinkage in grainland area per person.
- Eliminate the overgrazing that is converting grasslands to desert.
- Reduce soil erosion losses to below the natural rate of new soil formation.
- Halt the advancing deserts that are engulfing cropland.
- Check the rising temperature that threatens to shrink harvests.
- Arrest the fall in water tables.
- Protect cropland from careless conversion to nonfarm uses.

NO

Bjorn Lomborg

The Truth About the Environment

Ecology and economics should push in the same direction. After all, the "eco" part of each word derives from the greek word for "home", and the protagonists of both claim to have humanity's welfare as their goal. Yet environmentalists and economists are often at loggerheads. For economists, the world seems to be getting better. For many environmentalists, it seems to be getting worse.

These environmentalists, led by such veterans as Paul Ehrlich of Stanford University, and Lester Brown of the Worldwatch Institute, have developed a sort of "litany" of four big environmental fears:

- Natural resources are running out.
- The population is ever growing, leaving less and less to eat.
- Species are becoming extinct in vast numbers: forests are disappearing and fish stocks are collapsing.
- The planet's air and water are becoming ever more polluted.

Human activity is thus defiling the earth, and humanity may end up killing itself in the process.

The trouble is, the evidence does not back up this litany. First, energy and other natural resources have become more abundant, not less so since the Club of Rome published "The Limits to Growth" in 1972. Second, more food is now produced per head of the world's population than at any time in history. Fewer people are starving. Third, although species are indeed becoming extinct, only about 0.7% of them are expected to disappear in the next 50 years, not 25–50%, as has so often been predicted. And finally, most forms of environmental pollution either appear to have been exaggerated, or are transient—associated with the early phrases of industrialisation and therefore best cured not by restricting economic growth, but by accelerating it. One form of pollution—the release of greenhouse gases that causes global warming—does appear to be a long-term phenomenon, but its total impact is unlikely to pose a devastating problem for the future of humanity. A bigger problem may well turn out to be an inappropriate response to it.

Can Things Only Get Better?

Take these four points one by one. First, the exhaustion of natural resources. The early environmental movement worried that the mineral resources on which modern industry depends would run out. Clearly, there must be some limit to the amount of fossil fuels and metal ores that can be extracted from the earth: the planet, after all, has a finite mass. But that limit is far greater than many environmentalists would have people believe.

Reserves of natural resources have to be located, a process that costs money. That, not natural scarcity, is the main limit on their availability. However, known reserves of all fossil fuels, and of most commercially important metals, are now larger than they were when "the Limits to Growth" was published. In the case of oil, for example, reserves that could be extracted at reasonably competitive prices would keep the world economy running for about 150 years at present consumption rates. Add to that the fact that the price of solar energy has fallen by half in every decade for the past 30 years, and appears likely to continue to do so into the future, and energy shortages do not look like a serious threat either to the economy or to the environment.

The development for non-fuel resources has been similar. Cement, aluminum, iron, copper, gold, nitrogen and zinc account for more than 75% of global expenditure on raw materials. Despite an increase in consumption of these materials of between two- and ten-fold over the past 50 years, the number of years of available reserves has actually grown. Moreover, the increasing abundance is reflected in an ever-decreasing price: *The Economist's* index of prices of industrial raw materials has dropped some 80% in inflation-adjusted terms since 1845.

Next, the population explosion is also turning out to be a bugaboo. In 1968, Dr Ehrlich predicted in his best selling book, "The Population Bomb", that "the battle to feed humanity is over. In the course of the 1970s the world will experience starvation of tragic proportions—hundreds of millions of people will starve to death."

That did not happen. Instead, according to the United Nations, agricultural production in the developing world has increased by 52% per person since 1961. The daily food intake in poor countries has increased from 1,932 calories, barely enough for survival, in 1961 to 2,650 calories in 1998, and is expected to rise to 3,020 by 2030. Likewise, the proportion of people in developing countries who are starving has dropped from 45% in 1949 to 18% today, and is expected to decline even further to 12% in 2010 and just 6% in 2030. Food, in other words, is becoming not scarcer but ever more abundant. This is reflected in its price. Since 1800 food prices have decreased by more than 90%, and in 2000, according to the World Bank, prices were lower than ever before.

Modern Malthus

Dr Ehrlich's prediction echoes that made 170 years earlier by Thomas Malthus. Malthus claimed that, if unchecked, human population would expand exponentially, while food production could increase only linearly, by bringing new land

Figure 1

Slowing Up

World population 1750–2200*, bn

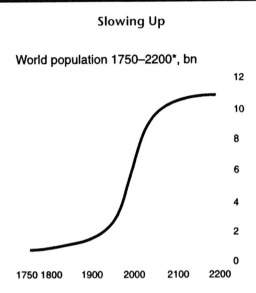

*UN medium-variant forecast from 2000

Source: UNPD

---

into cultivation. He was wrong. Population growth has turned out to have an internal check: as people grow richer and healthier, they have smaller families. Indeed, the growth rate of the human population reached its peak, of more than 2% a year, in the early 1960s. The rate of increase has been declining ever since. It is now 1.26%, and is expected to fall to 0.46% in 2050. The United Nations estimates that most of the world's population growth will be over by 2100, with the population stabilising at just below 11 billion (see Figure 1).

Malthus also failed to take account of developments in agricultural technology. These have squeezed more and more food out of each hectare of land. It is this application of human ingenuity that has boosted food production, not merely in line with, but ahead of, population growth. It has also, incidentally, reduced the need to take new land into cultivation, thus reducing the pressure on biodiversity.

Third, that threat of biodiversity loss is real, but exaggerated. Most early estimates used simple island models that linked a loss in habitat with a loss of biodiversity. A rule-of-thumb indicated that loss of 90% of forest meant a 50% loss of species. As rainforests seemed to be cut at alarming rates, estimates of annual species loss of 20,000–100,000 abounded. Many people expected the number of species to fall by half globally within a generation or two.

However, the data simply does not bear out these predictions. In the eastern United States, forests were reduced over two centuries to fragments totalling just 1–2% of their original area, yet this resulted in the extinction of

Figure 2

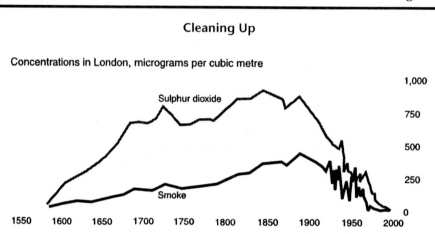

Cleaning Up

Concentrations in London, micrograms per cubic metre

Source: B. Lomborg

only one forest bird. In Puerto Rico, the primary forest area has been reduced over the past 400 years by 99%, yet "only" seven of 60 species of bird has become extinct. All but 12% of the Brazilian Atlantic rainforest was cleared in the 19th century, leaving only scattered fragments. According to the rule-of-thumb, half of all its species should have become extinct. Yet, when the World Conservation Union and the Brazilian Society of Zoology analysed all 291 known Atlantic forest animals, none could be declared extinct. Species, therefore, seem more resilient than expected. And tropical forests are not lost at annual rates of 2.4%, as many environmentalists have claimed: the latest UN figures indicate a loss of less than 0.5%.

Fourth, pollution is also exaggerated. Many analyses show that air pollution diminishes when a society becomes rich enough to be able to afford to be concerned about the environment. For London, the city for which the best data are available, air pollution peaked around 1890 (see Figure 2). Today, the air is cleaner than it has been since 1585. There is good reason to believe that this general picture holds true for all developed countries. And, although air pollution is increasing in many developing countries, they are merely replicating the development of the industrialised countries. When they grow sufficiently rich they, too, will start to reduce their air pollution.

All this contradicts the litany. Yet opinion polls suggest that many people, in the rich world, at least, nurture the belief that environmental standards are declining. Four factors cause this disjunction between perception and reality.

Always Look on the Dark Side of Life

One is the lopsidedness built into scientific research. Scientific funding goes mainly to areas with many problems. That may be wise policy, but it will also create an impression that many more potential problems exist than is the case.

Secondly, environmental groups need to be noticed by the mass media. They also need to keep the money rolling in. Understandably, perhaps, they sometimes exaggerate. In 1997, for example, the Worldwide Fund for Nature issued a press release entitled, "Two-thirds of the world's forests lost forever". The truth turns out to be nearer 20%.

Though these groups are run overwhelmingly by selfless folk, they nevertheless share many of the characteristics of other lobby groups. That would matter less if people applied the same degree of scepticism to environmental lobbying as they do to lobby groups in other fields. A trade organisation arguing for, say, weaker pollution controls is instantly seen as self-interested. Yet a green organisation opposing such a weakening is seen as altruistic, even if a dispassionate view of the controls in question might suggest they are doing more harm than good.

A third source of confusion is the attitude of the media. People are clearly more curious about bad news than good. Newspapers and broadcasters are there to provide what the public wants. That, however, can lead to significant distortions of perception. An example was America's encounter with El Niño in 1997 and 1998. This climatic phenomenon was accused of wrecking tourism, causing allergies, melting the ski-slopes and causing 22 deaths by dumping snow in Ohio.

A more balanced view comes from a recent article in the *Bulletin of the American Meteorological Society*. This tries to count up both the problems and the benefits of the 1997–98 Niño. The damage it did was estimated at $4 billion. However, the benefits amounted to some $19 billion. These came from higher winter temperatures (which saved an estimated 850 lives, reduced heating costs and diminished spring floods caused by meltwaters, and from the well-documented connection between past Niños and fewer Atlantic hurricanes. In 1998, America experienced no big Atlantic hurricanes and thus avoided huge losses. These benefits were not reported as widely as the losses.

The fourth factor is poor individual perception. People worry that the endless rise in the amount of stuff everyone throws away will cause the world to run out of places to dispose of waste. Yet, even if America's trash output continues to rise as it has done in the past, and even if the American population doubles by 2100, all the rubbish America produces through the entire 21st century will still take up only the area of a square, each of whose sides measures 28 km (18 miles). That is just one-12,000th of the area of the entire United States.

Ignorance matters only when it leads to faulty judgments. But fear of largely imaginary environmental problems can divert political energy from dealing with real ones. The table, showing the cost in the United States of various measures to save a year of a person's life, illustrates the danger. Some environmental policies, such as reducing lead in petrol and sulphur-dioxide emissions from fuel oil, are very cost-effective. But many of these are already in place. Most environmental measures are less cost-effective than interventions aimed at improving safety (such as installing air-bags in cars) and those involving medical screening and vaccination. Some are absurdly expensive.

Table 1

The Price of a Life

Cost of saving one year of one person's life – 1993$

Passing laws to make seat-belt use mandatory	69
Sickle-cell anaemia screening for black new-borns	240
Mammography for women aged 50	810
Pneumonia vaccination for people aged over 65	2,000
Giving advice on stopping smoking to people who smoke more than one packet a day	9,800
Putting men aged 30 on a low-cholesterol diet	19,000
Regular leisure-time physical activity, such as jogging for men aged 35	38,000
Making pedestrians and cyclists more visible	73,000
Installing air-bags (rather than manual lap belts) in cars	120,000
Installing arsenic emission-control at glass-manufacturing plants	51,000,000
Setting radiation emission standards for nuclear-power plants	180,000,000
Installing benzene emission control at rubber-tyre manufacturing plants	20,000,000,000

Source: T. Tengs et al, *Risk Analysis,* June 1995

Yet a false perception of risk may be about to lead to errors more expensive even than controlling the emission of benzene at tyre plants. Carbon-dioxide emissions are causing the planet to warm. The best estimates are that the temperature will rise by some 2°-3°C in this century, causing considerable problems, almost exclusively in the developing world, at a total cost of $5,000 billion. Getting rid of global warming would thus seem to be a good idea. The question is whether the cure will actually be more costly than ailment.

Despite the intuition that something drastic needs to be done about such a costly problem, economic analyses clearly show that it will be far more expensive to cut carbon-dioxide emissions radically than to pay the costs of adaptation to the increased temperatures. The effect of the Kyoto Protocol on the climate would be minuscule, even if it were implemented in full. A model by Tom Wigley, one of the main authors of the reports of the UN Climate Change Panel, shows how an expected temperature increase of 2.1°C in 2100 would be diminished by the treaty to an increase of 1.9°C instead. Or, to put it another way, the temperature increase that the planet would have experienced in 2094 would be postponed to 2100.

So the Kyoto agreement does not prevent global warming, but merely buys the world six years. Yet, the cost of Kyoto, for the United States alone, will be higher than the cost of solving the world's single most pressing health problems: providing universal access to clean drinking water and sanitation. Such measures would avoid 2m deaths every year, and prevent half a billion people from becoming seriously ill.

And that is the best case. If the treaty were implemented inefficiently, the cost of Kyoto could approach $1 trillion, or more than five times the cost of worldwide water and sanitation coverage. For comparison, the total global-aid budget today is about $50 billion a year.

To replace the litany with facts is crucial if people want to make the best possible decisions for the future. Of course, rational environmental management and environmental investment are good ideas—but the costs and benefits of such investments should be compared to those of similar investments in all the other important areas of human endeavour. It may be costly to be overly optimistic—but more costly still to be too pessimistic.

POSTSCRIPT

Is Mankind Dangerously Harming the Environment?

Though a number of works (see below) support Lomborg's argument, his evidence has come under heavy attack (see Richard C. Bell, "How Did *The Skeptical Environmentalist* Pull the Wool Over the Eyes of So Many Editors?" *WorldWatch* [March–April 2002] and *Scientific American* [January 2002]). The issue of the state of the environment and prospects for the future have been hotly debated for over 30 years with little chance of ending soon. Two key issues are the potential impacts of global warming and the net effects of future agricultural technologies, which will be used to feed growing populations with richer diets. On the former, see Douglas Long, *Global Warming* (Facts on File, 2004); Robert Hunter, *Thermageddon: Countdown to 2030* (Arcade Pub., 2003); John Theodore Houghton, *Global Warming: The Complete Briefing*, 3rd edition (Cambridge University, 2004); Andrew Simms et al., *Up in Smoke?: Threats from, and Responses to, the Impact of Global Warming on Human Development* (New Economic Foundation, 2004); and the journal *The Ecologist* (March 2002). Ronald Bailey and others debunk the global warming "scare" in his edited book, *Global Warming and Other Eco-Myths: How the Environmental Movement Uses False Science to Scare Us to Death* (Prima, 2002). See also Patrick J. Michaels, *Meltdown: The Predicatable Distortion of Global Warming by Scientists, Politicians, and the Media* (Cato Institue, 2004). On food production issues and agriculture technologies, see Lester R. Brown, *Outgrowing the Earth: The Food Security Challenge in the Age of Falling Water Tables and Rising Temperatures* (Earth Policy Institute, 2004); Bread for the World, *Are We on Track to End Hunger?: 14th Annual Report on the State of World Hunger* (Bread for the World Institution, 2004); and On agricultural technologies, see Vaclav Smil, *Feeding the World: A Challenge for the Twenty-First Century* (MIT Press, 2000).

Paul R. Ehrlich and Anne H. Ehrlich wrote *Betrayal of Science and Reason: How Anti-Environmental Rhetoric Threatens Our Future* (Island Press, 1996) to refute statements by those who do not agree with the messages of the concerned environmentalists. Julian Lincoln Simon counters with *Hoodwinking the Nation* (Transaction, 1999). For a debate on this issue see Norman Myers and Julian L. Simon, *Scarcity or Abundance? A Debate on the Environment* (W. W. Norton, 1994).

Publications that are optimistic about the availability of resources and the health of the environment include Ronald Bailey, ed., *The True State of the Planet* (Free Press, 1995) and Gregg Easterbrook, *A Moment on the Earth: The Coming Age of Environmental Optimism* (Viking, 1995). Publications by some who believe that population growth and human interventions in the environment have dangerous consequences for the future of mankind include Joseph Wayne Smith, Graham Lyons, and Gary Sauer-Thompson, *Healing a Wounded World* (Praeger, 1997); Douglas E. Booth, *The Environmental Consequences of Growth* (Routledge,

1998); and Kirill Kondratyev et al., *Stability of Life on Earth: Principal Subject of Scientific Research in the 21st Century* (Springer 2004); and James Gustive Speth, *Red Sky at Morning: America and the Crisis of the Global Environment* (Yale University Press, 2004).

Several works relate environmental problems to very severe political, social, and economic problems, including Michael Renner, *Fighting for Survival* (W. W. Norton, 1996); Michael N. Dobkowski and Isidor Wallimann, eds., *The Coming Age of Scarcity: Preventing Mass Death and Genocide in the Twenty-First Century* (Syracuse University Press, 1998); and one with a long timeframe, Sing C. Chew, *World Ecological Degradation: Accumulation, Urbanization, and Deforestation, 3000BC–AD2000* (Roman and Littlefield, 2001). An important series of publications on environmental problems is by the Worldwatch Institute, including two annuals: *State of the World* and *Vital Signs.*

ISSUE 20

Is Globalization Good for Mankind?

YES: Johan Norberg, from "Three Cheers for Global Capitalism," *The American Enterprise* (June 2004)

NO: Herman E. Daly, from "Globalization and Its Discontents," *Philosophy & Public Policy Quarterly* (Spring/Summer 2001)

ISSUE SUMMARY

YES: Author Johan Norberg argues that globalization is overwhelmingly good. Consumers throughout the world get better quality goods at lower prices as the competition forces producers to be more creative, efficient, and responsive to consumers' demands. Even most poor people benefit greatly.

NO: Herman E. Daly, professor at the School of Public Affairs at the University of Maryland, does not object to international trade and relations, but he does object to globalization that erases national boundaries and hurts workers and the environment.

$\mathbf{A}$ really big issue of today is globalization, which stands for worldwide processes, activities, and institutions. It involves world markets, world finance, world communications, world media, world religions, world popular culture, world rights movements, world drug trade, etc. The focus of most commentators is on the world economy, which many believe promises strong growth in world wealth. Critics focus on the world economy's negative impacts on workers' wages, environmental protections and regulations, and national and local cultures. Many say that it is easy for Americans to feel positive toward globalization because America and its businesses, media, and culture are at the center of the globalized world, which ensures that America gains more than its proportional share of the benefits. But the real debate is whether or not globalization benefits all mankind. When the whole world is considered, there may be far more minuses to be weighed against the pluses. It is hard to settle this debate because so many different dimensions that are incomparable must be included in the calculation of the cost-benefit ratio.

The concept of globalization forces us to think about many complicated issues at the same time. There are technological, economic, political, cultural, and ethical aspects of globalization. Technological developments make possible the communication, transportation, coordination, and organization that make economic globalization possible. Political factors have made this a relatively free global economy. Restrictions on trade and production have been greatly reduced, and competition has greatly increased. The results have been increased production and wealth and celebration in financial circles. But competition creates losers as well as winners, so peoples throughout the world are protesting and resisting economic globalization. Many are also resisting cultural globalization because their own cultures are threatened. They feel that the global culture is materialistic, sexualized, secular, and egocentric—and they may be right. But many also consider the strengths of the global culture, such as championing human rights, democracy, and justice.

In the selections that follow, Johan Norberg reports on the benefits of the global economy and counters many of the arguments against globalization. His main argument is that the global economy stimulates faster economic growth, which improves the standard of living of all groups. Herman E. Daly opposes globalization and favors the alternative of internationalization. Both involve the increasing importance of relations among nations, but globalization erases national boundaries while internationalization does not. The negative effects of globalization, he states, are standards-lowering competition, an increased tolerance of mergers and monopoly power, intense national specialization, and the excessive monopolization of knowledge as "intellectual property."

Johan Norberg  **YES**

Three Cheers for Global Capitalism

Under what is rather barrenly termed "globalization"—the process by which people, information, trade, investments, democracy, and the market economy tend more and more to cross national borders—our options and opportunities have multiplied. We don't have to shop at the big local company; we can turn to a foreign competitor. We don't have to work for the village's one and only employer; we can seek alternative opportunities. We don't have to make do with local cultural amenities; the world's culture is at our disposal. Companies, politicians, and associations have to exert themselves to elicit interest from people who have a whole world of options. Our ability to control our own lives is growing, and prosperity is growing with it.

Free markets and free trade and free choices transfer power to individuals at the expense of political institutions. Because there is no central control booth, it seems unchecked, chaotic. Political theorist Benjamin Barber speaks for many critics when he bemoans the absence of "viable powers of opposing, subduing, and civilizing the anarchic forces of the global economy." "Globalization" conjures up the image of an anonymous, enigmatic, elusive force, but it is actually just the sum of billions of people in thousands of places making decentralized decisions about their own lives. No one is in the driver's seat precisely because all of us are steering.

No company would import goods from abroad if we didn't buy them. If we did not send e-mails, order books, and download music every day, the Internet would wither and die. We eat bananas from Ecuador, order magazines from Britain, work for export companies selling to Germany and Russia, vacation in Thailand, and save money for retirement by investing in South America and Asia. These things are carried out by businesses only because we as individuals want them to. Globalization takes place from the bottom up.

A recent book about the nineteenth-century Swedish historian Erik Geijer notes that he was able to keep himself up to date just by sitting in Uppsala reading the *Edinburgh Review* and the *Quarterly Review*. That is how simple and intelligible the world can be when only a tiny elite in the capitals of Europe makes any difference to the course of world events. How much more complex and confusing everything is now, with ordinary people having a say over their own lives. Elites may mourn that they have lost power, but everyday life has vastly improved now that inexpensive goods and outside information and different employment opportunities are no longer blocked by political barriers.

To those of us in rich countries, more economic liberty to pick and choose may sound like a trivial luxury, even an annoyance—but it isn't. Fresh options are invaluable for all of us. And the existence from which globalization delivers people in the Third World—poverty, filth, ignorance, and powerlessness—really is intolerable. When global capitalism knocks at the door of Bhagant, an elderly agricultural worker and "untouchable" in the Indian village of Saijani, it leads to his house being built of brick instead of mud, to shoes on his feet, and clean clothes—not rags—on his back. Outside Bhagant's house, the streets now have drains, and the fragrance of tilled earth has replaced the stench of refuse. Thirty years ago Bhagant didn't know he was living in India. Today he watches world news on television. The stand that we in the privileged world take on the burning issue of globalization can determine whether or not more people will experience the development that has taken place in Bhagant's village.

Critics of globalization often paint a picture of capitalist marauders secretly plotting for world mastery, but this notion is completely off the mark. It has mostly been pragmatic, previously socialist, politicians who fanned globalization in China, Latin America, and East Asia—after realizing that government control-freakery had ruined their societies. Any allegation of runaway capitalism has to be tempered by the observation that today we have the largest public sectors and highest taxes the world has ever known. The economic liberalization measures of the last quarter century may have abolished some of the recent past's centralist excesses, but they have hardly ushered in a system of laissez-faire.

What defenders of global capitalism believe in, first and foremost, is man's capacity for achieving great things by means of the combined force of market exchanges. It is not their intention to put a price tag on everything. The important things—love, family, friendship, one's own way of life—cannot be assigned a monetary value. Principled advocates of global economic liberty plead for a more open world because that setting unleashes individual creativity as none other can. At its core, the belief in capitalist freedom among nations is a belief in mankind. . . .

Today, we hear that life is increasingly unfair amidst the market economy: "The rich are getting richer, and the poor are getting poorer." But if we look beyond the catchy slogans, we find that while many of the rich have indeed grown richer, so have most of the poor. Absolute poverty has diminished, and where it was greatest 20 years ago—in Asia—hundreds of millions of people have achieved a secure existence, even affluence, previously undreamed of. Global misery has diminished, and great injustices have started to unravel. . . .

･✿･

This progress is all very well, many critics of globalization will argue, but even if the majority are better off, gaps have widened and wealthy people and countries have improved their lot more rapidly than others. The critics point out that 40 years ago the combined per capita GDP of the 20 richest countries was 15 times greater than that of the 20 poorest, and is now 30 times greater.

There are two reasons why this objection to globalization does not hold up. First, if everyone is better off, what does it matter that the improvement comes faster for some than for others? Only those who consider wealth a greater problem than poverty can find irritation in middle-class citizens becoming millionaires while the previously poverty-stricken become middle class.

Second, the allegation of increased inequality is simply wrong.

The notion that global inequality has increased is largely based on figures from the U.N.'s 1999 *Human Development Report*. The problem with these figures is that they don't take into account what people can actually buy with their money. Without that "purchasing power" adjustment, the figures only show what a currency is worth on the international market, and nothing about local conditions. Poor people's actual living standards hinge on the cost of their food, their clothing, their housing—not what their money would get them while vacationing in Europe. That's why the U.N. uses purchasing-power-adjusted figures in other measures of living standards. It only resorts to the unadjusted figures, oddly, in order to present a theory of inequality.

A report from the Norwegian Institute for Foreign Affairs investigated global inequality by means of figures adjusted for purchasing power. Their data show that, contrary to conventional wisdom, inequality between countries has continuously *declined* ever since the end of the 1970s. This decline has been especially rapid since 1993, when globalization really gathered speed.

More recently, similar research by Columbia University development economist Xavier Sala-i-Martin has confirmed those findings. He found that when U.N. figures are adjusted for purchasing power, they point to a sharp decline in world inequality. Sala-i-Martin and co-author Surjit Bhalla also found independently that if we focus on inequality between *persons*, rather than inequality between *countries*, global inequality at the end of 2000 was at its lowest point since the end of World War II.

Estimates that compare countries rather than individuals, both authors note, grossly overestimate real inequality because they allow gains for huge numbers of people to be outweighed by losses for far fewer. For instance, country aggregates treat China and Grenada as data points of equal weight, even though China's population is 12,000 times Grenada's. Once we shift our focus to people rather than nations, the evidence is overwhelming that the past 30 years have witnessed a strong shift toward global equalization.

•⦿•

One myth about trade is the notion that exports to other countries are a good thing, but that imports are somehow a bad thing. Many believe that a country grows powerful by selling much and buying little. The truth is that our standard of living will not rise until we use our money to buy more and cheaper things. One of the first trade theorists, James Mill, rightly noted in 1821 that "The benefit which derives from exchanging one commodity for another arises in all cases from the commodity received, not the commodity given." The only point of exports, in other words, is to enable us to get imports in return. . . .

Trade is not a zero-sum game in which one party loses what the other party gains. There would *be* no exchange if both parties did not feel that they benefited. The really interesting yardstick is not the "balance of trade" (where a "surplus" means that we are exporting more than we are importing) but the *quantity* of trade, since both exports and imports are gains. Imports are often feared as a potential cause of unemployment: If we import cheap toys and clothing from China, then toy and garment manufacturers here will have to scale down. But by obtaining cheaper goods from abroad, we save resources in the United States and can therefore invest in new industries and occupations.

•✦•

Free trade brings freedom: freedom for people to buy and sell what they want. As an added benefit, this leads to the efficient use of resources. A company, or country, specializes where it can generate the greatest value.

Economic openness also leads to an enduring effort to improve production, because foreign competition forces firms to be as good and cheap as possible. As production in established industries becomes ever more efficient, resources are freed up for investment in new methods, inventions, and products. Foreign competition brings the same benefits that we recognize in economic competition generally; it simply extends competition to a broader field.

One of the most important but hard to measure benefits of free trade is that a country trading a great deal with the rest of the world imports new ideas and new techniques in the bargain. If the United States pursues free trade, our companies are exposed to the world's best ideas. They can then borrow those ideas, buy leading technology from elsewhere, and hire the best available manpower. This compels the companies to be more dynamic themselves.

The world's output today is six times what it was 50 years ago, and world trade is 16 times greater. There is reason to believe that the trade growth drove much of the production growth. One comprehensive study of the effects of trade was conducted by Harvard economists Jeffrey Sachs and Andrew Warner. They examined the trade policies between 1970 and 1989 of 117 countries. The study reveals a statistically significant connection between free trade and economic growth. Growth was between three and six times *higher* in free-trade countries than in protectionist ones. Factors like improved education turned out to be vastly less important than trade in increasing economic progress.

Over those two decades, developing countries that practiced free trade had an average annual growth rate of 4.5 percent, while developing countries that practiced protectionism grew by only 0.7 percent. Among industrial countries, the free traders experienced annual growth of 2.3 percent, versus only 0.7 percent among the protectionists. It must be emphasized that this is not a matter of countries earning more because *others* opened to *their* exports. Rather, these countries earned more by keeping their own markets open.

⋅⟨◉⟩⋅

If free trade is constantly making production more efficient, won't that result in the disappearance of job opportunities? When Asians manufacture our cars and South Americans produce our meat, auto workers and farmers in the United States lose their jobs and unemployment rises. Foreigners and developing countries will increasingly produce the things we need, until we don't have any jobs left. If increasing automation means everything we consume today will be able to be made by half the U.S. labor force in 20 years, doesn't that mean that the other half will be out of work? Such are the horror scenarios depicted in many anti-globalization writings.

The notion that a colossal unemployment crisis is looming began to grow popular in the mid 1970s. Since then, production has been streamlined and internationalized more than ever. Yet far more jobs have been created than have disappeared. We have more efficient production than ever before, but also more people at work. Between 1975 and 1998, employment in countries like the United States, Canada, and Australia rose by 50 percent.

And it is in the most internationalized economies, making the most use of modern technology, that employment has grown fastest. Between 1983 and 1995 in the United States, 24 million more job opportunities were created than disappeared. And those were not low-paid, unskilled jobs, as is often alleged. On the contrary, 70 percent of the new jobs carried a wage above the American median level. Nearly half the new jobs belonged to the most highly skilled, a figure which has risen even more rapidly since 1995.

So allegations of progressively fewer people being needed in production have no empirical foundation. And no wonder, for they are wrong in theory too. Imagine a pre-industrial economy where most everyone is laboring to feed himself. Then food production is improved by new technologies, new machines, foreign competition, and imports. That results in a lot of people being forced to leave the agricultural sector. Does that mean there is nothing for them to do, that consumption is constant? Of course not; the manpower which used to be required to feed the population shifts to clothing it, and providing better housing. Then improved transport, and entertainment. Then newspapers, telephones, and computers.

The notion that the quantity of employment is constant, that a job gained by one person is always a job taken from someone else, has provoked a variety of foolish responses. Some advocate that jobs must be shared. Others smash machinery. Many advocate raising tariffs and excluding immigrants. But the whole notion is wrong. The very process of a task being done more efficiently, thus allowing jobs to be shed, enables new industries to grow, providing people with new and better jobs.

Efficiency does, of course, have a flip side. Economist Joseph Schumpeter famously described a dynamic market as a process of "creative destruction," because it destroys old solutions and industries, with a creative end in view. As the word "destruction" suggests, not everyone benefits from every market transformation in the short term. The process is painful for those who have invested in or are employed by less-efficient industries. Drivers of horse-drawn cabs lost out with the spread of automobiles, as did producers of paraffin lamps when electric light was introduced. In more modern times, manufacturers of typewriters were put out of business by the computer, and LP records were superseded by CDs.

Painful changes of this kind happen all the time as a result of new inventions and methods of production. Unquestionably, such changes can cause trauma for those affected. But the most foolish way to counter such problems is to try to prevent them. It is generally fruitless; mere spitting into the wind. Besides, without "creative destruction," we would *all* be stuck with a lower standard of living. . . .

A review of more than 50 surveys of adjustments after trade liberalization in different countries shows clearly that adjustment problems are far milder than the conventional debate suggests. For every dollar of trade adjustment costs, roughly $30 is harvested in the form of welfare gains. A study of trade liberalization in 13 different countries showed that in all but one, industrial employment had already increased just one year after the liberalization. The process turns out to be far more creative than destructive.

If there are problems resulting from unshackled capitalism, they ought to be greatest in the United States, with its constant swirling economic transformations. But our job market is a bit like the Hydra in the legend of Hercules. Every time Hercules cuts off one of the beast's heads, two new ones appear. The danger of having to continue changing jobs all one's life is exaggerated: The average length of time an American stays in a particular job actually increased between 1983 and 1995, from 3.5 years to 3.8. Nor is it true, as many people believe, that more jobs are created in the United States only because real wages have stagnated or fallen since the 1970s. A growing proportion of wages is now paid in non-money forms, such as health insurance, stocks, 401(k) contributions, day care, and so forth, to avoid taxation. When these benefits are included, American wages have risen right along with productivity. Among poor Americans, the proportion of consumption devoted to food, clothing, and housing has fallen since the 1970s from 52 to 37 percent, which clearly shows that they have money to spare for much more than the bare necessities of life. . . .

Advocates of protectionism often complain of "sweatshops" allegedly run by multinational corporations in the Third World. Let's look at the evidence: Economists have compared the conditions of people employed in American-owned facilities in developing countries with those of people employed elsewhere in the same country. In the poorest developing countries, the average employee of an American-affiliated company makes *eight times* the average national wage! In middle income countries, American employers pay *three times* the national average. Even compared with corresponding modern jobs in the same country, the multinationals pay about 30 percent higher wages. Marxists maintain that multinationals exploit poor workers. Are much higher wages "exploitation"?

The same marked difference can be seen in working conditions. The International Labor Organization has shown that multinationals, especially in the footwear and garment industries, are leading the trend toward better working conditions in the Third World. When multinational corporations accustom workers to better-lit, safer, and cleaner factories, they raise the general standard. Native firms then also have to offer better conditions, otherwise no one will work for them. Zhou Litai, one of China's foremost labor attorneys, has pointed out that Western consumers are the principal driving force behind the improvements of working conditions in China, and worries that "if Nike and Reebok go, this pressure evaporates." . . .

·◈·

Corporations have not acquired more power through free trade. Indeed, they used to be far more powerful—and still are in dictatorships and controlled economies. Large corporations have chances to corrupt or manipulate when power is distributed by public officials who can be hobnobbed over luncheons to give protection through monopolies, tariffs, or subsides. Free trade, on the other hand, exposes corporations to competition. Above all, it lets consumers ruthlessly pick and choose across national borders, rejecting companies that don't measure up. . . .

Companies in free competition can grow large and increase their sales only by being better than others. Companies that fail to do so quickly go bust or get taken over by someone who can make better use of their capital, buildings, machinery, and employees. Capitalism is very tough—but mainly on firms offering outdated, poor-quality, or expensive goods and services. Fear of established companies growing so large as to become unaccountable has absolutely no foundation in reality. In the U.S., the most capitalist large country in the world, the market share of the 25 biggest corporations has steadily dwindled over recent decades.

Freer markets make it easier for small firms with fresh ideas to compete with big corporations. Between 1980 and 1993, the 500 biggest American corporations saw their share of the country's total employment diminish from 16 to 11 percent. During the same period, the average personnel strength of American firms fell from 17 to 15 people, and the proportion of the population working in companies with more than 250 employees fell from 37 to 29 percent.

Of the 500 biggest enterprises in the United States in 1980, one third had disappeared by 1990. Another 40 percent had evaporated five years later. Whether they failed to grow enough to stay on the list, died, merged, or broke up, the key lesson is that big corporations have much less power over consumers than we sometimes imagine. Even the most potent corporation must constantly re-earn its stripes, or tumble fast. . . .

❧✿❧

Many people fear a "McDonaldization" or "Disneyfication" of the world, a creeping global homogeneity that leaves everyone wearing the same clothes, eating the same food, and seeing the same movies. But this portrayal does not accurately describe globalization. Anyone going out in the capitals of Europe today will have no trouble finding hamburgers and Coca-Cola, but he will just as easily find kebabs, sushi, Tex-Mex tacos, Peking duck, Thai lemongrass soup, and cappuccino. . . .

The world is indeed moving toward a common objective, but that objective is not the predominance of a particular culture, rather it is pluralism, the freedom to choose from a host of different paths and destinations. The market for experimental electronic music or film versions of novels by Dostoevsky may be small in any given place, so musicians and filmmakers producing such material could never produce anything without access to the much larger audience provided by globalization.

This internationalization is, ironically, what makes people believe that differences are vanishing. When you travel abroad, things look much the same as in your own country: The people there also have goods and chain stores from different parts of the globe. This phenomenon is not due to uniformity and the elimination of differences, but by the growth of pluralism everywhere. . . .

❧✿❧

In the age of globalization, the ideas of freedom and individualism have attained tremendous force. There are few concepts as inspiring as that of self-determination. When people in other countries glimpse a chance to set their own course, it becomes almost irresistible. If there is any elimination of differences throughout the world, it has been the convergence of societies on the practice of allowing people to choose the sort of existence they please.

Global commerce does undermine old economic interests, challenge cultures, and erode some traditional power centers. Advocates of globalization have to show that greater gains and opportunities counterbalance such problems. . . .

Lasse Berg and Stig Karlsson record Chinese villagers' descriptions of the changes they experienced since the 1960s: "The last time you were here, people's thoughts and minds were closed, bound up," stated farmer Yang Zhengming. But as residents acquired power over their own livelihoods they began to think for themselves. Yang explains that "a farmer could then own himself. He did not need to submit. He decided himself what he was going to do, how and when. The proceeds of his work were his own. It was freedom that came to us. We were allowed to own things for ourselves."

Coercion and poverty still cover large areas of our globe. But thanks to globalizing economic freedom, people know that living in a state of oppression is not natural or necessary. People who have acquired a taste of economic liberty and expanded horizons will not consent to be shut in again by walls or fences. They will work to create a better existence for themselves. The aim of our politics should be to give them that freedom.

NO

Herman E. Daly

Globalization and Its Discontents

Every day, newspaper articles and television reports insist that those who oppose globalization must be isolationists or—even worse—xenophobes. This judgment is nonsense. The relevant alternative to globalization is internationalization, which is neither isolationist nor xenophobic. Yet it is impossible to recognize the cogency of this alternative if one does not properly distinguish these two terms.

"Internalization" refers to the increasing importance of relations among nations. Although the basic unit of community and policy remains the nation, increasingly trade, treaties, alliances, protocols, and other formal agreements and communications are necessary elements for nations to thrive. "Globalization" refers to global economic integration of many formerly national economies into one global economy. Economic integration is made possible by free trade—especially by free capital mobility—and by easy or uncontrolled migration. In contrast to internationalization, which simply recognizes that nations increasingly rely on understandings among one another, globalization is the effective erasure of national boundaries for economic purposes. National boundaries become totally porous with respect to goods and capital, and ever more porous with respect to people, who are simply viewed as cheap labor—or in some cases as cheap human capital.

In short, globalization is the economic integration of the globe. But exactly what is "integration"? The word derives from *integer*, meaning one, complete, or whole. Integration means much more than "interdependence"—it is the act of combining separate although related units into a single whole. Since there can be only one whole, only one unity with reference to which parts are integrated, it follows that global economic integration logically implies national economic *dis*integration—parts are torn out of their national context (dis-integrated), in order to be re-integrated into the new whole, the globalized economy.

As the saying goes, to make an omelet you have to break some eggs. The disintegration of the national egg is necessary to integrate the global omelet. But this obvious logic, as well as the cost of disintegration, is frequently met with denial. This article argues that globalization is neither inevitable nor to be embraced, much less celebrated. Acceptance of globalization entails several serious consequences, namely, standards-lowering competition, an increased tolerance of mergers and monopoly power, intense national specialization, and the excessive monopolization of knowledge as "intellectual property." This article discusses these likely consequences, and concludes by advocating the adoption of internationalization, and not globalization.

The Inevitability of Globalization?

Some accept the inevitability of globalization and encourage others in the faith. With admirable clarity, honesty, and brevity, Renato Ruggiero, former director-general of the World Trade Organization, insists that "We are no longer writing the rules of interaction among separate national economies. We are writing the constitution of a single global economy." His sentiments clearly affirm globalization and reject internationalization as above defined. Further, those who hold Ruggiero's view also subvert the charter of the Bretton Woods institutions. Named after a New Hampshire resort where representatives of forty-four nations met in 1944 to design the world's post–World War II economic order, the institutions conceived at the Bretton Woods International Monetary Conference include the World Bank and the International Monetary Fund. The World Trade Organization evolved later, but functions as a third sister to the World Bank and the International Monetary Fund. The nations at the conference considered proposals by the U.S., U.K., and Canadian governments, and developed the "Bretton Woods system," which established a stable international environment through such policies as fixed exchange rates, currency convertibility, and provision for orderly exchange rate adjustments. The Bretton Woods Institutions were designed to facilitate *internationalization, not globalization,* a point ignored by director-general Ruggiero.

The World Bank, along with its sister institutions, seems to have lost sight of its mission. After the disruption of its meetings in Washington, D.C. in April 2000, the World Bank sponsored an Internet discussion on globalization. The closest the World Bank came to offering a definition of the subject under discussion was the following: "The most common core sense of economic globalization . . . surely refers to the observation that in recent years a quickly rising share of economic activity in the world seems to be taking place between people who live in different countries (rather than in the same country)." This ambiguous description was not improved upon by Mr. Wolfensohn, president of the World Bank, who told the audience at a subsequent Aspen Institute Conference that "Globalization is a practical methodology for empowering the poor to improve their lives." That is neither a definition nor a description—it is a wish. Further, this wish also flies in the face of the real consequences of global economic integration. One could only sympathize with demonstrators protesting Mr. Wolfensohn's speech some fifty yards from the Aspen conference facility. The reaction of the Aspen elite was to accept as truth the title of Mr. Wolfensohn's speech, "Making Globalization Work for the Poor," and then ask in grieved tones, "How could anyone demonstrate against *that?*"

Serious consequences flow from the World Banks' lack of precision in defining globalization but lauding it nonetheless. For one thing, the so-called definition of globalization conflates the concept with that of internalization. As a result, one cannot reasonably address a crucial question: Should these increasing transactions between people living in different countries take place *across national boundaries* that are economically significant, or *within an integrated world* in which national boundaries are economically meaningless?

The ambiguous understanding of globalization deprives citizens of the opportunity to decide whether they are willing to abandon national monetary and fiscal policy, as well as the minimum wage. One also fails to carefully consider whether economic integration entails political and cultural integration. In short, will political communities and cultural traditions wither away, subsumed under some monolithic economic imperative? Although one might suspect economic integration would lead to political integration, it is hard to decide which would be worse—an economically integrated world *with,* or *without,* political integration. Everyone recognizes the desirability of community for the world as a whole—but one can conceive of two very different models of world community: (1) a federated community of real national communities (internationalization), versus (2) a cosmopolitan direct membership in a single abstract global community (globalization). However, at present our confused conversations about globalization deprive us of the opportunity to reflect deeply on these very different possibilities.

This article has suggested that at present organizations such as the International Monetary Fund and the World Bank (and, by extension, the World Trade Organization) no longer serve the interests of their member nations as defined in their charters. Yet if one asks whose interests are served, we are told they service the interests of the integrated "global economy." If one tries to glimpse a concrete reality behind that grand abstraction, however, one can find no individual workers, peasants, or small businessmen represented, but only giant fictitious individuals, the transnational corporations. In globalization, power is drained away from national communities and local enterprises, and aggregates in transnational corporations.

The Consequences of Globalization

Globalization—the erasure of national boundaries for economic purposes—risks serious consequences. Briefly, they include, first of all, standards-lowering competition to externalize social and environmental costs with the goal of achievement of a competitive advantage. This results, in effect, in a race to the bottom so far as efficiency in cost accounting and equity in income distribution are concerned. Globalization also risks increased tolerance of mergers and monopoly power in domestic markets in order that corporations become big enough to compete internationally. Third, globalization risks more intense national specialization according to the dictates of competitive advantage. Such specialization reduces the range of choice of ways to earn a livelihood, and increases dependence on other countries. Finally, worldwide enforcement of a muddled and self-serving doctrine of "trade-related intellectual property rights" is a direct contradiction of the Jeffersonian dictum that "knowledge is the common property of mankind."

Each of these risks of globalization deserves closer scrutiny.

1. Standards-lowering competition   Globalization undercuts the ability of nations to internalize environmental and social costs into prices. Instead, economic integration under free market conditions promotes standards-lowering competition—a race to the bottom, in short. The country that does the poorest job of internalizing all social and environmental costs of production into its prices gets a competitive advantage in international trade. The external social and environmental costs are left to be borne by the population at large. Further, more of world production shifts to countries that do the poorest job of counting costs—a sure recipe for reducing the efficiency of global production. As uncounted, externalized costs increase, the positive correlation between gross domestic product (GDP) growth and welfare disappears, or even becomes negative. We enter a world foreseen by the nineteenth-century social critic John Ruskin, who observed that "that which seems to be wealth is in verity but a gilded index of far-reaching ruin."

Another dimension of the race to the bottom is that globalization fosters increasing inequality in the distribution of income in high-wage countries, such as the U.S. Historically, in the U.S. there has been an implicit social contract established to ameliorate industrial strife between labor and capital. As a consequence, the distribution of income between labor and capital has been considered more equal and just in the U.S. compared to the world as a whole. However, global integration of markets necessarily abrogates that social contract. U.S. wages would fall drastically because labor is relatively more abundant globally than nationally. Further, returns to capital in the U.S. would increase because capital is relatively more scarce globally than nationally. Although one could make the theoretical argument that wages would be *bid up* in the rest of the world, the increase would be so small as to be insignificant. Making such an argument from the relative numbers would be analogous to insisting that, theoretically, when I jump off a ladder gravity not only pulls me to the earth, but also moves the earth towards me. This technical point offers cold comfort to anyone seeking a softer landing.

2. Increased tolerance of mergers and monopoly power   Fostering global competitive advantage is used as an excuse for tolerance of corporate mergers and monopoly in national markets. Chicago School economist and Nobel laureate Ronald Coase, in his classic article on the theory of the firm, suggests that corporate entities are "islands of central planning in a sea of market relationships." The islands of central planning become larger and larger relative to the remaining sea of market relationships as a result of merger. More and more resources are allocated by within-firm central planning, and less by between-firm market relationships. Corporations are the victor, and the market principle is the loser, as governments lose the strength to regulate corporate capital and maintain competitive markets in the public interest. Of the hundred largest economic organizations, fifty-two are corporations and forty-eight are nations. The distribution of income within these centrally-planned corporations has become much more concentrated. The ratio of the salary of the Chief Executive Officer to the average employee has passed 400 (as one would expect, since chief central planners set their own salaries).

3. Intense national specialization   Free trade and free capital mobility increase pressures for specialization in order to gain or maintain a competitive advantage. As a consequence, globalization demands that workers accept an ever-narrowing range of ways to earn a livelihood. In Uruguay, for example, everyone would have to be either a shepherd or a cowboy to conform to the dictates of competitive advantage in the global market. Everything else should be imported in exchange for beef, mutton, wool, and leather. Any Uruguayan who wants to play in a symphony orchestra or be an airline pilot should emigrate.

Of course, most people derive as much satisfaction from how they earn their income as from how they spend it. Narrowing that range of choice is a welfare loss uncounted by trade theorists. Globalization assumes either that emigration and immigration are costless, or that narrowing the range of occupational choice within a nation is costless. Both assumptions are false.

While trade theorists ignore the range of choice in *earning* one's income, they at the same time exaggerate the welfare effects of range of choice in *spending* that income. For example, the U.S. imports Danish butter cookies and Denmark imports U.S. butter cookies. Although the gains from trading such similar commodities cannot be great, trade theorists insist that the welfare of cookie connoisseurs is increased by expanding the range of consumer choice to the limit.

Perhaps, but one wonders whether those gains might be realized more cheaply by simply trading recipes? Although one would think so, *recipes*—trade-related intellectual property rights—are the one thing that free traders really want to protect.

4. Intellectual property rights   Of all things, knowledge is that which should be most freely shared, since in sharing, knowledge is multiplied rather than divided. Yet trade theorists have rejected Thomas Jefferson's dictum that "Knowledge is the common property of mankind" and instead have accepted a muddled doctrine of "trade-related intellectual property rights." This notion of rights grants private corporations monopoly ownership of the very basis of life itself—patents to seeds (including the patent-protecting, life-denying terminator gene) and to knowledge of basic genetic structures.

The argument offered to support this grab is that, without the economic incentive of monopoly ownership, little new knowledge and innovation will be forthcoming. Yet, so far as I know, James Watson and Francis Crick, co-discoverers of the structure of DNA, do not share in the patent royalties reaped by their successors. Nor of course did Gregor Mendel get any royalties—but then he was a monk motivated by mere curiosity about how Creation works!

Once knowledge exists, its proper price is the marginal opportunity cost of sharing it, which is close to zero, since nothing is lost by sharing knowledge. Of course, one does lose the *monopoly* on that knowledge, but then economists have traditionally argued that monopoly is inefficient as well as unjust because it creates an artificial scarcity of the monopolized item.

Certainly, the cost of production of new knowledge is not zero, even though the cost of sharing it is. This allows biotech corporations to claim that they deserve a fifteen- or twenty-year monopoly for the expenses incurred in research and development. Although corporations deserve to profit from their efforts, they are not entitled to monopolize on Watson and Crick's contribution—without which they could do nothing—or on the contributions of Gregor Mendel and all the great scientists of the past who made fundamental discoveries. As early twentieth-century economist Joseph Schumpeter emphasized, being the first with an innovation already gives one the advantage of novelty, a natural temporary monopoly, which in his view was the major source of profit in a competitive economy.

As the great Swiss economist, Jean Sismondi, argued over two centuries ago, not all new knowledge is of benefit to humankind. We need a sieve to select beneficial knowledge. Perhaps the worse selective principle is hope for private monetary gain. A much better selective motive for knowledge is a search in hopes of benefit to our fellows. This is not to say that we should abolish all intellectual property rights—that would create more problems than it would solve. But we should certainly begin restricting the domain and length of patent monopolies rather than increasing them so rapidly and recklessly. We should also become much more willing to share knowledge. Shared knowledge increases the productivity of all labor, capital, and resources. Further, international development aid should consist far more of freely-shared knowledge, and far less of foreign investment and interest-bearing loans.

Let me close with my favorite quote from John Maynard Keynes, one of the founders of the recently subverted Bretton Woods Institutions:

> I sympathize therefore, with those who would minimize, rather than those who would maximize, economic entanglement between nations. Ideas, knowledge, art, hospitality, travel—these are the things which should of their nature be international. But let goods be homespun whenever it is reasonably and conveniently possible; and, above all, let finance be primarily national.

POSTSCRIPT

Is Globalization Good for Mankind?

Daly believes that the economy is inexorably connected to culture and politics. He therefore asks, "Will political communities and cultural traditions wither away, subsumed under some monolithic economic imperative?" Economic integration will spawn greater political integration and cultural integration, he concludes, theorizing that in globalization, power is drained away from national communities and local enterprises and aggregates in transnational corporations.

There has been an explosion of books on globalization recently. A bestseller is Thomas Friedman's *The Lexus and the Olive Tree* (Farrar, Straus, Giroux, 2000), which tells the story of the new global economy and many of its ramifications. Friedman sees the United States as the nation that is best able to capitalize on that global economy, so it has the brightest future. Other works that explore the role of America in globalization include Jim Garrison, *America as Empire: Global Leader or Rogue Power?* (Berret-Koehler Publishers, 2004); *Global America?: The Cultural Consequences of Globalization,* edited by Ulrich Beck et al. (Liverpool University Press, 2003); and Will Hutton, *World We're in: A Declaration of Interdependence: Why America Should Join the World* (W.W. Norton, 2003). Works that applaud globalization include Barry Asmas, *The Best Is Yet to Come* (AmeriPress, 2001); Diane Coyle, *Paradoxes of Prosperity: Why the New Capitalism Benefits All* (Texere, 2001); John Micklethwait and Adrian Wooldridge, *Future Perfect: The Challenge and Hidden Promise of Globalization* (Crown Business, 2000); and Jacques Bandot, ed., *Building a World Community: Globalization and the Common Good* (University of Washington Press, 2001).

Attacks on globalization are prolific and include Robert Went, *Globalization: Neoliberal Challenge, Radical Responses* (Pluto Press, 2000); William K. Tabb, *The Amoral Elephant: Globalization and the Struggle for Social Justice in the Twenty-First Century* (Monthly Review Press, 2001); Walden Bello, *Future in Balance: Essays on Globalization and Resistance* (Food First Books, 2001); Vic George and Paul Wilding, *Globalization and Human Welfare* (Palgrave, 2002); Gary Teeple, *Globalization and the Decline of Social Reform* (Humanity Books, 2000); Noreena Hertz, *The Silent Takeover: Global Capitalism and the Death of Democracy* (Free Press, 2002); Alan Tonelson, *Race to the Bottom: Why a Worldwide Worker Surplus and Uncontrolled Free Trade Are Sinking American Living Standards* (Westview, 2000); *Civilizing Globalization: A Survival Guide,* edited by Richard Sandbrook (SUNY Press, 2003); Richard P. Appelbaum and William I. Robinson (eds.), *Critical Globalization Studies* (Routledge, 2005); Berch Berberoglu (ed.), *Globalization and Change: The Transformation of Global Capitalism* (Lexington Books, 2005); Peter Isard, *Globalization and the International Financial System: What's Wrong and What Can Be Done* (Cambridge, 2005); and Robert A. Isaak, *The Globaliza-*

tion Gap: How the Rich Get Richer and the Poor Get Left Further Behind (Prentice-Hall, 2005).

For relatively balanced discussions of globalization see Arthur P. J. Mol, *Globalization and Environmental Reform: The Ecological Modernization of the Global Economy* (MIT Press, 2001), which points to the environmental degradation that results from globalization but also actions that retard degradation and improve environmental quality; Richard Langhome, *The Coming of Globalization: Its Evolution and Contemporary Consequences* (St. Martin's Press, 2001); Kamal Dervis, *Better Globalization: Legitimacy, Governance and Reform* (Brookings, 2005); Barbara Harris-White, ed., *Globalization and Insecurity: Political, Economic, and Physical Challenges* (Palgrave, 2002); Dani Rodnik, *Has Globalization Gone Too Far?* (Institute for International Economics, 1997); *Global Transformations Reader: An Introduction to the Globalization debate*, edited by David Held et al. (Policy Press, 2003); Tony Schirato and Jennifer Webb, *Understanding Globalization* (Sage, 2003); and *Globalization and Anti-globalization: Dynamics of Change in the New World*, edited by Henry Veltmeyer (Ashgate, 2004). For interesting discussions of the cultural aspects of globalization see Paul Kennedy and Catherine J. Danks, eds., *Globalization and National Identities: Crisis or Opportunity* (Palgrave, 2001); Tyler Cowen, *Creative Destruction: How Globalization Is Changing the World's Cultures* (Princeton University Press, 2002); Alison Brysk, ed., *Globalization and Human Rights* (University of California Press, 2002); and Elisabeth Madimbee-Boyi, ed., *Beyond Dichotomies: Histories, Identities, Cultures, and the Challenge of Globalization* (SUNY, 2002).

Contributors to This Volume

EDITOR

KURT FINSTERBUSCH is a professor of sociology at the University of Maryland at College Park. He received a B.A. in history from Princeton University in 1957, a B.D. from Grace Theological Seminary in 1960, and a Ph.D. in sociology from Columbia University in 1969. He is the author of *Understanding Social Impacts* (Sage Publications, 1980), and he is the coauthor, with Annabelle Bender Motz, of *Social Research for Policy Decisions* (Wadsworth, 1980) and, with Jerald Hage, of *Organizational Change as a Development Strategy* (Lynne Rienner, 1987). He is the editor of *Annual Editions: Sociology* (McGraw-Hill/Contemporary Learning Series); *Annual Editions: Social Problems* (McGraw-Hill/Contemporary Learning Series); and *Sources: Notable Selections in Sociology*, 3rd ed. (McGraw-Hill/Dushkin, 1999).

STAFF

Larry Loeppke	Managing Editor
Jill Peter	Senior Developmental Editor
Susan Brusch	Senior Developmental Editor
Beth Kundert	Production Manager
Jane Mohr	Project Manager
Tara McDermott	Design Coordinator
Nancy Meissner	Editorial Assistant
Julie Keck	Senior Marketing Manager
Mary Klein	Marketing Communications Specialist
Alice Link	Marketing Coordinator
Tracie Kammerude	Senior Marketing Assistant
Lori Church	Pemissions Coordinator

AUTHORS

ANN ROSEGRANT ALVAREZ, PhD, is co-chair of the Graduate Concentration in Community Practice and Social Action at the Wayne State University School of Social Work in Detroit, Michigan. Her research and teaching interests include community practice, multi-cultural community organizing, feminist practice, international social work, social work history and policy issues.

DAVID A. ANDERSON is a Blazer Associate Professor of Economics. He teaches many courses including law and economics, as well as the economics of crime. He is the author of *Environmental Economics* (Southwestern, 2004).

JEFFREY M. BERRY is John Richard Skuse Professor of Political Science at Tufts University. He is the author of *The New Liberalism: The Rising Power of Citizen Groups* (Brookings Institution Press, 2000) and *The Interest Group Society,* 3rd ed. (Addison-Wesley, 2001).

LAWRENCE D. BOBO is the Martin Luther King Jr. Centennial Professor at Stanford University where he is also director of the Center for Comparative Study in Race and Ethnicity and Director of the Program in African and African American Studies. He is a founding co-editor of the *Du Bois Review: Social Science Research on Race* published by Cambridge University Press. He is co-author of the award-winning book *Racial Attitudes in America: Trends and Interpretations* (Harvard University Press, 1997). His next book, *Prejudice in Politics: Public Opinion, Group Position, and the Wisconsin Treaty Rights Dispute,* will be published by Harvard University Press and is scheduled to appear in March 2006.

CLINT BOLICK is vice president of the Institute for Justice, has litigated many crucial school choice decisions. His book Voucher Wars: Waging the Legal Battle Over School Choice has just been published by the Cato Institute.

ROBERT H. BORK is a senior fellow at the American Enterprise Institute. He has been a partner at a major law firm, taught constitutional law as the Alexander M. Bickel Professor of Public Law at the Yale law school, and served as Solicitor General and as Attorney General of the United States. He is the author of the bestselling *Slouching Toward Gomorrah: Modern Liberalism and American Decline* (HarperCollins Publishers).

LESTER R. BROWN was the founder and president of the Worldwatch Institute, a non-profit organization dedicated to the analysis of the global environment. He served as advisor to Secretary of Agriculture Orville Freeman and served as administrator of the International Agricultural Service in that department. In 1969, he helped James Grant establish the Overseas Development Council. He is the author and coauthor of numerous books.

PATRICK BUCHANAN was a presidential candidate in 2000. Currently, he is a political analyst, television commentator, and the author of *The Death of the West* (Thomas Dunne Books, 2000), which focuses on the issue of immigration.

ANDREW G. CELLI, JR. is a lawyer practicing in New York City, and has served as chief of the Attorney General's Civil Rights Bureau from 1999 to 2003. He has recently published in the *New Republic*, "A Democratic Vision for the New Economy" (March 16, 2004).

MICHELLE CONLIN is a journalist and the editor of the Working Life department of *BUSINESS WEEK* magazine, where she covers workplace culture and careers.

STEPHANIE COONTZ teaches history and family studies at the Evergreen State College in Olympia, Washington. She is the author of *The Way We Never Were: American Families and the Nostalgia Trap* (Basic Books, 1992) and *The Way We Really Are: Coming to Terms With America's Changing Families* (Basic Books, 1997). She is coeditor of *American Families: A Multicultural Reader* (Routledge, 1998).

CURTIS CRAWFORD is the editor and co-author of the website www. DebatingRacialPreferences.org.

MARY CRAWFORD is a professor of psychology at the University of Connecticut. She is the author, with Rhoda Unger, of *Talking Difference: On Gender and Language* (Sage Publications, 1995) and *Women and Gender: A Feminist Psychology*, 3rd ed. (McGraw-Hill, 2000).

HERMAN E. DALY is a professor in the School of Public Affairs at the University of Maryland and the author of a classic on the subject of environmental economics, *Steady-State Economics: The Economics of Biophysical Equilibrium and Moral Growth* (W. H. Freeman, 1977). Recently he authored *Beyond Growth: The Economics of Sustainable Development* (Beacon Press, 1996) and *Ecological Economics and the Ecology of Economics: Essays in Criticism* (Edward Elgar, 1999).

CHRISTOPHER C. DeMUTH is president of the American Enterprise Institute for Public Policy. He is also editor, with William Kristol, of *The Neoconservative Imagination: Essays in Honor of Irving Kristol* (American Enterprise Institute for Public Policy Research, 1995) and coauthor of *The Reagan Doctrine and Beyond* (American Enterprise Institute for Public Policy Research, 1988).

G. WILLIAM DOMHOFF has been teaching psychology and sociology at the University of California, Santa Cruz, since 1965. His books on political sociology include *Who Rules America?* (Prentice-Hall, 1967); *The Power Elite and the State: How Policy Is Made in America* (Aldine de Gruyter, 1990); and *Diversity in the Power Elite* (Yale University Press, 1998).

BARBARA DORITY is president of Humanists of Washington, executive director of the Washington Coalition Against Censorship, and cochair of the Northwest Feminist Anti-Censorhip Task Force.

SUSAN DOUGLAS is the Catherine Neafie Kellogg Professor of Communication Studies at the University of Michigan and author of *Listening In: Radio and the American Imagination* (Times Books, 1999), *Where the Girls Are: Growing Up Female with the Mass Media* (Times Books, 1994), and *Inventing American Broadcasting, 1899–1922* (Johns Hopkins University Press, 1987).

SUSAN FALUDI is a Pulitzer Prize–winning journalist who writes for magazines such as *The Nation* and the *New Yorker.* She is the author of *Backlash: The Undeclared War Against American Women* (Random House, 1995) and

Stiffed: The Betrayal of the American Man (William Morrow & Company, 1999).

JOHN BELLAMY FOSTER is an editor of *Monthly Review*. He is author of *The Vulnerable Planet*, and co-editor of *Hungry for Profit: The Agribusiness Threat to Farmers, Food, and the Environment*, all published by Monthly Review Press.

FRANK FURSTENBERG is Zellerback Family Professor of Sociology at the University of Pennsylvania. He has written extensively on children, families, and public policy including with others *Managing to Make It: Urban Families and Adolescent Success* (University of Chicago Press, 1999).

JEFF GRABMEIER is managing editor of research news at Ohio State University in Columbus, Ohio.

SHARON HAYES is the author of *Flat Broke with Children* and is a professor of Sociology and women's studies at the University of Virginia.

RICHARD T. HULL is professor emeritus of philosophy at the State University of New York at Buffalo. He is editor of *Ethical Issues in the New Reproductive Technologies* (Wadsworth, 1990).

HUMAN RIGHTS CAMPAIGN is the largest national gay, lesbian, bisexual, and transgender political organization with members throughout the country.

KAY S. HYMOWITZ is a Senior Fellow at the Manhattan Institute and a contributing editor of *City Journal*. She writes extensively on education. Her latest book is *Liberation's Children: Parents and Kids in a Postmodern Age* (Ivan R. Dec, 2003)

CHRISTOPHER JENCKS is a professor of social policy at the Kennedy School at Harvard University and the author of many books on poverty and inequality, including *Rethinking Social Policy: Race, Poverty, and the Underclass* (Harvard University Press, 1992).

ROBERT KUTTNER is a founder and co-editor of *The American Prospect*, a longtime contributor to *The Atlantic*, and the author of *Everything For Sale: The Virtues and Limits of Markets* (Alfred A. Knopf, 1997).

LAMBDA LEGAL DEFENSE and **EDUCATION FUND** is a national organization committed to achieving full recognition of the civil rights of lesbians, gay ment, bisexuals, the transgendered, and people with HIV or AIDS through impact litigation, education, and public policy work.

BJORN LOMBORG is a statistician at the University of Aarhus and the author of the controversial book *The Skeptical Environmentalist: Measuring the Real State of the World* (Cambridge University Press, 2001).

BRUNO V. MANNO is a former assistant secretary of education and currently is senior program associate with the Annie E. Casey Foundation. He is the author, with Chester E. Finn, Jr. and Gregg Vanourek, of *Charter Schools in Action: Renewing Public Education* (Princeton University Press, 2000).

ROBERT W. McCHESNEY is the author of eight books on media and politics, professor of communication at the University of Illinois at Urbana-Champaign, and host of the weekly talk show, Media Matters, on WILL-AM radio. McChesney also writes widely for both academic and non-academic publications. He gives talks frequently on issues related to media and politics in the United States and world today.

WILLIAM McGOWAN has reported for *Newsweek International* and the BBC and has written for the *New York Times*, the *Washington Post, Columbia* Journalism Review and other national publications. A regular contributor to the *Wall Street Journal*, he is currently a senior fellow at the *Manhattan Institute.* He is also the author of *Only Man Is Vile: The Tragedy of Sri Lanka* (Farrar, Straus & Giroux).

MEREDITH MICHAELS is a writer and philosophy professor at Smith College. His books include *Twenty Questions: An Introduction to Philosophy*, 5th ed., with G. Lee Bowie and Robert C. Solomon (Thomson/Wadsworth, 2004) and *Fetal Subjects, Feminist Positions*, edited with Lynn M. Morgan (University of Pennsylvania Press, 1999).

BILL MOYERS is an author and television journalist. His recent book is *Moyers on America: A Journalist and His Times*, edited by Julie Leininger Pycior (New Press, 2004).

CHARLES MURRAY is Bradley Fellow at the American Enterprise Institute. He is the author of *Losing Ground: American Social Policy, 1950–1980*, 10th ed. (Basic Books, 1994) and *The Underclass Revisited* (AEI Press, 1999). He is coauthor, with Richard J. Herrnstein, of *The Bell Curve* (Free Press, 1994).

ETHAN A. NADELMANN is director of the Lindesmith Center of the Drug Policy Foundation, a New York drug policy research institute, and professor of politics and public affairs in the Woodrow Wilson School of Public and International Affairs at Princeton University. He is the author of *Cops Across Borders: The Internationalization of U.S. Criminal Law Enforcement* (Pennsylvania State University Press, 1993).

JOHAN NORBERG has been in charge since 1999 of ideas policy at the Swedish think-tank *Timbro* where he is editor of smedian.com, a Swedish-language journal of cultural affairs and ideas. His recent book is *In Defense of Global Capitalism* (Cato Institute, 2003).

DAVID POPENOE is a professor of sociology at Rutgers–The State University in New Brunswick, New Jersey. He is the author of *Disturbing the Nest* (Aldine de Gruyter, 1988) and *Life Without Father: Compelling New Evidence That Fatherhood and Marriage are Indispensable for the Good of Children and Society* (Martin Kessler Books, 1996). He is editor, with Jean Bethke Elshtain and David Blankenhorn, of *Promises to Keep: Decline and Renewal of Marriage in America* (Rowman & Littlefield Publishers, 1996).

JEFFREY REIMAN is the William Fraser McDowell Professor of Philosophy at American University in Washington, D.C. He is the author of *Justice and Modern Moral Philosophy* (Yale University Press, 1992) and *The Rich Get Richer and the Poor Get Prison: Ideology, Class, and Criminal Justice*, 6th ed. (Allyn and Bacon, 2001). He is also editor, with Paul Leighton, of *Criminal Justice Ethics* (Prentice Hall, 2001).

MICHAEL J. SANDEL is the Anne T. and Robert M. Bass Professor in the Political Science Department at Harvard. His recent book is *Public Philosophy: Essay on Morality in Politics* (Harvard University Press, 2005).

SAM SCHULMAN is a New York writer whose work appears in New York Press, the Spectator (London), and elsewhere. He was formerly publisher of Wigwag and a professor of English at Boston University.

BARRY SCHWARTZ is the Dorwin Cartwright Professor of Social Theory and Social Action and professor of psychology at Swarthmore College. He is the author of *The Costs of Living: How Market Freedom Erodes the Best Things in Life* (W. W. Norton, 1994).

MARGARET SOMERVILLE holds professorships in both the Faculty of Law and the Faculty of Medicine at McGill University, Montreal. She is Samuel Gale Professor of Law (as such, she is the first woman in Canada to hold a named Chair in Law) and the Founding Director of the McGill Centre for Medicine, Ethics and Law. She plays an active role in the world-wide development of bioethics and the study of the wider legal and ethical aspects of medicine and science.

ELIOT SPITZER has been New York's attorney general since 1999. He has advanced initiatives in environmental protection, public safety, civil rights, and consumer affairs. He often presses cases against the major Wall Street firms.

PETER SPRIGG serves as Vice President for Policy at the Family Research Council and oversees FRC research, publications, and policy formulation. He is also the author of the book *Outrage: How Gay Activists and Liberal Judges Are Trashing Democracy to Redefine Marriage* (Regnery, 2004), and the co-editor of the book *Getting It Straight: What the Research Shows about Homosexuality.*

JOHN STOSSEL works for the ABC news magazine *20/20*, has received 19 Emmy Awards and has been honored five times for excellence in consumer reporting by the National Press Club.

GREGG VANOUREK is vice president of KIZ, heads its Charter School Division, and is the author, with Chester E. Finn, Jr. and Gregg Vanourek, of *Charter Schools in Action: Renewing Public Education* (Princeton University Press, 2000).

ERIC A. VOTH is a physician and chairman of the International Drug Strategy Institute.

CLAUDIA WALLIS is editor-at-large at TIME. She has been both a writer and editor specializing in stories about health and science, women's and children's issues, education and lifestyle. She was the founding editor of *TIME for Kids.*

BEN WATTENBERG is a senior fellow at the American Enterprise Institute and is the author of *The First Universal Nation: Leading Indicators and Ideas About the Surge of America in the 1990s* (Free Press, 1991). He is coauthor, with Theodore Caplow and Louis Hicks, of *The First Measured Century: An Illustrated Guide to Trends in America, 1900–2000* (AEI Press, 2001).

MURRAY WEIDENBAUM is the chairman of the Weidenbaum Center at Washington University in St. Louis. He is also the author of *Business and Government in the Global Marketplace,* 6th ed. (Prentice Hall, 1999) and *Looking for Common Ground on U.S. Trade Policy* (Center for Strategic and International Studies, 2001).

JOEL WENDLAND is managing editor of *Political Affairs,* a monthly magazine of ideology, politics, and culture, and a member of UAW Local 1981 (national writers union) who has written for numerous publications. He also writes and maintains *ClassWarNotes.*

DAVID WHITMAN is a senior writer for *U.S. News & World Report* and the author of *The Optimism Gap: The I'm Ok—They're Not Syndrome and the Myth of American Decline* (Walker & Company, 1998). *Judgment: Does the Abuse Excuse Threaten Our Legal System?* (Basic Books, 1997); and *The Decline of Marriage* (HarperCollins, 2002).

SCOTT WINSHIP is a Ph.D. candidate in sociology and social policy at Harvard University. He studies inequality in scholastic achievement, the importance of single motherhood and family structure, and black-white inequality. He recently co-authored an op-ed on welfare reform in the *Christian Science Monitor.*

RON WOLK is a former vice president of Brown University and is chairman of the board of Editorial Projects in Education. He founded *Education Week* and *Teacher Magazine.* He edited with Blake Hume Rodman *Classroom Crusaders: Twelve Teachers Who Are Trying to Change the System* (Jossey-Bass Publishers, 1994).

PHILIP YANCEY serves as editor-at-large for *Christianity Today* magazine. He has authored numerous books, including *The Jesus I Never Knew* (Zondervan Publishing House, 1995) and *What's so Amazing About Grace?* (Zondervan Publishing House, 1997).

MATTHEW YGLESIAS is a fellow for *The American Prospect.* His column, Broadside, appears weekly.

Index